THE FIRST ONE

America during the Jack Johnson years

Patrick Desmond Cooper

Author's Note

By the beginning of the twentieth century, a brief thirty-five years after the end of the fratricidal Civil War that had cost it more than 600,000 of its finest and most idealistic young men, the United States had become the wealthiest and most powerful country in the world. That startling material success led many to conclude that America had been awarded a special dispensation by heaven, that God, as one influential Senator concluded, "had marked the American people as His chosen nation to finally lead in the regeneration of the world."

But America's nine million Negroes, as African Americans and other people of African descent around the world were then quaintly known, were not regarded as Americans. Therefore when Jack Johnson won the heavyweight title in 1908 from the Canadian Jack Burns in distant Sydney, Australia, the first black man to do so, his victory was not seen by white Americans as an American triumph.

To the contrary, black power of any kind was seen as a direct threat to the American way of life. The enforced docility of young black males had long been a major goal of official American domestic policy and Johnson represented a major threat to that policy. Perfectly reflecting the attitude of his white countrymen was the novelist Jack London who was sitting at ringside that night in Sydney. It was from his pen that the appeal first went out for the retired, undefeated champion, Jim Jeffries, to come out of retirement and regain the title for the white race. "There was no fight. No Armenian massacre could compare with the hopeless slaughter that took place at the Sydney Stadium today. But one thing now remains; Jim Jeffries must now emerge from his alfalfa farm and remove that golden smile from Jack Johnson's face. Jeff it's up to you. The white man must be rescued."

Jeffries, by far the most formidable of the 'White Hopes' recruited to separate Johnson from the heavyweight title, did not relish the role in which he had been cast. He had never been comfortable in the spotlight and initially made it clear that he was not interested in rescuing the white race. But Johnson's provocative behavior and offers of enormous sums of money soon made the pressure on the former champion to come out of retirement virtually irresistible. Declaring that he was responding to "that portion of the white race that has been looking to me to defend its athletic superiority," Jeffries finally agreed to get back in the ring and restore the natural order of things.

The First One is the story of that fight and the extraordinary events surrounding it, including Johnson's affairs, liaisons with and marriages to a lengthy list of white women, and his trial and conviction of White Slavery; events that unleashed extraordinary passions in this country and throughout much of the white world. More importantly it is a story about America at the dawn of the twentieth century. By almost any measure "The Fight of the Century" as it was billed, is still the most significant sporting event ever held in America, but it was also far more than a sporting event. No single event, of any kind, before or since, has ever commanded the entire country with as much passion and intensity. And not until the assassination of Martin Luther King, more than a half-century later, would a single event provoke such widespread rioting.

Whatever his intent, Jack Johnson's defeat of the white standard-bearer, Jim Jeffries, and his marriage to not just one but two white women (in his later years he married a third), were black America's first truly potent challenges to the ruling doctrine of white superiority. The Jack Johnson story has been told many times but never before as faithfully to historical accuracy, nor in the full context of the kind of country America was at the time, or with a full appreciation of the magnitude of the social and political challenge Johnson represented to the status quo.

Muhammad Ali's America was a far kinder and gentler place. Over the years America had slowly and grudgingly made space for its black citizens. By the 1960's white Americans no longer spoke, as they had a half-century earlier, with a single voice on the subject of race. Education, exposure and black activism and achievement had cracked the once solid wall of white solidarity. Before Ali there had been Johnson and Garvey and Dubois, and Jesse Owens, Joe Louis, Jackie Robinson, Philip Randolph, Martin Luther King, Rosa Parks, Malcolm X, and so many others.

Finally, this is not attempt to tell the entire Jack Johnson story. Instead it focuses on the years 1909 to 1913, the most momentous years of his remarkable life.

Prologue

In the soft light of the darkened bedroom Jack Johnson seemed strangely vulnerable. The heavily-muscled naked body, gleaming black against the pure whiteness of the crisp cotton sheets, was lined with disconcerting scars. Most had not been earned in the ring. They were instead eloquent testimony to a life of struggle and early poverty, of wounds treated by neglect and coffee grounds instead of the needle and thread of the surgeon. One, a long, thick, ugly line that ran all the way from the left knee to the upper thigh, was the legacy of his service as a stable boy and the brutal kick from a nervous horse that broke the femur and ripped open the delicate skin. The long, powerful arms, massive biceps bulging even in repose, rested limply at his side. And the surprisingly slender legs, finely sculpted by countless miles of roadwork, splayed passively across the bed, seemed curiously ill-equipped for the considerable task of conveying the massive torso and the large, round, cleanly-shaven head with the ridged tissue over both eyes where hair no longer grew.

Hours of frenzied lovemaking had already left him physically sated and the most momentous decision of his life was only hours away from implementation. But, as he watched his nineteen-year-old wife walk back to their bed, generous hips undulating and large, dark-violet eyes smoldering with a wild intensity than even he sometimes found intimidating, he knew that there would be very little sleep for them that night.

She wanted, she had told him repeatedly, the night to be perfect, a memory they would share and cherish forever. As she climbed back into the enormous four-poster bed and crawled on all fours like a giant cat towards him, her smoldering eyes fixed firmly on the midpoint of his body, her tongue slowly licking her full, pouty lips, he closed his eyes and waited. Familiar music, just barely audible, from a light opera he could not immediately identify floated gently across the room. Behind her, on the ornate Elizabethan dresser, the heady scent of lilacs wafted slowly from a trio of brightly colored candles set in heavy crystal holders. But all night it had been her scent, delicate and musky all at once, which had filled his nostrils and infused his brain with a fragrant, powerful aphrodisiac. And now, happy and exhilarated, she had no intention of allowing her thirty-four-year-old husband to fall asleep.

"Too tired for another round champ," she teased, as she reached, insistently, between his legs, and draped a firm, plump leg across his supine body. "Everybody tells me," she cooed, "that you'll never be satisfied with just one woman. But, that isn't true, is it champ, I'm more than enough woman for you, aren't I champ" she said in the breathless, little-girl voice she had practiced to perfection.

"You never get tired do you," Johnson replied, his voice soft and hoarse with a mix of lust and apprehension. His body had never failed him in such a situation before but he knew that everybody, even he, had their limits. Chuckling, as the heavyweight champion of the world groaned softly, his body responding quickly to the invasion of fingers educated in Chicago's finest brothels and to the tonguing and soft biting of his nipples, Lucille swung her heavy-hipped body over her husband and mounted him with a small cry of triumph.

As her soft, hot wetness enveloped him, he marveled again at her uncanny power to arouse him. Not only was he physically exhausted but the decision to flee the country was also proving to be far more emotionally devastating than he had expected. Before, going to Europe had been fun, liberating, but then he was always coming back home. Now everything was going to be different. The prospect of never seeing his mother again was sometimes too much to bear.

But, electrified by his young wife's artful caresses and playful challenge, the undisputed heavyweight champion of the world made a valiant attempt to unseat his squealing rider and assume his accustomed place on top. But Lucille, her square-jawed face flushed with passion, shoulder-length blonde hair damp from exertion, and wide, full-lipped mouth set in determination, would have none of it. Tonight, she would be in charge, the master. Slowing her frantic movements to press his shoulders back against the bed, she leaned forward and offered her generous breasts to his straining mouth.

"I am enough women for you, aren't I Jack," she panted, bearing down and brushing the tips of her swollen nipples, back and forth, against his rock hard chest. "You don't need any other woman to satisfy you, do you Jack." Then straightening up and resuming her frenzied rocking, Lucille announced in a voice low and thick with passion, her fingers moving from his nipples to her own. "I am the best you've ever had, isn't that so Jack. You've never had anybody like me, have you Jack. No nasty old French actress can do this to you Jack. What's her name Jack, the one who told the whole world that she wanted you to fuck her so bad, Gaby, or is it Gabay.

I've been practicing my French Jacques. *Je vais combler tous tes desire. Tu n'en voudras jamais une autre.* Does it make you hot Jack? What did she tell all the papers, that you made her desire utter fulfillment? Well, Jack that's what she wants from you, but that's what I'm going to give you tonight Jack—total utter fulfillment, utter, utter fulfillment. *Je deviend mi toutes celles qui t'ont donne du plaisir*. She wanted you to fuck her Jack but I'm the one fucking you and I'm not ever going to stop Jack. Never, ever, do you hear me Jack, never, ever. I'm going to show you what utter fulfillment is Jack. I'm never going to stop fucking you Jack, not ever. Do you hear me Jack, I'm never going to stop fucking you tonight Jack, I am never, never, ever going to stop. I can go all night like this Jack, you know that don't you Jack. That's what you really love about me, isn't it Jack, nobody has ever fucked you the way I do Jack, nobody else has ever been as good at it Jack. Do you know why Jack, because nobody, nobody loves it as much as I do Jack. You'll have to beg if you want me to stop."

"No, no, don't, don't stop, please don't stop," the world's greatest warrior pleaded as he moaned in the pain of ecstasy.

Spurred on, as she always was, by the sight of his rapture, Lucille further increased the speed of her gallop, and a long, low feminine wail, growing ever louder and higher, soon announced that the end of the furious ride was coming. With his eyes wide open and locked on to hers, his hips raised and pumping wildly to answer her call, the heavyweight champion of the world suddenly stiffened, then shuddered, and with one great groan slumped back onto the bed in blissful surrender.

In the sudden silence the soft, sweet strains of an operetta could once again be heard and the mysterious scent of lilacs began filling the room. After a long moment of quietly relishing her triumph Lucille slowly dismounted her steed, rolled onto her back, stretched in delight like some giant cat, all the while yawning without inhibition, turned on her side, draped an arm over her husband's body and with a tender smile wrapped a possessive fist around his wilting member.

"I am the best you've ever had, aren't I Jack, you've never had anybody like me, have you Jack" she asked in her most seductive voice, mischief dancing in her eyes. Then, without waiting for an answer, she raised her lips to his ear as her talented fingers resumed their voyage of exploration and whispered hotly, "because if you're still not sure they're a couple more tricks I know that I haven't shown you yet, they're a lot more things I want to do to you Jack, a lot more, a lot more Jack."

"*Oui mon amour, tu es certainement ma prefiree, tu es certainement ma prefiree,* you are truly the very best I've ever had," the heavyweight champion of the world fervently acknowledged, desperate to avoid another test of his manhood.

Minutes later as she slept peacefully at his side, her soft snoring barely audible, he reached over and with a little smile brushed a damp lock of hair from her eyes. He had been reluctant, he recalled with amazement as he watched her sleep, to get too involved with her when they first met because of her age. She was so very young and he usually preferred more sexually experienced women, but the sheer ferociousness of her passion and some special quality, he had not yet been able to define, had quickly won him over.

Very early in the relationship she had insisted that they sleep together, giggling in that wicked little-girl manner of hers as she said it, "absolutely buck-naked". And when, with a modesty that she had found both surprising and delightful, he had hesitated to sleep in the altogether, she had quickly gained his enthusiastic consent with the whispered confession that just the sight of their intertwined bodies, in the enormous mirrors surrounding their bed that he had bought at her insistence, black on white, hard on soft, thrusting and yielding, aroused her to heights of passion she had previously thought impossible.

She had hated the restriction of clothes, she had confessed with another giggle, for as long as she could remember. And she had laughed madly as she described the horror of her outraged and disapproving mother because she had discarded them, even as a child, at every opportunity. Curled up in his lap she had whispered in his ear, her soft tongue and sweet, warm breath insinuating and teasing, that she never tired of watching him in the gym, that just the sight of his muscles, so massive and powerful, rippling and moving like snakes under his skin, drove her completely wild.

And few things delighted her more than lying naked together in their huge bed and with crimson-tipped fingernails slowly trace the bulging muscles in his back, from the top of his powerful shoulders all the way past his lean waist to his narrow, swelling buttocks: thrilling at her power to arouse and control so much power and strength.

For Lucille the attraction had been immediate and powerful. She had decided from their very first meeting that she would have him and that nothing would get in her way: Not the fact of his marriage, not the fierce opposition of her mother and stepfather, not the disapproval of society or her friends, not even his reputation as a notorious womanizer. She had been confident right from the start that she knew just how to handle him. She had always understood men; had always known, even as a child, how to get what she wanted from them. And she always got what she wanted, always. In fact, so certain had she been that this time would be no different that it had not occurred to her, for even a single moment, that he would have been anything but delighted with her plan to make him her very own. And as usual, she had been proven right.

The music had stopped and the candles had burnt themselves out. Overhead the big ceiling fan groaned as it whirled tirelessly around and around and around. Perhaps, Johnson thought, as he watched its relentless but monotonous journey, if I count its rotations I'll finally be able to sleep. But after several fruitless minutes with the count already topping the three hundred mark he eased slowly out of the bed—Lucille was a light sleeper—and slipped on a pair of silk blue pajamas, matching bedroom slippers and a pale blue bathrobe. Quietly opening the door leading out of the room, he stepped into the corridor and without turning on a light made his way down the nearby staircase to the second floor and knocked softly but repeatedly on the first door to the right.

"Ma, Ma" he called after each knock, "are you sleeping."

"Not any more Jack," the surprisingly sprightly, little, dark-skinned woman answered as the door opened. "Is anything wrong son," she asked, a worried frown on her broad, almost unlined face as she took his massive hand in her small one.

"Are you sure this is the right thing Ma, I can still change my mind, its still not too late," he answered, his tone soft and plaintive, "I mean if I go I may never see you again, do you realize that Ma. If I stayed at least I'd be here with you and you could visit me and at worse I'd be out in a year and I could even win the appeal because the law may not even be according to the constitution."

"Jack," she replied, stepping into the corridor, her voice a fierce hiss as she looked up at her towering son, "I'll not have dose people shaming you dat way, throwing you in prison like a common tief and you the heavyweight champion of the world. An yu never know wat dey might do to you in dere. Yu may never leave dere alive. Dey sure didn't treat the white ones dat way. I'll not have it, and if your Pa was alive, even as godly as he was, he'd tell you the same thing too."

"But Ma, I may never be able to come back to America," Tina Johnson's son began, "What if..."

"Ssshh," she said, placing an index finger on his lips, "What and if nothing, trust more in the Lord Jack, he 'as all the power and he decides who gits the glory, man might think he do but he don't, only God decides, we jus' does our best and we leaves the rest to him, we learned all six of yu dat."

"Yes Ma, you and Pa," the heavyweight champion of the world acknowledged in a chastened voice, "you taught us right."

"Come Son," she said, taking him by the arm, "I know jus' what to fix to make yu sleep." Then, arms linked mother and son walked down the staircase to the first-floor kitchen.

Less than twenty-four hours later, standing on the platform of the brightly lit station in suburban South Englewood, black fedora pulled low over his face, Jack Johnson's palms were damp with apprehension. Nervously shifting his weight from one foot to another, he was trying, as unobtrusively as possible, to slink into the shadows cast by the boisterous, well-dressed young black men milling and jostling playfully around him.

A crisp breeze that had swept off Lake Michigan and crept into the interior of the city was cooling the early Chicago summer night, but the heavyweight champion's dark face was shiny with perspiration. He had known for months that nothing he did or said had gone unnoticed or unrecorded. His every movement had been monitored by the Secret Service agents who hung around his home and followed him through the streets: And even, he reflected bitterly, by some of his so-called friends whom they had recruited and paid to spy on his most private moments.

Like the other young black men crowding around him on the platform that night, the heavyweight champion of the world was carrying a large leather bag loaded with baseball equipment. But, unlike his carefree companions, the normally loquacious Johnson was uncharacteristically quiet; money and spies and God were on his mind. The arrangements that made what he was attempting that night possible had been expensive, very, very expensive: Almost all the cash he had been able to put his hands on, close to one hundred and forty thousand dollars, one hundred and thirty-eight thousand to be exact.

Every eventuality had been exhaustively discussed and taken

care of. Judge Carpenter had agreed to reduce his thirty thousand dollar bail by a half. His mother, who had used the house he had transferred in her name to secure the first fifteen thousand dollars of his original bond, would therefore not lose her home. His cash deposit would fully satisfy the reduced bond. Their tickets, his and Lucille's, which routed them from Chicago to the French port city of Havre, placed them outside the reach of the Canadian immigration authorities. And, he had been assured that the extradition treaty between Canada and the United States did not cover violations of the American White Slave Law. Benjamin Bachrach, his high-priced white attorney, had not been cheap but he had gotten the job done. The huge fees had been, he knew from his own experience, for far more than just legal advice. He understood only too well how the city worked. Just to open his saloon and to keep it open, his anger rising at the memory, he'd been forced to pay his alderman, "Hinky Dink" Kenna, a thousand dollars every month.

The spies on his mind were not so much the official ones, the Secret Service agents: they, he felt reasonably certain, had been taken care of. Carpenter's decision to reduce his bail, he was certain, had been the signal that the big men had decided to let him go, or at least not to actively stop him. In addition to the payments to Bachrach he had given $20,000 to Roy Jones and $30,000 to Sol Lewinsohn, the bagmen for the Bureau of Investigation and the District Attorney's office. Not that he trusted those thieving hypocrites to keep their word; DeWoody and Parkin were blackmailers and robbers but he knew that they preferred him out of the country rather than risk the possibility that Carpenter might set him free on bail to appeal their trumped up charge.

What was really concerning, Johnson concluded, his anger and anxiety rising as he nervously scanned the increasingly crowded platform while pulling the fedora covering the famous cleanly-shaven head even lower over his face, were the rabid citizen groups like the Law and Order League and their president, that self-righteous, hypocritical bitch, Alice Comstock. She and the members of her racist organization were the ones who were really responsible for most of his troubles. Pretending to be god-fearing

Christians when all the while they hated him just because of his color. God knows; he had done nothing to harm any of them or their friends and families. His only crime was to exercise his rights just like any other American, for refusing to be their kind of nigger. And for that they had been determined to get rid of him or destroy him, from the very beginning.

But what he would never forgive them and all the others like them for, he silently vowed, a deep vertical frown wrinkling his forehead and his eyes moisting as he again scanned the platform before glancing down at the heavy gold watch on his right wrist, was what they had done to poor Etta, the love of his life. They had killed her, snuffed out the life of one God's dearest, sweetest creatures, just as certain as if they had pointed the gun and pulled the trigger themselves: And if there was a just God the evil motherfuckers would pay for it many times over, would burn in the eternal fires of hell forever and ever; every last goddamned, fucking one of them. The dirty, lowdown fuckers had made her life so terrible, so goddamned miserable that she had decided that she no longer wanted to live: Just because she had dared to marry him, a black man. They had spread the most vicious lies and rumors about him; that he had beaten her; that she had killed herself to escape from him. And at the end the sick, twisted motherfuckers, who had driven her mad with their taunts and dirty lies, had claimed that what happened to her was living proof, a warning, of what would happen to any white slut who dared to cross the color line and marry a black man: That they would discover that even death was better than life with a black man.

One thing he had learned very early about America, he thought grimly, as he took one step even further backwards into the shadows while resisting the impulse to tug his hat even further down on his face, was that all the pious talk about morality and the rule of law was nothing more than bullshit. It was all about money and the privileges of white men, rich white men. In Chicago they didn't even bother to pretend. The so-called laws were only for the little people, the people who didn't have any money or know anybody. Even a black man with money was better off than a shit poor white man, most of the times anyway, although the poor bastards didn't even seem to know that the system was designed to fuck them, left and right and right up the middle. The ignorant bastards were too busy hating niggers to realize they were the real niggers.

But there was no honor among white men, he had discovered, not when it came to black men anyway. He had, he recalled, nodding his head in grim satisfaction, always kept up his part of the deal. Nobody could accuse him of playing the game like a nigger. His payments had always been on time, every month just like clockwork, nobody ever had to remind him that they were due. He had wanted the fuckers to trust him, just like they would a white man. He had tried his damnest to make them see that his word was as good as any goddamn white man's. And in any case the money hadn't even really come out of his pocket, not directly anyway. He had been, he thought smugly, a little smile briefly lighting up the flat, wide, almost oriental face, too fucking smart for that. He had sold the exclusive right to supply the Café de Champion with beer to one of the big breweries for the same amount of his protection money, one thousand goddamned dollars per month. It had been a good deal for everybody. He opened as late as he wanted. They made money, he made money, that was the way it was supposed to be.

But that had not meant anything, he remembered, his face quickly darkening with anger again, when they decided to fuck him for breaking their fucking golden rule; black men shall not fuck white women and no amount of gold shall change that. The money hadn't meant anything then: Or at least it wasn't nearly enough, not when everything was out in the open. They had even blamed him, the hypocritical fuckers, the ones who had known all along that his club had been a place not just for white women but also for white men who had a taste for the darker side to find what they were looking for, to have a little fun, for not being more discreet.

But then, he conceded, his face softening and his eyes growing moist again, he probably deserved every bit of the hell he'd been cast into. All of his troubles were probably God's judgment. His mother had warned him, God knows, so many times, that the big man upstairs expected more from those who had been given more. And no black man had been given more than him, not in America anyway. His dear father, she had often reminded him, might have been poor but he had been a true man of God, proud but in a humble Christian way, reliable and hardworking. A man even the rich white people of Galveston had respected. But he, Mr. Bigshot, had been too busy being a big shit to listen. What did she know? Well, she had been absolutely right: He had fucked up his life. Just the way she had warned him, over and over again, ever since he had won the title. *It is easier for a camel to pass through the eye of a needle, than for a rich man to enter into the Kingdom of God.*

Gus Rhodes, just two feet to the left, standing like a sentinel between the stairs leading to the platform and his uncle, could sense the champion's turmoil. From the corner of his eye he watched uneasily as a range of emotions, manifested in turn by tight-lipped little smiles, nods, frowns, scowls and grimaces, chased each other across the heavyweight champion's famously impassive face. Lurking just beneath the surface of Johnson's public mask of cool indifference, he knew only too well, was a very different reality. Excruciating, disabling headaches that the heavyweight champion had once described as "setting his brain on fire" and almost complete physical exhaustion, which left him too weak to even get out of bed for days at a time, had followed previous bouts of mental depression.

He had, poor fool, Gus remembered, shaking his head in lingering amazement at his uncle's naiveté, genuinely believed, despite his many statements to the contrary, that at some stage he would have been accepted by white America, if he continued to prove that he was the very best. That they hated him even more for beating their champions, that he would never be their champion whatever he did, however good he was, that they would always relentlessly try to destroy him, the realization had almost killed him. The man had never been content with the money and the admiration of his own people; he had always desperately wanted the approval of white Americans, even as he defied them. Etta and Grandma Johnson had been the ones who had kept him sane, stopped him from taking his own life. Etta had hardly left his side for a whole year. But Etta was dead now and his mother would soon be thousands of miles away and this new wife was just a child, a greedy, self-indulgent child.

Sensing his nephew's intense observation and understanding the source of his concern, Johnson turned, flashed a quick smile of reassurance and whispered: "Its okay Gus, I'm okay, everything is going to be okay."

Yes, he told himself, everything is going to be okay. He was, after all, not just the greatest fighter in the world but also the most famous man in the world. What further proof was required than the fact that in London, during the King's own coronation, he had attracted more attention than the very King himself. But it was also true, his throbbing brain insisted on reminding him, that even the princely sum of $138,000 would only buy so much official protection. They would not stop him themselves, he was pretty certain, or at least, fairly certain. That much, at least, he hoped to God, had been decided.

But he also had no illusions that if he was seen fleeing the country and was reported by any of the good citizens of Chicago, that the Bureau of Investigation and the District Attorney's office would do anything other than immediately order the police to apprehend him. The most dangerous part of his journey was right here in Chicago. If he could only manage somehow to get out of the city without being spotted, he had concluded after several long sleepless nights, he probably would make it across the border without any problem.

Which was why, when he learned that the Foster's Giants baseball team had scheduled a game in New York City, he had offered to pay all their expenses if they allowed him to route the train. Not only were all of the players black but also many of them were as big and muscular as he was and one Rube Foster, the owner of the team, had even on several occasions been mistaken for him. Tonight, he was just one of a big group of large black men: Lucille was leaving on another train, from another station. A big black man and a white woman traveling together were guaranteed to attract a great deal of unwelcome attention.

So, he told himself, taking a long deep breath, as he looked out on the vehicles moving steadily along the broad and straight park-like boulevard that was 87th Street, he had every reason to relax. After entering the two-and-one-half storey Gothic Revival building, he and his party had avoided the waiting room and had gone directly to the platform. Looking around at the gathering crowd, it seemed pretty obvious that their party had attracted little undue attention. White people, he reminded himself, knew little and cared less about black baseball players: To most of them the Foster's players were virtually invisible. Nevertheless, as he waited, lightly tapping the concrete floor with his right shoe in barely disguised impatience, glancing to his left and right, he furtively slipped the expensive gold watch off his wrist, pulled the diamond ring, bearing the symbol of his title, off his left index finger and swiftly stuffed them into the right hand pocket of his trousers: Both items had been used in the past by the police to identify him.

Then, as the train finally pulled into the station, the heavyweight champion of the world, accompanied by Gus, Rube and the entire team of the Foster's Giants, hurried aboard their private car. The train, which has been routed to Buffalo via New London, pulled out of the station, almost as soon as everybody was seated. Quickly dropping his pretense that he was just one of the fellows, Johnson whispered to Rube Foster, slapped a few of the players on the back and almost immediately made his way to the drawing room he had reserved. As the train sped through the night, he calmly went to bed fully dressed, except for his jacket and shoes, and promptly fell asleep; the events of the night before finally taking their toll.

PART ONE

ONE

In America, the twentieth century began auspiciously. In the nation's capital heavy snow had fallen steadily for several hours during the early hours of the morning. But as if directed by some celestial power the dark clouds and icy downpour had given way to clear skies and brilliant sunlight by mid-morning. To Turlough Daniel O'Brien, approaching from his hotel near Lafayette Square, the glowing White House, lit by the reflected light of the morning sun, seemed yet another happy augury of his and his nation's future.

And as his hansom rolled along the vast, asphalted expanse of Pennsylvania Avenue, lined with the silver-bearded poplar trees planted there a century earlier by the order of President Thomas Jefferson, the young newspaper reporter leaned back and smiled as he contemplated his good fortune, good fortune he had not always fully appreciated. He had been given the White House assignment just a few days before the Christmas holiday break. The paper's Washington correspondent, he had been told, was traveling out of the country and would be unavailable for several weeks and so he had been dispatched from New York. Just stepping into the vast marble lobby of the magnificent hotel in which he was staying had literally taken his breath away. At first he had been convinced that there must have been some kind of mistake, that his New England accent had confused his driver about the address of his hotel. But the polite front desk clerk had quickly assured him that he was in the right place, that people from the *Tribune* were always booked into that hotel.

Although he had fully understood immediately that his selection was a significant vote of confidence in him by his editor, he had not, initially, been entirely pleased. For months he had been planning to spend the holidays in Boston with his family. He had been particularly anxious to see his grandfather, Dermot Patrick O'Brien, who had not been well for several years. But the fierce old man had responded to Daniel's (that is what he was called by everybody but his grandfather who had given him his unusual first name) telegram explaining his dilemma by insisting that it was his grandson's responsibility to the family not just to accept the assignment but to prepare diligently to ensure that he would prove worthy of such a high responsibility. Coming home to see him, he made clear, was nice but the success of the O'Brien family in their adopted country was far more important to him.

The old man's telegram had prompted a gentle shake of the head and a small knowing smile from Daniel; his grandfather's response had not been entirely unexpected. He had grown up listening to fantastic stories about his grandfather's primary obsessions, the histories of Gaelic Ireland and of the O'Brien clan and its legendary founder, Brian Boru. Dermot O'Brien never tired of explaining and he never tired of hearing that the O'Brien's had emerged from what until that time had been a royal but obscure clan called the Dalcassians. The essence of the story, as Daniel remembered it in later years, was that from time immemorial another clan, the Eoghanacti, had ruled the southern half of the island. But the barbarians, as his grandfather called the Vikings, had defeated the Eoghanacti and broken their power and the Dalcassians, led by Brian and his older brother Mahon, had assumed the responsibility of defeating the foreigners. They had raised a great army and fighting fiercely and brilliantly had routed the barbarians, defeating them in battle after battle. Since they were of royal blood themselves, the Dalcassian brothers, with the support and acclaim of a vast majority of the citizens, had then rightfully laid claim to the throne they had so ably defended. But the Eoghanacti princes, unable to reconcile themselves to the loss of the throne, had treacherously joined forces with the barbarian Ivar, in an attempt to reclaim what they misguidedly believed had been willed to them in perpetuity from heaven. But Brian and Mahon had defeated the combined Eoghanacti-barbarian forces at the Battle of Sulcoit in 968. Then without stopping for rest the brothers had immediately marched on Limerick and in a great battle recaptured the city from the barbarians and forced the tyrant Ivar to flee like a wounded dog from the blessed soil of Ireland.

Although he was only the third of three children, younger by four years than Brian and by two than Kelley, by the time he was twelve Daniel was the only one of the siblings who was able to recall the names and dates of all the battles and the names of all the principal characters in their grandfather's stories with absolute accuracy. But that was not, primarily, because his memory was so much better than theirs; it was more that he had become almost as obsessed as his grandfather with the histories of Ireland and the O'Briens. Most nights as he laid in his bed in the tiny room he shared with Brian, oblivious to his brother's robust snoring, scenes of warriors in armor filling his head, he would often fall asleep while softly mouthing the names of the people and places that had come to mean so much to him.

He had relished the feel and sound of the Gaelic names as he rolled and twisted them in his mouth. And the stories, and the way his grandfather told them, had made an extraordinary impression on him as a child, inflaming his imagination and implanting an ambition to one day tell his own. Even when he was clearly not feeling well retelling the exploits of Ireland's greatest heroes never failed to rally the old man's spirits. The pale blue eyes, set deep in the broad face and normally almost entirely obscured by incredibly thick and unruly white eyebrows, would emerge from their hiding place flashing fire. His heavy brogue would become even more pronounced, and sometimes, on good days, he would almost leap out of his armchair, willing his arthritic legs to propel him around the room as he strode about gesturing eloquently like an actor on some grand stage. But even on those other days, when all he could manage was to rise slowly and painfully hobble a few steps here and there supported heavily by his walking cane, it was obvious that nothing in the world gave him greater pleasure than passing on the proud histories of ancient Ireland and the O'Brien family, which often seemed to them a single, seamless story, to his enchanted grandchildren.

Ahead, as he approached the North gate, Daniel could see that more than a thousand people, many of them the capital's most prominent private citizens, were standing four abreast in the snow, waiting patiently to pay their respects to the President of the world's newest imperial power. Another crowd, only slightly smaller, also waited outside the South gate; their size and evident enthusiasm a measure of the popular support the country's new imperial ambitions commanded. Despite the unexpected insurrection in the Philippines and the bitter opposition from anti-expansionists like the steel magnate, Andrew Carnegie, and the intemperate Senator Pettigrew of South Dakota, the American people as a whole were proving to be surprisingly enthusiastic imperialists.

As the clean, sharp smell of fresh sawdust drifted into the carriage through a crack in the window, Daniel waved self-consciously at the unusually large ground crew, some of whom had stopped working briefly, shading their eyes with gloved hands, to stare at the distinguished visitors. The men, bulky figures in heavy overcoats, faces partially obscured by misty clouds from their heavy breathing, had been laboring all morning to clear the snow from the pathways and to cover them with sawdust. Their considerable numbers and the unusually large contingent of blue-coated police officers stationed on the grounds and in every corner of the interior of the White House itself, was a signal of the importance of the occasion, and the White House's determination to manage it with the efficiency the country's new place in the world demanded.

Daniel O'Brien, and other white men of wealth, power, influence or promise, had every reason to be pleased with the state of the American nation on that first morning of the new century. In just one-half of a biblical lifetime, a collection of fratricidal states had become a single nation; a federal union had been converted into the American nation. And that nation, due largely to the spectacular rise of big business in the North was not only safe but prospering. The defeat of the South had not only altered the very concept of how the Union was to be structured, but had also radically changed how business was to be organized.

Before the war, federal aid to private enterprise had been strenuously resisted and successfully limited by the agrarian South.

As a result, economic enterprise had been both highly individualistic and of limited size. After the war, because of generous federal aid in the form of tariffs and subsidies, and favorable judicial decisions, which made it difficult for individual states to regulate business activity, big business increasingly became part of the American way of life.

The depression of 1893, which had crippled the economy for five long years, was now little more than a fading memory. The great corn crops from the fertile plains of Kansas; the unprecedented prosperity of the iron and steel industries; the enormous expenditures on transportation; the rapid advance in manufacturing inventiveness and efficiency; the dramatic increase in industrial output and the expansion of foreign trade; the vibrancy of the Stock Exchange; and the 93 billion dollars of bank clearings in 1899, eloquently proclaimed the birth of a new industrial giant.

America's dizzying rise to world power status had been propelled by the Spanish-American War, which lasted less than four months and cost less than 250 American lives. But that brief contest, that glorious little war, which officially began on April 25, 1898, when the Cuban coast was blockaded and ended on August 12, of the same year, when American troops, encountering almost no resistance from the Spanish, entered and occupied Manila, was a turning point in the nation's destiny. No longer would the country be satisfied just being a continental nation. Not only were Cuba, Puerto Rico, the Philippines and the Pacific island of Guam acquired; but more importantly, America's gaze was turned outward, as it became strategically supreme in the Caribbean and deeply involved in the international politics of the Far East.

In America, the nineteenth century had been a time of extraordinary, perhaps unparalleled change and achievement. A tiny fringe of Eastern States with five million people of, generally, very similar backgrounds had been transformed into a racially and ethnically diverse, continental nation of seventy-six million people. Nineteen million immigrants had been absorbed, if not always welcomed, and dispersed around the country. After a long, brutal and bloody struggle, the proud Native American tribes had been conquered and the rugged western frontier subdued. Big cities with towering buildings reaching further into the skies than the tallest trees had transplanted giant forests and seemingly endless prairies; and the geographic center of population had shifted an astounding 475 miles to the west.

Seeing all this, many Americans came to believe, perhaps understandably, that America was a special nation, a nation whose destiny was most memorably described by Senator Albert J. Beveridge of Indiana: "God has marked the American people as His chosen nation to finally lead in the regeneration of the world. This is the divine mission of America, and it holds for us all the profit, all the glory, all the happiness possible to man. We are trustees of the world's progress, guardians of its righteous peace."

Standing outside the North Gate among a small group of fellow black Americans but well apart from the ebullient white citizens waiting to be admitted into the nation's inner sanctum, a pensive Richard Alexander Barrington watched quietly as the Cabinet Ministers and ambassadors and statesmen from around the world, some graciously acknowledging the crowd with small waves from their ornate, handsome carriages, made their stately way along Pennsylvania Avenue.

The eighteen-year-old had lain awake for much of that final night of the dying century, watching the snow hurl itself in impotent rage against the windows of his bedroom, waiting impatiently for the first light of the sun to officially proclaim the birth of a brand new age. It would be many years before he would be able to identify the mysterious source of the unrealistic optimism that had made him almost giddy with anticipation on that first morning of the twentieth century, as merely the innocence and natural buoyancy of youth.

It was not that he did not understand what was happening in the city in which he and more than five earlier generations of his family had been born and raised. He had listened carefully, far more carefully than his studied air of careless indifference could have led them to suspect, to his parents and the other adults around him, and he had seen and experienced for himself many of the changes that were taking place in his city. He had been fully aware, or as much as somebody of his age could be, when he awoke that morning, that the relationship between the races, what little there was of it, was deteriorating and at a fairly rapid pace. And he knew only too well from the evidence of his own family, that some of the older people, especially those with the strongest ties to the white community, had begun to despair of the future.

But not him; he had felt that the confluence of his admittance to a famous university and the start of a brand new century were far more propitious of the future, at least his future, than the gloom that surrounded his elders. And so, with the boundless if untested optimism of the young, he had literally leaped out of bed that morning confident of his place in the glorious new century.

Despite the fact of his race Richard's confidence was not entirely misplaced. The Barrington's sat atop of what was locally known as the *crème de la crème* of black Washington society. Originally from Boston, the light-skinned family had lived as free persons in Georgetown for more than one hundred years, and a Barrington, a fact of which the family was immensely proud, had been one of the founders of the venerable Lotus Club. A club that, as the members frequently reminded the white community, antedated the whites-only Oldest Inhabitants Society by two full, gloriously ineradicable years. At a time when Washington was home to what many judged the most distinguished and brilliant assembly of Negroes in the world, the Barrington's were among the most distinguished and the most respected, by both races.

Many of the City's most influential black citizens had grown wealthy from catering, hotel-keeping and barbering, and wellknown from high profile political activity. But the reticent Barringtons had quietly restricted their professional and business activities to banking, real estate and medicine. Although for decades, a succession of luminaries, such as Frederick Douglass, Blanche Bruce, the Reverend Alexander Crummell, John Langston, and Mary and Robert Terrell, had been among their closest friends and associates, the family had deliberately maintained a low public profile, preferring to exercise influence indirectly and discreetly.

Richard's decision to apply to Yale, his father's alma mater, and his acceptance had surprised and delighted his parents. Not that they had ever doubted his ability, but he had led them to believe that there was nothing in the entire world he desired less than attending a white university his father held in high esteem. Howard, right there in their backyard, had seemed a far more likely destination. Peter and Catherine Barrington's youngest child, unlike his compliant and dutiful older brother and sister, had given his parents and siblings every reason to believe that there was almost nothing about Barrington traditions he either admired or wished to emulate; in fact, the very opposite seemed more likely. Whatever they held sacred he professed to find ridiculous. He had, as an example, frequently denounced their restraint and gentility as old fashioned and pretentious. But it was his palpable disdain for their long-held Episcopalian faith, his open contempt for their unquestioning acceptance of the social order, of the world as they found it, that they regarded as the most alarming and potentially the most dangerous.

The problem was that their youngest child, for reasons they did not fully understand, simply refused to behave like a Barrington. But it was not just his behavior that concerned them; it was his entire persona. The truth was, it was often whispered outside the immediate family, that it wasn't only that Richard did not behave like a Barrington, but that he hardly looked like one either, or for that matter, a Spyhax, his maternal ancestors, who were themselves descendants of Martha Washington. For a start, he was darker-skinned and bigger and broader than either of his parents or his siblings. Although individual parts, his medium-brown skin color, his 6'2" height, strong square face, short, blunt nose, loosely curled hair, wide, sensitive mouth, high, broad brow and wide-spaced brown eyes, could be traced to various ancestors, and his mother's unimpeachable reputation excluded even the hint of scandal, the net effect was often, for relatives and longtime friends of the family, quite startling. Nobody could remember ever seeing a Barrington or a Spyhax quite like him before. Even as a small child, he had radiated what grandmother Barrington had worriedly described as a "force of defiance."

As the twentieth century dawned, black parents, however light-skinned, affluent and well-connected to white America, had every reason to be worried about the future and safety of their children. Particularly those sons who, driven by what sometimes appeared to be irresistible hormonal urges, seemed determined to disregard the rigid conventions white America had designed to direct their behavior; who were inclined, despite the known danger, to challenge the power and prerogatives of white men by asserting their own manhood. For bold and ambitious young African Americans, the early decades of the twentieth century were not exactly the best of times.

More than 600,000 American men, many of them young, white and idealistic, had died, often heroically, on blood-drenched battlefields in a brutal contest for America's soul. Militarily, those who were said to believe that a nation conceived in liberty could not and should not survive half-slave and half-free had won that grisly and costly struggle. Three amendments to the constitution had seemed to give substance to those claims. The Thirteenth, Fourteenth, and Fifteenth Amendments had not only brought chattel slavery to an end, but had legally secured the full rights of citizenship, including the power of the vote, for American men of African descent. Nevertheless, in this new century, one-half of three score and ten years later, America still adamantly excluded every man, woman and child of known African descent from its circle of privilege. Possession of just one drop of that poisonous blood still negated every positive accomplishment.

Unfortunately, nothing in his upbringing or character had prepared Richard for a world where his choices and possibilities would be severely limited simply because of his race. Negroes, of his family's wealth and status, had understandably assumed that with the abolition of slavery the country had taken a decisive turn away from its virulent racial policies: And that educated and westernized Negroes of their type would link arms metaphorically, if not physically, with educated and liberal whites to lead the nation into a new era of tolerance and mutual understanding. In this new, enlightened America, Negroes like Richard would have had an equal opportunity at the fabled American dream. Even with the disappointments of the recent years, the Barrington children, like others of their background, had been raised with the expectation that they would be able, despite their race, to enjoy and exercise the prerogatives accorded to all full American citizens.

It was, perhaps, a combination of the force of these expectations and the inherent spirit of "inner defiance" that had so concerned his grandmother, which had led Richard to the North Gate of the White House that morning. For several weeks there had been a great deal of talk among the adults about the White House event, much of it lamenting the changes taking place in the country and the growing hostility against even the most distinguished Negroes. The memory of Frederick Douglass, who had daringly invited himself to Lincoln's second inaugural reception, was repeatedly summoned and stories of black congressmen and senators dancing with their wives at Ulysses S. Grant's second inaugural ball were repeated and embellished with relish. When he, Richard, tiring of listening to such impotent railings, had impudently suggested that they do something about it, he had been told, in what he regarded as dismissive and patronizing tones, that he simply did not understand that "things were different now and that he would understand more fully one day."

Stung by his curt dismissal, Richard had conceived of a plan, inspired by the legend of old family friend Frederick Douglass, whose portrait retained a prominent place in the Barrington drawing room, to simply invite himself to the White House ceremony. He had remembered reading in one of the local newspapers that invitations or passes were not required to enter the White House. The White House, the theory went, was the people's house and the people had almost as much right as the President himself to enter the house that had been bought and was maintained by the people's taxes. By that measure, Richard concluded, since very few white citizens contributed as much to the purchase and maintenance of the White House as his family did, he had at least as much right as almost any of them to visit the

White House whenever it pleased him.

Knowing that his parents would not approve of his plan and unwilling to openly defy them, Richard had kept it to himself. Although there were only seven years and five years respectively between his brother and sister and himself, Richard often felt that his older siblings belonged to a different generation, closer in attitude and outlook to their parents than to him. Their response, he had decided, would be very little different from his parents; confiding in either of them would almost certainly lead, he knew, to the information being passed on almost immediately to his parents.

So, he had dressed quietly, in the same dark suit, white shirt and blue tie he had worn to his interview at Yale, and after penning a brief note explaining that he was going to "observe the festivities at the White House," had slipped out of the house without attracting the attention of the rest of the family or the servants. Wrapped in his heavy woolen overcoat and with the snow on the ground melting rapidly under the relentless assault of the fierce sun, Richard had briefly debated the relative merits of walking or hailing a cab with himself. But the familiar sight of old Mister Jonathan, grayer and more wrinkled than ever, driving the same sturdy but now fraying hansom with which he had serviced the neighborhood for as long as he could remember, had quickly decided the matter.

He had mentally rehearsed a thousand times exactly how the bold deed would be done. He would behave, he had decided, just like any white person would. He'd simply walk up to the gate and without looking left or right, without pause or hesitation, nonchalantly step inside as if he owned the place. But that was before he had explained to the politely insistent Mister Jonathan exactly why he wanted to be driven to the front gate of the White House on this particular cold and snowy morning. The old man had been aghast, first staring at him as if he had lost his mind and then in the slow and patient voice normally reserved for the dull or the insane had carefully and ruthlessly exposed the folly of his plan.

"Dere's goin to be a big crowd of white people all lined up an waitin by de time we git dere," the old man had explained in the peculiar nasal drawl whose geographic origins neither Richard nor any other member of the Barrington family had ever been able to identify and which he had resolutely refused to disclose. After several years of futility the family had reached a consensus that the eccentric old man had probably invented it himself. "And ye'll have to git in line wid dem for one, maybe two 'ours or even more. An I can tell you right now, dere's no way dose white people goin to let you or, beggin your pardon Mistah Richard, any odder nigger, stand dere wid dem in dat line in front of de White House for all dat time. No way it goin to appen Mistah Richard."

Mortified that he had completely overlooked such an obvious scenario, Richard had only been able to manage a mild "Are you sure," in protest. And when the old hansom driver had offered to take him back home for the same fare he had merely asked instead to be let out down the street, well away from the White House and on the other side of the road. After paying and thanking the old man he had slowly made his way down Pennsylvania Avenue, barely glancing at the long line of white humanity snaking along the White House fence, too angry with himself to notice the curious and often friendly stares directed at the tall, imposing, well-dressed young man, who many assumed was probably a member of one of the more exotic diplomatic contingents from Latin America.

Inside, the old mansion was ablaze with sunlight streaming through every window and from the soft electric glow of its magnificent chandeliers. The slightly shabby but stately Red Room, richly furnished in the French Empire style introduced by President Monroe, was brightly illuminated by the sun and a gilded 36-light chandelier hanging from the middle of the ceiling. On this morning, the room's normal formality was relieved by garlands of smilax and clumps of palms and foliage plants interspersed with poinsettia blooms and rubber plants. Amidst this curious mix, representatives of all the great nations of the world, and some lesser ones, also waited patiently to pay their respects to the Twenty-fifth President of the United States.

Observing it all, some making notes and others simply staring, were a small contingent of ladies and gentlemen of the press. Among those carefully making notes was the tall, fresh-faced, fair-haired Daniel O'Brien, who was doing his best to contain his awe and growing excitement. Despite his awe, the White House that Daniel walked into that first morning of the twentieth century was hardly the imposing mansion it would later become. Designed originally as the home and office of the Chief Executive of a small republic, it had from Lincoln's time become increasingly inadequate for the demands imposed by the nation's expanding status. Modern conveniences: a steam-heating system, bathtubs with running water, a creaking elevator which ran on water pressure from a tank on the roof, telephones, and electric lighting, had been periodically added; but no concerted attempt had been made to adapt it to the realities of America's central place in the new century. Or even to repair the dangerous dilapidation into which it had slowly fallen, and which now threatened the safety of both occupants and visitors.

By tradition and in sharp rebuke to the aristocratic traditions of European rulers, the mansion and the President were expected to be readily accessible to the American people. Every day, until two o'clock, sightseers were permitted to prowl through the East Room, where the first occupants, John Adams and family, had dried their laundry on two "Ten Plate" stoves, and which Thomas Jefferson had partitioned to provide two rooms for his secretary, Meriwether Lewis, later to become co-leader of the Lewis and Clark expedition.

Every room on the first floor, except the dining room, was open, at some time, to visitors; and Grover Cleveland had been severely criticized for making even that private. And, on some days, when the East Room was filled with citizens admiring its massive crystal chandeliers and plush yellow ottomans, it was not uncommon for President McKinley, outfitted in his customary black Prince Albert coat, white waistcoat, which he fastidiously changed several times a day, boiled shirt, dark tie, high collar and striped pants, to go downstairs, station himself at the door, and shake the hand of every visitor as he or she took reluctant leave of what they clearly understood was the people's house.

The Army Engineers, the body to which the maintenance of the building had been entrusted, had warned ominously of the possibility of either fire or collapsing floors, or both, occurring during a large reception. Unimpressed, Congress continued to provide barely enough appropriations to mend carpets, upholstery and curtains. Peeling wallpaper in the state dining room and reception parlors, sagging furniture, faded drapes, creaking floors and shaky banisters, humiliated White House staffers and scandalized distinguished visitors. Even on the eastern wing of the second floor, where the six-room executive suite was located, the parade of generations of office seekers had weakened the floor beams, rendering them dangerously shaky.

Upstairs, in their spacious bedroom on the second floor of the west wing, on this first morning of the new century, the first couple were happily untroubled by the many inconveniences of the White House. Their private living quarters consisted of five bedrooms and two dressing rooms, but much of their time was spent here in the big northwest chamber where they slept.

The President, with the skilful assistance of his mulatto valet and personal factotum, William Sinclair, was already fully dressed in the white tie and tails prescribed by protocol for formal occasions. At a time when facial hair was highly fashionable, he was clean-faced, freshly shaven and waiting patiently for his Ida. He had awoken that morning in a particularly upbeat mood. He was not an emotional man but the new century seemed so full of promise, to offer so much for his administration and the country, that he was filled with what he felt was a justifiable sense of satisfaction and well-being. Unlike his jingoistic and young and inexperienced Assistant Secretary of the Navy, Teddy Roosevelt, he, the Civil War veteran who had seen the horrors of war up close and in person, had been a reluctant warrior, but he no longer had any doubts about the wisdom of the war. The letter from Horace Porter had neatly summed up what he himself had come to believe. Public men in Europe, the Ambassador had written, were saying that by taking control of a chain of island posts in the Pacific and capturing their trade, America had virtually taken control of that ocean and in so doing, had done in three months what the great powers of Europe had sought in vain to do for more than one hundred years.

Manila, afterall, was a perfect post from which to defend the country's interests in the Orient. Not only was it only a few days from the Chinese coast but also it was easily defended, and our command there removed the specter of Chinese or Russian armies at our back. And from his reception across the country, especially in the South where he, a Republican and Union Officer, had not expected anything like the welcome he had received, it was obvious that the common people agreed that America was simply taking its rightful place among the leading nations of the world. They fully agreed, with his own creed, he had come to realize, that it was America's duty to educate and civilize the Filipinos. Uplifting and Christianizing the backward people of the world was, they understood, the burden God, in his infinite wisdom, had placed on the white man.

Despite its size, its pale walls and carpeting and white upholstery, and the grandeur of a lofty painted ceiling and a carved marble mantel topped by an elegant mirror, this main bedroom managed somehow to seem cozy, even cluttered. Twin, thin-railed brass beds with white counterpanes and a pair of heavy, mirror-paneled wardrobes commanded much of the room; but the eclectic furnishings also included a sofa, two tufted easy chairs, a pedestal table on which stood a white-ruffled electric lamp that was plugged into the rickety chandelier overhead; and, incongruously, on either side of the table a cheap, spindle-backed wooden rocker.

Souvenirs, knickknacks, fringed scarves, ruffled pillows, photographs, and a portrait of little Katie, enshrined in an exquisite blue frame set with jewels, which the President had purchased that Christmas as a present for his wife, filled the walls and the mantelpiece and spilled over onto the chairs and sofa. Katie had died in 1876, the year her father had been first elected to Congress, when she was only four and a half, but now, almost a quarter of a century later, the pain of her parents had barely diminished.

The McKinley's were almost perfect representatives of their country and its most cherished fables. Neither royal birth nor lordly gifts of mind or spirit were to be, this tale went, overly admired in this land of the common man. He, the white everyman, born of modest circumstances, modestly educated and modestly gifted, except for the silver tongue which often laid a layer of sturdy commonsense on even the most banal sentiments; but devout, devoted, genial and persistent; living proof that any white, Christian, American boy of good character and Western European descent could, with a bit of luck, become President of the United States of America. She, the pretty sister, mindful daughter, dutiful wife, devoid of any noteworthy talents or ambitions but endowed with a modest fortune by a loving father. They, the first couple of the land, equal or more in power and prestige to the crowned heads of Europe, but resolutely unaffected in their supreme Americanness by the pomp and splendor of their temporary circumstances.

And, as he had been for almost all of their twenty-nine-year marriage, the President of the United States was deeply concerned that morning about the state of his wife's health. Remarkably, her health had improved as she had gotten older, and by her standards she had been fairly healthy since they had been in the White House. But large receptions were always an ordeal for her. During his term as Governor of Ohio and even here in the White House there had been minor convulsions in public. Elaborate precautions had been taken to make them as inconspicuous as possible. During dinners, she was usually seated to his right and he had become adept at nonchalantly covering her face with his napkin, a procedure that seemed to serve the dual purpose of concealing her distorted features and abbreviating the attack. When receiving callers she was never left alone, and on state occasions, her maid hovered close by, ready always to whisk her swiftly and discreetly away, through the Red Parlor and the State Dining Room and into the safety of the elevator, which led to the private quarters upstairs.

The constant fear, his and hers, was that someday one of her massive, frightening epileptic attacks would take place in the full view of the whole world. One of them, in 1888, had been so violent and prolonged, that her doctor had thought it unlikely that she would recover. But, today, she had assured him, was one of her better days. In truth, he thought, as he fondly watched the nimble fingers of her Swiss maid, Clara Thorin, touching and fluffing the Greek bob in which she wore her hair, Dr Bishop's bromides seemed to be worth their considerable price. The improvement in her health began after she became his patient, of that there could be no doubt. From his perch on one of the two tufted easy chairs, he marveled at the woman's speed and agility as she fussed over his wife's dress and hair, which had been cropped short years before, when the weight of braids and hairpins had become unbearable to her.

Despite the enormity of his duties, his wife still demanded his advice on her clothes, as she always had, and he was happy to comply however limited his contribution. It was his presence, he understood, that she really wanted, that she found so reassuring. To Ida, one of the most attractive features of the White House was the fact that her husband's office was only down the hall from their bedroom, enabling her to summon him quickly and easily.

Back downstairs, Daniel carefully noted that the members of the Cabinet and their wives and daughters had begun arriving by the south portico and that after depositing their coats and wraps in the state dining room they had all made their way upstairs, presumably to visit with the President and Mrs. McKinley. Since, unlike *The New York Times*, his paper had not sent a Society reporter to cover the activities of the cabinet ladies, he had decided after a brief debate with himself to do his best, however poor that was, to include them, even how they were dressed, in his report and hope for the best.

"At precisely 11 o'clock, and exactly on time," Daniel quickly scribbled in his manufactured shorthand, glancing at his watch as the sound of bugles heralded the approach of the President, *"the clear, sharp blast of bugles sounded the assembly, and the red-coated Marine Band struck up the stirring chords of Hail to the Chief."* Pleased with this opening sentence, he added the following as the Presidential party made its slow and regal entrance. *"At this signal, President and Mrs. McKinley, accompanied by the members of the Cabinet and their ladies, descended down the broad stairway, with the Secretary to the President, the stout and pompous, J. Addison Porter, assisting Mrs. McKinley, and took*

their places in the Blue Parlor." Then with an impish smile he drew two quick lines through the phrase *"the stout and pompous"*, to remind himself that that description of the President's powerful Secretary should not be part of his official report.

Unlike the adjoining Red Parlor, the Blue Parlor, glittering from the electric brilliance radiating from its French Empire gilt wood chandelier, was almost bare of decoration; the President and Mrs. McKinley having decreed that its pale blue loveliness should be admired without distraction. Two tall bouquets of white hyacinths, one topped with pink carnations and the other with a spray of pink orchids, were the only exceptions.

Daniel had prepared diligently for the assignment, just as his grandfather had ordered, by carefully studying the reports of previous years and learning the names and titles, and their correct spelling, of all the major personalities who were expected to attend the event. But he had quickly realized that describing what the ladies were wearing was well beyond his capabilities. That shortcoming was soon fixed with a whispered confession of boyish ignorance on matters pertaining to the fairer sex, blushing as he did so, to the stout but fashionably dressed Society reporter from *The New York Times*, who was only too willing to lend a helping hand to the handsome young man with the exquisite manners from the rival paper. With the assistance of his new friend Daniel was able to add the following to his narrative. *"Mrs. McKinley, in an elegant gown of pale mauve brocade with a string of diamonds clasped around her neck, as was her custom sat immediately in a large, throne-like blue velvet chair and remained seated throughout the proceedings. Next to the First Lady stood a phalanx of women, brilliantly gowned in brocade, silk, satin, lace, velvet and crepe: Mrs. Hay, wife of the Secretary of State; Mrs. Gage, wife of the Secretary of the Treasury; Mrs. Root, wife of the Secretary of War; Mrs. Griggs, wife of the Attorney General; Mrs. Smith, wife of the Postmaster General; Mrs. Long, wife of the Secretary of the Navy; Mrs. Hitchcock, wife of the Secretary of the Interior; and Miss Wilson, daughter of the Secretary of Agriculture. Behind the receiving line gathered the wives and daughters of Senators and members of Congress, and other officials, also all brilliantly gowned and coifed; discreetly attempting to outdo each other for attention from the powerful men and the ladies of the press, who were busy recording the details of each lady's dress and accessories."*

With everybody in place, the doors to the Red Parlor were finally thrown open. Then, as Daniel recorded, *"the Ambassadors and Ministers of Foreign Governments and their parties, resplendent in full Court dress, moved into the Blue Parlor to be greeted by the President and Mrs. McKinley. At their head, long, bushy white whiskers framing his round, florid face, marched Lord Pauncefote, the British Ambassador and Dean of the Diplomatic corps, accompanied by Lady Pauncefote and their four daughters. The elegant Secretary of State, John Hay, standing at the President's left, smoothly introduced each member of the diplomatic corps. "*

Daniel would be one of several reporters who would later describe the scene in the Blue Parlor that day as surpassing in brilliance anything that had been previously witnessed on American shores. His report would describe the impressive uniforms of the Russians and the Germans and the *"tastefully-flamboyant, sable-trimmed, purple cape of the Austrian-Hungarian Minister, Mr. Ladislaus Hengelmuller."* He told his readers that a *"slew of Oriental dignitaries, many of them exotically dressed in bright silks, added color and quaintness to the proceedings"* and he even noted that *"many of the surprisingly large number of women in the diplomatic corps were more than adequately attractive."*

But it was his description of the American participants that his editor would select for commendation. *"The blue and gold uniforms of the army; the black-plumed chapeaus of the navy; and the light blue uniforms and black helmets with red decorations of the marines,"* he wrote, *"Seemed, almost, to mock the somber duties they represented."* And he explained that *"the American army, now though swollen to four times its size during previous receptions, was represented by its smallest delegation in twenty-five years: Most of its officers being on active duty in the new colonies of the Philippines, Cuba and Puerto Rico."* He also noted the presence of veterans of the Mexican, Civil, and Spanish-American Wars and that *"pride of place was given to the dwindling few that had fought in the Mexican War."*

Daniel ended his article by declaring the event, which he claimed had been attended by exactly 3,354 persons, *"a resounding success and a pleasant augury for the new year and the new century."* It was a judgment that was enthusiastically shared by all the other major newspapers present that day. Not a single report acknowledged that although President McKinley was a disciple of Lincoln and a Republican, the party to which the vast majority of black Americans then claimed allegiance, that the attendees at the White House that first day of the twentieth century were all white or Asian. Not one commented on the fact that at the dawn of the new century not a single black man or woman would have been welcomed as a guest in the people's house. Not one thought it worth reporting, that whatever his personal inclination, that the President of the United States would not have dared to commit such an offense against the American people.

That sad litany was of course not news. It was simply the state of the American nation on the first day of the twentieth century.

A world away from the grandeur of Washington, a tall, lanky young man glided effortlessly along an eerily quiet shore, gracefully evading scattered mounds of debris, his lithe confident stride belying the cheap, fraying, ill-fitting clothes he wore. It was a perfect late September day on Galveston Island. Warm and sunny with billowy white clouds floating under a pale blue sky and a cooling wind blowing gently off the tranquil waters of the Gulf of Mexico. But the ebony-skinned runner, except for an occasional hollow-bellied, mangy dog ripping at a bloated, rotting carcass, was all alone, for as far as the eye could see.

At first, the well-worn heavy work boots barely caressed the coarse, dark-stained sand and the runner seemed oblivious of the devastation and the rotten-sweet stench of death all around him. Then as the distance mounted and the yards turned into miles, the beads of sweat turned into rivulets, the breathing grew ragged, the footsteps slowed and the clinging sand gradually tightened its grip. But the runner, eyes now focused and mouth set in grim determination, kept going, kept moving relentlessly forward. Jack Johnson was running for his life.

Only two weeks earlier the world as he knew it had been utterly and totally destroyed. Until then pugilism had been an occasional ambition pursued with only moderate effort and modest success. Starting from the tender age of seventeen, Johnson had made frequent but relatively brief forays to the big cities of New York, Chicago and Pittsburgh, centers of the still-new, almost completely unregulated and ruthlessly Darwinian world of professional pugilism. Run, in the main, by cold-eyed, flint-hearted white men, it was a world that devoured eager and naive young black men with pitiless ardor. Frequently unable to earn enough to even feed himself, the young Johnson might have been one of those unfortunates except for the always welcoming refuge of his family's Galveston home.

In 1900 Galveston was not just any town. Immensely successful, fabulously wealthy and inordinately confident of its future, it was on the first day of the twentieth century, as it had been for decades, the leading city in Texas and one of the wealthiest communities in the country. Surpassing even such famed east coast centers of affluence as Newport, Rhode Island. The site of a medical college and the first post office in the Lone Star State and its only deep-water port, Galveston was the hub of a booming cotton export trade. The bustling downtown area was dominated by large ornate buildings, and the financial center, The Strand, was widely known as the Wall Street of the Southwest. Well-maintained city streets led to imposing mansions of Greek Revival, Romanesque and Italianate designs. Packed streetcars ran at frequent intervals along the crowded beach and popular bathhouses dotted the gulf shoreline like an army of sentinels.

All of that changed forever on one brutally unforgettable night. On September 8 of that year one of the most powerful storms to ever strike the United States swept off the Gulf of Mexico and with scant warning rolled over the island from gulf to bay, relentlessly destroying everything in its path. It was, when it was finally over, even now more than a century later, the single deadliest natural disaster in American history. Violent winds exceeding 150 miles per hour, rain that poured out of the heavens in endless torrents, and tidal waves measuring almost sixteen feet, took the lives of at least 8,000 men women and children, many of them among the most prominent in the white community, and wiped away twelve city blocks, three-quarters of the entire city.

The Johnsons were luckier than most. Their sturdy little house at 808 Broadway was reduced to rubble, but, unlike so many others in the rest of the city, they did not lose a single member of their large and close-knit family. Patriarch Henry Johnson had had been born a slave in Maryland and could neither read nor write. And, although quite a bit smaller than his famous son, he had, at the behest of his owner, for the entertainment of other wealthy and jaded slave holders, become a fairly proficient bare-knuckle fighter. Henry's pugilistic career was far less successful than his son's however. In 1880, two years after Jack's birth the forty-two-year-old ex-slave, who had married a woman nineteen years his junior, was listed in the federal census report as a paralyzed laborer. Somehow, despite those formidable handicaps, Henry managed not only to find work as a janitor at a public school for black children but also to acquire a small plot of land in Galveston and to build a house on it. By the 1890's the ambitious and diligent ex-slave had become the janitor for the entire East School District, a job he held for the next decade.

Remarkably, in some way, at some stage in his unrelentingly harsh existence, this illiterate but sober man who had been a slave until his mid-20s, had embraced the traditional middleclass virtues of hard work, fidelity, piety and education. With his wife and partner Tina, who he had married while she was still in her early teens, Henry had raised six children—three others had died at birth—in, as the saying goes, the shadow of school and church. And all six, three boys and three girls, learned to read and write, a not inconsiderable achievement for Americans of the period, black or white.

The Johnson's home may have been poor in material comforts but by more spiritual measures it must have been uncommonly rich. In just nine short years this lanky, inexperienced young man would leave his shattered home and without money or sponsor and in defiance of persistent racism and against all odds travel across the country taking on all comers, honing his craft, relentlessly establishing himself as the best in the business. And when prejudice blocked his path to the title in the United States he would chase the champion across much of Europe before cornering and effortlessly destroying the unfortunate Tommy Burns in distant Australia.

Two

The early afternoon sun had cleared the towering hurdle of Mount Coot-tha and was just beginning its gentle descent across the pale blue Brisbane sky when a lone automobile conveying the new heavyweight champion of the world drove slowly through the semi-circular gateway of the main entrance to the immense Toowong Cemetery. Eight weeks after becoming the first black man to win the world heavyweight boxing title, Jack Arthur Johnson, had come to Queensland's newest and largest burial ground to pay quiet homage to another black fighter of immense talent, Peter Jackson, who, except for racism even more virulent and unbending than he himself had faced, would probably have deprived him of that signal historical honor.

The Black Prince, as the cultured and chivalrous Jackson had been admiringly named, had died almost eight years earlier of tuberculosis and heartbreak, three days before his fortieth birthday. Penniless and broken in spirit at the time of his death, only the intervention of friends and supporters had rescued the great West Indian boxer from a pauper's grave. Born on July 16, 1861 in the town of Christiansted on the tiny island of St. Croix, Jackson had begun his working life as a naval apprentice to a Danish merchantman at the precocious age of ten. Seven years and countless nautical miles later the able-bodied seaman would make his way to Australia and discover in himself a natural aptitude for the art of boxing so enormous that he would win the Australian heavyweight title after a mere year of tutelage.

Soon however racial hatred and no doubt fear and envy reared their ugly heads and not even the prospect of winning the heavyweight title proved sufficient to lure any of the top challengers. One, Jack "The Irish Lad" Burke, expressed the common sentiment of the time when he insisted that he would not lower his reputation by fighting a black man. Disheartened, unable to make a living in his adopted country and hoping for better prospects elsewhere, Jackson embarked on a 9,000 mile journey to the United States, arriving in San Francisco in April of 1888 aboard the Almeda.

At first, as in Australia, success came quickly. Throughout 1888 and 1889 he took on all comers, emphatically dispatching a string of opponents of both races. But soon, once again, as in Australia, racism would intrude to derail his blossoming career. America's first-ever sporting hero, the heavyweight champion of the world, the great John L. Sullivan, made it abundantly clear that he would not, under any circumstances, give Jackson a shot at his title, publicly declaring "I will not fight a Negro. I never have and never shall."

Undeterred by this latest setback Jackson took his campaign to London where he won the title of Champion of the British Empire. Returning to the United States he met the rising star James J. Corbett for what was then a world record purse of two thousand pounds. Despite the handicap of a sprained ankle that severely restricted his mobility, Jackson battled Corbett for sixty-one rounds over just more than four hours; at which stage the fight was declared, "no-contest," because neither man was physically capable of continuing.

A year later Corbett easily defeated Sullivan in the first heavyweight title bout fought with gloves. In the meantime Jackson had returned to England where he defeated Francis "Paddy" Slavin at the august National Sporting Club of London in what one historian described as "one of the most viciously contested fights ever held in England." In the audience for the tenth round knockout, and immensely impressed with Jackson's prowess, was what was described at the time as a large and representative assemblage of sportsmen, including many members of the British nobility; one of whom, Lord Lonsdale, had acted as Jackson's timekeeper. The stage seemed set for a return bout between Jackson and the new heavyweight champion of the world. But the new champion would have none of it, effectively drawing the color line against the man who had given him his toughest fight.

Finally realizing that he would never be given a chance to fight for the title for which he had campaigned for much of his adult life and now at the age of thirty-seven, his once formidable physical powers severely eroded by time, alcohol and disease, Jackson was defeated by a 23-year-old giant with a devastating punch, named Jim Jeffries. Three years later on the very day of what should have been his fortieth birthday he was laid to rest at Toowong.

The taxi had made its way through the avenue of bamboo trees that framed the entrance and was crawling carefully over the rugged and undulating terrain of the cemetery, past small, scattered groups of men, women and children, some of them tending gravesites, others merely enjoying what appeared to be picnics, when the newly crowned heavyweight champion of the world tapped the driver on the shoulder and asked, "Are you sure you know where to find it."

Johnson impatience was understandable. He had arrived in Brisbane that morning aboard the great Australian liner RMS Makura, now moored in Moreton Bay, to fulfill a series of public engagements and was due to reboard the vessel for Vancouver that very night. Just getting to the cemetery, which was located at the base of Mount Coot-tha, on the outskirts of the city, had taken more time than he had expected. Now, as the vehicle struggled along the winding roads that formed the boundaries of the various religious and cultural sections, the beauty and vastness of the heavily wooded two hundred and fifty acre site and the difficulty of finding a single gravesite there, became painfully apparent.

The driver was smoothly reassuring however. "Can you see that big stone at the top of the hill," he asked, pointing to a slender but imposing memorial to his left, "that was put up for Governor Blackall. Jackson is near here, on this side of the creek." Queensland's second governor, Samuel Wensley Blackall, was buried on Toowong's highest knoll on the third of January 1871. And, fittingly, his memorial was the largest and most prominent in the cemetery whose development he had championed and where he had asked to be buried, with appropriately commanding views of the city and the surrounding environs.

True to his word, within minutes the driver pulled up in front of an impressive two-meter high tombstone perched on top of a rise. "There it is," the driver announced triumphantly, "I told you we weren't too far away."

"Thank you," Johnson replied, "I'll be back in a minute." Then turning to his female companion, "Come on, Hattie, I want to take a closer look."

For a long solemn moment the heavyweight champion stood staring at Jackson's sandstone image, and then his head nodding in agreement silently mouthed the words from Shakespeare's Julius Caesar that had been selected as a tribute to the West Indian's life. "This was a man."

It was just after 4o'clock on the afternoon of March 9, 1909 and the Makura had just berthed at the Canadian Pacific Railway dock on the Vancouver waterfront after a 22-day trip across the Pacific. The year-old turbine steamship had ferried boxes and crates of coffee, butter, onions, coconut and eucalyptus oils, thousands of pieces of timber, exotica such as hides, pelts, legs of mutton and bales of sheepskins, plus 367 passengers, many of them returning from vacations in Hawaii. But the large crowd that had gathered at the pier, including a number of what one newspaper described as "camera fiends," who were everywhere, had come to get a glimpse of just one passenger, the new heavyweight champion of the world.

As he stood straight and tall on the deck, his massive, dark-coated frame silhouetted sharply against the clear, Vancouver skyline, Jack Johnson looked down at the waiting, impatient crowd and took a deep gulp of the chilly afternoon air. Sam may not have been right about much, he told himself, but he was right about one thing: I'm a very different man now than I was just three months ago.

Ten weeks, including three weeks at sea had given him a lot of time to think, to assess what he had accomplished, what it meant and how it would change his life. Barriers had been broken, but others, formidable ones, remained. Defeating a Canadian in a distant country might have made him, legally, the new heavyweight champion of the world. But many in the United States, particularly in the white community, would never accept him as such, he knew, until he met and defeated the man who had never been beaten in the ring, Jim Jeffries.

He had expected to win the title but, frankly, not that easily. The extent of his mastery had surprised even him. He could have finished Burns within a round or two if he had wanted to; but he had preferred to toy with the Canadian, to taunt him, to punish him. Burns, he recalled, the memory evoking a small, barely audible chuckle, had been game and tough because he had honestly believed that the longer the fight went the better was his chance of winning. Nigger fighters, the fervently held theory went, Johnson knew only too well, lacked stamina, were weak in the stomach and, of course, slow in the head.

The fight had been brutal and very, very, bloody. By the second round Burns' right eye had been discolored and blood had begun oozing out of his mouth. Halfway through the fight, his mouth hung open, his jaw swollen, probably broken. Blood from a dozen facial wounds ran down his shoulders, staining the carpet beneath his tottering feet. Between rounds his seconds had worked feverishly to keep him going, sponging his face with champagne to keep him going. But by the thirteenth it had become obvious to all, except possibly the two combatants, that Burns had nothing but courage left. Even the most bloodthirsty spectators, all male and almost to a man rabid Burns partisans, had begun yelling for the fight to be stopped.

Heeding their entreaties, the Sydney police had entered the ring at the end of the round but the champion, dreaming perhaps of landing one decisive punch to his tormenter's belly that would save his crown, stubbornly refused to concede.

In the fourteenth more punishment followed before, mercifully, a hard right cross knocked him off his feet and onto the canvas. Bravely, he had struggled to his feet at the count of eight, wobbly and stumbling blindly around the ring. Again the police had entered the ring: This time to end it, while Burns, still dazed and covered with blood, barely able to stand and hold his hands up, screamed with all of his remaining strength for another chance.

Inheriting the fabled crown, the mantle of Sullivan, Corbett and Jeffries, Johnson had conceded in one of his interminable internal dialogues, had changed him, as it would have, he had reminded himself, any other man. Not even the unrestrained viciousness of the racist Australian press had been able to completely dampen the joy of his conquest. He had been variously described as "a huge primordial ape," a "shaven-headed reptile," and "archetypal darkness." But one journalist, Randolph Bedford, had outdone his fellow racists with these memorable passages. "Yet the white beauty faced the black unloveliness, forcing the fight, bearing the punishment as if it were none... weight and reach were ebbing against intrepidity, intelligence and lightness...His courage still shone in his eyes; his face was disfigured and swollen and bloodied. He was still beauty by contrast—beautiful but to be beaten; clean sunlight fighting darkness and losing."

But, whatever they wrote, he had proven to the entire white world that their best man was no match for him, and now he had no intention of bending to their rules, to be limited by their ancient prejudices. He was the champion of the world and there was nothing they could do about it.

A small ironic smile dancing on his lips, he switched the walking stick he had been given by Aborigines in Australia from his right to his left hand and nonchantly folded the small, pale left hand of his female companion into his enormous, dark right one. "Remember, Mrs. Johnson," he said turning to her, mischief dancing in his eyes, "you're the former Nellie O'Brien of Philadelphia." Then, after a final appraisal of her curvy, buxom figure, fashionably attired in a dark, full length fur coat and a large hat covered with flowers, Johnson, in a heavy black overcoat over a dark grey suit, nodded his approval and quietly added: "Here they come, the gentlemen of the press, let's go meet them."

As the couple walked slowly down the gangplank hand-in-hand accompanied by flashing light bulbs and shouted greetings and questions, darting messengers squeezed through the crowd and delivered a small stack of telegrams to the new champion, who read them quickly, stuffed them into a pocket of his overcoat and stepped on land. The first black man to wear the coveted crown of heavyweight champion of the world had returned to the North American continent for the first time since his destruction of the former champion, Tommy Burns, in Australia.

Despite his poor treatment in Australia and the fact that his share of the fight proceeds had been humiliatingly paltry, $5,000 to Burns' $30,000, Johnson had every reason to feel good about himself that chilly Tuesday afternoon. True, the road to the title had been long and grueling. To get a shot at the heavyweight crown, the first ever for a black man, he had chased Burns around the world and fought for far less than any white man would have accepted. In a little more than two weeks he would be thirty-one years old, not young for a fighter. He had been fighting for fourteen years; but he had not just survived, he had prevailed. And, he knew with absolute certainty that the title would be his for many years; that no man on earth, black or white, was even close to being his equal in the ring.

On the ship but traveling separately from the champion and the woman who had been introduced to everybody on board as his wife, was Johnson's former manager, Sam Fitzpatrick. Johnson, Fitzpatrick would explain to anyone who would listen, was suffering from a severe attack of what he diagnosed as a "swelled head" since his defeat of Burns. Before that, the little, sharp-featured Irishman contended, Johnson had been content "to feed from the hand" but, as he would never tire of saying, Johnson "had gotten out of control" since winning the title. For his part, Johnson defended himself by saying that Fitzpatrick had been "too dictatorial," wanting to keep "too close a tab on his movements, insisting on being his guide and mentor from the time he left the breakfast table in the morning until he retired at night." When he, Johnson, had made it clear, that he did not intend "standing for such strict discipline," they had mutually decided to go their separate ways.

Then, there was the question of the erstwhile Mrs. Johnson; a relationship, of which Fitzpatrick made it clear, he heartily disapproved. Hattie McLay, who had worked as a prostitute in New York City, had been with Johnson while he pursued Burns around the world and although women were not allowed in the arena had been in Sydney with him when he won the title. She had also accompanied him on the piano, while he played the bass viola, during two warmly received concerts the champion gave aboard the Makura. But Fitzpatrick's objection to the relationship had nothing to with Hattie's sometime profession and everything to do with her race. He had been frank and straightforward about his absolute distaste for that kind of racial mixing. And that view, as the champion was now so clearly demonstrating, was not one that he any longer intended to give even the appearance of respecting.

Johnson's relationships with white women had begun several years earlier in Boston. There, while training, he met a young woman with whom he developed what must have been an emotionally substantial relationship. For not only did she share his home in that city but she had also willingly moved hundreds of miles across the country to be with him when he returned to Philadelphia, his home base at the time. But she was just the first of many such relationships. And, by the time he became champion, whatever allowance, however small, that he had been previously willing to cede to white America's social conventions, had evidently become too much for him to tolerate. Now, his relationships with white women, he had obviously decided, would be unafraid, open, and unapologetic.

"Yes, I will fight Jeffries," Johnson replied to the first question thrust at him, looking at his questioner in mild amusement, the ironic smile widening. "Nobody in the world is barred, and I don't believe that anyone boxing at the present time can get the decision over me or has any chance of knocking me out. About Jeffries I will talk in due time. What right has he got to claim the championship? That makes me laugh. When a mayor retires from office he's an ex-mayor, isn't he? Well, that goes for Jeffries. He's an ex-champion. If he wants to take a try at getting the championship back, all well and good, but he has to wait until I am ready to say the word."

"How soon will you be ready to meet the former champion," a

new questioner demanded, the tone of his voice clearly implying that Johnson might be trying to avoid his most dangerous opponent.

"I'm sick and tired of all this talk about Jeffries I see in the papers," Johnson replied, the voice still soft and even but the big smile shrinking. "You would think him the only one to be considered. I'm not making any restrictions, but Jeff will not get away with all the money, win, lose or draw. There will be a winner's end and a loser's end. I don't care what it is. He can cut the money sixty and forty or seventy-five and twenty-five percent, but I am going to have a word. I'm the champion, ain't I and I guess something is coming to me."

Warming to his subject, his smile returning, Johnson continued. "Burns wanted to make all the conditions when he was champion and I had to follow him all around the world. I knew I could get him and finally I had my show at Sydney. Burns got most of the money, but I'm the champion now. And if Jeffries really wants a go at me, as the papers say, I'm going to dictate that there shall be at least a winner's and a loser's end."

"It says here in the *Galveston Dispatch* that committees have been formed to arrange a parade and reception in Galveston to welcome you home. Did you know anything about that?" another voice asked.

"No," Johnson replied, his eyes sparkling, an uninhibited grin of pure pleasure baring his gold-tipped teeth, "But tell them I'll be there."

"What about Stanley Ketchel?" asked a little man, with bad teeth and sandy hair. "There is talk that you are going to give him a shot."

"It all depends on the offering," the champion replied expansively, "but I don't think anything can be done in that regard until after my theatrical engagements in England."

"It's being said in New York by a respected sporting man from Australia," a voice at the back of the gathering began, "that before the fight your manager had received an offer of $12,000 in cash to throw the fight to Burns. Can you confirm this story; is it true?

"Yes, I can confirm that story," Johnson said, turning serious, his voice grave, "but we turned them down cold. I don't think that's right. I don't know what they might have wanted to do, but you see they were afraid to come near me, and—-well, I don't think that kind of behavior is right."

"Where is Fitzpatrick; isn't he on the ship", a suspicious voice asked.

"He's on the ship, but he's no longer my manager," Johnson replied casually, "we've decided to go our separate ways."

"What caused the break-up," several voices, all speaking at once, demanded.

"I'd rather not say, maybe you should ask him," a suddenly reticent Johnson replied mildly, repeatedly refusing to add any further details.

"How was the trip," somebody asked, finally changing the subject.

"It was a great trip," Johnson responded enthusiastically, clearly grateful for the chance to move on to a less delicate topic. "Mrs. Johnson and I—glancing at his female companion standing demurely beside him—- even took part in a number of concerts on board. I played the bass viola, which, as some of you fellows know I don't do too badly with, and she accompanied me very nicely on the piano. But I must admit," he added cheerfully, "that sometimes, especially at night, the rolling of the steamer was too much for me. I have to say, all in all, that it probably got the decision."

"Did you give any concerts in Australia," a tall, thin, almost bald man, with a red bulbous nose and an incongruously large belly asked; his tone sardonic, almost mocking.

"Well, I wanted to give some selections at church entertainments there," Johnson answered, his voice earnest, the smile again fading. "I'm a churchman, belong to the Methodist church, but they did not seem to have much use for a colored man in the Methodist churches of that white Australia. They are good sports though," he quickly added, "they treated me fine, and I've got no kick coming. But on the surface," he continued, his voice turning malicious, "they seemed to think more of Tommy Burns after I had licked him, giving him such a licking as anybody ever had, than they did of me, and me the champion."

"What about that reference to Shakespeare, do you really read Shakespeare," another voice asked, the sneer barely disguised.

"That was a funny stunt about me finding comfort in Shakespeare's books and the Pilgrims Progress," Johnson agreed his voice soft and unperturbed. "But on the level I do read Shakespeare."

"Mrs. Johnson," somebody suddenly interjected, "what do you think of your husband.

"I'm very proud of him," Hattie McLay responded archly, moving closer to the champion and placing a possessive hand on his arm, "I think he is the greatest man in the world."

"Did you watch the fight?"

"I was very disappointed at not being permitted to see the fight at Sydney," she replied, moving even closer to the champion, tilting her head to look up at him, her eyes glowing, "my only consolation is that Mrs. Burns did not see it either."

"Jack, did you go into the Melbourne hospital as a charity patient," a new voice asked.

"Well, it was this way," Johnson began mildly, "I had some boils on my neck and kind of thought the Melbourne hospital the best place to go; but I could not go there as a charity patient. Why I drove there in my motor car."

"Did you pay for the treatment," the tall, thin man with the big belly and bulbous nose demanded his voice harsh and accusatory.

"Why, no," Johnson responded, a touch of irritation creeping into his voice. "It was a free hospital, wasn't it? And anyhow, I felt I was entitled to go there, for wasn't I paying an income tax of ten pounds, that's $50 a week on the two hundred and ten pounds I was getting a week for my theatrical work. Tommy Burns was getting more, but he had moving pictures. He was getting two hundred and fifty pounds a week. I kind of thought the income tax was sufficient to pay for what I got at the hospital. I offered to pay the doctor, anyhow," he added defensively, trying to win over the uniformly skeptical white faces, "but he wouldn't take my money. Then I wanted to send him some silk socks, but he wouldn't take them. I told him that men in America worth millions went to public hospitals, but he didn't seem to understand. Australia has no reason to complain about me, though," Johnson continued, the voice still mild but the big smile no longer reaching his eyes, "I have paid my income tax all the time and I raised a good deal of money for various charities while in Sydney. Yes," he acknowledged, holding up his open palm to deflect other questions, "there was some discussion by the hospital people and something got in the press. But gentlemen," Johnson said, taking Hattie McLay's hand, "my friends came all the way from San Francisco to welcome me back home and they have been patiently waiting, it is time for me to go."

"I'm truly sorry, "the balding, pasty-faced clerk began smoothly, practiced deceit radiating from every pore of his pudgy body, "but the hotel is filled to overflowing, there are no more rooms available." The heavyweight champion of the world on his first night back on North American soil since winning the title, accompanied by his "wife" and friends, were standing in the resplendent marble lobby of the St. Francis hotel, hoping to find suitable accommodation for the night. The hotel, Vancouver's finest, had a French chef and was housed in a new fireproof building with a stunning view of the harbor. It had been recommended to the champion as the place where people of his accomplishments and means stayed. And now tired but happy, he just wanted to go to bed.

The afternoon, after disembarking from the ship, had been a long but pleasant one; filled with food, laughter, story telling and reminiscing, and topped off with a visit to the home of a friend, George Paris, a jazz drummer and boxing instructor, where the group spent the early part of the night. But it had not been all fun, the champion had been eager to find out from the Californians what kind of opponent they thought Jeffries would make; repeatedly inquiring about the ex-champion's ability to get into shape.

"Are you sure you cannot find anything," Johnson replied affably, as he looked down at the little clerk with an enormous golden smile, and reached into an inside pocket of his obviously expensive overcoat to retrieve a bulging billfold, "money is not a problem, we can pay whatever the price is." Throughout Europe he had stayed in the finest hotels; even in Australia accommodation had not been a problem. Certainly, he thought to himself, here in North America they couldn't be refusing to have me because of my color, not now.

"It's not a matter of money," the clerk explained, faux smile firmly fixed in place, "all of our rooms are booked. Really, Mr. Johnson," he added with even more apparent sincerity, glancing nervously at the other members of Johnson's party who were eyeing him suspiciously," It cannot not be helped."

"The man says they are fully booked," the heavyweight champion of the world replied with a wan smile, turning away from the triumphant, now openly smirking clerk, "Let's try somewhere else."

"Jack, you don't believe that little worm, do you," Hattie asked, stepping forward and taking the champion's arm, her voice low but angry. "You know what's happening here, don't you," she demanded, disgust curling her lips. "They should be grateful to have you under their roof, but it's their loss not yours," she added, tossing her head and casting a cold, contemptuous look at a gawking guest.

"Well Hattie," Johnson answered his voice soft and uncertain, still more hurt than angry, "you may just be right. I was expecting more than this when I got home with the title. But you may just be right," he repeated, a little sadly, as they walked slowly through the glittering lobby, accompanied by dozens of disapproving stares. "We are going to find out soon enough," he added, as they stepped outside into the freezing night.

That night, as widely reported in the newspapers of the time, Johnson and his party would be turned away five more times: At the Hotel Irving with its electric elevator; at the Metropole, at the Rainier, and again at the Astor. In its report *The New York Times* wrote: *"The fighter took the turndown with good grace the first time, but when it was repeated in five other hotels, and especially $2 a day houses, he was abusive. Mrs. Johnson said little but* *plainly was disgusted at the turn of affairs. Later in the evening they obtained accommodations at the Dominion, a downtown hotel."*

Three

It was early morning and shafts of light from the young morning sun peered tentatively through the mottled clouds, filling the busy dining car with a ghostly glow. In the shifting, uncertain light, white-jacketed dining room attendants obsequetiously tended to fashionably dressed, pale-skinned men and women. Strong black hands smoothly delivered steaming silver platters to tables set with starchy white linens, glistening crystal and gleaming silverware.

Amid the din and clatter in this temple of wealth and luxury, but somehow apart from it, at a corner table at the end of the room closest to the private sleeping compartments sat four people, two very large men and their very well-dressed wives. Three of them, the two women and the smaller of the two large men, were deeply engrossed with breakfast and the kind of meaningless small talk common to people who know each other exceedingly well. Ignoring his companions and the quizzical glances of other travelers, the larger of the two large men stared intently through the mud-streaked window of the speeding train. He had spent much of the 20-hour trip from Chicago either sleeping or like that: locked in his own silent, private world.

Occasionally, his companions attempted to engage him in conversation but were rewarded with little more than a nod or a grunt.

"Aren't you eating darling, your pancakes are getting cold"

"Not hungry."

"Jim, what you're looking at, anything special out there."

"No."

"Jim, you think the crowd in New York will be anything like the one in Chicago."

"Hope not."

Normally, his appetite was, to put it gently, robust; but that morning he had done little more than pick at his plate, which was still overflowing with a normal favorite, light, fluffy, golden-brown pancakes, generously covered with thick, rich maple syrup. But, they, the people who knew him best, were neither alarmed nor offended. Not only was he, even at the best of times, a man of remarkably few words, but they also knew that the withdrawal was his way of coping with his great but unwanted fame; of zealously guarding whatever small zones of privacy he could manage; And of preparing himself for the relentless, endless scrutiny and pressure that they all knew would begin as soon as they arrived in New York City, then less than two short hours away.

Despite every appearance to the contrary, the big man, Jim Jeffries, retired, undefeated heavyweight champion of the world, enjoyed the comfort and isolation that traveling by first-class rail made possible. Except, of course, for those times when he was forced by necessity to use the public cars.

Although it had made its inaugural run less than seven years earlier, on June 15, 1902, the train on which the former champion and his party were traveling, the all-Pullman *Twentieth Century Limited*, was already the most famous of all American trains and the preferred method of travel in the East and mid-West for the most prominent men and women in the country. Beginning with the ritual unrolling of a symbolic red carpet down its platform in Grand Central Terminal, the *Twentieth Century's* policy was to spare no effort or expense in providing its rich and famous guests with the absolute ultimate in luxury travel.

A crew of almost seventy people, an average of fewer than two passengers for each crewmember, manned each train. In addition to a generous number of sleeper and dining car attendants, each train was staffed with an astonishing array of skilled help, among them maids, barbers, manicurists, valets, and male secretaries. On eastbound runs, the secretaries, all among the very best in their field, were routinely sent ahead to Elkhart, Indiana, where they transcribed closing stock prices and then boarded the *Twentieth Century* to report the market news, which for many of the wealthy passengers was absolutely vital information. Experienced professional planners arranged on-board meetings and parties with, often, remarkable dispatch and efficiency. For those with the means almost anything was possible aboard the *Twentieth Century.*

George Mortimer Pullman had not invented the sleeping car but he had, by the beginning of the twentieth century, transformed a good idea into the most remarkable transportation system in the world. Pullman had entered the sleeping car business in 1858; twenty years after the first sleeper had been introduced on the Cumberland Valley Railroad, later to become a part of the Pennsylvania Railroad. But it was not until 1865, when he completed the production of his legendary *Pioneer*, a triumph of American craftsmanship, that fate, in the guise of the assassination of President Abraham Lincoln, intervened in the sleeping car wars and propelled the Pullman's to the very top of the industry.

Lincoln's assassination the very year the *Pioneer* was completed, the location of the Pullman Company in Chicago, Illinois, Lincoln's home state, and the unprecedented high quality of the *Pioneer,* combined to win for the Pullman flagship the signal honor of carrying the great man's casket. *Pioneer's* association with the martyred president greatly enhanced its legend and before too long, probably before it was really fully deserved, the Pullman Company became, in the minds of the traveling public, the leading representative of its industry.

Riding in a Pullman Palace car, the exteriors painted a rich, dark brown to distinguish them from the drab coaches the masses had to be content with, was, decidedly, not cheap. At a time when the most highly skilled Americans earned less than one hundred dollars a month, a trip from Omaha to Sacramento cost an astounding one hundred dollars for a first class ticket and an additional four dollars a day for the privilege of securing a berth in a Pullman. Nevertheless, in mute testimony to the massively unbalanced distribution of wealth that has always been a feature of American life, demand was so great that within a year the Union Pacific would begin running as many as three sleeping cars on some trains and still be forced to turn away prospective customers.

Despite the high cost, a range of innovations introduced by Pullman, wider, convertible sofas and longer berths, provided comfortable sleeping space for all but the tallest and largest of men and made wealthy travelers increasingly eager to ride in them, regardless of the price. Tourists from around the world were properly impressed. So much so that British travelers, in particular, began peppering railway directors in their own country with letters imploring them "to take a leaf out of the Americans' book, and provide sleeping carriages for long night journeys."

Over the years, Jeffries, who had begun his working career as a lowly boilermaker, had grown fond of luxury and comfort. But long before he had become either rich or famous, traveling by train across the vast open spaces of the country had been a special delight. Although an indifferent student, at best, his youthful imagination had been captured by the stirring tales of Lewis and Clark, of the great Indian fighters and of the bold and fearless cowboys. Because of his great size, chosen profession and gruff demeanor, it was easy for those who did not know him well, and very few did, to mistake Jeffries for an unimaginative dullard, but nothing was further from the truth. Early in his life he had fallen in love with the sights, sounds and odors of the West. Nothing delighted him more than the simple pleasures of watching tumbleweed, in their thousands, wheel madly across the drying grass, and prairie fires blaze brightly against the distant horizon; listening to the hissing of fires rush across reddened ground: and inhaling the sharp-sweet smell of hay and dust and cattle and the elusive fragrance of wild flowers drifting through open windows. Those were the things he loved but in the real world he made his living as a fighter spilling blood.

It was just after nine o'clock on Wednesday morning, March 3, and Daniel O'Brien, was, as usual, running late. But this time, he told himself, glancing at his watch and tapping his fingers impatiently on the leather seat of the cab, the fault was not entirely his. Winter in the New York area had been remarkably mild all year but when he awoke that morning, he had not been certain that he would have been able to make it into the city at all. Only the importance of his assignment had dragged him out of bed and into the howling near-gale force winds and freezing rain that had battered savagely at his windows all night. But, by the time he left home, the raging storm had largely spent itself and the wheeling seagulls, just barely visible against the slate-grey sky, were angrily screeching their defiance for all to hear.

The still potent northwest winds had added several precious minutes to the trip across the grey, choppy North River from his home in Hoboken. The real problem began, however, when the pilot attempted to pull the 200-foot, double-decked ferryboat into its Manhattan berth. The wind and accompanying tide had turned the immense craft partially sideways as it approached its Manhattan dock.

Before the pilot could take corrective action, the redoubtable *Bergen*, the first propeller ferryboat built specifically for the North River, had begun bouncing madly, back and forth, from one side to another, like some mere child's toy. Daniel had always fancied himself the iron-stomached sailor but as he staggered out of the cabin, insides heaving, he knew that it was only the lack of breakfast that had prevented him from publicly despoiling that conceit. Many others on the craft, he had noted with a mixture of disgust and satisfaction, were not as fortunate that morning.

The downpour had almost completely stopped by the time he left the pier but with the competition for taxis fiercer than usual, getting one had taken even longer than it normally did. West Street had been filled with long lines of trucks, pulled by steaming teams of horses, straining and slipping on the icy streets, laden with merchandise bound to and from all parts of the country and the globe. But, sitting, and watching and listening as the taxi crawled through congested streets teeming with a dazzling variety of human types and an amazing array of vehicles, variously powered by horse muscle, electricity and motor, Daniel smiled as he remembered just why he had fallen in love with New York on first sight. The babble of languages and accents, the shouted curses, the impatient horns, the neighing of angry and frustrated horses, the mechanical grind and groan of shifting gears and screeching tires, unbearable, nerve-jangling noise to many, vibrant, pulsating urban music to him.

From his slow-moving cab Daniel watched the small crowd outside the towering, triangulated structure with sympathetic amusement. Many of the upturned faces were flush from the cold and the excitement of finally seeing for themselves the most famous building in all of the United States. Some of the more adventurous of them, in an effort to see to the very top of the 307-foot tower, had bent their heads so far backwards that a few had toppled over and fell, sprawling awkwardly on the ground.

Seven years after its completion, the Flatiron Building was still attracting far more attention than any other building in the city. Some of the attention was morbid, as some seemed convinced that there was a real danger that the slender structure would simply give way and fall over one day. One amateur architectural critic, commenting on the Flatiron's giant verticality, even calculated that if the building fell eastward it would almost reach Madison Avenue.

Although it was almost as familiar to him as his own home, the building that had been credited with revolutionizing American architecture had lost none of its allure for Daniel. No member of the press knew more or had written more admiringly about it than he had. Unlike many of the critics who had bemoaned the Flatiron's "disconcerting" break with the past; Daniel had been captivated by the technological advances that had made its construction possible. Reaching thirty-five feet underground, the twenty-storey edifice had been constructed of 3,680 tons of steel on an astonishingly tiny piece of triangular real estate. The fact that seventeen hundred office workers, more people than in many decent-sized suburban villages, worked daily on the site of that tiny piece of real estate never failed to amaze him.

Although it was not the tallest building in New York, the top floors of the Flatiron, in Daniel's enthusiastic if somewhat biased opinion, offered the most extraordinary panoramic views of the city. The mental pictures, from his first wide-eyed glimpse of the city from that great distance in the sky, were among his most precious. And sometimes when he was alone at night he would close his eyes and conjure them up, and awe and wonder would fill him up all over again. He had tried repeatedly to describe with mere words the magic of those first brief moments that had so captivated him, but, at least to him, without even a semblance of success, despite the considerable enthusiasm of his editor and the paper's readers.

"On one side of the Flatiron," he had written, in what he judged was his finest effort to capture the images burnt into his brain "is Broadway, which with the exception of trade routes is the longest commercial stretch on the face of the earth. On the other side is Fifth Avenue, which, without exception, is the richest thoroughfare in the world." But, he had explained, "from that distance in the sky both seemed extraordinarily small, terribly inconsequential, and almost mean. Moving purposefully about on them were creatures so tiny they appeared at first glance to be merely beetles and ants. But, more closely inspected the tiny creatures magically revealed themselves as taxis and human beings."

After a quick, brief stop at his office and a few fruitless minutes waiting for another taxi Daniel decided to walk to the Grand Central terminal, some ten blocks away, where Jim Jeffries, the former world heavyweight champion, was scheduled to arrive in a little more than twenty minutes. Although he was not one of their regular sports reporters, Daniel had been assigned the leading role in the coverage of Jeffries' arrival and stay in the city, to the displeasure of some on that desk.

Although covering the enormously popular former world champion was understandably seen by some of his less experienced colleagues as a plum assignment, Daniel knew from previous experience with the great man that the task, and task it was, posed a number of real challenges. Although not a word of criticism ever appeared in the newspapers, Jeffries was widely regarded by those in the know as an exceedingly difficult interview. The man had been a great champion, no doubt about it, but he was also, in the view of many, including Daniel, a boring, pompous ass.

Before his retirement even getting a simple statement out of him had been like pulling teeth. And, now, despite intense pressure the famously reticent Jeffries had, to date, refused to commit himself to challenging the new black champion or reentering the ring. He had come out of retirement from his Californian farm, he had announced, simply to go into vaudeville under a contract that had been reported to be worth the enormous sum of $50,000, for twenty weeks of appearances in the vaudeville theatres of William Morris, Inc. Nevertheless, the visit of the man who had been unbeaten during his entire ring career and now offered the whites of America a champion seemingly eminently capable of putting the upstart Johnson in his proper subservient place, had stirred up enormous public interest and speculation as to his future intentions. So much so that the *Tribune* had felt it necessary to ask him, one of their most experienced and talented correspondents to head up the reporting team.

Although he was not particularly fond of Jeffries the man, like almost every other white male in America, Daniel passionately wanted Johnson to be taught a lesson in respect by some white man. Therefore, despite some initial misgivings, he had gladly accepted the assignment. And as he made his way to the train station he was, despite the travails of the morning, in an exceptionally positive mood and looking forward, hopefully and a little eagerly, he admitted, to seeing for himself if Jeffries' physical condition and manner was that of a man who wanted to regain the heavyweight championship of the world.

Adjusting his dark blue overcoat against the wind whipping across 42nd Street, his thick shock of prematurely white hair flapping like the mast of a sailship in a storm, Daniel quickened his long, loose-limbed stride as he neared Bryant Park. Saturday night, he recalled happily, the sight of long red hair on an attractive young woman crossing to the other side of the street stirring up memories, had been almost perfect. The date with Bridget, he remembered, a smile softening the ruddy, square-jawed face, only their third, had gone remarkably well. Already, he sensed that despite the fourteen-year difference in their ages, that there was something special between them. Some mysterious chemistry, an ease, a special bond of understanding, which he had often heard of and read about but had not even remotely found with any other of the many women he had known. All that and beauty too, he thought, breaking into a grin.

The well-dressed young woman, who was bareheaded despite the weather, had in all likelihood crossed the busy street, he soon realized, to avoid the hordes of workmen at the site of the almost completed, new public library that was being built on the site of the old Croton Reservoir. Daniel had never seen anything quite like it. Neither had anybody else for that matter, since the monumental stone building, one of the finest examples of Beaux-Arts architecture in the country (two city blocks long- 390 feet across and 270 feet deep), was the largest marble structure ever constructed anywhere in the world. It had taken five hundred workmen some two years just to dismantle the massive reservoir and prepare the site.

Nothing, he knew, would please his parents more than news that he had finally found the right girl. At thirty-eight, he was still a bachelor and even his mother thought it was time to find a wife and produce a family. For years she had scoffed at criticisms of his wandering ways from other members of the family, pointing out that in the old country people rarely married as early as they did here in America. But, in the past several years, sometime shortly after his thirty-fifth birthday, even she had begun to drop the occasional pointed hint.

He had hoped, he thought, glancing again at his watch as he passed the elegant Manhattan Hotel, one of his favorite dining places, at the corner of Madison Avenue, to stop at Mendel's for a spot of breakfast before Jeffries' arrival: now that hardly seemed possible since the appointed event was a little more than fifteen minutes away. The renowned restaurant, one of a dwindling number of Jewish-owned businesses in Grand Central Station, was perhaps his favorite eatery in the city. Since dining out was one of his favorite activities, Daniel regarded himself, not unreasonably, as something of a gourmand. And, in his considered opinion not only was much of their menu well above average but also, as he recalled his last visit there for dinner with some pleasure, their oyster stew was extraordinarily delicious.

But the superb quality of the food was not the only reason dining at Mendel's was such a pleasure, Daniel reminded himself, as the massive Florentine structure of the new Grand Central Station came into view. He had loved visiting the old building and, frankly, missed it, although, he had been forced to admit, this new one, once you got accustomed to it, was far more efficient and had its own special charm.

But the old one had been exceptional. A single roof of iron and glass, more than 500 feet long and 200 feet wide, towering a hundred feet above the floor, combined with the immense wall of glass which had enclosed the northern end gave it, he had thought when he had first set sight on it, the appearance of a giant sun parlor. He had read somewhere that there were two acres of glass in the old roof and an additional two-thirds in the north wall: And he believed it. But whatever the facts were, the old building had been remarkably clean and bright, especially for a train station.

This new building or perhaps more accurately, the extensively renovated building (much of the interior had been unchanged) had converted, it was said, Grand Central Depot into Grand Central Station. In 1899, after twenty-eight years of service, it had become painfully clear to its principal owner's, the Vanderbilt's, that the old depot, with its three separate stations, could no longer cope with the enormous increase in commuter traffic pouring in from the newly burgeoning suburbs. An extraordinary exodus from city to suburb of some two million people, largely the better-off middleclass, had marked the final years of the nineteenth century. Long accustomed to spending much of the summer outside the city, these increasingly affluent Americans had fled the dirty and overcrowded city in record numbers, leaving behind only those who could not afford to go and the very rich, who owned summer and weekend homes outside of the city.

From a mere forty thousand in 1890, the number of commuters entering New York City had increased by 1900 to an astounding half-a-million persons every weekday morning. Most of them came by ferryboat from North New Jersey and Long Island and it was soon clear that if the railroads wanted to share in the new prosperity then every effort would have to be made to encourage migration to Westchester by enlarging Grand Central and improving the quality of the trip. Not only were the relatively few trains that could be fitted in on the twelve tracks usually extremely overcrowded but, in addition, the long-suffering passengers were often half-gassed to death in the Park Avenue tunnel.

First, the roof had been removed and the cast-iron masonry stripped from the red brick walls. Then, the walls were raised from three stories to six and faced with granite. Inside, the three stations were combined into one and the area, facing Forty-Second Street, which had been the New Haven station, became a single, vast waiting room in which all three railroads had separate ticket offices. To increase the number of tracks from twelve to twenty-one, seven per railroad, passengers who were once allowed to cut across tracks were now confined, in the English fashion, to considerably narrowed platforms and to a concourse that lay between the platforms and the new waiting room.

As soon as he crossed Park Avenue it became clear to Daniel that the crowd was much larger than he or probably anybody else had anticipated. Comprised almost completely, he noted as he drew nearer, of loudly enthusiastic white men and boys, with a sprinkling of curious Negroes on its fringes, it was so enormous that it had spilled over from 42nd Street, which was itself impassable, and was also blocking all the other streets around the station. Standing at the head of this boisterous assembly was a formal Reception Committee, made up of what he quickly estimated was about two hundred representatives of the leading sporting and athletic clubs in the city, many of whom were holding up signs on which the names of their organizations were prominently printed.

Standing alongside the Committee was a large and noisy brass band, whose enthusiastic if off-key renderings added immensely to the general atmosphere of manic celebration. Showing his press identification, to which nobody paid the slightest attention, Daniel pushed his way through the unruly crowd that was already pressing hard against the ropes erected by the overextended police to keep them away from the iron fence enclosing the terminal.

After several minutes of pushing and pleading to be allowed inside to do his job, the veteran journalist finally made his way through the police lines and entered the station through the noisy and crowded waiting room. The vast room, in which all three railroads had separate ticket offices, seemed only slightly less crowded than the streets outside, as some of the more enterprising or determined souls had gained entrance either through an unguarded door or by the special favor of station attendants. After quickly glancing at the board for arrival confirmation, Daniel slowly made his way to the platform where Jeffries' train, the *Twentieth Century,* was scheduled to arrive on time from Chicago, at 9.30 a.m.

To his surprise, as he slipped his notebook from a coat pocket and began jotting observations in a cramped left-handed script that even he frequently had trouble deciphering, Daniel realized that he too, against his better judgment, was being swept up in the excitement of the occasion. Although he regarded himself as proud an Irishman as any, Daniel, unlike the vast majority of his less knowledgeable compatriots, was not certain that Jeffries was still capable of meeting the challenge posed by fellow Irishman, Jack London. London's already famous column, written from ringside in Sydney after Johnson's destruction of heavyweight champion Tommy Burns, had electrified and galvanized white men of every ethnicity all over America. The final sentence had burned itself into Daniel's mind: *"But one thing now remains; Jim Jeffries must now emerge from his alfalfa farm and remove that golden smile from Jack Johnson's face. Jeff, it's up to you. The White Man must be rescued."*

Johnson, he knew, would have been a tough opponent for even the young Jeffries, before he retired. For this Jeffries, with more than four years of ring rust and maybe more than fifty pounds of additional weight, some even said that he was now over 300 pounds, the task, he feared, would be impossible. He regarded as uninformed nonsense all the talk about Jeffries' superior intelligence. While he had no special affection for Negroes, indeed he really didn't know any of them very well; his own observation was that, generally, they were far more intelligent than most whites claimed. Their speech, for example, was often deliberately misrepresented in the press as being far more uneducated and ungrammatical than the reality. His own paper, he knew full well, was one of the major offenders. Reporters routinely cleaned up the dialogue of whites, making them appear more intelligent and educated than they really were, while the opposite was done to the Negroes.

In fact, he thought, as he stepped onto the crowded platform, if he had to make a bet on the relative ring intelligence of the two men his money would be firmly on Johnson. Not that he particularly liked the man: nor thought he was a great fighter, not at all. Johnson, who he had seen fight several times and once interviewed was not an easy man to like. Behind the wide smile and occasionally ingratiating manner, there was, he had sensed, another face, far different from the public one, revealed only occasionally by the cold, watchful eyes. But, the man, it had to be admitted, was not, by any measure, unintelligent and in the ring he was a superb technician with great defensive skills.

In contrast, Jeffries, even at his peak, had never been a clever boxer, powerful and indestructible, but not clever. Some white reporters, Daniel was aware, taken aback by Johnson's ready wit and considerable verbal skills, had tried to make a distinction between what they labeled Johnson's cunning and real intelligence, which they were reluctant to ascribe to a Negro. That, to him, especially on matters pertaining to the ring, seemed a distinction without a difference and worse, a silly exercise in self-deception.

Looking around, he could see that among the jostling crowd on the track platform were a number of the city's most prominent sporting men, several of whom he knew quite well, including Professor Mike Donovan and Colonel Harry Perry Disbecker of the New York Athletic Club and John Conway, the president of the Irish-American Athletic Club. Also on the platform were a group of prosperous-looking, dark-suited men, whom, he assumed, from their comments and air of eager expectation, were personal acquaintances of the retired champion; several fellow journalists, instantly identifiable, he thought with some distaste, by their generally scruffy appearance; and a large group of red-capped smiling Negro porters, who had apparently, judging from their unusually large numbers, been dispatched not only to assist Jeffries and his party but also to help protect them from his most fervent admirers.

"Good morning, Mister O'Brien, you must be here for Mister Jeffries."

Turning around to face his greeter, Daniel found himself staring directly into the smiling, dark-brown, Irish-face of Patrick O'Neill.

"Yes, thank you Patrick and you must be here for the same purpose," Daniel answered, returning the smile and reaching out to shake the proffered hand.

"Yes Sir, I am part of that party," the tall, trim young man responded, indicating the other red-capped porters with a swivel of his head. "Have you met him before?"

"I certainly have, several times," Daniel replied, thinking again how much he liked this young Negro boy with the Irish name and face, "even saw one of his early fights before he won the title, right here in the city, at Madison Square Gardens."

"I've heard so much about him, is he as…" Patrick began, before the rest of the sentence was drowned out by the sharp, high blast of the approaching train's whistle.

"Excuse me sir," the young man politely concluded when it was once more possible to be heard, again holding out his hand, "but I believe that is my signal to get back to work." If all the Negroes were like that one, Daniel thought, as he watched the young porter move briskly to rejoin his fellow redcaps, there would be far less discrimination against them.

As the sleek *Twentieth Century* came to a full stop and the doors slowly opened, or so it seemed to Daniel, the veteran journalist pushed as closely to the train as he could, standing on tippytoes and craning his neck for a better view. "Well, he is certainly not the mountain of fat we were told he had become," Daniel muttered to himself in relief, as the surprisingly trim former champion, in the company of his wife and sparring partner, Sam Berger and Mrs. Berger, was engulfed by his delighted supporters. *From the sleek, hungry look of Mr. Jeffries,* Daniel jotted in his notebook, *it is my guess that we will soon be seeing the great battle for racial supremacy between the undefeated former champion and the Negro champion, Johnson, that so many of our citizens so heartily desire.*

In the waiting and baggage rooms and outside on the streets amongst the crowd massed behind the police ropes, the announcement of the arrival of the *Twentieth Century* with Jeffries and his party aboard had set-off an extraordinary surge of excitement. Despite the frantic efforts of the police contingent that had been bolstered by reserves, the sight of the big form stepping off the train triggered an enormous cheer and a huge surge that quickly swept aside the Reception Committee, broke down the ropes and threatened to tear down the iron fence enclosing the terminal.

As he walked off the platform surrounded by his smiling bodyguard of Negro porters, Jeffries, one big arm wrapped protectively around his wife, took a surprised look at the frenzied crowd outside the fence and stopped dead in his tracks. Realizing that there was no chance of getting out safely that way, the former champion quickly conferred with the station master, who had been part of his welcoming party at the platform, on finding another, safer way of leaving the station. After a hurried conference in the baggage room, which momentarily took them out of the sight of the crowd outside, Jeffries and his party emerged with a police escort, which managed to break open a passage to a taxicab parked on a side street, Depew Place.

Using his giant frame and every bit of his renowned strength to protect his wife from the relentless crowding, and simply nodding and smiling at the cheers, applause, and cries of "Get the nigger champ" and "Send the savage back to Africa" that greeted them, Jeffries and his party fought their to the waiting automobile. As the vehicle pulled away, trailed by plumes of white smoke, dozens of small boys and young men raced exuberantly behind it, testing each other and the new machine.

"Wow, goddamn Jim, do you believe the size of that crowd," Sam Berger, literally bouncing in his seat, barely able to restrain his excitement, asked his friend sitting placidly beside him. "That was even larger than the one at the depot in Chicago, don't you think. They really love you here Jim"

"It's not me those yaps want Sam. I'm just a nobody. It's the champ they're yelling for, not me, "Jeffries replied, with what must have been seen as surprising sharpness by his traveling companions, judging from their startled expressions, "Never forget that, I don't."

Although he had known him for many years, was one of his closest friends and had probably spent more time with him than any other person on earth, including his wife, Sam Berger, like the rest of the world, including Mrs. Jeffries, rarely knew what was on the big man's mind. Talking, even his friends were forced to admit, had never been his greatest strength. A deeply private man, who was happiest hunting and fishing and roaming the giant redwoods of his beloved California, Jeffries had never been comfortable in the white-hot glare of public attention. He despised and avoided the easy banter with reporters and fans that many of them expected, and, which, in contrast, Johnson had developed into something of an art form and often used as a weapon. He had always preferred to let his fists do his talking, and strongly felt that what he did in the ring should be enough.

But, he had never expressed any particular animosity towards the fans before and so Sam was surprised and a little concerned at the apparent bitterness in his friend's voice. After noting with relief that the driver had apparently not overheard the remark, Berger turned to look at his friend, who was staring fixedly through the window, his face an impassive mask.

"Jim," he said softly, almost in a whisper, leaning toward the expressionless Jeffries, "remember what I said to those reporters in Chicago. Whether or not you return to the ring, remember you've been away for four years and you're thirty-four years old, depends entirely on whether you can get in the kind of shape, which would make it possible for you to be at your best. Nobody expects you, I wouldn't want you to, wouldn't let you, get back in that ring if you weren't in the best shape of your life."

"Thanks Sam," Jeffries responded, finally turning from the window with a small smile for his friend and his concerned wife, who had been throwing nervous glances in his direction. But, just then the group of boys, making their way nimbly through the traffic, their numbers now considerably diminished, caught up with the taxi and began pounding on the driver's window. As he lowered it, irritably, to shoo them away, one of the older boys shoved his head inside and yelled, his face red and contorted with excitement and mischief, "Get the nigger champ, get the nigger."

That kind of sentiment, Jeffries thought, shaking his head as he returned his attention to the towering landscape, was exactly what he feared. He knew very well, despite what Sam or anybody else said, that the pressure on him to return to the ring and reclaim the title for the white race would soon become irresistible. Already a bunch of pesky newspaper writers who had never stepped in a ring or even thrown a punch in their lives were saying that he had some kind of moral responsibility to the Caucasian people. Some of the bastards had even gone as far as hinting that unless he stepped back into the ring and took the title back from Johnson that he would be seen as a coward. But as angry as these demands had made him, he also knew that unless some other white fighter defeated Johnson fairly soon it was going to be up to him to do so.

He had been reluctant to come out of retirement at all, even for these theatrical appearances and had stoutly resisted the first offers. Leaving his ranch and getting back into the ring was a nightmarish idea but, finally, the money had been impossible to refuse. At least fifty thousand dollars, for merely showing up and going through some training routines, far more than he had ever earned for any of his fights as champion. And so he had accepted, reluctantly, but only on the understanding that it was not a commitment to return to the ring. Nevertheless, he had begun training to get some of the weight off, to get some of his wind and timing back, at least to look like a fighter again. Getting back in decent shape had been surprisingly easy and he had lost about twenty-two pounds in just a few months, but defeating Johnson, he knew, would take a lot more than decent condition.

"We're here Mr. Jeffries," a cheerful voice with a pronounced Irish brogue announced from somewhere above his head. Startled, Jeffries looked up into the smiling face and the pale blue eyes of their driver, who had already gotten out of the cab and was in the process of opening the passenger doors. Lost in his reveries, the former champion had been unaware that the taxi had stopped outside the Broadway offices of the William Morris Company.

"I guess there is a lot on your mind these days, eh champ." Flushing with embarrassment, as he noticed that the others were already standing on the pavement outside, Jeffries hurried out of the cab and began reaching into his trouser pocket.

"No money Mr. Jeffries, I wouldn't think of it, just shaking your hand is enough for me," the driver said, sticking out his pudgy right hand. "I'm an Irishman too, just like you, as you no doubt can tell. Let me tell you something," he added, the pleasant smile disappearing as he stepped closer to the former champion, his eyes mere slits, his voice a low, harsh hiss. "The title belongs to us, not to them godforsaken savages. But it's more than that champ, let me tell ya. A nigger beats a white man in the ring and suddenly they're all as good or even better than us. Then there's no respect from none of them for none of us. Niggers are like that, you should hear some of them already, you've got to put that fucking nigger in his place."

"Thank you," Jeffries replied noncommittally, his expression even more guarded than usual, as he quickly stepped away after a brief, perfunctory handshake. Then, after looking around to identify the source of the applause that had greeted his appearance, he hurried on to the sidewalk where his wife and the Bergers were patiently waiting.

They're everywhere, he thought, as he waved to the crowd gathering outside the building, everywhere, but inside will be even worse. Then placing his arm around his wife, he nodded to Sam, who also took his wife by the hand and together the foursome walked slowly into the building. There, as reported in the newspapers the next morning, Jeffries spoke to newspaper reporters for nearly two hours "but sidestepped every question as to his intentions except as to his vaudeville engagement, which opens here next Monday."

The *New York Times* concluded its report on Jeffries' arrival this way:

"Jeffries, with clear eyes, a good color and quick movements, looked big and strong; but was not by any stretch of the imagination fat. He looked to weigh close about 250 pounds, but his clothes hung on him so loosely that he laughingly said that one of the first things he would have to attend to would be seeing a tailor about new clothing. After talking for nearly two hours to newspaper reporters, who passed in procession, each with new questions, Jeffries had not been interviewed. The substance of what he said was:

I have been training lightly for several weeks and have reduced my weight to about 245 pounds. In fact I have taken so much weight off that I have got to purchase a new suit of clothes. Each day I find that I can box faster than the day before, and I am delighted to find that my wind is in good shape. I feel first rate, but I can't say definitely whether again I will enter the ring or not. I have been out of the ring four years, and that may make it impossible for me to attain strict championship form again."

Four

According to the Pottawattomie Indians, who in 1835 finally relinquished control of the befouled, marshy rim of Lake Michigan that was to become the city of Chicago, "The first white man to settle at Chickagou was a Negro." During the seventeenth century white men of all kinds, trappers, priests, and explorers, had passed through this forbidding and unpromising territory. But it was a handsome, well-educated, French-speaking Negro, Jean Baptiste Point de Saible, who, sometime around 1790, established the first permanent settlement.

Very little is known of du Saible's background. By one account, he was from what is now Haiti and had planned to establish a colony of free Negroes on the shores of Lake Michigan. By another, he was the descendant of a Negro slave and a French fur-trader in the Northwest Territory. What is known is that for sixteen years he lived with his Pottawattomie wife Catherine and their daughter Cézanne at the present site of the city of Chicago.

It is doubtful that the first black heavyweight champion of the world knew anything about this earlier black pioneer when he made the decision to settle in Chicago. But he may have known a little more about the hundreds of Negroes who, fleeing slavery, had poured into the city, an important terminal along the Underground Railroad, between 1840 and 1850. The federal Fugitive Slave Law of 1793 had made the harboring of a fugitive or the prevention of his or her arrest, a criminal offense, punishable by a fine of $500. Consequently, the Illinois Black Code had required every Negro who remained in the state not only to post a bond of one thousand dollars but also carry a certificate of freedom on his or her person at all times. Nevertheless, throughout the Forties and Fifties, a few churches and several homes in Chicago had served as stations on the Underground Railroad.

For this brave activity, carried out by a union of whites, church people and political radicals, and Negroes holding free papers, the city was derisively described as "a nigger-loving town," and "a sink hole of abolition" by angry planters in the lower Mississippi Valley and residents of southern Illinois, a proslavery stronghold.

Despite this reputation as a city of refuge, at the time of the great Chicago fire, in 1871, the Negro community numbered a mere 2,500 residents and was largely confined to an area three blocks long and fifteen blocks wide. The great fire, which destroyed 17,000 buildings and left 100,000 people homeless, spared the Negro neighborhood, but not the adjoining Central Business area and the world-famous Red-Light District. As a result, a majority of the city's gamblers and prostitutes took refuge in the Negro neighborhood, where they remained even after the city was rebuilt.

Three years later another fire ravaged the city, concentrated this time in the Negro neighborhood. Consequently almost half of the black families were dispersed among the white residents, but a new Negro community also arose from the embers of the old. There, in a long, thin sliver of land, bordered on one-side by a prosperous white neighborhood, and one the other by that of the "shanty Irish," the vast majority of Chicago's black residents and their major institutions would be concentrated during the next forty years.

In 1909, when Jack Johnson arrived in Chicago, Negroes were still a mere two percent of a population that had already surpassed the two million mark. Of that number, the vast majority were people of Northern European descent. Of those, the Irish who, fleeing famine and English oppression, had first started arriving during the first great wave of immigration in the 1840s, were the most numerous. Next were the Germans, themselves victims of the suppression of the democratic revolutions of 1848. The third largest group was the British contingent—English, Welsh and Scots. But by 1890, the stream of Northern European immigrants had begun drying up. Their place was soon taken by Italians and Eastern Europeans, particularly Poles and Jews. This "new immigration," which also included smaller numbers of Hungarians and Greeks, reached a floodtide during the first decade of the twentieth century.

In 1909, the emergence of the so-called Black Belt was still several years away.

"It is Negroes like these," Richard Alexander Barrington muttered softly to himself, distaste curving his wide mouth," who give our entire race a bad name." The targets of Barrington's bad-tempered disapproval were scores of strutting black men garishly outfitted in peg-leg trousers, polka-dot hosiery, boldly designed shirt fronts and what appeared to be masculine versions of the cabriole hat. The peacocks were among hundreds of black Chicagoans of both genders who had gathered outside the State Street train station to greet the first black man to wear the coveted crown of heavyweight boxing champion of the world.

The train, from St. Paul, was already two hours late but it was an almost cloudless, beautifully mild morning and the long delay had done little to dampen the festive mood of the noisy crowd. Many of them seemed to have come prepared with homemade sandwiches and beverages of various kinds. But Richard Barrington was not accustomed to waiting and he was not in the best of moods.

Being surrounded by large numbers of Negroes, especially the very dark-skinned, generally uneducated kinds at the station that morning, still made him uncomfortable, despite his best efforts. It was unseemly, he had told himself again and again, for one to be more comfortable with members of another race, especially one as hostile to the interests of all Negroes as even the most refined white Americans had become. But so far nothing had worked and it was only his general determination to see through to the end any undertaking he began and a grudgingly acknowledged interest in seeing Jack Johnson in the flesh that kept him there.

Richard Barrington was decidedly not, as he had assured several questioners who had wondered just who this tall, well-dressed young black man was, in Chicago to meet with Jack

Johnson. He was in Chicago on business, he had explained without elaboration, repeatedly explaining that the timing was purely coincidental. But his denials were hardly convincing, in fact their effect was the very opposite of what he intended; understanding nods and winks greeted every one. Everybody knew that with his expensive clothes, cultivated speech and air of quiet authority that he was someone special, the kind of Negro the new champion could now do business with.

Richard Barrington had come to Chicago on family business several days earlier. His father's sudden death a little more than a year before and his mother's visible decline since had dramatically changed his life. He had assumed his current position as President and Chief Executive Officer of the Barrington Development Company with the full if reluctant agreement of his brother and sister. Their votes for him had been cast as a favor to their mother and because neither wanted the post for themselves. Like their father before them, his brother and sister were talented and successful physicians with little interest in or flair for business. And with his undergraduate and law degrees from Yale, they were unable to convincingly argue that he was not at least nominally qualified, although they (even as children the two older Barrington siblings had always seemed of a common mind) had quietly raised the question of his comparative youth and inexperience with their mother.

His elevation had been entirely his mother's idea and, initially, he had been almost as uneasy with the prospect of trying to fill her rather large shoes as his siblings clearly were. He too had pointed to his youth, he was almost a decade younger than both Paul and Constance, but also to the additional fact that he had never gotten along particularly well with either of them and was quite different, temperamentally, and in just about every way he could think of, from both. This clear evidence of shared antipathy between her youngest and two older children had not dissuaded their mother, to the contrary it had seemed only to serve as a spur to her efforts to persuade him to accept the position, as if binding them together in a web of mutual interests and obligations would be an antidote for their distaste, if not active dislike of each other. She had not hesitated to deploy every weapon at her disposal, alternately threatening and cajoling, but it was her use of what her children called "the guilt card," reminding them of the heavy burden she had carried virtually alone since their father's sudden death, that had been, by far, the most effective.

Unable to resist their mother's pleas, the Barrington children had agreed to her proposal that Richard would take over the daily management of the company, and that she and they would become active members of the board. But it had been quickly evident that the siblings' many differences extended to their views on investment strategy. As a condition of accepting the post Richard had insisted that he be allowed considerable leeway in making decisions, as long as he was successful. The older Barrington children, who had given their consent to the stipulation had, however, immediately and strenuously opposed their brother's first proposal to the board as the new chairman, to dismantle the family's considerable real estate portfolio and to reinvest the proceeds in the stock and bond markets.

But, despite a reasonable amount of success with the fairly limited amounts of capital that had initially been made available to him-- he had just missed the huge bull market that had ended in 1906--his siblings had continued to resist a wider involvement in the markets, repeatedly describing his original proposal as "radical and reckless." And when he had pressed them to explain their objections in specific terms or to propose an alternative plan of action, they had finally made it clear that what they really opposed was his penchant for, as they put it, "changing things." What they really wanted, they let him know, was to keep things just as they were.

Over a period of decades the Barringtons, one of Washington D.C.'s most successful and respected black families, had quietly put together a substantial real estate empire much of it in the Georgetown area, where the family had lived as free persons for more than a hundred years. Historically, the Barringtons had never expected their real estate investments to generate a substantial income stream; their professional incomes had always provided far more than they needed. The rents on their properties were kept as low as possible, usually just enough to pay the mortgages and a modicum of maintenance. Property was not bought to be sold; property was bought to be held in trust, to build security, stability, respectability and long-term prosperity.

Owning property had always been particularly important to families such as the Barringtons; land had long been the most tangible expression of their status as freemen. During slavery black freemen had lived in a precarious civil state: neither slave nor truly free. Slave owners had viewed them with suspicion and hostility, as bad examples for their own bondsmen and in the nation's capital a variety of laws and ordinances had been passed to restrict their freedoms and "keep them in their place." As early as 1795 they had been denied the right to assemble in groups of seven or more. And The Ordinances of the Corporation of Georgetown, printed in 1811, allowed free blacks to be fined fifteen shillings for speeding as compared to the "seven shillings, six pence if an apprentice, indentured servant, or slave," was found guilty of the same offense.

But they had always been allowed to buy property and that one freedom, far more than any other, had always affirmed to them that they were in fact, by law, different from their less fortunate brethren, who were themselves mere property, to be bought and sold by other men.

Over the years, because of the constant, crushing uncertainties of their situation, many of the most financially successful of the freemen had learned not to flaunt their wealth; had discovered, sometimes by harsh example, the wisdom of avoiding the attention and envy of less successful whites. As a consequence wealthy, free-colored families such as the Barringtons had developed the habit of maintaining extremely low public profiles and had generally restricted their investments to their own communities and institutions. But Richard, ever impatient with tradition, had decided to break with the past, arguing with typical brashness that holding large amounts of low-performing residential real estate in poor black neighborhoods was a miserable idea and certainly not the way for the family to maximize its return on its considerable investment.

Like other affluent, college-educated young men of the period, the vast majority of whom just happened to be white, Richard had decided that far better returns awaited the bold and the informed in the booming stock and bond markets. And unlike his siblings, he was completely unfazed by the unpleasant, but to him, irrelevant fact that the hostility of the white community had grown substantially ever since the collapse of the brief racial honeymoon of the Reconstruction period. In fact one of the features of the money markets that appealed to him most was their relative anonymity. It was probably the only area, he figured, where the color of his money mattered far more than the color of his skin.

His interest in the markets had begun with what he had described to a few friends as a series of "transformative" articles—they had helped to transform his view of how the world of commerce really worked—that he had read in *Everybody's Magazine* shortly after graduating from Yale. The articles had been written by Thomas Lawson, the man who had organized the copper trust, Amalgamated Copper, in association with Standard Oil. Lawson, the son of a Nova Scotia carpenter who had left school at the age of twelve to work in Boston's Wall Street, had been a financial prodigy, if such a category exists. Starting from scratch with nothing, by the time he was sixteen he had amassed the considerable fortune, for the period, of $60,000, by speculating in rail stocks on the Boston Exchange. Before he turned thirty Lawson had made his first million on Wall Street in New York.

Amalgamated Copper had been organized in 1899 and by 1904 Lawson had broken with the Standard Oil forces and created a sensation by issuing advertisements in newspapers denouncing what he called the "System." In one typical ad in the New York *Daily Tribune,* headlined **Amalgamated Stockholders— Warning**, Lawson wrote: "I advise every holder of Amalgamated stock to sell his holdings at once before another crash comes. Another slump may carry it to 33 again or lower. It may go higher, but this is no affair of mine. From the moment of publication of this notice all those who have looked to me for advice must relieve me of further responsibility. As the people who look to me for advice are scattered all over this country, I know no other way than this to simultaneously notify them of what I have learned."

This highly public rift with Standard Oil had prompted the editor of *Everybody's Magazine* to ask Lawson to write a series of articles, a sort of "true confession" about the inside workings of high finance in the United States. Lawson readily agreed but with one stipulation: he would receive no fee but the magazine would spend a minimum of $50,000 to advertise the series. The magazine accepted the condition and Lawson added more than five times as much from his own pocket to bring the series to the attention of as wide a public as possible. The millionaire financier explained his motivation for writing the series in an ad in the *New York Post* of June 21, 1904 headlined **The Story of Amalgamated Copper.** "I have unwittingly been made the instrument," he wrote, "by which thousands upon thousands of investors in America and Europe have been plundered. I wish them to know my position as to the past, that they may acquit me of intentional wrongdoing; as to the present, that they may know that I am doing all in my power to right the wrongs that have been committed; and as to the future, that they may see how I propose to compel restitution."

Attempting to put into words exactly why the articles had had such a profound impact on him, Richard had explained that until he read them the world of high finance had been a mere abstraction, a mysterious world reserved for a handful of exceptional white men. The articles, he said, had lifted the veil of secrecy, had made him understand that it was all just a game, a scheme, that clever men had invented to detach less clever men and women from their hard-earned money. But the numbers involved in the Amalgamated Copper debacle were so enormously mind-boggling that Richard, like hundreds of thousands of other Americans, had been riveted from the opening sentence of the series which read as follows: "Amalgamated Copper was begotten in 1898, born in 1899, and in the first five years of its existence plundered the public to the extent of over one hundred millions of dollars."

Lawson's second sentence was almost as savage and unforgiving. "It was a creature of that incubator of trust and corporation frauds, the State of New Jersey, and was organized ostensibly to mine, manufacture, buy, sell and deal in copper, one of the staples, the necessities of civilization."

He then explained that Amalgamated Copper was a "corporation with $155,000,000 capital, 1, 5550,000 shares of the par value of $100 each," and that the "entire stock was sold to the public at an average of $115 per share ($100 to $130), and in 1903 the price had declined to $33 per share."

Then he named names, very, very big names, some of the giants of American business. "From its inception it was known as a Standard Oil creature, because its birthplace was the National City Bank of New York (the Standard Oil bank), and its parents the leading Standard Oil lights, Henry H. Rogers, William Rockefeller, and James Stillman."

Unblinkingly, Lawson then laid the blame for the massive fraud squarely at the feet of those estimable gentlemen. Amalgamated, which he confessed had been constructed with plans that he had laid out, had, he wrote with all the grief and regret of a father lamenting the crimes of a murderous son, "from its birth to present writing been responsible for more hell than any other trust or financial thing since the world began. Because of it the people have sustained incalculable losses and have suffered untold miseries. But for the existence of the National City Bank of New York, the tremendous losses and necessarily corresponding profits could not have been made." Had his plan been followed, he added, "there would have been reared a great financial edifice, immensely profitable, permanently prosperous, one of the world's big institutions."

Lawson claimed that his plans had been "perfected" as a "broad and comprehensive project, having for its basis the buying and consolidating of all the best-producing copper properties in Europe and America, and educating the world to their great merits as safe and profitable investments," but had been hijacked by a band of greedy and ruthless men, who had never intended to follow his blueprint and had deliberately misled and "taken in" the public. If his readers were to understand the "the torturous course of Amalgamated," he explained, it would be necessary for them to know the true nature of the "giant creature" called Standard Oil.

To underline how much of the mechanisms of the financial

world was hidden from the people at large, Lawson began by revealing a fact about the company that was well known on Wall Street but unknown to the public: "that there are two Standard Oils." There was, he explained, "Standard Oil, the corporation which deals in oil and things which pertain to the manufacture and transportation of oil, and Standard Oil, the giant, indefinite system which sometimes embraces all the Standard Oil group of individuals and corporations and sometimes only certain of the individuals."

In an attempt to describe this curious creature in terms the average man could understand, Lawson explained that it was comprised of "a group of money-owners—some individuals and some corporations—who have a right to use the name Standard Oil in any business undertaking they engage in." The right to use the name, he pointedly added, "is of priceless value, for it carries with it assured success." Standard Oil, the seller of oil to the people, he wrote, "transacts its business as does any other corporation, but it plays no part in my story." The story of Amalgamated Copper was about the other Standard Oil, the "larger and many times more important system."

There were only three men, he continued, "who can lend the name Standard Oil, even in the most remote way, to any project, for there is no more heinous crime in the Standard Oil decalogue than using the name Standard Oil unauthorizedly. The three men are Henry H. Rogers, William Rockefeller and John D. Rockefeller." But while these giants of American commerce stood alone atop the giant pyramid, below them were an "army of followers, capitalists and workers in all parts of the world, men who never require anything more than the order, Go Ahead, Pull Off, Buy, Sell, or Stay where you are, to render as absolute obedience and enthusiastic cooperation as though they knew to the smallest detail the purposes which entered into the giving the order." And last but not least in the Standard Oil army, Lawson claimed, were the "countless hordes of politicians, statesmen, law makers and enforcers, who, at home or as representatives of the nation abroad, go to make up our political structure, and judges and lawyers."

What made the mammoth institution work "with the ease and smoothness of a creature one-millionth its size and without noise or dissension, he explained, was "a basic law, from which no one, neither the great or the small, is exempt. In substance it is: Every Standard Oil man must wear the Standard Oil collar. "

This collar, he added, "is riveted onto each one as he is taken into the band, and afterward can only be removed with the head of the wearer."

Additionally, Lawson wrote, every Standard Oil man had to agree to abide by the rules of the following Code or face instant dismissal.

Keep your mouth closed, as silence is gold, and gold is what we exist for.

Collect our debts today. Pay the other fellow's debts tomorrow. Today is always here, tomorrow may never come.

Conduct all our business so that the buyer and the seller must come to us. Keep the seller waiting; the longer he waits the less he'll take. Hurry the buyer, as his money brings us interest.

Make all profitable bargains in the name of Standard Oil, debatable ones in the name of dummies. Standard Oil never goes back on a bargain.

Never put Standard Oil trades in writing, as your memory and the other fellow's forgetfulness will always be reinforced with our organization. Never forget our Legal Department is paid by the year, and our land is full of courts and judges.

As competition is the life of trade—-our trade; and monopoly the death of trade—our competitors' trade, employ both judiciously.

Never get into a butting contest with the government. Our government is by the people and for the people, and we are the people, and those people who are not us can be hired by us.

Always do right. Right makes might, might makes dollars, dollars make right, and we have the dollars.

While conceding that there was an element of exaggeration in Lawson's description of the scope and reach of Standard Oil's power and influence, brought on quite likely, he felt, by the man's desperate, almost psychological need to minimize his own responsibility for the catastrophic failure of Amalgamated Copper, by the end of the series Richard had concluded that the essential elements of the story were true. He, afterall, was not one to harbor any illusions whatsoever about the willingness of men of their kind (meaning rich white men) to prey on their fellow humans, to violate every tenet of basic human decency in their pursuit of wealth. The very history of his people in America was a living testimony to that awful fact.

But more prosaically and to the point, the story Richard knew, fitted perfectly into the prevailing philosophy of many of the country's business leaders. At Yale he had become acquainted with that philosophy, courtesy of William Graham Sumner, the august professor of sociology and perhaps the country's leading proponent of Darwinism. Sumner, himself a graduate of Yale, who had studied ancient languages and history at Gottingen and Anglican theology at Oxford, had been a deacon and then a rector at a number of Episcopalian churches before being appointed professor of political and social science at Yale in 1872. Despite, or perhaps because of, his theological background, Sumner fully accepted the harsh view of human nature and existence that underpinned the basic propositions of Malthus and Ricardo and the classic economists. He firmly believed, as he wrote that "constraint, anxiety, and possibly tyranny and repression characterized all social relations" and that "the law of population combined with the law of diminishing returns constituted the great underlying condition of society."

He disdained sociologists of the "progress" school such as his great ideological adversary Lester Ward, one of the founders of the National Liberal League, dismissing their concerns about alleviating poverty and other forms of human distress as mere sentiment. To Sumner, suffering and toil had been the great teachers of mankind. To him it was clear and obvious "that if we should try by any measures of arbitrary interference and assistance to relieve the victims of social pressure from the calamity of their position we should only offer premiums to folly and vice and extend them further."

At Yale, Sumner's lectures had left Richard with a welter of conflicting emotions. The professor's enthusiastic embrace of "scientism," the belief that science, not religion, provides the most rational and reliable means of explaining both the natural and human worlds, made absolutely perfect sense to him. "Each of the sciences," Sumner would explain in his rumbling bass voice, "which, by giving to man greater knowledge of the laws of nature, has enabled him to cope more intelligently with the ills of life, has had to fight for its independence of metaphysics." Sociology, which he defined "as the science of life in society," was, he explained, "Only the most recent science to engage in that struggle and since it claims as its field of investigation an immense range of subjects of the first importance, the struggle was bound to be severe."

But, he was also often repelled by Sumner's undisguised contempt for the poor and the powerless. The professor usually ended his lectures by reaffirming his conviction that what he described as "misplaced sentiment" was far more dangerous to society than leaving it alone to its own "laws" of development. "The old classical civilization," he would lecture the often-spellbound students, his voice rising just ever so slightly in volume, the sweeping arm gestures growing just a little wider, "fell under an irruption of barbarians from without. It is very possible, maybe even possible that our civilization may perish by an explosion from within. For a century the sentimentalists have been preaching notions of rights and equality, of the dignity, wisdom, and power of the proletariat, which have naturally filled the minds of ignorant men with impossible dreams. The thirst for luxurious enjoyment has taken possession of us all. That thirst, when combined with the notion of rights, of power, and of equality, and, as is so often the case, dissociated from all concepts of industry and economy, inevitably produces the foolish and dangerous notion that man is being robbed of his rights if he has not everything he wants and desires. And perhaps even more dangerously to the health of the civilization, that he is a fool if, having the power of the State in his hands, he allows this state of things to last. Then we have socialism, communism, and nihilism and the attendant danger of being trampled underfoot by a mob which can only hate what it cannot enjoy."

Lawson's series of articles had dramatically connected Sumner's theories and lectures with business practices in the real world, made Richard acutely aware of how little he really knew and just how much he needed to learn to prepare himself for combat in this Darwinian world and had sent him to law school.

It was the sudden hush that fell over the crowd as the doors to the Pullman opened, Richard would later tell friends, which made him realize just how much Jack Johnson meant to the average Negro. When asked to describe his first impression of the new heavyweight champion in the flesh, Richard would admit to being, to his not inconsiderable surprise, quite favorably disposed. No doubt fully aware of the intense scrutiny of the audience at this his first appearance in front of a large and largely supportive crowd since capturing the title, Johnson had left the train as if stepping onto a stage.

He had dressed carefully and with what can only be described as conservative flamboyance for his starring role. "He's wearing a grey fedora, just like mine," a smiling admirer in the crowd whispered, as the champion stepped jauntily and alone, big, gold-tipped smile flashing, onto the platform.

"And look at the field glasses over his shoulder. Reckon he wants them to look for Jeffries," a wit in the crowd, wearing a particularly inventive version of the cabriole hat, added, drawing guffaws and twitters of amusement from those around him. Even as he spoke, a group of men and women, evidently previous acquaintances, no longer able to contain their excitement, rushed forward with outstretched arms to greet the champion, yelling, "Jack, Jack."

While the old acquaintances flaunted their friendship with the champion with noisy hugs and hearty backslaps, others, less fortunate had to be content with formally shaking the great man's hand and gravely announcing, "proud to meet you Mr. Johnson:" And then promptly retiring to a respectful distance.

Despite themselves, the white reporters were clearly

impressed with the champion's demeanor and bearing. The next day, one paper would describe the champion this way: "*There was a hush as the conqueror of Tommy Burns alighted from the Pullman. His eye was keen, his step jaunty. There was lithe strength apparent in every movement, and his smile showed appreciation of mingling again with his old friends.*"

Asked about the whereabouts of his white wife, Johnson told the reporters that she had left the train at Milwaukee to visit friends. Regarding the fight with Jeffries, Johnson was equally brief: "I am willing to fight, everybody knows that. Sixty percent to the winner; forty to the loser-that looks about right to me."

That said the champion turned on his heels and walked, surrounded by friends and admirers, to a waiting automobile. To be whisked away, as the newspapers reported,"*To the home of his friend J.B. Williams, 2252 State Street, a section of the city in which many colored people make their home.*"

The south side theatre was filled to capacity with a rainbow of happy, jubilant, Negro faces. For those fortunate enough to be there that cold, wintry, March night, they were—and to a man and woman they fully understood—- participating in living, glorious history. For, in all of history as they knew it, nothing even remotely similar had ever previously happened to any other member of their race. True, other black men had won world-boxing titles before, but those were for the lower, far less regarded weight divisions: The little men, not the vaunted crown of the heavyweight champion, unchallengeable symbol the world over of male power and strength.

But dotted, here and there among the expectant dark faces, were pale ones with very different expressions. These, the men and women of the white press, who had come to take a further measure of the black champion, and to find out more about a question of enormous interest to them: Where was his white wife?

Behind the stage, in his dressing room, despite the big, easy smile, Johnson was a worried man. His reception all over the city by the white population had been cordial enough. But, from what he had learned from friends, nothing even remotely approaching the enormous crowd that had greeted Jeffries only two weeks earlier.

Jeffries' enormous popularity was hardly his greatest concern however. Something, he knew, had to be done about Hattie. She was a hell of a woman and he enjoyed her company, in bed and out. But her drinking, which had long been worrisome, had finally gotten out of control. And her erratic and sometimes abusive behavior, he was convinced, was going to cause him serious embarrassment, sooner or later. A few months ago he could have afforded to ignore such matters. But not any longer, the spotlight was evenbrighter and hotter than anything he had he had imagined or expected. Having a white wife was enough of a problem; what he didn't need, he had decided, was the hassles of one who misbehaved in public.

"Johnson weighs in his street clothes 215 pounds and while he looks big enough ordinarily, he loomed up like a giant on the theatre stage. "That is how the *Chicago Tribune* described the champion as he stood in front of the enraptured crowd describing the difficulties that had been placed in his path during his quest for the title.

"But I overcame them all," he said nodding with satisfaction, his voice emphasizing *all*, "and I am proud to be the first colored man to hold the world's heavyweight championship, "he added, to cries of approval and a standing, sustained ovation.

"And I want you all to know," he said after the cheering had finally ended and most of the crowd had retaken their seats, "that when the time comes to defend it I will do so to the *best* of my ability." Again, like a seasoned politician or a trained actor, Johnson was able to stir up the crowd to another round of cheering and shouting by simply emphasizing a particular word.

"Jeffries is the man I want to meet next," he assured them, "and I hope to meet him right here in the United States, he proclaimed, his voice rising.

"Talk sah, talk," a big, bass voice boomed from the back of the hall to more wild applause and cries of "that's right, that's right."

"As the champion I am entitled to have something to say about the terms, but I would not ask any opponent, black or white, to accept treatment similar to that given to me by Burns. All I want is a winner's and loser's end, with, of course, a reasonable guarantee," Johnson added quietly, as sounds of sympathy and agreement flooded the big room.

"There is no prospect of Jeffries making any announcement as to his intentions for some time," Johnson continued, to cries of derision and laughter, "and I have no desire to meet anyone else."

"Dat white boy's no fool, he knows what's good fer him," a feminine voice shouted. "He knows who his master be," a masculine one responded.

"I want you to know," Johnson added, as the room grew quiet, "that stories that I am under some kind of an obligation to the National Sporting Club of London are false, and I have no contract to meet Sam Langford over there, as has been stated. My theatrical contracts call for my appearance some time this year, but the dates are moveable to suit my convenience. I have a number of offers in this country, which, if I accept, will take up about twenty weeks of my time."

To them, that night, he was a revelation. The simple but extraordinary sight and sound of a black man, impeccably-dressed, well-spoken, standing up in public, bold and unafraid and unapologetic, in front of hundreds of people, while white reporters listened carefully and took notes: Talking openly about *his* convenience, and whether or not he was going to accept offers from people they knew could only have been white, drove many in the audience, who had never seen or heard of any such thing before or even thought it possible, to their feet, hoarsely shouting support and encouragement.

"Tell them."

"You the champion."

"You the champion, now."

"Only you can decide."

"It's our time now."

"I want to make some very personal remarks now," Johnson began after the excitement had subsided, his voice grave. "Despite what you've heard or read, my wife is not a white woman, neither was her name Nellie O'Brien. She was born in Mississippi, her maiden name was Adele Smith, and she was reared in Philadelphia. We were married two and a half years ago in a small Nevada town."

"I have always believed," he said, looking straight ahead, an injured note creeping into his voice, "that a man was entitled to some privacy in family matters, but so many wrong statements have been made that I felt like making no contradictions. I cannot understand why I have been misrepresented so frequently, as I have tried at all times to conduct myself in a manner that, at least, would call for courteous treatment."

"Don't you worry none love, we understan' what's going on," a large, yellow-complexioned, buxom woman, wearing an enormous hat, sitting near the stage shouted, leaping to her feet and directing a hard stare at a white reporter seated nearby.

"We know what's going on, don't we," she demanded of the audience, as she turned fiercely to face them. "We know how it is, don't we."

"Dats right champ, dose white people 'ate it sometin' powerful dat a nigger has taken away dey crown from dem," a bug-eyed, wizened, little, blue-black man of indeterminate age, answered fervently. "Dey tink dat it belongs to dem, by right of dey color," he added to laughter and applause.

Listening to Johnson's amazing performance from his seat near the back of the room, Richard Barrington turned to his companion with a little bow of acknowledgement. "You were right," he said to Robert S. Abbott, the founder and editor of the *Chicago Defender*, one of the men whom he had traveled to Chicago to see. "He is quite extraordinary; he certainly is not your typical ignorant Negro fighter or fighter of any color for that matter. I must admit that there is a lot more here than many of us thought."

"I must be honest," Abbot replied, getting to his feet, "I was certain that you would have been surprised at how intelligent and articulate he was, but what he did tonight surpassed even my expectations. Come on let me introduce you to him. He is as curious about Negroes like you as you are about him. He doesn't meet many of your kind you know."

Concurring on the impressiveness of Johnson's performance, the *Chicago Tribune* reported the next day: "The champion was introduced to an audience of his own race at a south side theatre at night, and as an orator proved himself far superior to Jeffries."

FIVE

When the notorious "One-Eye Jimmy" Connelly, the longtime greeter of patrons at the Silver Dollar Saloon, shook his hand and welcomed him to that Chicago institution on a icy-cold March night, Jack Johnson stepped into a world that had traditionally been unrelentlessly hostile to men of his race. By his side, a wide grin advertising his delight, was the man who had made it possible, the failed politician and aspiring fight manager, George Little.

For Little, who despised everything about the distant province to which he had been exiled for his political failures, the black heavyweight champion represented a, literally, golden opportunity. Banished to distant Columbus, Ohio, by his employer "Hinky Dink" Michael Kenna, for his inadequacies as a political infighter, Little had quickly realized that the managerless and socially ambitious Johnson was the perfect vehicle for his triumphant return to Chicago.

The Silver Dollar was a special place, the favorite watering hole of some of the city's more influential citizens. The saloon had acquired this enviable status because its owner, "Bathhouse" John Coughlin was not just one of the richest and best-known men in Chicago, but also because he was one of the most powerful politicians in the city, and, unquestionably, the most corrupt and influential. By building an organization of police officers, saloonkeepers, gamblers, pimps, pickpockets and brothel owners, the former bathhouse attendant and his political partner, "Hinky Dink" Kenna, had long controlled the votes and graft in the First Ward and the Levee.

The aldermen had built an enviable power-base for themselves in Chicago by reliably delivering an enormous number of votes, frequently more than the actual number of voters, to the Democratic Party machine every Election Day. The men were a marvelous team, but, physically, two Irishmen could hardly have been more different. Bathhouse was an enormous, bull-necked man with a huge paunch and a big, broad face, while everything about Hinky Dink was slight, his legs, his shoulders, even the lines on his thin, drawn face.

Legend had it that the name of the saloon, one of the most popular spots in the Levee, had been inspired by William Jennings Bryan's fiery "Cross of Gold" speech, in which the Democratic Party's presidential candidate in 1896 had passionately defended free silver coinage. To ensure that the thousands of customers, who passed through the saloon's doors each month, understood the reference, Alderman Coughlin had decorated the ceiling and walls with giant replicas of silver cartwheels, as dollars were then popularly known.

"I told you that any friend of mine would be welcome here," Little whispered, as they made their way to the crowded, noisy bar.

The arrival of such an odd couple would have attracted more than average attention under any circumstance. But, it was soon obvious from the stares, many hostile, some merely curious, of the mostly male clientele and the sudden, pregnant silence, that the new heavyweight champion of the world had been recognized.

The uneasy silence was soon broken however by a gruff, booming disembodied voice, which carried through the entire room. "Welcome Mister Johnson, yer a man after me own heart I can see," it announced from somewhere behind and to the right of the enormous mahogany bar. Following close behind was the owner of the voice, the alderman John Coughlin, who added: "I'm second to none, as anybody will tell yer, in my appreciation of any man who knows a thing or two about style for the masculine gender."

Despite his constantly swelling waistline, the once-trim alderman had remained, improbably, a dude, a fashion horse, so confident of his own good taste that he had not hesitated to publicly criticize the Prince of Wales for being "a lobster in his taste." The Prince's outfits, Coughlin had boldly opined to a reporter, "Was all right fer playin' baccarat and puttin' his coins on the right hoss at the races. But when it come down to mappin' out style for well-dressed Americans, he's simply a faded two-spot in the big deck of fashion. People, they been followin' his lead cause no other guy has the nerve to challenge him for the championship...now I'm out for first place and you'll see his percentage drop."

Although it is difficult to conceive of someone capable of remarks of such monumental inanity striking fear in anybody, it was clear, from the tightening of the small, almost lipless mouth beneath the full mustache, that was precisely the effect that Coughlin's mere presence had on the short but powerfully-built Little. "Champ," he said, turning to Johnson who was resplendently turned out in a pale ivory suit of English provenance, in a voice that seemed even to his ear far too loud and much too falsely jovial, "let me introduce you to another champion, the champion dresser of America and the world, Mister John Coughlin." Despite years of determined effort his voice, he also told himself with a small shiver of self-loathing, had shook and quivered, determined, as it had on so many previous times, to betray his innermost thoughts and to make it impossible for him to succeed in the brutal world of Chicago deal-making.

In fact, Little's self-flagellation was hardly necessary; in truth he had every reason to be nervous. This was no honest poker match between equal players. In this game Coughlin held all the aces; his moves were the only ones of consequence. How the political boss responded to the black heavyweight champion, and it would be, as he knew from painful experience, arbitrary and almost purely instinctive, would decide his future. Whether or not he would become Johnson's next manager and be allowed to redeem himself, depended entirely on Coughlin's whim. He had represented himself to the new champion as the man who could open all the doors that were normally locked to a black man in Chicago, heavyweight champion of the world or not. And, as he knew, the keys to those doors were tightly locked in the ham like fists of the bombastic and unpredictable alderman.

He had done all he could to make the meeting successful by pointing out to his old mentor, Hinky Dink, that the ownership and control of the heavyweight champion, that was both how he envisioned the role of manager and how he attempted to sell it to his political masters, was an enormous asset that in their hands could make them all a great deal of money. Despite his pleas, however, the men had been unwilling to commit themselves beyond agreeing to meet with Johnson at the Silver Dollar Saloon. That was recognition enough for a nigger, whoever he was, they had insisted. Anything beyond that would have to wait.

Despite the fearsome reputation, there was nothing about the ridiculous figure waddling ponderously towards them that inspired fear or even respect: that is until he was close enough for you to look directly into the pale, almost expressional eyes. Then, the raw intelligence and cold calculation, in such stark contrast to the absurd utterances and comical appearance, was, as many had found, startling, even disconcerting. Coughlin, by his own flamboyant standards, was dressed Little saw with some relief, fairly conservatively. Nothing could have been worse for his cause, than Johnson, openly responding, as other strangers had, with amusement or even worse, contempt, when first confronted by the spectacle Coughlin presented. He had explained to the champion, as delicately as he could, that the alderman was a little bit, maybe more than a little bit, eccentric and colorful in his selection of clothes. Still, the dove grey tailcoat and matching trousers, the Kelly green vest with white checks, the brown silk shirt and the yellow bulldog-toed shoes might have seemed more than a little over the top to the uninitiated. But, at least he had left at home such startling fashion innovations, Little thought gratefully, as the patent-leather dancing pumps with green tops, the Irish green, striped Prince Albert cutaway and the plaid waistcoat with white buttons.

"Mister Johnson, as you can see fer yerself," Coughlin announced, pointing to his green vest, in the same loud, gruff tone he had used from the back of the room, although he was now a little more than a foot away: "I'm a proud Irishman, and Jeffries is too."

The big room had gone completely quiet and every head was turned to see if this was going to be a meeting or a confrontation.

The collar around Little's muscular neck was, suddenly, as

tight as a noose and rivulets of cold sweat crawled painfully down his back. His narrow-set eyes seemed to be staring intently at each other. Slowly, almost imperceptibly, he stepped back one pace away from Johnson, like a man preparing to move out of the line of fire.

Only the two big men, similar in height, but representing very different kinds of power, now standing so close together they could have embraced or grappled without taking another step, seemed oblivious to the tension crackling in the room.

"I want to let you into a little secret, Mister Coughlin," Johnson replied, flashing his golden smile and leaning forward slightly, confidentially, "something I've never divulged to the public before, something my daddy told me when I was no higher than my knee."

"What, Mister Johnson," Coughlin said, in a slightly startled voice, as he took a small step back.

"I know you can't tell, with my complexion, from just looking at me," Johnson continued, the famous smile getting ever larger, "but I swear on my daddy's grave that there's some Irish blood running in these veins too, at least that's what my daddy told me. And you can see," Johnson added, pointing to his pale green tie and matching vest and socks, "that I too am a proud Irishman."

The whisper of the ceiling fans and two quickly muffled coughs were the only sounds in the room. The brief silence seemed endless. Long seconds passed and the two men stood looking into each other's eyes.

"You're not shitting me now Mister Johnson, are you," Coughlin finally replied, a small smile tugging at his enormous cheeks.

"I shit you not, Mister Coughlin," Johnson responded, this time with just a hint of a smile.

"Well shit," the Alderman said, with a chuckle and threw his enormous right arm around Johnson's shoulders, "then yer even more welcome to this Irish saloon. Yer're a good man, Mister Johnson, we can do business with you."

The benediction having been given, the room, as if by magic, sprung to life again. Little reappeared at the champion's side, smiling triumphantly, his exile, he knew, was finally over. Voices were raised again, only louder; people coughed again, only bolder. Glasses and bottles clicked and shook and rattled. A plaintive, Celtic folk song began playing in the background. And hard-eyed men, some with flushed faces, came forward to congratulate the new manager and meet the new champion.

In a sumptuously furnished room in the back of the saloon Hinky Dink Kenna, hair as white as his pale, pasty skin, looked up from the tidy stacks of papers on the roll-top desk, as his partner abruptly pushed open the door with the sign that warned in gilded letters, No Entry, Private Office, and lumbered inside.

"So what did you think of Little's fighter," the sad-faced little man with the slanted eyebrows asked. The tone was mild but the large violet eyes, simultaneously guarded and alert, watched carefully as Coughlin sat heavily in the big armchair across the room: which groaned loudly in a futile protest against the sudden imposition of that considerable weight.

"We can do business with him," Coughlin responded, nodding his massive head in reinforcement.

"But," Kenna prompted, raising a soft, slender, bejeweled right hand to his chin, sensing from their long and close association, that there was more to be said.

"It's just too bad that a man like that had to be a nigger," Coughlin replied, shaking his head. "It's really too bad," he muttered to himself as he leaned back in his creaking chair and sighed, heavily.

It was Saturday night and Belle Schrieber was bored and depressed. The prospect of spending the entire weekend in her gilded cage was sometimes more than she could bear. Not even the fact that she was wearing an expensive evening gown and a golden necklace sparkling with real diamonds was of any help. True, the money she was now making, more in a single week than she had in five months in the straight world, was far more than she had ever expected, and one of her several specialties, abusing and humiliating rich masochists had been enormous fun, for a while.

In the early days, the sight of men of the type who once held enormous power over her groveling naked at her feet, begging pathetically for the crumbs for her attention, had not only absolutely delighted the former stenographer, but it had also done wonders for her then fragile self-esteem. Not coincidentally, the 23-year-old bottle blonde had become, in a remarkably short time, the most requested girl at the Everleigh Club, which almost since its opening more than nine years earlier had been widely regarded as the most luxurious brothel in the world.

But sometimes, she thought, as she stared sympathetically at the singing canaries in their golden cage across the room, she just wanted to get away from the whimpering old men and their soft, useless cocks and find a man who really knew how to fuck. And tonight was one of those times. But the rules were strict and rigidly enforced at the Everleigh: you didn't just leave when you wanted to. If you did there was no coming back. And for the kind of money that could be made here, there were scores of girls lining up to replace every one that left.

No less an authority than the *Chicago Tribune* had described the Everleigh Club this way: "No house of courtesans in the world was so richly furnished, so well advertised, and so continuously patronized by men of wealth and slight morals." And the coldly judicial report of the Vice Commission of Chicago described the Everleigh as "probably the most famous and luxurious home of prostitution in the country."

But it was not just the gaudy splendor of the Everleigh Club that truly set it apart from all other such establishments. Sharing the distinction was the unusual backgrounds and social pedigree of the owners, the extraordinary sisters, Aida and Minna Everly, among the most successful madams on record. When they retired, still in their thirties, the sisters were said to have accumulated a million dollars in cash, some two hundred thousand dollars in jewelry, enough furniture to equip a small hotel, and books, paintings, rugs, statutes, and other valuable articles for which they had paid a hundred and fifty thousand dollars.

The daughters of a wealthy Kentucky lawyer, the sisters had received a finishing school education before marrying two brothers, generally described as Southern gentlemen, before either was twenty years old. But, before long, the fun-loving sisters, who alternately claimed to have been mistreated by or to have been bored with their traditional Southern husbands, had run off to Washington D.C., where they joined a theatrical troupe, and for a year or so traveled around the mid-West playing small roles in popular melodramas. It is not clear how financially successful this endeavor was, there were rumors that they had become high-class prostitutes. Certainly, the vast majority of the actresses of the period were forced to supplement their meager earnings with part-time prostitution. But, whatever the case, it seems likely, that at least, the untimely death of their father, when they were only twenty-two and twenty-four respectively, and a subsequent inheritance of $35,000, had rescued them from a fate that women of their background normally regarded as worse than death.

The sisters, according to this same rumor, used that money to open their first brothel near the Trans-Mississippi Exposition in Omaha. By the time the Exposition closed the $35,000 had more than doubled to $80,000 and the canny sisters, now spelling their name Everleigh, were ready for bigger things. After spending several months investigating prospects in New York, New Orleans, and San Francisco they decided, on the advice of their good friend, the Washington D.C. madam, Cleo Maitland, whose own establishment catered to the lonely men of the House and the Senate, to move their operations to the Levee in Chicago's First Ward.

The business they purchased, at 2131 Dearborn Street, was housed in an enormous, three-storey structure of some fifty rooms that had been put together, from two adjoining houses, as a high-class brothel during the Colombian Exposition in 1890 by the renowned old madam, Lizzie Allen. Another madam, Effie Hankins, had bought out Lizzie after the fair and it was from Effie, a good friend of Cleo, that they had bought the business. The Everleighs bought the lease, fixture and girls for fifty-five thousand dollars, paying twenty thousand dollars down, with the remaining due in six months. They then immediately discarded the fixtures and discharged the girls. Carpenters and decorators were hired and the whole place refurnished and redecorated and an entirely new staff of girls, many of them new to the city, was hired.

Business, right from the grand opening on a freezing cold night on February1, 1900, had been excellent, grossing more than a thousand dollars on the very first night and subsequently, frequently reaching five thousand dollars a night. Even wellborn men were astounded at the Everleigh's glittering opulence: curtains of golden silk, great divans and easy chairs upholstered in silk damask, thick and expensive Turkish rugs and carpets, solid mahogany tables covered with slabs of imported marble, gold spittoons, solid silver dinner service, gold-rimmed china and crystal glassware, golden trays and champagne buckets, tablecloths of Irish linen and Spanish drawnwork, magnificent paintings and tapestries, and a half-dozen pianos, one of them specially gilded and made to order at a cost of fifteen thousand dollars.

Word of the Everleigh's splendors traveled quickly around the country and the world. American sophisticates claimed that by comparison the celebrated Mahogany Hall of Washington D.C., the famous Clark Street house of Carrie Watson, and the finest brothels in New York, San Francisco, and New Orleans were merely squalid hovels, and European visitors said it surpassed anything to be found in Paris.

From long association with that particular subspecies, satisfying the needs and fantasies of wealthy males was something the sisters understood perfectly. The women were chosen as carefully as the furnishings. The rigorous selection process began with a personal interview with Ada. "I talk with each applicant myself," she explained. "She must have worked somewhere else before coming here. We do not like amateurs. Inexperienced girls and young widows are too prone to accept offers of marriage and leave. To get in a girl must have a good face and figure, must be in perfect health, must understand what it is to act like a lady. If she is addicted to drugs or to drink, we do not want her." Implied but unstated was another vital qualification Ada was too well-bred to publicly admit but one on which she privately insisted: only the most skilled, those willing and able to engage in almost every possible variety of sex the Club's often jaded clients might want, were even considered.

Close attention was also paid to the quality of the food and the alcohol, and these too were substantially upgraded. The sisters, upstanding Southern girls as they were, and being far more comfortable with Negro servants than their predecessors, brought in a staff of well-trained, obsequesious, "darkies" to ensure that the gentlemen callers received the excellent service that their money deserved.

The price of the very best was not cheap. Guests knew in advance that a visit would cost the enormous—for the period—sum of least fifty dollars, and often a great deal more. A single bottle of wine, for instance, was twelve dollars downstairs and fifteen in bed, a full weekend, a staggering five hundred dollars. But for the wealthy and powerful men who frequented The Everleigh Club the high prices only added to its allure: it ensured, like their social clubs, that only a certain class of gentlemen would be admitted.

Although naturally bawdy, Belle was intelligent and well spoken and knew how, when she wanted, to present herself favorably. More importantly, as her enormous popularity, particularly with older gentlemen of certain sexual tastes proved, she was certainly extremely skilled in even the most esoteric vices. Her success had very little to do with beauty, at least not of the conventional type. Although her more devoted clients would often describe her as "beautiful" and "stunning," more neutral observers would have regarded the designation "striking" as being far more accurate. The secret of their devotion to her had more to do with her instinctive sadism and the skills she had quickly developed in the use of the whip and the crop.

Initially, the very notion that men of position and authority would pay large sums of money to be verbally and physically abused by her had seemed bizarre and even a little perverse. But she had been intrigued and more than willing when the matter was raised by Ada, especially when she learned that she would make more money performing these "special" services, usually without even taking off her own clothes. Other girls in the house also offered these "special" services, but none, she had been assured by grateful customers, with anything approaching her skill and enthusiasm.

But as enjoyable practicing those skills sometimes were, they did little more than arouse her deeply passionate nature. What I really need now, she acknowledged morosely, as she sat at the bar in the glittering Gold Room, one of twelve theme rooms in the brothel, is a real man, a man of the kind, she knew from experience, that she was unlikely to find in a place like the Everleigh. She wanted a man who knew what he was doing and who would not be put off by the fact that she too knew what she was doing and what she wanted. Men, she thought, wrinkling her short, blunt nose in disgust, only seem to come in two types, those who wanted to be dominated and those who wanted to dominate, and tonight, she wanted neither. After swallowing a half of her glass of wine with one quick gulp, she turned to her companions and rhetorically asked:

"Do you know what I really need tonight, right now?"

"A real man with a strong, firm body, a big, hard cock and lots of stamina," three feminine voices shouted in unison, gigglingly repeating a list of physical qualifications she had previously mentioned. Flanking Belle were "Jew Berha" Morrison to her left and Lillian St. Clair and Virginia Bond to her right. The four women, although not really friends, often found themselves, for reasons none of them could adequately explain, spending a great of time in each other's company.

"Well it's been a long time," Belle responded with a lopsided smile. Titling her head well back she drained the remaining half glass of wine with another long, unladylike swallow, and then placed it down hard on the polished surface of the bar. She could at least get too drunk to feel anything, even if Ada and Minna disapproved. She was their best girl, what the fuck could they do if she had a little too much to drink: let her go?

"Give me another bottle Joe," she shouted tipsily to the wiry, dark-skinned Negro bartender, who was grinning widely, displaying an almost perfect set of white teeth: "Same thing as before."

"What about him," the giggling "Jew Bertha" demanded in a

slightly accented voice, pointing a long, manicured index finger at Joe behind the counter.

"Maybe, but first we have to check if he has a big, hard cock," Belle answered with an evil grin, reaching for Joe's crotch as he approached the counter with the new bottle.

"Now, now Miss Belle, you know how Miss Minna and Miss Ada is about dem sorts of things," Joe replied, a huge smile belying the mildly disapproving tone, as he stepped right up to the counter and made absolutely no effort to avoid Belle's grasping fingers.

"Oh my God, it's true what they say," Belle squealed, as her fingers found their target and squeezed. "You've got to feel this," she added, to no one in particular.

"Let me go first," Virginia suddenly announced, rising unsteadily to her feet. "Come over here Joe, she demanded, leaning over the counter, her tongue thick from several rounds of brandy. "I want to feel this for myself," she added in boozy explanation as she tore his zipper open, reached inside his pants and grabbed.

"No, no, oh Jesus Christ Miss Virginia, Miss Minna don't allow dis kind of thing," Joe pleaded desperately, his eyes widening in an almost comical mixture of lust and panic as she pumped and fondled.

"Look at what I've found," she said in the delighted tones of a little girl who has just finished unwrapping an unexpected gift. Giggling madly, she pulled the now tumescent cock free and impatiently tugged at it.

Across the room, a graying, elegant, Negro in a dark suit, white shirt and a carefully-tied red bowtie, walked delicately up to the gold piano, gleaming dully in the dim light, and looked anxiously around the almost empty room. Then, with a disdainful shrug of his head in the direction of the commotion, he took his seat without even acknowledging the women at the bar. Behind him, against the wall, scores of gold fish swam around energetically in three enormous fish bowls set on elaborate gold stands.

"Joe, you're nothing but a fucking slut," Belle shouted happily, drawing a deep gasp from the bartender, whose hips had begun an involuntary dance to the rhythm of Virginia's relentless hand. "You don't even care whose doing it to you, do you bitch."

"When you're done with the whore, let me have a go at him too," Lillian St. Clair noisily added, as the women roared with laughter. "If there's anything left of the slut," she added, to even more laughter.

Growling fiercely the big car leapt ahead, cutting effortlessly through the night as the driver gunned the powerful engine, repeatedly swinging the long-nosed automobile past startled lines of slower moving vehicles. "Jesus Christ, champ, do you always drive like a bat out of hell," the clearly nervous passenger asked, as the driver expertly pulled the snarling vehicle into the parking space. "What kind of car is it, anyway?"

"A Thomas-Flyer, the racing model," the heavyweight champion of the world proudly replied, as the car shuddered to a stop." I love to speed, man, one day I'm gonna race. Are you sure about this shit man," he asked, suddenly turning to face his companion. "Everybody knows these motherfuckers don't allow men of my color into this place."

Little leaned back in the plushly upholstered seat and smiled smugly. "Champ," he began, rubbing his hands together, satisfaction oozing from every pore of his compact, muscular body. "You've got to understand what we're dealing with here. This is the Levee, the First Ward, nothing happens here, and I mean nothing, that we don't want to happen and everything happens that we want to happen. It's that fucking simple, champ, I shit you not." Smiling cockily, he swung his stocky legs out of the low-slung car and added, "We own this fucking place, lock stock and fucking barrel."

Johnson glanced at his new manager appraisingly, uncoiled his long legs from beneath the dashboard, stood up and carelessly slammed the door shut behind him. "So, what is the plan then," he asked, affecting a confidence that was betrayed by the slight quiver in his voice. "We are just going to go in, look around, select some of the girls and then take them back to our place."

"Or, we could close down the entire fucking place for a while and have all the fucking girls for ourselves champ, what the fuck do you think about that," Little asked, his tone light and jovial. All was well with his world.

"Damn, are you serious man, all of them?" Johnson asked, as he threw another appraising glance at his partner, and evidently reassured, slapped his knee in delight at the prospect, his eyes sparkling. "I like how you think man," he said quietly, his tone suddenly serious as the glowing Little nodded appreciatively.

"Champ, I wouldn't fucking joke about such a serious matter," Little replied with a wink. "I only joke about religion and politics, pussy is fucking serious business," he said, chuckling appreciatively at his own little joke.

"That's big man. You know," the smiling Johnson said, draping his right arm affectionately around the smaller man's shoulders. "We are going to get along just fine, you know what I mean. But tonight man, to give it you straight, I just want a woman, or two. You know what I mean."

"Just two, is that all man," Little asked in a bantering voice, as they walked up to the steps and rang the bell. "Tell you what," he said, as they waited, "let's get us three or four and I'll have at least one, maybe two, depending on how you feel. Does that sound fair?"

"You're on man," Johnson replied, the big golden smile getting bigger "I told you I like the way you think."

Within seconds the heavy door creaked open and a very old Negro, dressed in what appeared to be an even more ancient formal dress coat, welcomed them with a stiff bow of his snow-white head, a slightly raised eyebrow the only visible sign of his surprise and irritation at the unusual racial make-up of his guests; chauffeurs, however well-dressed, did not usually accompany their employers inside. "Good evening sah, may I take your hat and coat," the old man said stiffly, looking directly at Little, allowing himself only the faintest of smiles, his entire being radiating disapproval. It was quickly evident that as far as he was concerned Johnson— who was obviously not well-trained having entered the foyer ahead of his employer—did not exist.

"It is Mistah Little, isn't it sah, we haven't seen you for quite a while," the gravel-voiced old man added politely, managing somehow to make his welcome sound like an interrogation.

"I was out of town for a while Carter," Little answered, his face reddening from the certain knowledge that the old man and many others knew that he had been exiled in disgrace. "But," he added, quickly regaining his composure and gesturing grandly at Jackson, who was standing uncomfortably in the imposing entry foyer, "I'm the manager of the new heavyweight champion of the world, Mister Jack Johnson."

Instantly, as if a bolt of lightning had struck him, the old man's entire countenance underwent an extraordinary transformation. Quickly discarding the carefully constructed Uncle Tom mask he always wore in the company of white folks, the suddenly animated doorman, literally rushed over to the heavyweight champion, his eyes beaming. "It's a pleasure to meet you Mistah Johnson," he said, sticking out a bony, wrinkled hand, "Mah name is Carter Williams and I never thought ah'd ever have such an honor."

Beaming with pleasure, Johnson enthusiastically took the bony old hand in his and was about to reply when Little interrupted.

"Carter, I want you to do me a favor," he said, "I want you to tell Miss Minna that I'm here with Mister Jack Johnson and that we've come here directly from the Silver Dollar. She'll understand."

"Straight from the Silver Dollar sah," the old man repeated, his eyes widened with surprise and something approaching awe as the full import of what was about to happen slowly sunk in. Here again was something he never expected to see in his lifetime, a black man being welcomed into the Everleigh Club.

"And Carter," Little added in a conspiratorial whisper, placing a friendly hand on one of the doorman's bony shoulders, "We want three or four of your best girls, any recommendations?"

"Three or four sah?" the old man asked, confusion clear in the watery old eyes, looking from Johnson to Little and back again, as if by counting the two men repeatedly he might find the ones he had missed. Then, seeing the sly smiles on both men, the old man smiled himself, understanding finally dawning. "Oh, I see, sah," he finally responded, this time looking straight at Johnson.

Evidently discomfited by the old man's confusion, Johnson stepped toward him, pulled a bulging billfold from a coat pocket, extracted a few bills, pressed them into the doorman's outstretched right hand, and in a surprisingly gentle tone said, "Here's a little something for your troubles Mister Williams."

"No trouble at all sah, Mistah Johnson, " the old man said brightly, as he pocketed the bills with a pleased smile after a quick glance to check the denominations. "There a young lady, Miss Belle," he began, "she's our best gal sah I think you may just take a shine to her sah, and sah," he added, winking, "she has some very nice friends with her right now."

Six

For many years one of the proudest boasts of the original Puritan, Congregationalist, founders of the Massachusetts Bay Colony was that not a single person of Irish blood had participated in the American Revolution against the British. The inhabitants of New England at the time of the revolution, successions of Harvard-trained, New England-bred historians had assured their proud, Anglo-Saxon readers, were wholly English. Not a single county in England, they were told again and again, to their enormous gratification, had purer English blood than theirs.

While these claims were certainly not true, Irish men had participated in every aspect of the Revolution and immigrants from both the northern and southern parts of the country had been in the colony since the mid-1770s, it accurately reflected the intense animosity of the Anglo-Saxon population, who then, almost unanimously, regarded the Irish as members of a barbaric and inferior race. Because of this, the earliest Irish immigrants had generally avoided Boston and its environs, preferring less populated areas of New England, such as Bangor, Belfast, and Limerick in Maine; Dublin, Londonderry, and Hillsboro County in New Hampshire; and Orange County in Vermont.

While all people of Celtic descent were viewed with disdain, Irish Catholics were particularly detested. The Ulster Irish, primarily Protestant descendants of Scottish settlers who had been planted on lands confiscated from Irish rebels by King James 1, were viewed somewhat differently. The fact that they were Protestants not Catholics; that they spoke English rather than Gaelic; that they were merchants, commercial farmers and enterprising businessmen; made them and their lifestyles far more compatible with the traditional Puritan work ethic, and rendered them, therefore, far more acceptable to their Anglo-Saxon overlords.

Centuries of bitter military and political conflict between English invaders and Irish defenders in the old countries had taken an enormous psychic toll. To the self-righteous and hypocritical English Puritans, despite their own rebellion against the British crown, not only were the Irish Papists practitioners of a heretical and blasphemous religion, but they were, also, such dangerous political subversives that they had to be excluded from the liberties extended to other European settlers. As one particularly egregious example, in Massachusetts, by a law enacted by the General Court in 1700, Catholic priests were subject to imprisonment and even death if found anywhere in the colony.

It took the unofficial but invaluable assistance of the French Catholic king, Louis XV1, during the struggle with Britain to make Catholicism slightly more acceptable in the colonies. And it was only when the French government agreed to recognize the fledgling nation and extended a formal treaty of military and commercial alliance to it in the early months of 1778, that most Americans began adopting a more tolerant attitude to their traditional enemy.

Forbearance of a handful of sophisticated French Catholics did not, however, translate into acceptance of hordes of poor and uneducated Irish ones. The charm and piety of two French priests, Fr. Francois Antoine Matignon and Fr. Jean-Louis Lefebvre de Cheverus, had so captured the affections of a majority of the citizens of Boston that by March of 1800 the Catholic Church was able to break ground for the construction of its first church in that city. But when, after 1815, an average of 20,000 Irish Catholics began arriving in the United States each year, many of them making their way to the Commonwealth of Massachusetts, Bostonians became increasingly alarmed.

But the storm was yet to come. The Great Famine of the 1840s and 1850s brought death and starvation to Ireland and ignited a massive new wave of immigration. Hundreds of thousands of Irish peasants, packed into the stinking bellies of dilapidated cargo ships like slaves and cattle, fled the ancient and exhausted soils of Europe for the safety and promise of the New World. In just one year—1847—-Boston, which had been struggling to absorb four to five thousand immigrants a year, was suddenly engulfed by a tidal wave of more than thirty-seven thousand refugees, most of them officially listed as Irish laborers.

Unfortunately Boston offered few economic opportunities for the unskilled, however strong and willing. And many of the new arrivals were weak and pallid, half-starved, and disease-ridden. Unlike many other American cities, which were just then in the throes of developing an industrial base, by the middle of the nineteenth century Boston was already an old city and its capital investments had long been dispersed to outlying areas such as Waltham, Lowell, and Lawrence. Long after New York and Philadelphia and even newer western cities like Chicago and St. Louis, had become major metropolitan centers capable of absorbing frontiersmen and immigrants alike, Boston, now more than two hundred years old, tenaciously retained its distinctive Anglo-Saxon-Protestant character.

The warning issued in 1850 to the city's taxpayers by Mayor John Prescott Bigelow, that: "Foreign paupers are rapidly accumulating on our hands," that large numbers of "aged, blind, paralytic, and lunatic immigrants who have become public charges on our public charities," was an early indication of the problem that would come to be known as the "the Catholic Menace." The vile and disgusting conditions of the slums in which they were forced to live was not seen as an inevitable result of their lack of opportunity and extreme poverty, but of confirmation of their laziness and moral turpitude.

The Civil War provided the Boston Irish with just the opportunity they had long been waiting for. "We Catholics have only one course to adopt, only one line to follow," the local Irish newspaper, *The Pilot*, instructed its readers on January 12, 1861. "Stand by the Union; fight for the Union; die for the Union." And they did: With few exceptions, the Irish loyally supported the Lincoln administration, although most had been members of the Democratic Party from the time of Jefferson and Jackson. But, they would fight, they made abundantly clear, to save the Union, not to free the slaves. Many would distinguish themselves in the all-Irish

9th Regiment, which, with its distinctive green banners, carved out a reputation for always being in the forefront of the fighting.

After the war a series of enormous construction projects, including the laying out of the South End and the filling in of the Back Bay, gave many Irish workers their first real opportunity to earn a regular day's pay. This new prosperity and new forms of transportation such as the horse-drawn streetcar allowed them to move out into the suburbs, create whole new residential neighborhoods, and, in time, become a major political force.

Nothing had really changed, Daniel O'Brien thought sadly. He had spent the first six years of his professional life in Boston, it was where he had gotten his first job in journalism, but he had never felt comfortable there and now some fourteen years since his departure for New York he still didn't. He had made a few hurried visits back for family events but this was his first extended trip. Visiting Brian and his family was nice and the automobile show had been spectacular, even better than New York's or Chicago's. Of course he had not included that little bit of opinion in the short piece he had prepared for his paper. He had pointed out however, that the eight-day show, the seventh annual, had been attended by some 150,000 people, which along with the range of exhibits and the number of sales completed there, made it the largest of its kind in the country. But just being in Boston, Daniel ruefully acknowledged to himself, was still enough to depress him and darken his mood. In New York he was a real American, here he felt he was just an Irishman living in America. Coming a full week before Jeffries' arrival had been a mistake, already he could hardly wait to leave.

But that, he reminded himself once again, as he watched, out of one eye, the enormous black horse prancing happily down West Broadway like a thoroughbred, head held high, nostrils flaring wide, was totally impossible. Covering Jeffries here, he knew, was about a lot more than just boxing. His paper and he had heartily concurred, was convinced that the kind of welcome extended to the popular former champion would be an important gauge of the current state of Irish-Yankee relations in this ethnically divided city. And based on some of what he had already learnt and heard around town, Jeffries' reception here would be somewhat less than rapturous. Even some members of the Irish community were becoming impatient with the former champion's obdurate refusal to commit to meeting Johnson. Suspicion was growing that he intended to do no more than take his fat earnings from his theatrical appearances and return to his alfalfa farm in California.

To Daniel, nothing spoke more eloquently about Irish impotence in Boston than the very event he was attending that morning; the celebration of the One hundred and Thirty Third Anniversary of the evacuation of Boston by the British army: And on St. Patrick's Day, no less. From every appearance the peculiar local holiday would be celebrated for at least another one hundred years. The police had told him that almost a quarter of a million men, women and children had attended last year's event and even more were expected this year. And from what he had been able to see, their estimate was, sadly, not overly optimistic. Judging from the festive crowds jamming the sidewalks, almost the entire city was in the streets. The authorities had also said that the route was going to be one of the longest and best looking in the history of the holiday; and those claims also seemed to be true. Most of the houses along the route, certainly along West Broadway, were elaborately decorated with the national colors and paintings of former presidents of the country, governors of the state and naval and military heroes. Brian, himself a city employee, had also confirmed that more of the city's major thoroughfares were going to be involved than in any other previous year of which he was aware.

Even Mother Nature seemed to be on the side of the organizers. Snow had fallen steadily until sunrise but by 9 o'clock the weather had cleared. And just after noon, when the crowd began assembling along the parade route, the sun had broken out from behind its stifling prison of low-hanging, grey-mottled clouds to bestow its benediction on the city. For somebody who had grown up in Worcester at a time when proud Irishmen had been marching on St. Patrick's Day for more than a decade, it was humiliating to the extreme that the same rights had not been won in Boston so many years later. Not that there had not a battle in Worcester about the wisdom of having a St Patrick's Day march. But the opposition had come from other Irish groups, not from the Yankees. For years the temperance men had voted against it, on the basis that it provoked the disgraceful drinking and brawling that had stained the good name of the Irish people in the United States.

Eventually, however, after years of fierce debate, the men of the Ancient Order of Hibernians and their allies had won the day. Their father, like his father before him, had been a proud and committed member of one of their militia companies: The Hibernian Rifles and Guards. And the triumph of those who, in their father's words, "were not ashamed to call themselves Irishmen," had filled him with exultation. One of Daniel's favorite mental pictures and one that he almost unfailingly conjured up when thinking of his parents, was of that proud Irish immigrant marching briskly down Main Street, back ramrod straight, surrounded by hundreds and hundreds of identically dressed Irishmen. The sight of all those men, row after row of them, outfitted in freshly-ironed green tunics and trousers, spiked and plumed helmets set firmly on their heads, putteed feet stepping in unison, had been, even he in his youthful arrogance had been forced to admit, amazingly impressive.

Daniel's sour mood that morning had not been helped by severe sleep deprivation. The day's events, which had begun noisily before dawn, precisely at six, with the roar of cannons and the pealing of bells throughout the South Boston and Dorchester districts, had prematurely interrupted his fitful sleep. Brian had, of course, insisted that he stay with him and his family in their modest but tidy three-bedroom home in the Dorchester area. Although he would have been far more comfortable staying in one of the many fine hotels in the city and his paper was paying all of his expenses, he had, somewhat reluctantly, agreed.

Not that he had not been looking forward to spending as much time as possible with Brian and his family, he really had been. It had been almost fifteen long years since they had seen much of each other. A few hurried visits home, to the funeral of their grandfather, the wedding of their sister and the most recent one, three years ago for their father's sudden serious illness, had not afforded much time or opportunity for more than casual conversation. But he had over the years grown accustomed to sleeping in far greater comfort than the narrow bed, thin mattress and small room, which Brian had commandeered from his older son, offered.

Nevertheless, the first few days had been fun, a great deal of fun. At first it seemed, to the open-eyed wonderment of Brian's attractive wife, Erin, and their two boys, who had previously only caught an occasional glimpse of their quite famous relative, that the two grown men had in some mysterious manner reverted to their long-departed childhoods, talking, joking, laughing, even giggling. They had stayed up for much of those first nights, hardly sleeping, eating, drinking, and endlessly talking. They had updated each other about their new lives, but, mostly, they had talked about the past, about the declining health of their parents, whom, like their sister, still lived in Worcester, and had reminisced about the old days in that benighted city, now seen in the tinted glow of time, by mutual agreement, as their golden years.

As children they had been very close, but even then, very different, in both temperament and physical appearance. Brian, older by four years, had been the good son, a kind, thoughtful, mindful child, and the longest serving altar boy in the city; the kind of boy proud parents and teachers expected or at least hoped, in poor Irish Catholic families, to one day be called to the blessed service of the Church. Of him, a far different, much less pleasant fate had been feared, if not quite expected. True, inspired by his grandfather's tales of ancient Ireland and the O'Brien clan, he had been an avid reader and a good and sometimes even brilliant student, but also, too often, a brawler, quick to try finishing with his fists the innumerable arguments his acerbic tongue and quick temper initiated.

Brian, his enormous, big brother, he recalled, glancing fondly over at his towering brother, who was standing to his left with a huge arm draped protectively over each son, had also been his special champion, guarding him with a fierce devotion. Very, very rarely with his fists, that was decidedly not Brian's style and was almost never necessary, but, usually, with a quiet word and his calm, massive, presence. His brother's great size, intimidating physical power and flaming red hair, had made such an enormous impression on the young Daniel that he had often thought of him as the reincarnation of the legendary founder of the O'Brien clan, the warrior king Brian Boru, in whose memory he had been named.

Less than twenty yards away, on the other side of the street from the O'Brien's, a small, nimble, sandy-haired boy in a blue coat, egged on noisily by playmates on the ground, had clambered out too far on the wet and slippery limb of one of the large trees lining West Broadway and had suddenly lost his footing, screaming as loudly as he could as he fell. Bystanders in the immediate vicinity, from both sides of the street, had rushed to his assistance and for a brief moment the parade was forgotten. But with the appearance of the coast artillery, resplendent in their heavy blue coats, capes turned back, red lining showing, the onlookers' eyes were soon redirected to the primary spectacle. The sailors from the four battleships in the harbor followed immediately behind the coast artillery. Smartly outfitted in blue pea jackets and matching blue watch caps and leggings, their rollicking gait contrasting sharply with the steady stride of the artillerymen who had preceded them.

For Daniel, one of the most disturbing aspects of the trip was the realization that his big brother still evoked in him the same powerful mixture of love and bewilderment that he always had. Everything had changed but nothing had. As much as he loved and admired Brian, he had never really understood what made him tick and, he had finally, reluctantly, admitted to himself, he still didn't. Despite all the time they had spent talking during the past several days he had not, he had been forced to concede, gotten any closer to solving the unfathomable puzzle that Brian had always been to him. Perhaps their sister, Kelly, had been right that the problem was not with Brian but with him. With Brian, she had said, and very unlike him, he had added, what you saw was what you got. There was no puzzle to unravel, no mystery to solve.

Understanding Brian, she had pointed out, with more than just a little touch of impatience, required nothing more than accepting him for the simple, caring, unpretentious human being that he so obviously was.

And when he had responded with a cry of frustration, that was exactly what he was trying to do, figure out his brother, so he could accept him for whoever he was, Kelly had looked hard at him for a long moment, incredulity filling her enormous, wide-spaced, grey-green eyes that was so much like their mother's, before spilling slowly over to her slender, oval face. And then she had laughed loudly, and, he thought pityingly, and said something he had carried with him all these years, like a sore that would not heal. "Poor Danny, you always knew more than the rest of us, but you really don't know anything you can't find written down in one of those books of yours, do you? "

From anybody the gibe would have stung. Coming from his beloved sister, who he knew had not meant to be cruel, the observation had been particularly painful, precisely because it was unaccompanied by any sign of ill will. To Kelly and the rest of the family Brian, with all his seeming incongruities and contradictions, was simply Brian. Just as, as Kelly also pointed out, he Daniel, with his own odd ways was just Daniel. But even as a child, even when he had been filled with gratitude and overawed by his brother's great size and strength, a little part of his brain had been critical of what he had seen as Brian's inexplicable passivity. And as they grew older and his appreciation for Brian's gentleness, quiet intelligence and wry sense of humor increased, so had his puzzlement at his big brother's obeisance to authority, from wherever source it came.

Brian had accepted without question such, in his Daniel's carefully considered opinion, absurdities such as the Virgin Birth, the Resurrection and Ascension, the Transfiguration, Holy Water, the Holy Mary and Holy Communion, and even the totally inane concept, which none of the silly priests had ever been able to explain, of a Holy Ghost. None of that anti-rational, anti-scientific, paganistic, nonsense for him, simply because naïve, parochial, religious zealots wrote them on pieces of parchment more than a thousand years ago. To him the world was often a ridiculous, highly imperfect place and those in charge of it not to be believed or trusted. Brian's unquestioning acceptance of what he was told, of the world as he found it was, to him, inexplicable, maddening.

As thunderous waves of applause followed the blue jackets down West Broadway, Daniel turned to his brother, who had happily joined in the applause, and asked: "Brian, doesn't it bother you even a little bit that on March 17, 1909, the only parade in Boston has nothing to do with St. Patrick's Day."

"Danny," Brian responded in his surprisingly high tenor, his eyes twinkling as he looked directly at his brother, "I know that this might surprise you, but I do, just a little bit. Let me tell you something else, Danny" Brian added, his eyes slightly narrowing, the twinkling fading, "I too am a proud Irishman, and these here," his massive head nodding in the direction of his sons, "are also being raised to be proud Irishmen, just like Granddaddy and Dad would have wanted it. Don't you ever forget it."

Brian had not moved nor raised his voice but the space between them had somehow narrowed and for the first time in his life Daniel was, suddenly, afraid of his brother. This is what the others saw, he thought, as he visibly flinched from the quiet menace and backed away, his knees shaking.

"One more thing, Danny," Brian added, the eyes twinkling again, "We, the Irish people, are going to do just fine here, we are already doing a lot better than you think, just wait and see. One day, Danny, we are going to be masters of this city, just you wait and see."

It was Monday, March 22, late in the afternoon, when Daniel walked into the smelly, steamy, overcrowded gymnasium at the Armory A.A. in Boston. The mingled stink of liniment, male sweat, and tobacco and an orchestra of gruff male voices shouting and swearing, filled the air. In the middle of a large group of sweating men, most far too grey and paunchy to be regulars at any place of exercise, sat the undefeated, retired heavyweight champion of the world, Jim Jeffries, already hard at work although he had arrived in town only that morning.

Hundreds, rather than the thousands in Chicago and New York, had greeted him at the Boston station. And representatives of the theatrical agents had whispered nervously that ticket sales for his engagements were slow. If his trip were going to be successful, a lot of work, they had warned, still had to be done.

The workout had begun with short but vigorous sessions of rope skipping, shadow boxing, and the pulling of chest weights. Now, seated on a backless campstool with his feet braced in front of him, the former champion was in the middle of a routine that Sam Berger had announced to the crowd was called the "Salome." After bending backwards until his head almost touched the ground behind him, the big man then slowly swung his body sidewise, then in a partial circle, before, to loud applause, finally bringing himself back to a sitting position.

Perhaps to demonstrate that despite his silence he had every intention of getting into the kind of championship form it would take to defeat Johnson, or, more likely, to ensure that his engagements were well attended, Jeffries, dripping with sweat, went straight into another routine. While he laid flat on his back, Berger repeatedly tossed the big medicine ball at him. Pulling his legs back until his knees almost touched his stomach, he drove his legs forward so powerfully that the heavy leather sphere shot back with such force that each time Berger was almost knocked to the floor.

After the hour-long workout was over, despite the warm applause of the many fans that went away convinced that their champion would soon reclaim the heavyweight title for their race and the smug satisfaction on his own face, Jeffries, as taciturn as ever, still refused to say anything about a possible fight with Johnson. That piece of ticket-selling promotion, as usual, was left to the glib Berger, who smilingly told the assembled newsmen that he was willing to wager with any of them, that when Jeff got ready that there would be a fight and that then Johnson would be repaid with interest for some of his recent statements.

"Jeff, you know," he said, his voice light and confident, "has never yet told anybody in advance what he was going to do to any prospective opponent."

Leaning forward slightly with a wink, his voice a confidential whisper, as if readying himself to share some profound secret with the newspapermen, Berger continued: "Take it from me boys that Jeff would not have left his alfalfa ranch if he didn't intend eventually to meet Johnson. Jeff is too fond of his home to ever leave it, unless he wanted to bring back the championship to a white holder."

As the reporters nodded in agreement, Berger pressed his point. "But he'll not enter the ring until he is certain that he'll be able to do himself and our people full justice. You all understand that don't you. He realizes fully, as you all do too, what it would mean to get into the ring unless in the best of condition, and that he'll never do. When Jeff finds himself, he will be there, and then Mr. Johnson will probably wish that the big fellow was somewhere else."

To demonstrate just how much progress he was making in his campaign to return to the ring, Jeffries then invited the formerly skeptical reporters to his hotel suite. There, as recorded by the *Boston Herald*, he proved to the now captivated press corps that getting into the kind of condition needed to meet and defeat Jack Johnson was only a matter of time. "Jeff looked surprisingly well—much better in fact than was expected. In his rooms at the hotel he stripped for the newspapermen, and instead of showing evidence of his long layoff he looked as if he was only 20 to 30 pounds above his normal fighting weight."

Back in his own hotel room, into which he had moved the day after the parade, Daniel sat at the big desk and wrote: *Turning around the previously skeptical opinions of his intentions proved far less difficult for the former heavyweight champion than anticipated. In fact, it took just a single hour of gymnasium stunts on the first day of his arrival to do so. Perhaps, as some area residents of Irish extraction strongly believe, the prejudice against Irish Americans is not as strong as in previous years or as we in far-off New York were led to believe or feared.*

The five-mile road run, from the Chestnut Hill reservoir to the

Armory, had been surprisingly easy despite the heavy footwear and bulky clothing that he had been obliged to wear as protection against the wintry conditions. It had been years since he had done anything nearly as strenuous and he had been worried that the cold air would have been extremely hard on his California-conditioned lungs. But now, after fifty-six minutes of steady running, Jeffries' was perspiring freely and his only discomfort was stiffness in his feet from the unaccustomed activity. He had started slowly, cautiously, moving with a steady, easy gait. But, as he warmed to the task he had increased his speed and had even, occasionally, broken into sprints for distances from twenty to one hundred yards; the quick starts designed to approximate the movements used during a ring encounter.

Jeffries' run attracted large and enthusiastic crowds. The *Boston Herald* reported on Thursday, March 25, that: "Several times along the roads the crowds of youngsters became so great that it was necessary for Jim to seek safety in flight, only to soon have another group of youngsters at his heels. On his return to the Armory A.A. Jim was perspiring freely, but his wind was surprisingly good, considering the exertion."

Berger, a former top heavyweight himself, had struggled to keep pace with his friend during the run, but also looking remarkably fresh, quickly took control of the press briefing in the Armory. "Tomorrow he will go in another direction and he'll increase the distance of the run each day until he covers ten or more miles," he announced, while Jeffries looked on silently.

"It's great to get out into the air and work, he added. "One hour of this will do more good than a week inside." Behind him, Jeffries nodded in silent but pleasant agreement.

But by the following day both the weather and Jeffries' mood had changed, dramatically. The morning began with the city locked in the throes of one of the worse storms of the winter, high winds and heavy rain making roadwork impossible. And Jeffries was fuming at the news that Johnson was heading toward Boston to demand a personal response from him. To the former champion the very idea that Johnson would dare to confront him personally was impertinent and intolerable.

"Even if I make up my mind whether or not I will fight him," the former boilermaker haughtily declared to the assembled newspapermen, as he sat on a backless stool in the gymnasium with an enormous dumbbell in each giant paw. "I will have nothing to do with him. I have no business to discuss with him, and certainly I would not receive him socially."

As usual, Berger was a lot more talkative. Among other pronouncements, he warned Johnson to stay away "or else there would probably be no battle in the ring in which the world's title was at issue." Listening closely to Berger's harangue, Daniel jotted in his notebook: *"The clear implication of the statement is that if the men come face to face there might be an impromptu affair without the benefit of purse or rules. But as we know this will never happen, there is too much at stake, far too much money at risk. I am more convinced than ever before that there will be a fight between Jeffries and Johnson, the only real questions now, I believe, are when and where"*

PART TWO

Seven

The roar and power of the wind rushing toward them at more than fifty miles an hour was overwhelming; like nothing the tight-lipped passengers in the big, open top touring car had ever experienced before. Only the smiling driver seemed unaffected. Ahead, the road turned sharply to the left but instead of slowing the driver swung the nose of the powerful vehicle into the bend, downshifted expertly in one fluid motion, and accelerated. Growling menacingly the 1909, six-cylinder Arrow Pierce leapt forward, shuddering wildly as the screaming rear wheels struggled to maintain contact with the asphalt. A high-pitched, feminine scream from behind the driver rose above the shrieking of the tires. Unperturbed, the driver, big smile in place, nonchalantly righted the vehicle with a deft flick of his right wrist, glanced at the young, blonde woman sitting stoically beside him and winked.

Stunned silence followed. Finally, after a long moment a slightly quavering, masculine voice from the backseat shouted, "Goddamn it Jack you just scared the holy shit out of Lilly. I swear you turn into a goddamned maniac whenever you get behind the wheel of a car," the man added, placing an arm around the ashen-faced woman trembling at his side.

"That's just because we're late for the game and I'm umpiring, remember that George," the heavyweight champion of the world replied mildly, glancing over his shoulder at his passengers. "Were you really scared Lilly," he asked, his tone suddenly solicitous, of the raven-haired woman, who was trying, unsuccessfully, to smile bravely. "Belle wasn't," he continued, "were you Belle."

"I wasn't scared at all, I love to speed," the blonde woman replied with a disdainful, unsympathetic toss of her head, "I told Lilly that you drove fast. She knew what to expect."

"I'm fine now, really," Lillian St. Clair said, smiling

reassuringly, "I'll get used to it."

The two-lane road between Cedar Point, Indiana and downtown Chicago had straightened out and seemed to stretch dead straight ahead as far as the eye could see. Smiling broadly Johnson tilted his head to look at Lilly's reflection in his rear view mirror. "Are you sure about that," he asked, "because this is as good a strip as any to find out if that salesman fellow was telling me the truth that this baby can go seventy-five miles an hour."

"Jesus Christ Jack," George Little yelled, "you're the fucking heavyweight boxing champion of the world, not the fucking champion racing car driver of the world. Besides if we get stopped by a cop now we'll never fucking make the game on time."

"Dammit George you're as bad as a little old lady, do you know that," Johnson replied, his tone light and bantering, "Never letting me have any fun."

"Well that's my job you fucking maniac," Little responded, a big smile lighting up the normally dour face, "that's what I do, take care of you, keep you out of trouble."

"Aren't they a lovely couple," Belle said laughing, as she turned to look at Lilly, "I'm surprised they even bothered to take us with them."

"Yeah," Lilly replied grinning, obviously now fully recovered, "so very much in love."

"You know what these ladies are hinting at with all this talk about man love, don't you George," Johnson quickly answered, looking over his shoulder to cast a conspiratorial wink in his manager's direction. "You wouldn't think *they'd* be so, what is the word, reticent about it though," he added pointedly, trying to prompt a rejoinder from the uncomprehending Little.

"Don't you start down that road Jack," Belle said levelly, as she turned to look directly at Johnson, "I know how your mind works, always going, always scheming, always trying to turn around anything anybody says to your advantage. I told you before I don't do that."

"Don't do what, what are they talking about" Little asked in a perplexed tone of nobody in particular. "

"You know, silly, the backdoor thing," Lilly replied, slipping her arm through Little's and resting her head on his shoulder.

"Damn Jack, why didn't you just say straight out that you were talking about ass fucking. You're not a straight talking man Jack, I don't always get you man."

"I know George, I know," Johnson said quietly.

Being the heavyweight champion of the world was turning out to be quite a lot less than he had expected. In the five months since his return to the United States with the title the reality had fallen far short of his expectations. Most white newspapers had steadfastly refused to acknowledge his new status, describing him merely as a Negro pugilist. He had been arrested repeatedly, sometimes for speeding, sometimes for just being a black man driving an automobile even wealthy whites envied. He had been denied service in restaurants and nightclubs, and hotels all across the country had turned him away. It had become painfully clear over the months that although they weren't even sure that Jeffries intended to fight again; as far as the vast majority of white Americans were concerned the title still belonged to the retired champion. Even some sections of the black community had not exactly welcomed him with open arms. Many of the better-educated, more affluent elements, he knew, strongly disapproved of his attitude and his lifestyle. And he had been strongly advised, even warned, to be less cocky and more deferential to white authority.

But what was most troubling, most galling, to him was that Jeffries was making a lot more money off his title than he himself was. Jeffries' newfound popularity, he knew, was due entirely to the fact that a Negro had won the heavyweight title. If he had not won the championship nobody would have cared if Jeffries had never left his alfalfa farm again. The large crowds that were turning out all across the country to see his vaudeville act were motivated more by a burning hatred of him than by any previous admiration for the former champion. But, by every report he had received, the crowds in most cities were so large that Jeffries was certain to earn substantially more than the $50,000 he had been guaranteed, more than $60,000, perhaps as much as $65,000 to $70,000, some had speculated, a sum at least twice as much as any fighter had ever received for actually getting into the ring with a real opponent.

In the meantime he, the heavyweight champion, had earned less than $10,000 from two six round bouts and a few thousands more from a few exhibitions and vaudeville appearances. It had also become painfully clear that George was a great guy but not much more. Almost immediately after that night in April at the Everleigh Club he and George had taken up with Belle and Lilly. Both women had left their positions with the Everleigh to travel with the two men, Belle as Mrs. Johnson and Lilly as Mrs. Little. When they were not on the road the two couples shared Little's home not far from the Levee and a rented cottage at Cedar Point, Indiana, a fraying summer resort about twenty-five miles from Chicago that was popular with residents of the Levee. They'd had a lot of fun together but it had become obvious that if was ever going to make real money that he was going to have to take a far more active role in his own management, which would mean relegating George to a lesser role, perhaps as a confidante and advisor.

Despite the torrid overhead sun and sweltering humidity, crowds of well-dressed black men and women had started gathering along 39th Street and South Wentworth Avenue from just after midday, fully two hours before the scheduled start of the game. And since many had come directly from work and had skipped lunch, business for vendors outside the ballpark was unusually brisk. Tickets for the contest, between the Leland Giants and the Cuban Stars, had been on sale all week and the *Chicago Defender* had warned several days earlier that seats for this rare Thursday event were selling fast and that, at the start of the week, 1,500 had already been taken.

The tickets were a hot item in the Chicago black community not just because a high quality of baseball was expected from the two superb teams, but also because, as the *Defender* had announced, "*A great array of Society Visitors and Home Folks Will be in Attendance at Provident Hospital's Great Benefit.*"

Foremost among the distinguished visitors expected to attend, the paper had gleefully announced, were, Mrs. Booker T. Washington, who would have a box seat, and the reigning heavyweight champion of the world, Jack Johnson, who would be umpiring the game. Just getting in therefore was not enough, getting a good seat as close as possible to the box seats and the field was absolutely essential.

The importance of the occasion was underlined by the fact, as the *Defender* had also announced, that the game was being played at South Side Park, the home of the White Sox, the white American Major League team, instead of the far smaller Auburn Park, the Leland Giant's home field. The paper had also been at pains to point out that the management of White Sox Park, as South Side Park was also known, had "given the use of the grounds free of charge in order that Provident may continue to do the good work it has done in the past."

At the turn of the twentieth century baseball had no rivals for the affections of the American sporting public, black or white; boxing was, at best, a distant second. But the relatively high regard in which white baseball players were held by the nation at large did not extend to their black counterparts. Major League baseball was strictly segregated, Rube Foster's creation of the Negro National League was still two decades away, and making a living playing baseball was a dubious proposition for black baseball players, however talented. Nevertheless, black baseball, however limited in scope and organization, was not just a rare source of entertainment for the millions of black Americans who were locked out of most places of amusement by white racism, but was, also, a platform for nascent black entrepreneurship. Barnstorming tours across the country and abroad, to Cuba and Mexico, playing exhibition games against other black teams and, occasionally, even white major league teams, gradually transformed black baseball from a weekend enterprise into a full-time operation.

Curiously however not all of organized baseball was segregated; in some cities black teams were allowed to compete in white semi-professional leagues. In 1909, the Leland Giants, which had been founded in 1905 by Frank Leland, one of the early black baseball entrepreneurs, entered the overwhelmingly white Chicago City League and won the title resoundingly.

The principal instrument of that victory was the same Rube Foster who would become the "father" of black baseball, be enshrined in the Baseball Hall of Fame and play a crucial role in Jack Johnson's escape to Paris after his conviction on White Slavery charges. In 1909, long before he had climbed to such exalted heights, Foster was both a dominating pitcher and the inspired manager of the Leland Giants. Born Andrew Foster on September 17, 1879 in Calvert, Texas, to a preaching father and a gospel-singing mother, the future Hall-of-Famer first came to widespread public attention in 1903 as a member of the Cuban X-Giants. That fall, Foster, who had developed a nasty screwball thrown with a submarine delivery, amazingly won four games during a seven-game series against the Philadelphia Giants for the "Colored Championship of the World." In 1907, the peripatetic Foster, who had first played in Chicago in 1900, returned to the city and the employment of Frank Leland with whom he had had a stormy relationship, but this time as both player and manager.

Leland, a light-skinned graduate of Fisk University needed help, badly. He had just been elected Cook County Commissioner and although only thirty-eight his health was already failing. The dark-skinned Foster, who had demonstrated his organizational skills while still in grade school, lost little time assuming almost total responsibility for the team, adding the booking of its games to his list of responsibilities. He also extensively overhauled the team's roster. First by releasing many of the players from the previous season, despite Leland's objections, then by inducing several of the best players from the Philadelphia Giants, the team he had been with the previous season, to renege on their contracts and join him in Chicago.

To attract top teams to Chicago, the shrewd Foster instituted what was then the novel arrangement of allowing the visitors to select from either an equal share of the gate receipts or a substantial guarantee. He also embarked on an aggressive, ambitious, barnstorming schedule that transformed the Leland Giants from the ranks of the stay-at-homes to the Midwest's top touring team. In two years, the Giants, traveling in their own private Pullman car to uphold their reputation as an elite independent black club, covered 4,465 miles playing both black and white teams in Memphis, Birmingham, Fort Worth, Austin, San Antonio and Houston. By 1909 they were ready to take on all-comers, including the white Major League team, the Chicago Cubs, to whom they lost three very closely contested games that October.

EIGHT

Alicia Barrington was exhilarated; the morning had gone extremely well, Chicago was full of extraordinary works of architecture, many of them far surpassing anything she had previously seen in either Washington D.C. or New Orleans. And as she strode briskly along State Street, bareheaded under the blazing midday sun, unopened parasol tucked away in her handbag, fine beads of perspiration gathering on her exquisitely formed brow, she could hardly wait to tell Richard about her adventures of the morning. She had briefly considered hailing a taxi but had decided to continue walking, all the way to the hotel, because there was just so much to see and she loved walking.

It was the look of outraged disapproval on the faces of the approaching older couple as she neared her destination at the Palmer House hotel, where she was staying with her husband, which had warned her that her whistling had become somewhat more audible than she had intended. In her twenty-six years on earth, she had been told, often by complete strangers, at least a thousand times, or so it sometimes seemed, that whistling was unladylike, even an abomination to the Lord. But to the college professor and enthusiastic cyclist, whistling, particularly when she was as happy as she was that morning, was almost as natural as reading or breathing. And, typically, she had adamantly refused to bow to what she regarded as unwarranted and impertinent intrusions in her personal affairs.

She had learned to whistle early, long before she had become aware of the many taboos and restrictions that directed the behavior of people of her gender. To the amazement of Uncle Eddie her first music teacher, who had either been oblivious, or, perhaps more likely, indifferent to such social conventions, she had quickly mastered the difficult breathing techniques that are the essence of the art. And by the time she was five she had been able to reproduce the most complex tunes and arias. Eddie, her father's younger brother, had been a brilliant musician; by general consensus one of the most talented and promising concert pianists and composers the city of New Orleans had ever produced, and a highly skilled and enthusiastic whistler.

As a young man great things had been predicted and expected of him. His performances as a teenager playing piano in the pit of the Theatre d'Orleans had been the stuff of legend. The city had, afterall, awarded an older cousin, who many thought was less talented, a scholarship that allowed him to continue his musical education in France.

The cousin had been admitted to the highly prestigious Conservatoire de musique in Paris, where he studied voice, music, and composition, eventually becoming a respected composer and the director of the orchestra of L'Alcazar in Bordeaux. Eddie had been expected to follow in his footsteps, but his extremely prickly and uncompromising personality had alienated many potential patrons, particularly in the white community. Consequently, not only did he fail to get the financial support he would have needed to study abroad but his professional opportunities had been severely restricted. The inevitable disappointments had led to an early death, from alcohol and heroin abuse.

Alicia had prepared her itinerary with her customary thoroughness, carefully calculating not just how far her stops were from each other, but also how much time would be required at each of them. She had dressed just as carefully, donning sensible brogan shoes, and a tailored jacket with a slightly-shortened, matching, pleated skirt, deliberately eschewing fashion for ease of movement. She had pulled her long, lustrous mane of dark hair back from her face in a tight ponytail, and except for the faintest brush of face powder and an almost imperceptible touch of mascara had avoided applying make-up altogether. It had occurred to her as she dressed that morning in their luxuriously decorated, oversized rooms at Palmer House that her mother and grandmother would have been scandalized, if they had been there to witness such blatant disregard of the standards expected of a proper lady dressing to go out in public. But they might not have, she had eventually concluded, since they had raised her to be, almost, their diametric opposite.

They were, her mother and grandmother freely acknowledged, anachronisms, relics of a bygone time and a vanished place. Both were, albeit in different degrees, products of that peculiar antebellum New Orleans institution known as placage that allowed wealthy white men to openly keep free women of color as mistresses. For a brief moment in history, between 1790 and 1865, it had not been uncommon for young white Creole men of means in New Orleans to set up colored mistresses in houses of their own. And, frequently, sire numerous mixed-race children before settling down with white women to raise their legitimate families.

But, since some of these relationships were based on genuine affection, they were sometimes extremely long lasting; continuing long after the man had married. The children of these unions generally took their white fathers surnames and many were supported by them, some even inheriting large sums upon their deaths. The most fortunate sons were sent to Paris to be educated but, generally, however beautiful and talented, daughters were not as fortunate. Their highest aspirations were to become the next generation of mistresses for wealthy, white Creole men.

These mixed-race people, known in legal documents as *gens de couleur* and *femmes de couleur* respectively, had French names, generally spoke French and did not consider themselves black, but rather Creoles of color. Their elaborate caste system was based, primarily, on skin shade and like all mixed-race groups they varied enormously in skin tone, facial features and hair type. A mulatto was the offspring of a black and a white, a griffe of a mulatto and a black, a quadroon of a white and a mulatto and an octoroon of a white and a quadroon. But those were simply the best-known terms; there were many others, quaterons, briques, and even more. In fact toward the end of the eighteenth century the French colonial government in Saint Dominique, the original home of much of the city's free, mixed-race population, registered some sixty combinations of white and Negro blood and, remarkably, gave a name to each.

A quateron, as an example, was thirty-two to fifty-seven parts black and seventy-one to ninety-six parts white, a result that was possible from twenty different combinations, among which was the mating of a white and a marabout. A marabout was approximately eighty-eight parts black to forty-four parts white. But given the vagaries of the laws of Malthusian genetic inheritance, however satisfying the classifying of such minute distinctions might have been to the bureaucratic mind, they often did little to predict actual physical appearance. Light-skinned mulattoes could be and often were lighter than dark-skinned quadroons and even octoroons, for example.

The story of Alicia's grandmother, Henrietta Seligny, an olive-skinned woman of surpassing beauty whose precise degree of black-white admixture was almost impossible to determine, was a fairly familiar one during the placage era. Her family had fled Saint Dominique, the western half of the island Christopher Columbus had called Hispaniola, in 1803, shortly before the French were driven out of the country by the bloody, twelve-year slave insurrection that ended with the establishment of the Republic of Haiti. During the eighteenth century the colony, widely known as the Jewel of the Antilles, was the wealthiest and most productive French overseas possession. Its rich soil and the labor of a half million black slaves on large sugar and coffee plantations created enormous fortunes for the planters who lived in extraordinary luxury and spent much of their time in Paris. Known locally as *grand blancs,* they had never considered settling permanently in the colony; Saint Dominique was simply a place to get rich quickly.

Not surprisingly, therefore, the slaves of Saint Dominique were treated far more brutally than in almost any other slaveholding society on earth, including the West Indies and the southern United States. As a result their death rates so greatly exceeded their birth rates that the planters were obliged to import twenty thousand new slaves from Africa every year simply to keep the workforce level. Which meant, of course, that not only would a significant majority of the slaves in the colony be foreign-born but also that there were few, if any, bonds of affection or familiarity between them and the country's white citizens.

In addition to the wealthy white plantation owners and their slaves there were two other groups in the colony; a lower class of white people, or *petit blancs*, and a class of freemen, or *affranchis*, which included some full-blooded blacks but was comprised primarily of mixed race descendants of white landowners and black slaves. It was to this latter group that the Seligny's belonged. Although the *affranchis* were an economically powerful group, often wealthy enough to own large estates and slaves of their own, and many were highly educated, sometimes in France, they were socially and politically impotent; obliged to give precedence to whites in all circumstances and forbidden to vote or hold political office, despite being required to serve in the militia.

In sharp contrast, the *petit blancs*, who were not nearly as well educated nor as wealthy, had full political rights since political activity was the sole preserve of whites, whatever their social and economic class. The intense animosity between the *affranchis* and the *petit blancs* that this anomaly created was exacerbated by the shock waves launched by the French Revolution of 1789, which inspired the *affranchis* to petition Paris to extend the political equality proclaimed in the "the Rights of Man" to them.

The revolution in France ripped the fragile social fabric of the colony apart and split the whites and the nonwhites down the middle. The *grand blancs*, with everything to lose, fiercely opposed the Revolution. The *petit blancs*, with a lot to gain, passionately supported the concept of equality and fraternity for themselves, but just as strongly rejected it for the *affranchis* and the slaves. The *affranchis* believed that they too should be included in the magical circle of opportunity but were afraid of widening it to include the slaves. And the slaves, the vast majority of the colony's population, led by the remarkable Toussaint L'Ouverture, listened and waited and planned. The future of Saint Dominique, they knew, belonged to them.

The Seligny's, who had owned a medium-sized coffee plantation and more than two hundred slaves in Saint Dominique, did well in New Orleans but were unable to duplicate the same level of success they'd had in the colony. But this was not because of a shortage of talent or a lack of effort or commitment to their new country. Henriette's grandfather, Alexandre Seligny, despite his relatively advanced age of forty-six, had volunteered his services to the United States during the War of 1812 against Great Britain, and had been slightly wounded while fighting in the Battle of New Orleans as a member of the Second Battalion of Free Men of Color. The Second Battalion, which was comprised completely of colored refugees from Saint Dominique and Cuba and had been organized by Seligny's close friend and fellow Saint Dominique refugee Joseph Savary, played a crucial role in the defeat of the far larger British forces, and was lavishly praised for its skill and bravery by Major General Andrew Jackson, the American commander and future President of the United States.

The mixed-race refugees also made substantial contributions to the artistic life of New Orleans, excelling in music, sculpting, painting, and poetry: And they were largely responsible for the extraordinary blossoming of artistic life there during the early part of the nineteenth century that made it one of the most picturesque and exciting cities in America. But nothing, not their light skin color, not their disdain for the slaves of their own race and uncritical embrace of the white community, not even their manifest accomplishments in the United States and Europe, could change the fact that in America they were black, Negroes, condemned to, at best, a second-class citizenship. Forced to add the initials "H.C.L." to their signatures, a mark of their inferior social status as *Hommes de Couleur Libres*.

Since even in America deeds were not enough, since it was so clear that destiny was decided by skin shade, lightening the color of their children and grandchildren became an obsession for many of the *hommes de couleur libres*. But since marriage between the races was illegal and impossible even the most ambitious and accomplished of these free colored families came to embrace an institution, placage, which would have shamed almost any other society on earth. An institution which joyously offered up the flower of their young womanhood to a hostile race, to white men, as mistresses and playthings.

The most desirable girls were usually introduced to their

potential white lovers by their mothers at another unique New Orleans institution, the so-called Quadroon Ball, or as it was known among the *hommes de couleur libres* themselves, the Bal de Cordon Bleu. The first ball was sponsored in 1805 by "Quadroon" mothers, quadroon being a catch-all term to describe light-skinned women in general, as a sort of coming-out party for their daughters; and although they were public the only invited guests were white men of means. Scores of these balls, invariably described as gay and lavish, were thrown every year. October was the beginning of the social season among Creoles of both races and quadroon and white balls were held almost every night until Ash Wednesday.

But it was not all wild fun and bacchanalia at the quadroon balls; they were after all, at least for the sponsors, more about business than pleasure. Strict rules governed the conduct of all the parties involved. The young women were expected to be flirtatious but decorous, after making their choices the men were expected to be forthright and generous in negotiating the terms of support with the mothers, who themselves were expected to be firm but reasonable.

For reasons unrecorded by history, but probably because it was too strong a reminder of the widespread prostitution that had been the primary source of social contact between whites and free persons of color in the colony, the Seligny's, unlike most of the Saint Dominique refugees, had not immediately embraced the idea of offering their daughters to white men at the balls. It had not been until 1848, the year Henriette turned eighteen, that the first Seligny attended a Quadroon Ball. She had been selected several times that year, Henriette would recall many years later, but she had not, to the outrage of some in her community, agreed to any of the proposals.

She had always known that marriage was out of the question with any of *them* but she had rejected her mother's patient argument that even white girls frequently had to settle for *mariages de convenance* and that dowries were an established fact. She had stubbornly refused to accept anything less than what the *hommes de couleur libres* called a *mariage de la main gauche*, a left-handed marriage, a love affair, a meeting of hearts. She found her *mariage de la main gauche* the following year in the person of a stockily built, intense, young Frenchman of medium height with flashing dark eyes and a shock of thick dark hair.

The attraction had been immediate, mutual and powerful but it had been evident right away that it was based on more than just lust. They spent most of the evening talking instead of dancing. Except for their different races or more accurately a few shades of skin color, they quickly discovered that they were uncannily alike, in both background and interests. Like hers, his family had fled Saint Dominique and they shared a common passion for poetry and music and, of all things, gardening.

She had been, she had assured her skeptical granddaughter, deliriously happy, at least for a while. For the first few years Andre Rillieux, for that was his name, had been afire with plans for them to marry secretly, to leave the country, to find someplace where their love would be accepted. She had been gratified and reassured at this evidence of his devotion but had lovingly, laughingly, rejected them as sweet but impractical. In time, however, starting with the birth of their first child, a son, which did not happen until the fifth year of the relationship, things began to change, perhaps because she had started to change. She was no longer a love struck girl but an intelligent young woman keenly aware of her vulnerable status. Andre regularly spent more than a half of the year in France and when he was in New Orleans it was his habit to visit the little townhouse on Rue de Rampart he had bought her about three or four times a week. In the beginning those visits and the little gifts of perfumes and jewelry he brought her from Paris were the very center of her universe.

But, by the time their second child, a daughter, came along just being together and talking about *his* plans, *his* ideas, *his* dreams, was no longer enough. Now she wanted to talk about the children's future, she wanted their lives to be different, better than hers, the idea that her daughter, their daughter, would have to settle for a *mariage de la main gauche* she found deeply upsetting. But it was soon evident that in this area they were not alike at all, he wanted things to remain just as they were, could not understand why she was, as he put it, suddenly so dissatisfied and unhappy. Gradually, he began spending more time in France and when he was in America came to visit them less frequently and stayed for fewer hours, sometimes not even staying for the entire night.

Finally, one day, while he was in Paris, she received a letter from him informing her that he had gotten married and would no longer be able to continue their relationship. He had decided, the letter continued, to be generous to her and the children and that he had made arrangements to pay off the mortgage on the house on the Rue de Rampart and have the title transferred to her. He would also, it added, be sending them a small but sufficient enough amount each month to take care of their basic needs. And he did, faithfully, until the children were grown but he never visited or wrote to them or even asked about them although she was careful, in the letters she sent to him every three months or so, to keep him informed about how well they were doing, making sure, if nothing else, that he knew that his money was being well spent.

The Civil War changed everything for the Seligny's and their fellow refugees. When it began they were *hommes de couleur libres,* admittedly socially inferior to whites, but unquestionably superior to the blacks and the slaves. When it ended there were no longer any intermediate group, no free people of color, just blacks and whites, you had to be one or the other. Many of those who were light-skinned enough moved north to start anew as members of the white race; the others mostly stayed in New Orleans and other parts of the state, at least for a while, and tried to figure out how to live in America as Negroes. Not only did the Quadroon Balls and the placage system die with slavery and the Confederacy but for the first time in several generations the fairest, most desirable women of the former *hommes de couleur libres* were available to men of their own kind.

Which is why Henriette's very light-skinned daughter, Harriet Rillieux, was available to marry the brown-skinned Michel Lambert, himself the son of an artistically gifted Saint Dominique refugee family. Michel's brother Eddie and several cousins were among the most brilliant musicians in the city and he himself was an enormously talented painter and sculptor. At thirteen he had been apprenticed to a stonecutter and within five years was so accomplished that he received several commissions to produce statues for St. Louis Cathedral, a few of which were elaborately praised by the local newspapers. Restless and ambitious and dissatisfied with his prospects in the city, the twenty-one-year-old left for Paris in October of 1873 to continue his studies. There, he rented a studio in Montparnasse and began studying at the Ecole des Beaux-Arts, where he stayed for four years.

After a great deal of success in France Michel returned to New Orleans to wide acclaim in early 1880 and shortly thereafter was introduced to the twenty-three-year-old Harriet Rillieux. Every bit as beautiful as her mother and even more selective, Harriet had rejected numerous offers of marriage, several of them from sons of the city's elite light-skinned families. But Michel, older, worldly, and enormously self-confident, was unlike anybody she had ever met and before long they were married.

Their second child, Alicia, born in 1884, was a perfect little replica of her mother physically; a boy, Alexandre, named in honor of his great, great, grandfather, Alexander Seligny, had arrived eighteen months earlier. Preternaturally grave and wise from the moment she left the womb, Alicia was the kind of child who made it easy to believe in the concept of reincarnation. Just hours after her birth her grandmother took one look at the little girl with the full head of hair and the unwavering, inquisitive stare and declared her "an old soul," someone who "had been here before." Nobody was more smitten with the baby than her delighted father, but despite the acclaim he had received on his return from Paris, Michel had been finding it increasingly difficult to make the kind of living he had expected and needed to support his growing family. Convinced that his race was an insuperable handicap in post-Reconstruction America Michel finally decided to return to Paris in early 1887, promising to send for his family as soon as he was able.

Urged on by her mother, who, understandably, associated France with her own painful memories, Harriet had briefly considered asking Michel to stay in the country and find a way of making a living in America, even if it meant abandoning his precious artistic career for something more practical, like farming. But she had decided against it, she knew him too well, loved him too much, to ask that of him. His psyche, she knew, was too fragile to survive such a profound admission of failure; plus, she had thought, smiling to herself as she tried to picture him in the fields behind a plow, he would not have been a very good farmer.

The first letters were long and full of hope and packed with the details of his progress and plans. He had again rented a studio in Montparnasse, very near to his old one, was working hard, had already received a few commissions, was in discussions with a major gallery to show some of his pieces and hoped to be able to send for them within less than a year.

Initially, the letters had come regularly, once every two weeks or so; but within six months they began slowing down to less than once a month. What was even more alarming to Harriet than the decline in the frequency of the letters was the marked change in their tone; the sunny optimism was suddenly gone. Sensing that something was terribly wrong she began bombarding him with her own letters, at least once a week despite the expense of the postage, showering him with the good news about how well the children, particularly the precocious Alicia, were doing at school and with their music lessons. Repeatedly he assured her that everything was going well, insisting that it was simply taking longer than he had expected to make the arrangements to send for them.

Then, one day, after not hearing from him for almost two months a letter arrived from Paris that was clearly not in his distinctive and beautiful handwriting. Inside was the terrible news that confirmed her most fevered nightmares: Andre was dead, from a bullet to the head, apparently by his own hand. A note had been found near the body, addressed to Harriet, asking her to forgive him. The letter was from somebody who introduced himself as a friend, one Jacques Durel, himself a painter, who Andre had mentioned in a couple of his letters. Andre's friends, Durel explained, had taken the liberty of arranging his funeral, which, unfortunately, as a matter of necessity would have already taken place by the time the news of his death arrived in America.

They would be arranging, the letter added, to return certain of his personal effects to her. Durel also offered what he regarded as a possible explanation for his friend's actions. Andre had been deeply depressed about negative reviews of his most recent work by critics who had once been among his strongest supporters, and the subsequent cancellation of a few of his commissions. What was particularly sad, Durel said, was that the critics were completely wrong. Andre's new work, he assured her, was even more powerful and accomplished, just different, more impressionist, as his vision grew and expanded. His friends had begged him to ignore the critics, pointing out how often they had been wrong about even the greatest artists, predicting that in time they would change their mind about him too. The problem, Andre had repeatedly replied, was that he had run out of time.

The formal decision to leave New Orleans was not made that horrible day the letter arrived but the seeds were sown. Harriet would never forgive the city she would blame for the rest of her life for betraying and killing her beloved husband. It was the indifference and blindness of its citizens, their failure to appreciate his wonderful talent, she would believe until the day she died, that had really been responsible for his death. So when it became obvious that both children were unusually academically gifted it had been easy to begin thinking about moving to a city with better educational facilities for its children of color than was available in New Orleans. Ironically, Andre's tragic death had led to a major re-evaluation of his work and Harriet was able to raise a fairly substantial sum of money, more than he had earned during his entire lifetime and far more than she had thought possible, by agreeing to sell several of his pieces, including four he had done of her and the children. As painful as it had been to part with them, it was, she was certain, what Andre would have wanted her to do.

He had just turned away from the front desk, where he had gone to make arrangements for transportation to the ballpark, when he saw her hurrying across the marble floor of the enormous, mirrored lobby of the Palmer House hotel and the sight, literally, took his breath away. The most beautiful thing about her, he thought, as she broke into a little run as their eyes locked on each other, was how lightly she wore her beauty. It was, of her many virtues, the one he admired most. And although they had been married for more than a year, just looking at her across a room filled with strangers was still enough to send his pulse racing.

"Oh Richard," Alicia said, as they embraced in the crowded room, "am I very late, were you very worried."

"Just a tiny little bit sweetheart," he conceded, smiling, oblivious to the curious stares they were attracting, "but I knew your itinerary was, let us say, just a little bit ambitious. Did you see everything?"

Individually, both Richard and Alicia Barrington were extremely attractive people. Together, as a couple, even in a setting, as they were that day, where very few people of their race were either welcome or comfortable, they never failed to turn heads, and attract the most intense interest and, frequently, even admiration.

"Not really, "she replied, laughing lightly, placing her hand in his, "I hate to admit it but I didn't even get near the Lincoln Monument or the Hull House. There was so much to see downtown."

"You mean like Marshall Field's and Carson, Pirie, Scott," Richard said teasingly, as they began making their way across the foyer.

"Well Mister Barrington," Alicia replied affecting an exaggerated professorial tone, "they are not just department stores as you probably know, both are what those of us who are knowledgeable of such esoteric matters call landmark buildings. The Carson, Pirie building merges beauty and function perfectly and is an excellent example of Louis Sullivan's, he is the architect, genius for architectural ornamentation. As for Marshall Field's the neo-classical design is quite remarkable and…"

"Am I to understand Professor Barrington," Richard responded in an equally pompous voice, quickly falling into the spirit of the familiar game, "that you are advancing the preposterous claim that it took you all morning to tour these structures that you *allege* are architectural masterpieces."

"Allege, Sir, allege," Alicia said, feigning outrage, "that comment hardly does you any credit. It only reveals, I must tell you Sir with absolute frankness, how little you know of such, how should I put it, artistic and cultural matters. If you were as knowledgeable as you pretend you would have long realized that the seamless intersection of form and function that these buildings embody is the very definition of art."

"Even conceding what you say is true Professor Barrington," Richard replied, looking at his wife in frank admiration, "and I must confess a certain…ah…grudging respect for your cleverness at verbal formulation if not for your architectural knowledge, the real point, which of course you're doing your best to obscure, is that you were doing more than admiring the fluted Ionic columns at Marshall Fields. Admit it; you were shopping, at least admiring the new fashions."

"Again dear Sir," Alicia began her rejoinder, her tone both playful and comically sad, "I must point out that you are in serious error. Although you are correct that I did not spend the entire morning worshipping the architectural delights of Marshall Field's and Carson, Pirie, Scott, your assumption that, ergo, I was shopping is both presumptuous and wildly inaccurate. If you must know I spent the earlier part of the morning becoming acquainted with the techniques of skyscraper skeletal construction, which I assure you are endlessly fascinating. Why, at the Marquette and Manhattan Buildings…"

"Skyscraper construction techniques? Really?" Richard said, clearly surprised and impressed, "did you really?"

"No, of course not ninny," Alicia replied in her normal tone, giggling girlishly, a triumphant smile covering her face. "But they are beautiful buildings; I really had a good time darling. How was your morning, did your meeting with Mister Abbott go well?"

As they neared the entrance to the ornate elevator, Richard, smiling broadly, leaned over and whispered in his wife's ear: "The meeting with Robert went fine but I'm going to get you for this as soon as we get upstairs."

"Is that a promise Sir?" Alicia asked in a coquettish tone,

turning to look directly at her husband, "Are you sure you will be able to keep it, last night was quite strenuous and you may not yet have fully recovered. At your age..."

"At my age, why, you little minx," Richard replied in mock indignation, "I'll show you what an old man of twenty-seven is capable of."

Just then the door to the gearless traction electric Otis elevator slowly opened and the attendant, a huge coal-black Negro, whose vast bulk seemed to occupy at least a half of the available space, greeted the waiting guests with a dazzling smile and a warm "Welcome folks to the only thoroughly fireproof hotel in the United States," delivered in a surprisingly high-pitched voice. Suppressing smiles summoned by the incongruity of that tiny voice emerging from such an enormous human being, the Barringtons stepped into the creaking piece of machinery and pressed themselves into a far corner to make room for the others. As it began its slow ascent Alicia pressed herself against her husband, whispered: Promises, promises, promises," and reached down and pinched him on the bottom.

It was fast and furious and was over in just ten minutes but it was also they both agreed one of their best times yet. A year of marriage had obviously not been enough to make up for the two long years they had waited, barely touching each other for weeks at a time, terrified that they would be unable to control themselves. Waiting until they were married had been very important to both of them. Initially, they had decided to risk being late for the game but a telephone call from Robert Abbott that arrived at the very moment they entered the room had altered that plan. The founder and majority shareholder of the *Chicago Defender*, which in just a few short years had become one of the leading black newspapers in the country, had decided, he informed Richard, to pick them up himself, in just over thirty minutes; but nothing, at that stage, could have kept them from each other. Now, as they began getting ready after lightning-fast baths they could not keep their eyes off each other.

Her pale brown skin still damp, warm, and glowing, Alicia hurried out of the bathroom and still entirely naked sat down at the dressing table and with long, quick strokes began brushing her hair: Which tumbled down her narrow back, past her slim, firm shoulders in glossy, black waves, so thick and dark that she had often been mistaken for a Native American, or in the language the question was usually phrased, an American Indian. In the gilded mirror she watched Richard watching her, saw the familiar longing cloud his eyes and tighten the muscles around his mouth, and felt her nipples harden and the opening at the juncture between her legs moisten in response.

"Alicia, let me help you brush your hair," Richard offered, his thickening voice betraying his gathering lust. He had already slipped into one the new Porosknit skivvies she had bought for him and the mesh knit fabric of the summer bodysuit clung tightly to his lean but muscular body, revealing all of his secrets. And so as he walked towards her the evidence of his arousal was on full display.

"And what do you intend to do with that," she asked quietly, her voice soft, yielding, her eyes fixed on his bulging tumescence.

"Oh God," Richard replied, glancing down as if surprised by the response of his own body. I'd better put it in my pants; Robert will be here at any time."

"You must really think a lot of this friend of yours, this is supposed to be a second honeymoon, remember," Alicia said, as she glanced at the clock on the dressing table. "We still have a little more than ten minutes," she added suggestively, as she turned to face him, her eyes smoldering with invitation.

"I know sweetheart but that is not even enough time for you to get dressed," Richard answered, his voice full of reason and good sense but his eyes fixed unblinkingly on his wife's engorged nipples. "And," he added, his voice beginning to quiver as his eyes drifted down to her barely parted legs, "I soon won't care if Robert and the whole world are waiting if you keep looking at me like that."

"Are you sure it's my eyes that's bothering you Richard," Alicia asked softly, her legs opening slightly wider, "that's not what you've been looking at."

"Jesus, Alicia, what are you doing to me," Richard said

plaintively, "I'm not going to be able to function for the rest of the day now. Robert will probably believe that I've suddenly lost a large piece of my mind."

"Don't blame me, that thing started it," Alicia replied with a little smile as she closed her legs and pointed to his still rigid member. "But I'll stop tormenting you by getting dressed," she added, rising from the chair, her full, round buttocks rolling gently as she walked slowly across the room to the enormous walk-in closet near the hallway door.

"Do you know you are an evil woman," Richard asked, his eyes following every step of her provocative journey.

"Tell me about this Robert that you're so willing to suffer for, who is so important to you that you're willing to disappoint your wife," Alicia said teasingly as she disappeared into the closet. "He must be a very special guy."

"I think so," Richard replied as he stepped into his pant suit, "Our backgrounds are very different but we have a lot in common."

"Is that why you like him so much," Alicia interrupted from inside the closet, "Because he reminds you of yourself. Talk about high self-esteem, your mother really did a good job."

"You know that's not what I meant you little minx," Richard replied with a smile as he pulled on the long-sleeved white shirt. "He has a law degree too but he doesn't practice. In his case though it wasn't his choice, he tried to find work all over the Midwest but nobody would hire him as a lawyer, he had been the only Negro in his class of seventy and he couldn't even get admitted to the bar. Nobody would hire him as a printer either for that matter, although he had quite a bit of experience in that area also. Seems his stepfather was in the publishing business, founded a paper called the *Woodville Times*, if my memory serves me right on that."

"Is that where he got the money to start the *Defender*," Alicia asked from inside the closet, "I mean from his stepfather," she added.

"No," Richard replied, bending over to pick up from the bed the blue tie with the tiny red dots Alicia had selected earlier, "his stepfather had died by the time he started the *Defender*. Actually it's quite a story really. He began with a total capital of twenty-five cents, which is what he needed to buy paper and pencils."

"Twenty-five cents, do you believe him" Alicia asked skeptically.

"Well, he rented office space on State Street, borrowed a card table and a chair and arranged to have the paper printed on credit, so in that sense it was more than twenty-five cents but still it is an impressive story you must admit."

"And he did it all by himself, put out an entire paper without any help, without any staff," Alicia replied, her skepticism clearly undiminished.

"He did have one staffer, his landlady's teenage daughter, but that was it," Richard answered as he straightened his tie in front of the full-length mirror. "Why do you find it so hard to believe, it was just a little paper, a few pages then but he must have known what he was doing because he's bested three other papers that were there when he started."

"Maybe you've never heard darling but most men exaggerate, even lie and I'm just doing my little wifely duty, trying to protect you and your money from...."

"Our money," Richard corrected, "and in any case as I've told you before," he continued, picking up the Omega wristwatch from the dressing table, briefly admiring its silver double-hinged case and railway minute track before strapping it onto his right wrist, "it's not a lot of money involved, just a few hundred dollars and the paper is doing very well, I've seen the numbers, they're pretty good, we're going to do alright with it. I'm pretty hardheaded when it comes to money sweetheart, believe me, you know what I'm trying to do with the family's real estate investments in DC don't you. I've been accused of being the absolute opposite of kindhearted there."

"So is this what you're doing with Mister Abbott and the other gentleman we're meeting today, what's his name, Foster, conscience money as your sister suggested," Alicia replied as she emerged from the walk-in closet in a stunning full-length dress of soft, clinging fabric in a delicate "eau de nile" shade. "Well Sir, what do you think," she asked, pirouetting in a half circle and smiling prettily at the admiration spreading over her husband's face.

"God, you're so beautiful," Richard replied, his eyes glowing, "you're even more beautiful now than when we first met and I thought you impossibly beautiful then. I must be crazy to be even thinking about business right now. As to my dear sister," he added, a touch of exasperation in his voice, "she willfully misrepresents what I've tried to explain to her and Peter at least a dozen times, my investment philosophy if you will."

"An entire philosophy devoted to a matter as prosaic as investing money Sir," Alicia teased, as she examined an enormous, wide-brimmed hat, "and you've never taken the time to explain it to me, perhaps you thought my poor female brain incapable of comprehending such complex, manly matters."

"I must confess," Richard responded, smiling broadly at his wife, "that when I look at you it is hard to think of matters as mean and hard as interest rates and rates of return."

"Au contraire Sir," Alicia replied archly, pointing to the platinum-set diamond earrings dangling from her ears, a first anniversary gift from him, "It is then that you should."

"Oh God," Richard began, laughing, "I cannot decide which I find more appealing, your body or your brain."

"Why choose Sir, when you may have both," Alicia replied, casting a coy look at her husband from beneath the elaborate hat she was trying to set on her head with a dangerous-looking, foot-long hatpin.

Before he could frame an adequate response the phone on the bedside table rang and moving quickly Richard picked it up before it rang a second time, listened briefly and replied, "We'll be down in a minute Robert." Turning briskly to his wife, he added, "You're perfect sweetheart, our ride has arrived, let's go my dear." Then taking her hand in his as they stepped into the corridor he leaned over and said "I'll tell you more later about the *principles* that guide me when I invest our money, maybe you'll have some advice."

"I just might," she replied, smiling enigmatically at her

husband as they walked to the elevator.

The white and maroon flag of the Leland Giants was being raised and the Eighth Regiment Band was striking the first stirring strains of the Star Spangled Banner, the patriotic song the lawyer and diplomat Francis Scott Key had written almost a hundred years earlier, when Robert Abbott and his guests, Richard and Alicia Barrington, arrived at the packed White Sox Park Stadium. Key, an amateur poet, had written the lyrics in 1814 after witnessing the fierce and relentless bombardment of Fort McHenry in Baltimore by British ships in Chesapeake Bay during the War of 1812. Ironically, Key's inspired poem had become popular across the nation only after it was put to the tune of, *To Anacreon in Heaven*, an English drinking song. The song proved to be particularly popular with military bands and by the beginning of the twentieth century it was frequently played at public events.

Out on the field, batting practice and all other pregame warm-up activities had ceased and most of the players were standing still, some with right palms covering their hearts. But in the pavilion, as Abbott and the Barringtons were being escorted to their reserved box seats, almost everybody remained seated and the hot dog and peanut vendors were just as busy as ever. The Star Spangled Banner, which Key had originally titled "In Defense of Fort McHenry," would be made the national anthem by a Congressional resolution on March 3, 1931.

Conversation during their brief ride from the hotel to the south side ballpark had been strained and awkward. The normally loquacious and supremely self-confident newspaperman was clearly not himself. Judging from the evidence of his slack-jawed awe when he first laid eyes on her in the hotel lobby and his bumbling incoherence since, he had clearly been intimidated by Alicia's extraordinary beauty and regal bearing. And her professorial habit of wrapping even casual conversation in an academic patina had not helped. But now, as they settled into their seats, painfully aware of how awkward and gauche he must have seemed to her and determined to present himself in a better light,

Abbott was casting about in his mind for a way to redeem himself.

Initially, Alicia, who was seated between the two men, had been coolly amused by the familiar response she had provoked in the man her husband had spoken so admiringly of. But prodded by Richard's meaningful glances she decided to do what she could to ease the considerable tension.

As the final strains of the song faded she gently leaned her head towards their host and in the softest and most alluring tone she could muster said, "Mister Abbott, this is really very pleasant, it was very nice of you to invite us here. I'm deeply impressed with that wonderful band, the song is a favorite of mine and they play it extremely well, are you able to tell me anything about them."

"Why yes, of course, Mistress Barrington," Abbott replied enthusiastically, his mood brightening considerably. "They're very good aren't they," he agreed, pleased to have been handed a subject on which he was an unquestioned expert. "They're attached to the Eighth Regiment Infantry, which is part of the Illinois National Guard. The Eighth has an interesting background. During the Spanish American War the War Department sent them to Cuba along with the regular Negro Regiments and two other Negro guard regiments because of the view, widely held, I've been reliably informed, in much of the Government, that Negro troops have a greater immunity to yellow fever than their white counterparts."

"Is that so Mister Abbott," Alicia replied, leaning a bit closer, her tone suddenly reassuming its normal crispness, genuine interest illuminating the large hazel eyes. "Do you believe that there is a scientific basis for such a view? Do you know if their experience shed any light on the question?"

"Now, now Alicia," Richard interrupted as the discomfited looking newspaperman struggled to formulate an answer, "Robert is many things, newspaper reporter, historian, visionary businessman, but he is not a scientist. You must excuse my wife's enthusiasms," he added, leaning across his wife to smile reassuringly at his obviously uncomfortable friend, "but the spirit of inquiry gets the better of her sometimes."

"I must assure you Madam," Abbott replied, turning to Alicia, an uncertain smile flitting on and off his wide, dark face, "that as a New Negro and a modern man that I have nothing but the greatest respect and yes, admiration, for educated and intelligent women, such as yourself, especially, I would like to add, when they are of our race."

A smiling Alicia was about to respond when a stir in the crowd attracted their attention. Jack Johnson, wearing an obviously expensive light-colored summer suit, accompanied by two much smaller male companions, one black and one white, had entered the building and like a king strolling among his subjects was slowly and majestically moving in their general direction, occasionally pausing to exchange a few pleasantries and to shake an eagerly offered hand.

"That is a man who knows how to make an entrance," Alicia said admiringly. "I assume that is the famous Mister Jack Johnson."

"Would you like to meet him," Abbott offered his voice somewhat more confident, "your husband already has as he may have told you. And I thought they both found each other far more interesting and sympathetic than they might have thought likely. Isn't that so Richard", he added, turning to his friend who nodded affirmatively. "I must tell you Mistress Barrington," he said, warming to his subject, "that he has been grossly misrepresented by the white papers; he is quite different from the image they've portrayed, quite different."

"I have no doubt that you are right in that judgment Mister Abbott. How could I refuse such an offer," Alicia replied in a tone that implied she would be gracious enough to consent. "But who is that elegant lady he's talking to, is that Mrs. Washington? Richard told me she'd be here."

"I tell you what," Abbott replied, rising from his seat and holding out a pudgy hand to Alicia, his tone suddenly firm and decisive, "Let us go and say hello to both of them. They'd be angry and disappointed if they found out that I kept the Barringtons of Washington to myself. It's a small circle of us you know," he added in a confidential tone, bending over to whisper to his guests, "and we've got to keep in touch with each other."

"You're right of course Mister Abbott," Alicia replied with a tiny smile as she reached up to accept the outstretched hand.

"Lead the way Robert," Richard cried gayly, as they rose and followed him down the aisle.

NINE

On those rare nights when young Patrick O'Neill had an hour or two to spare from his two jobs, just strolling along that magical mile and a half of Broadway popularly known as the Rialto, occasionally buying an ice cream cone or a cold bottle of coca-cola, was usually enough to revive his flagging spirits. Just losing himself in the vast crowds that surged up and down the fabled strip under the brilliant white lights cast by the newly-installed mantle gas lamps, he had discovered, allowed him in some indefinable way to maintain his sanity and hold on to what sometimes seemed his impossible dream of fame and fortune.

A few cents was all he could normally afford. All the money he made as a porter at Grand Central Station, every cent of it, the modest salary and all of the tips, went to his mother to help care for his three younger siblings. Long years of backbreaking labor in other people's homes, scrubbing floors, cooking, washing and ironing, had left her virtually crippled with arthritis and barely able to take care of her own home and children; working outside was out of the question. Their father, a half-caste seaman, the son of an Irish seaman, had died five years earlier at sea under suspicious circumstances when Patrick was seventeen and the youngest of the children only three years old. All of the money for his own personal needs came from his second job playing piano at the renowned Marshall Hotel on West 53rd.

Despite growing discrimination, segments of the black population in New York had become relatively well-educated and affluent as the twentieth century began. The development of new musical styles and the increasing sophistication of this new class of Negro had led to the development of a vibrant night life centered around hotels such as the Marshall and the Maceo, both owned by enterprising black men. These new fashionable centers of social activity and entertainment, where dinner was served to musical accompaniment and tables had to be booked in advance to ensure service, had largely replaced the old clubs further downtown that had been almost completely deserted by the smart set. Most of the patrons at these new clubs came not just for the food and the music but also to get a close-up look at the famous, the actors, musicians, composers, writers and the better-paid vaudevillians, who also frequented these new centers of entertainment.

The old downtown clubs had prospered at a time when a majority of the black population lived in that part of the city. When New York was first settled, African Americans, like all the other racial and ethnic groups in the city, lived at the southernmost tip of Manhattan. As late as 1880 they had been concentrated in the Greenwich Village and Little Italy neighborhoods, where Patrick himself lived until shortly after his father's death, on and around Minetta Lane and on Sullivan, Bleecker, Thompson, Carmine and Grove Streets. But just ten years later the center of the black population had shifted considerably northward, to the upper Twenties and lower Thirties west of Sixth Avenue. And by 1900 another northward shift had been made, to West Fifty-Third Street and to San Juan Hill (West Sixty-First, Sixty-Second and Sixty-Third streets.)

As he did almost every time he walked the Rialto Patrick started at its southernmost tip, at Madison Square Park at 23rd Street. On most nights he would take his time, moving slowly, stopping frequently, leisurely prolonging the experience. But tonight was different, tonight he had a few dollars to spend and instead of merely strolling aimlessly along, he was going to the Victoria Theatre on 42nd Street to see the newly released film of the sensational fight between Jack Johnson and Stanley Ketchel that everybody was talking about. Patrick's interest in prizefighting had been aroused by Johnson's assumption of the heavyweight crown and by meeting both Johnson and Jeffries at Grand Central Station. Like most of the young black men in his neighborhood, he was a fierce if discreet fan of the new heavyweight champion.

Not that young O'Neill disliked whites, far from it; he had been raised to be friendly and polite to everybody, and he generally enjoyed his interactions with the majority of them. Tips comprised a significant percentage of his wages at both jobs and most of his best tips came from satisfied white male customers at both places. In fact it was an unusually generous tip of five dollars from a slightly inebriated white patron at the Marshall, who had tipsily assured him that he was very talented and would be very famous one day, which had made his little outing possible.

Although his position at the Marshall paid even less, at least for now, than his day job, Patrick felt privileged just being allowed to play there. He had not received any formal musical training and he was well aware that he had gotten the job over several talented musicians with vastly superior training and experience. He had been taught to play the piano at seven by eighteen-year-old Frances Higgins, the daughter of one of his mother's employers. He had been an only child for much of his pre-teen years and had habitually accompanied his mother to the enormous Washington Square townhouse on weekends and at other times when he was not in school, where he earned small sums for running simple errands.

And when he was not busy, which was often, he would listen for long hours in rapt attention while the young lady of the house, who he thought impossibly beautiful, her long, slim fingers dancing over the keys, coaxed the most heavenly sounds he had ever heard from the highly polished piece of furniture he soon learned was called a piano.

Finally, one day, intrigued and impressed by the quiet young boy's intense interest, Frances had asked if he wanted to give it a try and he had shyly but eagerly assented. His prodigious natural talent had been immediately evident. To her astonishment he was able after a very short time to reproduce a fair facsimile of the melodies he had heard her play. Over the next few months he began visiting almost daily and although she preferred the early Romantics, such as Schubert and Mendelssohn, she also introduced him to the old masters, particularly Chopin, Bach, Brahms and Beethoven, and to rudimentary theory and composition. Within a year she had pronounced that her protégé had made so much progress that his technical proficiency had already surpassed her own.

She spoke to his mother and explained how rare a talent like his was and urged her to find a way to allow him to continue his musical education. She told them about the National Conservatory of Music in America, founded just ten years earlier right there in New York City by Jeannette Thurber, to support and encourage indigenous musical culture. She explained that because of the financial support of wealthy businessmen such as Andrew Carnegie and Theodore Thomas, talented students under the age of twenty-four of any race were sometimes admitted without charge if they could not afford the modest fee. The National Conservatory, she said, was the perfect place for the talented eight-year-old.

And to encourage him, to make him understand that his race was not an insuperable handicap to a successful musical career, Frances recounted the remarkable story of Elizabeth Taylor Greenfield, the soprano and former slave who was sometimes called the Black Swan by her enthusiastic fans. Elizabeth was probably born as slave on a plantation in Natchez, Mississippi in 1817 and as a child accompanied her mistress to Philadelphia. There the mistress, a Mrs. Greenfield, fell under the influence of the militantly anti-slavery religious organization, the Society of Friends, or as they are better known, the Quakers. Founded in 1643 by George Fox, a shoemaker from Leicestershire, England, the Society of Friends regarded all humans as equals and were not only the first religious group to denounce slavery but also adamantly refused to permit any of their members to own slaves. Accordingly, Mrs. Greenfield freed her slaves after joining the organization but Elizabeth chose to stay with the woman who had encouraged her to develop her extraordinary musical talent and as a tribute to her former mistress took her last name as her own.

Elizabeth continued her musical training after Mrs. Greenfield's death in 1845 and six years later gave her first public concert in New York and followed that successful debut with a tour of several cities from Boston to Chicago. A testimonial concert in Buffalo raised enough money to finance the former slave's trip to Europe for additional training. Elizabeth's voice, full, rich and resonant, with a remarkable 27-note range, was hailed as astonishing and a number of famous and powerful individuals, including Harriet Beecher Stowe, Lord Shaftesbury, and the Duchess of Sutherland, who became her patroness, assisted her in various ways. After touring cities in the East and Midwest, Elizabeth traveled to England in 1854 where her performances were lavishly praised by the English press. Finally, that same year, the woman who had been born in slavery thirty-seven years earlier, was invited to Buckingham Palace to perform for Queen Victoria.

Patrick had been captivated by Elizabeth's story. Visions of himself playing the piano for applauding crowds and a smiling woman with a large crown filled his head as he lay tossing and turning in bed at nights. His mother, whose early skepticism had been erased by amazement and pride when she first heard her son play the piano, had been determined to do what she could to get him admitted to the National Conservatory. But his father, who normally spent more time at sea than at home, would hear nothing of what he called "such female foolishness," when first approached for his permission. Brusquely declining every invitation to hear his son play so he could judge the boy's talent for himself, Patrick's father insisted that not only would the boy not be going to any kind of music school but that he was to "forthwith cease wasting his time on idle activities" that were not producing a single penny for the family. If his son had such skilful and artistic hands, he declared, then the boy should learn to use them for something practical and useful, like carpentry or some other trade, that would make a man of him and allow him to make a decent living in the future.

Although the physical resemblance between his father and himself was quite remarkable—relatives claimed that he was the spitting image of his father as a child—Patrick had never really liked the man he saw only occasionally, had never really been comfortable with him, probably because he had been aware from his earliest recollections that the gruff giant who sometimes replaced him in his mother's bed was somehow disappointed in him, somehow disapproved of him. Years later his mother had confirmed his intuition. The problem, she had explained, was that his father, especially because they looked so much alike, had expected his first born child, his first son, to be more like him in other ways as well. And, instead, they were very, very different, temperamental opposites in fact.

His father had been a taciturn, unsentimental man who prided himself, above all other qualities, on his toughness, both mental and physical. And it was how he judged other men, the degree to which they possessed this vital trait, and very early on he found the little replica of himself his loins had produced, who he had expected to be an extension of himself, wanting.

Patrick had been a sensitive, moody, high-strung child, who cried easily and often, always hyperaware of what others thought, hypersensitive, he had been told. As he began his stroll along the Rialto, which took its name from the strip's namesake theatre on 30th Street, Patrick smiled ruefully as he remembered how nervous his father had always made him and how angry he'd been, how much he had hated his father when he refused to allow him to attend the National Conservatory. His happiest times had always been when his father was away and he had been alone with his mother. However long the hours she had worked, however tired she was, she'd almost always find the time every night to indulge in their favorite pastime, singing. Mostly she sang and he listened, usually cuddled up against her, to the high, sweet voice that made him both happy and sad. His absolute favorites were the spirituals she had learned as a child in Mississippi, particularly "Swing Low, Sweet Chariot", which he insisted she include in every session.

It was the only song in her repertoire in which he did not attempt to join. Instead, he would often close his eyes, sometimes brimming with tears, as she sang the bitter-sweet chorus:

Swing Low, sweet chariot

Coming for to carry me home

Swing low, sweet chariot

Coming for to carry me home

In her voice, untrained and not very strong but melodic and remarkably expressive, the young boy heard all the pain and suffering of his long oppressed people. And, on some nights, when his mother's day had been particularly long and hard, her close-eyed, heartfelt rendition of the first verse would leave him sobbing openly.

> I looked over Jordan
>
> And what did I see,
>
> Coming for to carry me home
>
> A band of angels coming after me
>
> Coming for to carry me home

"Swing low, sweet chariot" was not the only song that sometimes brought tears to his eyes; his mother's personal favorite "Nobody knows the trouble I've seen" would often do the same. But he liked it less because he found it too disturbing. His mother's voice would become a plaintive wail and her body would sway from side to side as she sang the refrain again and again and again.

> Nobody knows the trouble I've seen
>
> Nobody knows but Jesus
>
> Nobody knows the trouble I've seen
>
> Glory Hallelujah

Even as a child he had understood that when she sang this song the emotion in her voice was deeply personal. And as he listened to her lament her fate and watched the tears flow slowly down her sad, lovely face it would sometimes seem that his heart would break and he had fiercely promised himself that he would take care of her as soon as he could.

> Sometimes I'm up,
>
> Sometimes I'm down
>
> Oh, yes, Lord
>
> Sometimes I'm almost to the ground
>
> Oh, yes, Lord
>
> (Refrain)

I never shall

Forget that day

Oh, yes, Lord

When Jesus washed my sins away,

Oh, yes, Lord

(Refrain)

He had been, he thought smiling to himself again as neared 30th Street, what would have been described as a sensitive and imaginative child and for a fleeting moment he even felt a little bit of sympathy for his father. Poor man, he thought, to have been presented with such an odd child when all he wanted was a normal son.

Although he had spent his entire twenty-two years in New York, Patrick was certain that nothing else in the world was even remotely like the Rialto, which, depending on who you were talking to, ended either at the Broadway Theatre at 41st Street or a block further north, at the southern border of what had been Long Acre Square until the *New York Times* relocated its headquarters to the triangle between Broadway, 42nd and 7th Avenue on April 9, 1904.

The strip was a glittering, bustling city in itself that truly came alive only at night. It was where the rich and the famous happily rubbed shoulders with streetwalkers, panhandlers and dope fiends; where both the mighty and the humble met on common ground. On any given night, among the teeming mass of humanity surging anonymously through its streets, could be found the most brilliant Wall Street financiers, the most successful industrial magnates, the greatest stars of the theatre, the most famous jockeys and pugilists, the most widely read journalists, the most beautiful chorus girls and kept women, the most reckless gamblers. What one observer of the period described as "notorious votaries of pleasure, the cynosures of a vast, prosperous public."

Scores of theatres, nightclubs, gourmet restaurants, hotels, shops, and sawdust bars provided an amazing array of food, drink and entertainment. The theatre was particularly well represented. Many of the streets off those eighteen or nineteen blocks of Broadway offered a different theatrical specialty; from the beautiful Lyceum on 24th, which presented the latest drawing room melodramas, to the Victoria Theatre on 42nd, America's greatest vaudeville house. The Fifth Avenue Theatre, just above 24th Street, routinely presented the biggest stars of the day in tailor-made extravagances. Four of the finest theatres in the city, the Rialto, Wallick's, Daly's and The Standard, were located on 30th Street. Both the Rialto and Wallick's offered realistic melodramas that quite often imaginatively explored social issues such as marriage, politics and crime. Daly's, presented Shakespeare's most popular plays in permanent rotation and its neighbor, the Standard, was the American home of the works of Gilbert and Sullivan. Further north, on 39th Street, stood the crown jewel of the strip, the magnificent Metropolitan Opera House, where the greatest opera stars, including Arturo Toscanini and Enrico Caruso, regularly performed to rapturous, sold-out crowds.

One of the features of the Rialto that Patrick was most fond of was that not all of the entertainment took place in the clubs and theatres. The streets were often just as lively and interesting and a lot less expensive. Every night performers, of all kinds and of every level of talent and ability, commandeered the street corners, singing, dancing, reciting or merely posing. He knew that most of them were there, primarily, to showcase their acts, hoping to be discovered by some talent scout or casting director from one of the theatres and to be invited to perform inside. But whenever he could afford it he'd leave a few cents in the always waiting hat or box of one of the more talented performers; afterall, better than most, he understood the importance of tips.

As he neared 39th Street, shivering slightly from the chilly October wind, Patrick pulled his fraying coat tightly around his slim body and smiled at the sight just ahead of him. Three plump, middle-aged couples, evidently visitors to the city, inhibitions loosened by alcohol, were dancing wildly—what he judged to be some version of the polka—to the energetic but discordant accompaniment of a violin played by a tall, emaciated looking man with a long, mournful face in a long, dark greatcoat. Soon, as he paused to watch, the dancing visitors were surrounded by dozens of other men and women, many with drinks in hand, some with arms around each other, shouting encouragement and good-natured insults, much of it profane, in a polyglot of languages and accents.

Watching too was a small group of heavily-powdered prostitutes, who had been parading openly in front of the handful of opulent brothels that dotted the northern reaches of the Rialto. One of the prostitutes, a slim, young blonde girl with a narrow, angular face and bold eyes sauntered over to Patrick, a wide smile of invitation on her rouged, thin lips.

"You're such a lovely, big fellow," she said, the voice high, flat and nasal, her accent pure Brooklyn. "I had a boyfriend once who looked just like you," she added as she sidled closer, reaching up to fondle and stroke the bicep of his right arm. "It won't even cost you nothing but the hotel. You'll have the best time ever, I promise. I love chocolate," she whispered, moving even closer, her tongue and breath warming his ear, as she ran the nails of her fingers up and down his leg.

"I can't, I can't," Patrick replied, backing away from her probing fingers on suddenly trembling legs, battling the hot flames of desire coursing swiftly through his healthy, young body.

"Why," she asked hotly, her fingers brushing against his rising erection, "I can tell you like me."

"I have a girlfriend," he lied hoarsely, as he hurried away with his face burning and his body shaking, looking straight ahead, not daring to turn around. Knowing that if he did so all of his resolve, all of his promises to his mother, would be lost.

Minutes later, standing in the long line outside the brightly lit Hammererstein's Victoria Theatre at 42nd Street and Broadway, Patrick took a long gulp of the chilly autumn night and tugged at the ends of his jacket, trying his best to cover the persistent, painful bulge at the front of his pants.

Once inside the ornate foyer of the eleven-year-old theatre,

Patrick, eager to get the best possible seat, pushed his way through the multi-racial crowd and quickly made his way upstairs to the second balcony. He would have preferred a downstairs seat with its superior view of the screen and that night he could have afforded the two dollar price. But, although in New York Negroes were legally entitled to sit in any section of the theatre, by custom this right was rarely exercised and when it was the theatre management generally made life extremely uncomfortable for the unfortunate offender.

The heavyweight title bout between Johnson and middleweight champion Stanley Ketchel had generated enormous interest throughout the country and the film of the unexpectedly exciting battle had been eagerly awaited by fight fans and ordinary citizens of both races across the country. Johnson's lackluster title defenses against Philadelphia Jack O'Brien, Tony Ross and Al Kaufman, had made many white Americans confident that the black champion was merely an interloper who would soon be put in his place. Before the fight criticism of his character and behavior poured in from every quarter. Throughout the year, as Jeffries had slowly worked himself back into fighting shape, the black champion had seemed far more interested in celebrating his good fortune than in training. He had entered the ring against O'Brien and Ross in poor condition and overweight.

Some newspapers even reported that he had been drinking the night before the O'Brien fight; but he had, nevertheless, handled both men easily. Kaufman, a former blacksmith, was a big, strong, experienced heavyweight, a far more formidable opponent than either O'Brien or Ross. Although Johnson had managed to get himself into somewhat better condition for this fight he had still been overweight and only modestly more interested. Kaufman had trained hard and entered the ring in superb condition but throughout the fight, despite a valiant effort, he was unable to penetrate Johnson's defense, landed only a half-dozen clean punches and was badly beaten.

If the earlier bouts had exposed what his critics saw as flaws in his character, the fight with Ketchel had revealed what had been interpreted by those same critics as weaknesses in his physical capabilities. Although he was regarded by some as the greatest middleweight who ever lived, Ketchel, who had once been described as having a face that could only be found in an insane asylum or a prison death house, was only 5 feet, 9 inches tall and weighed about 160 pounds. The promoter Jim Coffroth had asked Johnson to carry his smaller opponent for a while; the fight was being filmed and a quick knockout would significantly reduce revenues from that source. Johnson, who had been frequently involved in similar arrangements in the past—being asked by promoters to carry smaller or less talented white fighters was not an uncommon occurrence for him—was happy to comply since his purse included a share of the film revenues. To him it was just good business; unlike the mean, ferocious Ketchel, who had been aptly nicknamed "The Assassin," blood and pain were not high on his agenda.

The fight, which according to the reports had been witnessed by fashionably attired ladies and men of almost every nation, was the biggest California had seen in many years. Ketchel, who one reporter had described as a savage and an exception to the human race, was usually portrayed as the villain; being hissed at and booed was his customary fare. But pitted against the black champion, he had been transformed, for one of the few times in his career, into the crowd favorite, and when unaccustomed, thunderous cheers greeted his entry into the ring, the man of whom it had been written-*he could never get enough blood*- was overcome by racial pride and tears had streamed down his wild-eyed, brutal face.

As had been and would be true of every occasion that he entered the ring in the United States as heavyweight champion, a chorus of catcalls and crude racial insults had greeted Johnson's arrival. Nothing he did to improve his popularity made any difference. Not the American flag he draped around his waist, not the cool smile he offered his detractors. These small gestures of reconciliation had only served, perversely, to arouse more passionate denunciation from the sea of pale, hostile faces. Nothing less than his defeat and utter destruction, those eyes made clear, could sate such terrible hatreds.

For the first eleven rounds Johnson, like a cat with a rat, had toyed with the smaller man, striking him at will but generally just confusing him with feints that were so deceptive that Ketchel began, according to one report, *"Whipping his gloves to and fro sidewise and blinking as though punches were coming from he knew not where."* But, determined to honor his part of the agreement, Johnson allowed a number of openings to pass unexploited. And, not once did he throw an uppercut, his best punch.

Round twelve began routinely, with Johnson meeting Ketchel's bullish attacks with one brisk jab after another. Then, according to reports, somebody in his corner yelled, "Now then, Stanley", and the challenger almost simultaneously unleashed a vicious, roundhouse right hand punch that seemingly curved around Johnson's neck and landed with an enormous thud on the temporal bone behind his ear. The champion fell as if struck by a bullet, partially breaking his fall with his right hand, and landing clumsily on the carpet. But, with the hostile crowd on its feet roaring, and Ketchel, sensing blood, moving in for the kill, Johnson leapt to his feet—deals and promises now forgotten—before the count even began and met the challenger's rush with a volley of lethal punches.

One punch, a right uppercut, thrown with unrestrained power, landed squarely on Ketchel's open mouth with such force that the leather of Johnson's glove was torn open by the challenger's teeth. This time it was Ketchel's turn to fall, *like a man shot through the heart,* according to one report, but, unlike Johnson, he landed heavily on the canvas and remained motionless while the referee completed the count.

> *"He was as lifeless as a log, and a look of concern spread over Johnson's face. After the referee completed his count, Ketchel's cornermen rushed into the ring and carried him to his corner. Johnson seemed worried but smiled with relief when Ketchel regained consciousness."*

To Johnson's numerous critics and detractors, the knockdown by the much smaller Ketchel was proof positive that the black champion lacked the moral and physical fortitude to stand against the superhuman Jeffries; that his flesh and spirit would quickly wither under such powerful bombardment. To his admirers and supporters, almost all other Negroes, his recovery and deadly response were evidence of his remarkable recuperative powers and underappreciated power when aroused. Not surprisingly, the film became a hot item, a kind of Rorschach test, extremely popular with both races for very different reasons.

The fight films, as reported by *The New York Times* on the morning of Tuesday, October 26, 1909, "*Were remarkably clear, and showed every movement of the two pugilists. Joe Humphreys, the announcer, who made his initial appearance as a lecturer, described the battle and incidents in connection with it during the exhibition.*"

Although, as the *Times* also reported, "There was a difference in opinion among the big crowd of spectators as to the knockout blow which ended Ketchel's heavyweight championship aspirations," Patrick was one of the members of the audience that had lustily cheered Johnson's performance, particularly the lightning fast blow that ended the fight. "The sensational climax," the newspaper had reported, "is so sudden that many of the spectators hardly realized it. The pictures show Johnson floored by Ketchel. The colored fighter appears to be struggling somewhat as he faces Ketchel upon arising, but quick as a flash Johnson's right hand shoots out and lands on the side of Ketchel's head. The latter drops like a log and lies on the canvas-covered floor on his back, with his arms and legs stretched out at full length."

As he walked out of the theatre that night with a newly-minted pride in his race swelling his heart, young Patrick O'Neill vowed that the next time Johnson fought he would be watching the fight itself instead of the film.

Ten

The newsroom of the Tribune was abuzz with a swirl of frenetic activity. Phones rang unanswered while men and women hurried back and forth, and unseen, disembodied voices shouted, snarled, and cajoled. Sitting quietly amidst this maelstrom, at a desk tucked away in a distant corner of the vast, high-ceilinged room, Daniel O'Brien picked up the copy of the British magazine *Boxing* his editor had left him, glanced at the attached note urging him to read the piece on Johnson as soon as possible, and with a small sigh opened it to the dog-eared page.

It had been more than seven months since he had last seen Jeffries and since then there had been periods when he had doubted his original optimism that a fight between the former and present champions was inevitable and that the only questions were when and where. But the former champion was back in town after a long trip to Europe, Johnson was on his way from Chicago, and it now seemed inevitable that within the week the two men would be finally signing to meet in the most eagerly anticipated fight in the history of pugilism.

But he was no longer certain that he wanted to dive back into that particular hornet's nest and all the demands it would make on his time and attention. Not just when his relationship with Bridget was going so well. Over the past several months his work load had lessened quite a bit and he had been able to spend a lot more time with her and things had reached the point where he was planning, in the very near future, to ask her to spend the rest of her life with him.

Despite his own strong feelings in favor of Jeffries regaining the title, as he began reading the British editorial, Daniel was taken aback by the intensity of the emotions the black fighter seemed to provoke in white men all over the world.

> "With Johnson's decisive decision over Ketchel," the editor had written, "the road is cleared for the long expected battle between the black champion and the great hero, the only man to whom we can look to wrest back the title for the dominant race. It is not so much a matter of racial pride as one of racial existence which urges us so ardently to desire the ex-boilermaker's triumph.
>
> The colored races outnumber the whites, and have hitherto only been kept in subjection by a recognition on their part of physical and mental inferiority.
>
> But a great change has come over the situation of late years. The Russo-Japanese War proved that a coloured people could conquer a white nation in war even under modern conditions and ever since there have been signs of unrest among the subject nations, displaying itself in India, in the Philippine Islands, and elsewhere. Then came Jack Johnson's great triumph over Tommy Burns and White and Black stood before the world in suddenly inverted positions again.
>
> Here we are, the hitherto dominant race, compelled to recognize that an American negro, the descendant of an emancipated slave, is the principal figure, our acknowledged master at the one great physical sport in which actual personal superiority can ever be authoritatively tested. Does anyone imagine for a moment that Johnson's success is without its political influence, an influence which has only been checked from having full vent by the personality of Jim Jeffries?
>
> Jeff may smash Johnson when they meet...and by so doing restore us to something like our old position. We shall never quite regain it, because the recollection of our temporary deposition will always remain to inspire the coloured peoples with hope. While if, after all, Johnson could smash Jeffries—But the thought is too awful to contemplate."

"Jesus Christ, it's only a goddamned fight," Daniel said aloud to no one in particular as he slammed the magazine onto his desk in disgust. "This is going much too far."

At the nearest desk, plump, balding, Geoffrey Hewlett, one of the paper's top crime reporters, looked up in surprise at the uncharacteristic outburst from his normally low-keyed colleague. "What's going on O'Brien, talking to yourself is one thing but shouting that's serious," he said in a jovial tone, pushing back in his chair, stubby fingers still hovering over the keys of his battered typewriter.

"Nothing really," Daniel answered, smiling wryly in embarrassment, "just this ridiculous guy in England seems to be claiming that Western civilization as we know it will end if Jeffries doesn't, as he puts it, smash Johnson and regain the title for the white race. I hope Jeffries wins too but it's just a fight, right?"

"I'm not sure about that," Hewlett answered, the smile fading quickly from his big, apple-cheeked face. "He may just be right; one fight may not end Western civilization, but believe me if that nigger beats Jeffries things are going to change, and not for the better, at least not for us, mark my words."

"Change, in what way Geoff," Daniel asked, a touch of exasperation entering his voice. "Are they suddenly going to have more wealth, more power, more influence, better education, better jobs, exactly what's going to change? How is one fight, regardless of the outcome, going to change any of that?"

"I'll tell you what's going to change," Hewlett replied heatedly, his big face reddening, "they're going to change, they're changing already. Let me tell you a little story; a few nights ago I went to see the fight film, the one with Ketchel, over at the Hammerstein. A half of the place, at least, was full of fucking niggers, and you should have seen them, dressed to the nines and strutting around as if they owned the goddamned place. Believe it or not but some of them were even bold enough to sit downstairs and none of the fucking cowardly ushers said a single word. But what can you expect when the fucking owner is a Jew. A couple of the nigger bucks even had white girls with them, walking around hand in hand like it was the most natural thing in the world.

Prostitutes of course, but just the same it's fucking dangerous. Mark my word prostitutes are just the start; soon they'll be going after decent white women, our women. I tell you we've got to stop them now, not next week, not tomorrow, but right now, believe me."

"Come on now Geoff, don't you think you're being more than a little melodramatic," Daniel responded, smiling indulgently at his colleague. "I agree that it's a little offsetting to see Negro men consorting in public with white women but you said it yourself, those are prostitutes. I don't believe for a moment that any decent white woman, none that I know of anyway, would willingly involve herself romantically with any Negro man. It's simply unthinkable."

Now too agitated to sit but wary of attracting any attention other than the mildly curious glances his raised voice had already drawn from several of their colleagues at nearby desks, Hewlett walked over to Daniel and lowered his voice to a hiss.

"Unthinkable? You obviously have no idea of the incredible things going on in this country," Hewlett said, his face red and contorted, "Let me give you just one little example. There's a play happening right now, I mean its playing currently, at, I think, the New Theatre on Broadway called, get this, "Nigger." Now there was a time in this country…"

"And this offends you?" Daniel asked, interrupting the tirade, "I don't understand why of all people that would bother you."

"Let me finish, please," Hewlett replied, his voice quiet but grim, "this play has been described by both black and white critics as a great play. And do you know what happens in this allegedly great play that supposedly rings true because it is shockingly truthful and purports to lay bare the illegitimate relationships that supposedly exists between whites and blacks in this country?"

"No, but I'm sure you're going to tell me," Daniel replied, his voice a mix of sarcasm and weary resignation.

"Yes I'm going to," Hewlett responded, as he pulled a nearby chair to the front of Daniel's desk and plopped down heavily onto it, "because you of all people need to know what's really happening in this country, at least in this city. Thank god, I don't believe the rest of the country is as bad, yet. Anyhow, here is what happens. For three acts, not in one isolated scene mind you, but for three acts, a white woman, not a prostitute, an actress and by all accounts one of some renown and ability, and by the measures we normally use in judging these matters, a decent white woman, makes what, one reviewer described as ardent and passionate love to a Negro. And all of this takes place legally, in public, night after night, and not just in front of Negroes, as you would expect. But also in front of white men and, god help us, what we would normally describe as decent white women, all of whom pay good money to watch this humiliating and degrading spectacle. And you tell me that you think it is unthinkable that the likes of Jack Johnson and his kind won't soon be after our decent white women and that they might not receive a warmer welcome from some of them than you or I could ever have believed possible."

During Hewlett's outburst Daniel had become increasingly uncomfortable. Although he shared some of the general Irish antipathy to Negroes and had his own questions and doubts about their intellectual abilities and temperament, he found his colleague's open and unabashed racism both distasteful and unsettling. His grandfather, an ardent disciple of the great Daniel O'Connell, had frequently spoken out against his own people's "harsh and unconscionable treatment" of Negroes. O'Connell, known throughout the length and breath of Ireland as the Liberator, had founded the Catholic Association, the first mass political party in history and was an ardent and relentless opponent of slavery and American hypocrisy. The Catholic Association, which was supported by small dues collected every week in Catholic churches throughout Ireland, had been formed to overturn the restrictions against Catholic participation in public life and O'Connell had recognized the parallels between the struggles of the Irish in Ireland and Negroes in the United States.

Ireland's antislavery traditions were strong and ancient, dating back to the Council of Armagh in 1177, which had prohibited Irish trade in English slaves. The fact that for seven centuries not a single slave had set foot on Irish soil was a source of enormous pride for most Irishmen. When O'Connell first entered Parliament in 1830, with only one other Irish member for support, he had been approached by a representative of the West India interest with a deal. His silence on the slavery question for the support of their twenty-seven members on Irish issues. Unhesitatingly, the great man had replied, "Gentlemen, God knows I speak for the saddest people the sun sees; but may my right hand forget its cunning, and my tongue cleave to the roof of my mouth, if to save Ireland, even Ireland, I forget the Negro one single hour."

O'Connell's extraordinary response was not surprising. A year earlier, in denouncing what he saw as American hypocrisy he had fearlessly and eloquently declared: "Let America, in the fullness of her pride wave on high her banner of freedom and its blazing stars...In the midst of their laughter and their pride, I point them to the negro children screaming for their mother from whose bosom they have been torn... Let them hoist the flag of liberty, with the whip and the rack on one side, and the star of freedom on the other."

Hewlett's passionate outburst had been followed by a long moment of awkward silence. Finally, Daniel had looked his grim-faced colleague in the eye and to his own surprise had quietly replied: "Perhaps the difference between us," he had said, his grandfather's tales of the Liberator flooding his mind, "is that I guess I just don't really feel that strongly about it. I may not approve personally but, you know, we are all God's children."

The morning was misty, chilly and grey. But Central Park was ablaze with the deep, rich colors of fall. Infinitesimal shades of russet-orange, of yellow, purple, and gold, seduced and assaulted the senses. In the southeastern corner of the massive oasis, a mere stone's throw from bustling Fifth Avenue, graceful crabapple trees wrapped in gold and orange, hummed with life. Gaily clad robins and mockingbirds busily fed on pale green and cherry red fruits dangling invitingly from welcoming branches. While neighboring forsythia shrubs--damp foliage a riot of yellows and purples--but sadly devoid of fruit of any color, and adorned with only an errant flower bell or two, looked on in empty, envious silence.

Although the newly ascendant sun had not yet entirely banished every remnant of the night, the busy birds were not the only forms of life moving purposefully in the 843-acre park. Scores of far larger, two-legged creatures, some on foot and others on cycles, a smaller number of hansom carriages, and an occasional automobile, moved determinedly back and forth along the gently curving pathways that criss-crossed the magnificent man-made forest. Two of the two-legged creatures on foot, who had been moving faster and longer than the others, puffing wispy clouds of exertion, one trailing the other by an ever increasing distance, finally slowed as they approached the comma-shaped body of water, nestling unobtrusively below the 59th Street entrance, called the Pond.

Jim Jeffries was tired but pleased. Although the small growth in his left nostril had caused some minor discomfort the early morning run had gone as well as he could have hoped. After a brisk warm-up walk down Riverside Drive that had begun, the way he liked it, at the very crack of dawn when the air was still fresh and clean. He and Sam had gone for about five miles at a very strong pace, far faster than he had been able to manage in years. Sam had long been the superior runner but today he had not been able to keep up. His performance, especially his ability to hold a long sprint towards the end of his run had been gratifying. It was clear that his hard work at Carlsbad, despite the extravagances in Paris, were beginning to pay off.

His hard, lean appearance on his return from his ten-week European trip had shocked and delighted all of his friends. Just the astonishment on Sam's face when he met Freida and himself on the ship had made all the effort worthwhile. In Carlsbad, he had gotten up early every morning, laced up a light pair of boots and had hit the road, often going for as long as ten miles, most of it through the beautiful forests of that fabled German city, and best of all, always alone and unnoticed. And although he had not laced on a glove even once during the whole time he had been away he had worked diligently in the gymnasium most afternoons, hardening his muscles, chasing away the ugly flab. Astonishingly his weight had even dropped below 220lbs before spiking to 228 in France but now, he told himself as he tried unsuccessfully to pinch the firm, taut flesh around his waist, he was sure that it could not be any more than about 225.

One of the reasons he and Freida had chosen Carlsbad to spend much of their time was all the wonderful things they had heard about the city's healthful waters, and they had not been disappointed. Just soaking in it had somehow made them both feel better, healthier. And drinking copious amounts of the carbonic water, despite the unpleasant taste, had not just calmed and soothed their stomachs; it was not exaggerating to say they had been rejuvenated. He had particularly enjoyed just walking around unrecognized, listening to the bands in the drawing room of the hotel and in the city's large, lovely parks.

It had been there in Carlsbad that he had first begun to feel something like his old self again, like a real fighter again, not just somebody putting on a show for entertainment. It was there as he felt the rebirth of his body that he had finally decided that he was ready to face his greatest fear, stepping in the ring with that disgusting loudmouth, that coal-black nigger, Jack Johnson. First, it was the improvement of his wind that had surprised him, suddenly one morning his legs had no longer felt dead and heavy after a hard, fast run. For some time he had been able to handle long slow runs intermingled with short sharp sprints but any attempt to maintain a good pace for any reasonable distance had left him weak and gasping. Another morning, to his enormous delight, he had discovered that the ugly bulge around his waist had completely gone. In the gym the weights grew increasingly lighter and his arms and legs increasingly stronger.

Of course, he thought, as he slowed his jog to a walk and waited for the struggling Sam Berger to catch up, he was still nowhere near where he was when he last fought in New York, when he won the title from Fitz Fitzsimmons at the Seaside Sporting Club on Coney Island, a little more than ten years before.

Despite his massive size Jeffries had always been an outstanding athlete. He had been a very good sprinter as a youngster, several times running a hundred yards in eleven seconds. He had been a relatively inexperienced and fairly clumsy

24-year-old when he had been selected by Fitzsimmons as his opponent for his first title defense. The champion had obviously expected the youngster, with only twelve previous fights to his credit, to be an easy mark. But Jeffries had trained hard for six months and had gotten himself in the best shape of his life. Every day he had done between ten and fifteen miles on the road and boxed a dozen or more rounds, and three days before the fight he had run twelve miles without stopping, "Just to see if my wind was good," as he later recounted to friends.

The English-born Fitzsimmons, who had won the title by knocking out the popular Jim Corbett in the fourteenth round in Carson City, Nevada, on March 17, 1897, had also been the middleweight and light heavyweight champion. He was 37-years-old, stood just under six feet, weighed a mere 167 pounds and had not fought for two years when he met Jeffries on June 9, 1899, but he entered the ring a prohibitive 3-1 favorite. Jeffries skills were that lightly regarded by the odds makers; and for very good reason. In 1898, after an impressive campaign on the Pacific Coast, the youngster's handlers had pronounced him ready to invade the far tougher turf of New York. To ensure that his debut was as sensational as possible, they had announced that he would be meeting two men, in two 10-round bouts, on the same night.

As planned, the announcement attracted widespread attention and the Lenox Athletic Club was filled to overflowing on the night of the fights. Jeffries' opponents, Steve O'Donnell, a white Australian, and, Bob Armstrong, a black American, had been carefully selected. O'Donnell's chief claim to fame was that he was said to be the great Peter Jackson's favorite pupil, and Armstrong was old and well past his prime. Armstrong had been selected to go first and eager to make a good impression on his first outing in the East, young Jeffries had tried for a quick knockout. But the wily Negro, still tough and durable and wise in defensive tactics, had refused to cooperate. Bobbing and weaving and blocking and feinting, rarely throwing punches of his own, he had made the bout a nightmarish experience for the powerful, young Californian, who according to one observer "had not quite mastered the art of accurate delivery."

The punches that did find their mark landed primarily on what one paper described as Armstrong's "iron head." Jeffries was awarded a 10-round decision but his hands were so badly swollen that he could not put on the gloves for the second fight, and the bout with O'Donnell had to be cancelled.

The judgment of the watching sportswriters had been swift and harsh. With good-humored contempt they had, to a man, rated him as strong and willing but hopelessly clumsy. Deeply mortified, the shy young man, hurt and angry, quietly returned to the West Coast, nursing a grudge against newspaper reporters that not even all the subsequent lavish praise would ever appease.

But the gods of fate were on his side, his inept and embarrassing performance had a silver lining; it gained him a shot at the heavyweight title. The champion had watched the fiasco from ringside and after two years of inactivity Fitzsimmons was determined to make a cautious reentry to the ring and the big, ponderous Californian seemed the ideal opponent. The Englishman may have been undersized but he was crafty, moved extremely well, hit with surprising power with both hands from all angles, had perhaps the deadliest left hook in the business and was said to possess an uncanny knowledge of the human anatomy, knowing just where to place his punches for maximum effect.

On the night of the fight, the champion, who had been fighting since Jeffries was five years old, bald pate gleaming under the lights, entered the ring with a belt of American flags wrapped around his slender waist. Fitzsimmons went on the attack from the start, slashing with both hands, trying to open up the crouching challenger. Initially, squatting low with his head tucked in behind his shoulder and his massive left held in front of him, looking every bit like what one contemporary writer described as "the jib boom of a ship," Jeffries was content to fend off the champion's frenzied attacks. His unorthodox style had been developed to protect himself against Fitzsimmons' crippling solar-plexus punch, and it worked wonderfully well.

Nothing the champion did was able to penetrate the challenger's turtle-like defense. Lefts and rights, hooks and uppercuts, thrown with murderous power, exploded harmlessly off

Jeffries' powerful shoulders and the top of his enormous head. The Californian's answer was to keep stabbing his piston-like jab into the Englishman's face. In the second round Fitzsimmons received his first demonstration of Jeffries's great power; a straight left lifted him off his feet and dumped him unceremoniously on the seat of his trunks. But the champion was far from done and in the fifth he got his big chance to end the bout. A sizzling right hand finally penetrated Jeffries' defense and opened a bone-deep cut over the challenger's right eye. Then, as Jeffries pawed at the spurting blood, the champion steadied himself and threw his best punch, the solar-plexus, the one that had toppled Corbett and won him the heavyweight title.

The big Californian had temporarily abandoned his crouching defense and was standing straightup when the punch landed squarely in the pit of his stomach. At that moment the legend of his indestructibility was born. The champion stepped back and waited for the challenger to fall, as all of his opponents, when struck by that terrible blow, had. But nothing happened, almost nothing; Jeffries merely blinked and pressed forward relentlessly. "Fitz," one writer noted, "might just as well have tried to put the Rock of Gibraltar on its side."

By the eleventh round it was clear that the challenger's youth, great strength and enormous stamina was far too much for the aging champion. A short left, of the kind he would have easily avoided earlier, landed squarely on the fading champion's chin and Jeffries, right hand cocked, moved in quickly for the kill. But another blow from the young Hercules was unnecessary, the Englishman had already been demolished and he crumbled slowly to the ground as the new champion watched, marveling at what he had accomplished.

In Central Park, Jeffries paused and glanced behind him but Berger was still not in sight. They had run together on even terms for most of the way but the steep grades of the final mile had been hard on his friend and Berger had not been able to match the former champion's strong pace at the end. Then, as he waited, apparently energized by his performance that morning and the memory of his youthful accomplishments, Jeffries dropped nimbly to the ground and began a series of rapid, seemingly effortless pushups, his powerful arms pistoning his huge body up and down as he counted: "One…two…three…four…five…six…seven…eight…nine…ten," inhaling and exhaling noisily in short, explosive blasts of breath.

After a brief rest that was taken lying face down on the damp, leaf-covered park floor, the former champion had just begun his second set of pushups when Berger staggered slowly into view, breathing heavily, his hands on his hips, his face pale and drawn.

"Holy shit Jim," Berger gasped weakly, "are you trying to kill me, running like that and then I see you lying there, flat on your face, I thought you had a heart attack like the one I'm about to have."

Without waiting to finish the second set of pushups, Jeffries leapt to his feet and moved quickly towards his friend, his face soft with concern.

"Jesus Christ Sam, why didn't you just stop" he asked, as he wrapped a supportive right arm around his friend's waist and led him to a nearby bench. "Are you alright man, you look like dog shit," the former champion added, as Berger groaned slightly and stretched out flat on his back.

For a long moment there was no response from the exhausted man, just labored breathing and the concern on Jeffries's face began to change into panic. "Are you alright Sam," he asked again, this time bending over the bench to place two fingers at the base of Berger's throat, testing the rate of his pulse.

"I'll live Doctor Jeffries," Berger finally replied with a little smile, pleased and amused at his friend's solicitousness, "I'm just getting a little too old for this shit. But you," he added, sitting up, the smile getting wider, "are obviously getting younger, that was one hell of a run."

"It was all that work in Carlsbad," Jeffries replied with a little grin, "I haven't felt this good in a long time, a very long time."

"You look good too champ, you look damn good," Berger said, getting shakily to his feet. "A lot of people are going to be surprised when they see you on Friday, a lot of people, especially that fucking nigger," he added vehemently.

"He'd better watch what he says on Friday, always talking a lot of shit. I don't care who's there, I'm going to ram my fucking fist down his goddamned nigger throat if he's not careful," Jeffries growled.

"Forget the fucking nigger, don't let him bother you, that's exactly what he wants," Berger advised in a curt, dismissive tone. Then, with his arm draped across his friend's massive shoulders, he began moving them towards the nearby 59th Street exit. "Let's get some rest," he added, in a suddenly much lighter tone, "we have to be at the gym in a couple of hours and the great Ethel herself will be there."

"I know," Jeffries replied, and blushed.

When he walked into the crowded Jack Cooper's gymnasium, Daniel couldn't help thinking back to when he had last seen the former champion, at the Armory A.A. in Boston, and marveling at how very different the whole mood around the former champion seemed. In Boston, the dark cloud of Jefferies' seething resentment, at being forced to leave his beloved alfalfa farm to defend the honor of the white race, had hung over his camp like an impending thunderstorm. Now, in New York, it was immediately obvious, in the smiles and easy laughter that greeted the casual visitor, that something important had changed.

That something, Daniel realized the moment he saw the former champion, was a dramatic change in Jeffries' appearance and attitude. Gone was the heavy clothing that seven months earlier had camouflaged softening muscles and a flabby belly. Now, stripped to the waist and sweating profusely as he slammed thunderous punches into the heavy punching bag, he seemed almost the champion of old, massive muscles rippling dangerously with every movement. But even more remarkable than the trim waistline and jawline were the smiles and good-natured laughter; gone too, with the flab, at least for the moment, were the scowls and hard stares that had often made approaching him a newspaperman's nightmare.

The former champion's new training environment was every

bit as dramatically different as was his attitude and appearance. The Armory, an unpretentious male preserve, which reeked of stale sweat and tobacco, had seemed ill-cast as the camp of the man to whom an entire nation was looking to for redemption. In notable contrast, Cooper's Gymnasium, the scrupulously clean, lavishly equipped physical training headquarters of many of the nation's finest professional athletes, seemed eminently suited for that starring role.

Women, especially attractive, well-dressed ones, would have seemed entirely out-of-place at the Armory, but at Cooper's gymnasium their presence seemed perfectly natural and normal. And on this day one of the most beautiful and famous women in America, the actress Ethel Barrymore, of the renowned acting family, was in attendance, accompanied by her youthful new husband, the stockbroker Russell G. Colt, to cheer on her close friend. The glamorous couple had made a quick trip from Boston for the specific purpose of watching the former champion prepare for his bout against champion Jack Johnson.

Evidently impressed by what she saw, the 30-year-old star of the American and British stage, who had been described by newspapers of the time as "a close follower of the fighting game," enthusiastically voiced her support of the white fighter to the enthralled newspaper reporters, as a sweating Jeffries' looked on in pleased silence.

"I have known Jeff for five years," she told the assembled throng, in a voice that had a touch of an English accent, as they furiously took notes, "and he is in as good condition now as he ever was. If he is going to fight that black bluff now is the time to get to him. I hope he'll kill him."

Blithely demonstrating her knowledge of boxing, the actress, who asked to be addressed as Mrs. Colt, added, "I have watched Jeff's blocks and swings and every one of those moves says goodbye to Mistah Johnson. I'm willing to back Jeff tomorrow against any one in the world. I think he can beat Johnson right now. I'll back him to win easy."

After Miss Barrymore's departure the newspapermen turned their attention to the beaming former champion.

"Can you beat him," one small fellow with a wispy moustache and a surprisingly big voice demanded bluntly from the back of the crowd of reporters.

Jeffries' smile disappeared and his face hardened slowly as he looked in the general direction of his inquisitor. "That nigger can never lick me," he answered, his tone as hard and dispassionate as stone. "Did you ever see him fight," he asked, directing the question to the reporters as a group. "Well, I have, two or three times. He stands flat-footed as a washerwoman. Let me tell you no man earth who stands flat-footed can ever lick me. They've got to get up on their toes to do that. The man who stands flat-footed in the ring is licked before he ties on a glove, if the other man is anything near his equal."

"Did you know that John L. Sullivan said that Johnson will beat you," another voice from the crowd asked. But, before the big Californian could reply, another voice responded that "John. L. Sullivan has also been quoted as saying that you will win." The enormously popular Sullivan, the first heavyweight champion of the world, would have been an unlikely supporter of the black champion. Not only had Sullivan refused to fight Peter Jackson but he had criticized Tommy Burns for stepping into the ring with Johnson, calling the Canadian money-mad and a "man who upsets good American precedents."

The "Boston Strong Boy," as Sullivan had been dubbed for his prowess as a barroom brawler in his native city, had been deeply upset at Johnson's victory in Australia. Determined to restore the title to the white race, Sullivan had played a major role in the agitation for a Great White Hope. Early in 1909, before Johnson even returned to the United States, Sullivan, who had been forced to file for bankruptcy several years earlier, had announced that he was the front man for a syndicate that was willing to put up $75,000 for a Jeffries-Johnson fight. If Jeffries could not be lured back into the ring, he would, he had announced, "find someone."

"Well that's better," Jeffries replied quietly, getting to his feet. "Johnson," he explained, his tone thoughtful, his voice even, "has only one punch." Standing flat-footed with his feet wide apart, he made a slight movement of his hand that looked vaguely like an uppercut. "This is it. I have 400 punches and every one of them better than his best. I can hit anywhere from anywhere, short or long range, from the hip or the shoulder or anywhere else. I have two hands. He has one. I can send 'em in from away off, or pound 'em in with two inches play, Johnson can't."

What in the world had been responsible for this amazing transformation, Daniel wondered, as he watched and listened to the former champion's calm, self-confident performance. Pulling a battered notebook out of the breast pocket of his jacket, he scribbled the opening paragraph of his report.

> *For those of his numerous supporters who may have harbored any doubt, however small and fleeting, that former champion Jim Jeffries would ever be able to return to anything remotely resembling his former dominating form, yesterday's performance must have been very reassuring. It certainly was to this reporter. Not only was the big Californian in wonderful physical condition as he breezed through a grueling workout at Cooper's Gymnasium. But, even more important, was the calm confidence with which he explained and demonstrated why the current champion will go down to certain defeat when they finally get together sometime next year.*

Eleven

Daniel awoke from a fitful sleep frozen with fear. He could not believe, he thought, as he listened to the dreaded sounds coming from the front of his house, that this was happening to him again, not after all the precautions he'd taken. The fierce, powerful blows, booming in from all the way down the hall, were shaking the walls and rattling the windows of his bedroom. He knew the front door, despite the reinforcements he'd had done, would be unable to withstand such relentless, brutal pounding much longer and would break and shatter at any moment. The gun, he had cleaned and loaded and placed so carefully just before he went to bed, was, somehow, just like all the other times before, not under his rumpled, sweat-stained pillow.

He heard the door give way and knew that this time there was nothing he could do, that there was no avenue of escape, and that he was totally and absolutely helpless. He'd barred the windows and the back door against them but he had only, he now despairingly realized, created his own prison. And now he could hear the murmur of the familiar voices and the echo of the heavy steps start down the long, narrow hallway and grow louder as they drew nearer and nearer to his bedroom door. His fluttering heart leapt into his throat, choking off every breath and the sound of his own heartbeat was deafeningly loud.

He desperately wanted to move, to do something, anything, even scream, but his body, except for his eyes and ears, ignored the entreaties of his frantic brain and he could only watch and wait. Then the door was thrown open with a fearsome bang and they— how many he still could not tell—stepped loudly inside. As he watched helplessly he could again see the flash of white teeth against the angry black faces. The mouths opened and many words were uttered but in his panic all he could discern was the same accusing ones he'd heard the nights before. *"You of all people Daniel O'Brien should have known better,"* they chanted in unison over and over and over again, as they stood at the side of his bed and stared down on him through hollow, vacant eyes.

And he wanted, with all his heart, to tell them that he was not what he seemed, that, unlike the others of his kind, he meant them well. But even then, in bitter betrayal, his treacherous mouth still would not answer the pleadings of his heart or brain. It was only when, on not getting an answer, the angry faces began moving threateningly towards his bed that he was, thankfully, finally able to scream. And it was the sound of his own anguished voice that finally woke him up, shivering pitifully, and washed in cold and clammy sweat.

Daniel had expected a good crowd but nothing like the one that confronted him when he walked into the banquet hall of the Albany hotel on the Friday afternoon of October 29, 1909. Although he was almost ten minutes early the big room was already filled to overflowing with dark suits, white faces and a thick haze of blue smoke.

There was not, Daniel noted, as he pushed his way through the noisy, expectant crowd, a single dark face to be seen anywhere in the vast sea of excited countenances. It must be pretty hard on him, he found himself thinking, to be almost always surrounded by hostility and hatred. He didn't like the man but one had to admit, he told himself, that it took quite a bit of tough-mindedness for Johnson to handle himself with the aplomb he invariably demonstrated in public. There probably isn't a single person in this room, he thought, who wants him to win or even wishes him well.

He had just managed to get himself a drink, a long whisky sour, and was returning to the area of the room reserved for members of the press when the entire room seemed to erupt into wild and prolonged cheering. After taking a long swallow of the iced drink and resting his glass on the polished surface of the enormous table in front of him, Daniel hurriedly pulled his notebook out of his jacket pocket and began recording his impressions of the event in a virtually indecipherable left-hand script:

> *At exactly at three o'clock yesterday afternoon and precisely on time a burst of cheering, which reached every corner of the crowded banquet hall of the Albany hotel on Broadway, signaled the arrival of former champion, Jim Jeffries, for the signing of articles for his upcoming bout with the present champion, Jack Johnson. Wearing a thin serge suit, the big Californian strode down the middle of the room, not speaking as is his custom, but smiling and nodding to his left and right to acknowledge the cries of welcome that followed his every footstep. A few daring souls even reached out to slap the great, broad back. Less bold souls were content to scurry as close as possible to their hero.*
>
> *The effect of his hard training, much of it reportedly in secret during his trip to Carlsbad and Paris, was immediately obvious in his trim waistline and brisk but light footsteps. Connoisseurs of the fight game seemed particularly interested in these two aspects. They stared at his waistline, they admired it and told each other how brief it is and how much it said of his physical conditioning, which they unanimously agreed must be excellent. One particularly enthusiastic hero-worshipper, almost besides himself in ecstasy, loudly proclaimed to his fellow enthusiasts that not only were the big man's "light as a feather" movements eloquent testimony of his outstanding physical condition but so too were the brilliance of his eyes and the tone of his clear, bronzed skin.*

Johnson's entrance, fifteen minutes later, provoked a very different response. The reigning heavyweight champion of the world made his way to the table where the papers were to be signed in a room that had suddenly gone eerily silent. Daniel had finished his first drink and was halfway through a second when the abrupt hush enveloped the room. The deafening silence was, he knew, even before Johnson and his small party came into view, an unmistakable signal that the black champion had arrived. Replacing his drink on the table Daniel once again began recording his impressions:

> *Jack Johnson, the black heavyweight champion of the world, the first man of his race to hold this most coveted of titles, arrived fifteen minutes late to a welcome every bit as eloquent in its way of the sentiments of the fight fans of this city as the one given to Jeffries. But in place of the joyous shouts that greeted the Californian the Negro was met with a silence so complete, so hostile, that even that redoubtable pugilist was for a short while almost completely unnerved. To his considerable credit, it must be reported that Johnson soon recovered his traditional composure and by the time he took his place at the signing table, a mere six feet away from Jeffries, he seemed entirely relaxed and quite jovial. To the unbiased observer the black champion made an impression every bit as favorable as Jeffries'. Johnson is as tall as the former champion but fully thirty pounds lighter and there is something of the grace and power of the panther in his long, easy stride, and If his confidence faltered today it was only for a brief moment.*
>
> *What this reporter found more interesting than the physical appearances of the two men or the reaction of the fights fans of this city and believe to be more relevant to the eventual outcome of the fight was the attitude of the two fighters to each other. Jeffries made little effort to disguise his strong dislike of Johnson. The moment the black champion appeared the Californian's smile froze. I have seen him in other similar situations when he was indifferent or friendly or merely polite to the enemy, but never like this. Down came the heavy black brows in the fiercest of frowns and he glared at the champion it what seemed to this reporter to be genuine anger. Johnson's feelings are far less clear; apart from his momentary discomfort he seemed his usual jovial, unrevealing self.*

> *What is clear is that Jeffries will approach this fight as he has no other; those who may have doubted his will to recapture the title or even to get back in the ring can rest assured that if desire and determination are enough that the heavyweight title will be returned to the white race in due time. What is far less clear, at least at this moment, is if it will be.*

This report, Daniel told himself as he plopped his notebook on the table and picked up his drink, is probably not going to be too popular in either the newsroom or with many of the paper's readers, most of whom were impatient with anything less than absolute belief in and support for a Jeffries victory. A lot of them are probably out there in this audience standing in front of me, he thought as he gazed through the blue haze of cigarette smoke at the white faces intently following the proceedings. But it was what I believe and I need to sleep at night and grandpa would approve, he consoled himself. Just then, the man to his immediate right, a writer for *Harper's Weekly*, a little man with a bright red bowtie and tobacco-stained fingers and teeth, leaned over so closely Daniel could almost taste his breath, rancid from both tobacco and garlic, and with a big smile whispered conspiratorially:

"Doesn't he just look so frightened, almost like he expects a scolding or even a whipping?"

"Who," Daniel asked, recoiling involuntarily, his tone unexpectedly sharp, his nose crinkled in distaste.

"Why Johnson of course, don't you think so," the little man replied a bit uncertainly, clearly surprised by Daniel's response and attitude, the crooked smile slowly vanishing.

"No, I don't," Daniel replied and pointedly looked away, ending the discussion.

At the head table Johnson, clicking two red dice he carried in his right hand and smiling affably at his companions at the table, had done much of the talking. The two sides had quickly agreed to award the fight to the club, organization or person offering the best financial inducement, that bids would be submitted on December 1, 1909 at 3:00 p.m. at the Albany and that each club, organization or person making a bid for the contest had to have a representative present who would be required to post $5,000 in coin or certified check to make good any and all stipulations of the bid.

The naming of a referee had been a little more contentious. George Little, Johnson's manager, had wanted to name one right then and there. But Jeffries speaking for the first time had suggested they wait to allow the winning bidder some input into the decision.

"Let the club that gets the bid have a word," he had said. "They've got as much at stake as we have. Let it wait."

When his manager adamantly rejected Jeffries' suggestion Johnson had been conciliatory.

"Well, let it go," he had urged, "that's all right."

The champion had been more adamant on the question of the length of the bout. His concern had been that a club in San Francisco, where bouts were limited to twenty rounds, might win the bid and he wanted a fight to the finish. To the immense satisfaction of the highly partisan crowd, many of whom seemed to have been reluctantly supportive of Johnson's position, Jeffries, sensing the mood of the crowd, had finally overridden the objections of his advisors, who seemed to believe that a shorter bout favored the former champion, by boldly declaring:

"So far as I go I don't care if it's six, ten, twenty, or a hundred rounds; but I know what the public will demand, and I am going to see that they get it—it means a finish."

Demonstrating their complete and utter confidence in their champion's prowess, the crowd had then erupted into raucous, prolonged cheering that ended only after Bob Murphy, the manager of the hotel and the temporary stakeholder, repeatedly pounded the table for order.

The sides had then quickly agreed to the division of the purse, seventy-five percent to the winner and twenty-five percent to the loser, but clashed briefly on the matter of the side bet. Both fighters were supposed to put up $5,000 each as a side bet, but when Jeffries slapped five $1,000 bills on the table, the champion was only able to produce $2,500, all the money he had in the world, he claimed. The challenger then repeatedly insisted that he produce the full amount.

Unabashed, smiling broadly and prominently displaying the pair of red dice in his right hand, Johnson had made a counter proposal.

"I'll tell you what I'll do Mr. Jeffries," he'd said, we'll throw the dice to see whether you get my money or whether I have to put up five thousand." Smiling thinly Jeffries declined the offer and waived the requirement.

The parties then had quickly agreed that the contest would take place no later than July 5, 1910 and would be fought under straight Marquis of Queensbury rules with five ounce gloves. The final item before the signing of the articles of agreement was the matter of billing: that is whose name should go first on the agreement and on all references to the fight. On this question the previously affable and conciliatory Johnson absolutely refused to budge.

"I am the present champion and my name should go first," he insisted, to the glowering annoyance of the former champion and the loud disapproval of many of his supporters in the crowd.

As the crowd began filing out of the room Daniel made the final entry in his notebook:

For those of us who believe that character is at least as important as physical ability in determining the outcome of great physical contests, an incident at the very end of the proceedings today told us a great deal about Johnson's. For most of the afternoon the Negro champion adhered to the traits we've usually assigned to members of his race, seemingly happy and care-free even in the face of the unyielding hostility of the almost entirely white crowd (I spotted two black faces other than Johnson's). But on the final point, when the document was to be signed, Johnson refused to give way, quietly but firmly insisting that as champion his name should be placed first. Some would dismiss this as just another example of his race's addiction to pomp and display but the fact that this distinction was as avidly sought by the white challenger gives the lie to this charge.

Johnson, as some of us are reluctantly discovering,

possesses a far more complex personality than many of us previously believed or is generally attributed to men of his race. I have concluded after careful observation that the Negro is a serious, determined man and should be taken very seriously. I predict that the contest with Jeffries, the great white standard bearer will be a titanic one and, best of all, it will happen in just seven short months.

Twelve

He had finally gotten the opening piece right to his complete satisfaction and Patrick O'Neill slumped back in his chair in utter relief, his body aching and head throbbing from the long hours of concentrated effort. After considerable deliberation he had decided to begin with *Maple Leaf*, despite the obvious risks, instead of a lesser known work. Not only was it an extremely difficult piece for even a player of his technical proficiency to master, as he had discovered to his chagrin, but even more worrisome was the distinct possibility that even success could spell disaster.

If he was not careful everything that followed, the rest of the entire program, might be nothing more than one long anticlimax and he had been asked to play solo for the entire dinner period. But he really wanted to start on a high note and he had come to believe that some of Joplin's other pieces (he was particularly fond of *Cascades, Nonpareil, Ragtime Dance, Sunflower Slow Drag*, *The Entertainer, Paragon Rag* and *Heliotrope Bouquet*) although far less popular, were even more beautiful than the phenomenal *Maple Leaf*, and that he would, indeed, with a little luck, be able to sustain the interest and attention of his discriminating and demanding audience.

Patrick's decision to dedicate the entire program to Joplin's compositions was his way of responding to the stormy debate John Philip Sousa had ignited with his comments that ragtime music was dead and that the public was tired of it. The famed, white bandmaster had been quoted in Lester Walton's column in the *New York Age* as saying something to the effect that ragtime had had dyspepsia or the gout long before it died and that it had been overfed by poor nurses. Good ragtime, he'd claimed, had been buried by a half a million imitators and as a result the people were sickened with the stuff and as a consequence he had not played a single piece of it all season.

Clearly annoyed at the criticism, probably because of the source, the editor of the *Age*, the city's leading black newspaper, had pointedly reminded his readers that syncopated music was purely of Negro origin. And he had not only written to some of the younger and more successful colored composers asking them what they thought of Sousa's utterances on the subject but had also published several of the responses. To a man they had rejected Sousa's charges. J. Tim Brymn, the Musical Director of the Smart Set Company, drew a distinction between "low-class" ragtime songs and those of a "higher and more artistic order" and described ragtime as the true American music.

In a similar vein, Will H. Dixon, while agreeing that "there are many worthless compositions thrown on the market today," pointed to the outstanding work of men like Will Marion Cook, J. Rosamond Johnson and Harry T. Burleigh, who he described "as one of the greatest Negro composers America has produced," to refute Sousa's claims. Mr. Burleigh, he wrote, "has just finished a piano cycle, the theme of which is taken from Darky folk-songs with syncopated rhythm." I am confident, he added, "that Mr. Sousa, after reading the score of Mr. Burleigh's cycle, would know that it was the product of a master mind."

Chris Smith was more dismissive, writing in to point out that while "we have been hearing the same thing for ten years" his own ragtime compositions had met with tremendous success, with several of them selling in excess of a half million copies. But the most eloquent description of ragtime's elemental appeal came from Thomas Lemonier. If it is true that the public is tired of it, he wrote, "The public has tired of nature, the sweet song-birds, the music of the trees etc. Ragtime music is the only real melody that thrills the heart and moves the feet. The old Southern Negroes knew nothing of notes nor high art, yet they sang, and all who heard them stopped to listen. To such music, which some term ragtime, people will listen and dance to their heart's content. It stimulates when the works of the old composers will not. We don't ask which is the sweeter—the warble of the birds or the sighing of the trees—its all music. So is ragtime. We often forget grand opera and all that and come down to nature and dance as did the warriors of old from the music of the heart, not of the brain. Long live ragtime and long live the works of the old masters. Let the people have both."

Patrick had not always been a fan of ragtime; in fact, before discovering Scott Joplin's exquisitely crafted piano rags he would have been more likely to agree with Sousa than his critics. Not that some of it wasn't quite good, in a popular sense, but Joplin compositions, he had discovered to his delight, transcended the limitations he'd assumed applied to all forms of popular music, and was as melodically rich and as structurally complex and subtle as the most acclaimed classical pieces.

Discovering Joplin had been quite a revelation for the ambitious young black man. Until then he had never even considered the idea of musical composing. Although he greatly admired the song-writing abilities of some of the great Negro minstrels like James Bland, who wrote such standards of the time as *"Carry Me Back to Old Virginny," "Oh, dem Golden Slippers," "In the Morning by the Brightlight,"* and *"In the Evening by the Moonlight,"* and some of the younger writers such as Ernest Hogan and the musical comedy stars Cole and Johnson, serious composing was something he had associated with others, mostly with dead, white European men. Joplin changed all of that.

As eye-opening as his discovery of Joplin's genius was the realization that a piano rag was, at least for him, more difficult to master than a Chopin or Beethoven sonata. The problem was getting his brain wrapped around the concept of a syncopated rhythm and commanding his right and left hands to perform very different tasks, at the same time. Everything he had played before, from Bach to the blues, featured a strong, steady and predictable beat. Ragtime, on the other hand, was subversive and unpredictable. But it was, he knew, this very unpredictability, the deliberate flaunting of the rules that made it so compelling.

Music, as he knew it before Joplin, was always divided into beats and regular measures with a three four time (ONE two three ONE two three).Important events, like changes in the melody, always happened on beat ONE. But not in ragtime. A piece could begin conventionally, with the first two measures establishing a three four time and that would be followed by measures where the note began on beat ONE but the second note would begin on note three or where nothing would happen on beat ONE, but where there is a note on beat two. So instead of ONE two three ONE two three ONE, you have ONE-THREE-TWO-ONE.

But even more difficult than adjusting his brain to the inspired randomness of ragtime, had been getting his left hand to pound out the steady "boom-chic" bass and chord patterns while his dancing right hand coaxed the syncopated tunes from the sullen keys. But once he managed to overcome his old limitations the results were magical. In the music, arousing and delightful, that flowed from the piano he heard echoes not only of the old masters but of the songs he had been taught by his mother.

Just playing well that night Patrick knew would not be good enough, nothing but his very best would suffice. It was not just because he would probably be meeting the man he admired above all others but it was also going to be a rare opportunity to showcase his skills before a lot of very important people. He had been told only a few days earlier that there was going to be a special guest, the new heavyweight champion of the world, at the club that Friday night.

The word that Jack Johnson would be having dinner at the Marshall had spread like wildfire and in less than a day every seat at every table had been booked. Many of those coming to dinner were fans of the champion, but not all. But whether they admired him or not, supported him or not, they, the smart set, the fashionable Negroes of New York, all knew that Johnson's mere presence was an absolute guarantee that the Marshall would be the place to be on Friday night, October 29, 1909.

Thirteen

In the sometimes mysterious world of the black community, the word had been spread rapidly, somehow, that the heavyweight champion of the world was on his way. So when the big, late model automobile pulled up in front of the imposing structure at 235 35th Street and disgorged its passengers--three very large black men, the smallest of whom was the heavyweight champion of the world--the surrounding blocks were already lined with excited and cheering fans.

Traveling with Johnson were the only two other black men at the signing ceremony at the Albany hotel, the two black faces in the crowd, Barron Wilkins and Joe "Baby John" Souchon. Notably absent from the group was Johnson's white manager, George Little, who had been deliberately excluded from the special meeting Wilkins had organized and to which they were heading.

As the men slowly made their way through the admiring crowd which had quickly gathered around the car, the lithe figure of the heavyweight champion was dwarfed by the massive ones of his companions. After a few minutes of back-slapping and handshaking outside, the men entered the building and went directly to a door leading to the basement of Barron's Café, one of several businesses, including the Little Savoy Hotel, operated by Wilkins in the big building. The familiar lucky horseshoe and a bold-lettered sign over the basement door brought a fond smile from the champion: NO ONE ENTERS THESE PORTALS BUT THE TRUE IN HEART SPORTS, it warned.

For the nomadic heavyweight champion of the world the building at 235 West 35th Street was as close to a home as he had anywhere in the world and it served as his headquarters whenever he was in New York. Wilkins, the sole proprietor of the hotel and the cafe and the gambling operation in the basement, where the real money was made, was a close friend and supporter who had partially financed Johnson's relentless pursuit of Tommy Burns across Europe and Australia. Now he had put together a meeting of the heavyweight champion of the world and a roomful of many of the leading black gamblers in the country, men who wanted, urgently, to speak frankly and directly to the heavyweight champion himself about a matter of transcendence importance.

Wilkins was uniquely qualified for the task he had set himself. In addition to their long and close friendship and the critical financial support he had supplied during Johnson's quest for the title, Barron Wilkins was perhaps the most influential black man in New York. His influence had nothing to do with political power or public acclaim. He held no public office of any kind and was not wellknown by the general public of either race. Instead, it was due entirely to the large sums of money he regularly paid to the city's white power structure, police and politicians, to protect his expansive and extremely profitable gambling business.

Although all forms of gambling were then illegal in New York City, as in much of the nation, Wilkins' operation, which included both bookmaking and "policy" banking, operated openly and without harassment. The city's police department had long used a well-defined formula, which was based on the size of the operation, to determine the amount of graft that a gambling parlor had to pay to remain open. Despite their high cost these payments, which amounted to informal licenses and remained in place across the reigns of successive mayors and police commissioners, were usually paid promptly and without protest. The predictability of the size of the payments and the reliability of New York's policy, provided casino operations with a stability that was often missing in other cities, where the size of graft payments often varied from administration to administration, or where, occasionally, reform-minded politicians completely closed down all gambling operations.

The men who were waiting on the heavyweight champion of the world were a curious lot, high-living, free-spending dandies, most of them; "sports," and "flash niggers," as they were called. It was easy to disparage, to underestimate these seemingly mindless, frivolous, flamboyant black men in their ankle-length fur coats, fancy jewelry and expensive, brightly-painted sports cars. And not surprisingly, not just whites but the establishment of their own race held them in exceedingly low regard. But it was also a terrible if understandable mistake. For, like the man they had gathered to meet, they wore their easy smiles and seemingly careless ways as masks to disguise a steely determination to live in America on their own terms, as men unbowed, unbroken and untamed.

Although none of the two dozen or so men at Barron Wilkins that day were at the time still formally involved in the horseracing industry, several of them had been employed, at various times, as either jockeys or trainers or in a few cases both. Many of them, despite their unorthodox appearances, were genuine experts in the sport of kings and one of them, Johnson's other traveling companion, big Joe "Baby John" Souchon, was an acknowledged authority on thoroughbred pedigree. A former employee and protégée of the great black jockey and trainer William Walker, Souchon claimed to have been a fairly successful jockey himself before—like his mentor—turning to training when he became too tall, because of a late growth spurt that had added an astonishing nine inches to his then 5' 7" frame after his fifteenth birthday, and too heavy to ride.

Walker had won the "match of the century" at Churchill Downs in 1878 aboard *Ten Broeck* and had ridden in four Derbies, winning on *Baden-Baden* in 1877. His post-riding career had been even more distinguished. Widely regarded, among racing aficionados of both races, as perhaps the country's leading authority on matters of thoroughbred breeding and conformation, Walker had become a wealthy man serving as a consultant to prominent Kentucky breeders such as John E. Madden. Souchon had worked for Walker as an assistant trainer for years, traveling around the country with him to the prominent sales, learning from his master's encyclopedic knowledge of the industry.

But, despite the horseracing background of many of their members, the men as group were not committed to any particular form of gambling. Most of them were just as likely to be found playing a hand of stud or draw poker, as calculating the odds on a thoroughbred at Saratoga or Aqueduct, or even placing a "gig" or a "saddle" on a policy bet.

Policy was an illegal lottery that had been introduced in Chicago in 1885 by a man nicknamed Policy Sam. Despite widespread anti-policy laws which began appearing as early as 1901, it flourished across the country until legal numbers games such as state lotteries supplanted it. The game, which in the early years allowed wagers to be placed for as little as one cent per number or two cents per saddle (a two-number combination) and three cents per gig (a three-number combination), became so popular with African Americans that eventually the term "policy" implied an African American clientele.

Other racial and ethnic groups had different names for similar games. Among Italian-Americans a similar game was called "the numbers." Cuban-Americans in New York called their lottery, "bolita."

But policy bets were, in the main, for the casual gamblers, the anonymous toilers, the washerwomen and the parlor maids, the messengers and the ditch diggers, little people sporting calluses and dirty fingernails, the expectant poor, divining dreams to change their hardscrabble luck, desperately hoping to turn a handful of cents into a pocketful of dollars. The men gathered at Barron's Cafe were made of far more pragmatic, calculating, and tough-minded stuff. While always careful to pay proper obeisance to lady luck, they had invented themselves, primarily, through native wit, persistence and daring. Which was why the achievements and exploits of their fellow sport, the heavyweight champion of the world, appealed so powerfully to them. They didn't just admire him or just understand him; he was them, writ large, with the whole watching world for a stage. And so, earlier and more clearly than most, they had realized that there were fortunes to be made or lost on the day, if it ever came, of the great showdown between their great black champion and America's Great White Hope.

What they wanted to know, to hear directly from the man himself, was that he was going to fight to win, that there would be no deals whatever the pressure or temptation. Wild, ugly rumors that the fight was going to be fixed, that his white manager was secretly working for the other side, that he had agreed to throw the fight for an enormous, unspecified amount of money, that he was not going to knowingly lose the fight but that he would be poisoned or weakened in some fiendish if unknown way, that white people would never let him win, that they were planning something, anything, to stop him from beating yet another white man, especially this one who was carrying all their hopes, were already spreading like wild, poisonous mushrooms throughout Negro communities all over the country.

"They're waiting in the back room," Wilkins said, turning his head to look over his shoulder at the heavyweight champion trailing slightly behind him, as the three men stepped into the long, darkened, almost completely deserted front parlor. "Sent everybody home except these lucky two," he explained with a small smile, pointing at two slim, youngish men in white shirtsleeves standing somewhat nervously in the rear of the low-ceilinged 30-foot room, "they take care of our accounting and banking and their work can't wait. Plus they wanted a look at you up close, didn't you boys," Wilkins added, as both men smiled shyly and nodded diffidently in silent agreement.

"Well fellows, that's important work, accounting and banking, and knowing Barron here you men have to be pretty sharp to be working for him in that area," a smiling Johnson said, reaching out a big right hand to the beaming duo.

"I've made a few changes back here since you were here last," Wilkins explained, as he opened the door to another large, if somewhat smaller room with a far higher ceiling, again glancing back at the champion who had finally extricated himself from the two accountants. In sharp contrast to the plainly appointed front parlor, which was dominated by a long counter and had linoleum covering the floor, this one was obviously designed for a more affluent clientele and was far more richly furnished.

The floor was lushly carpeted, small wooden tables and upholstered chairs were carefully arranged around the room and the expansive walls were covered with the signed photographs or lithographs of black America's most renowned celebrities. Those of Frederick Douglass and Peter Jackson and Isaac Murphy, who won the Derbies of 1888, 1890 and 1891, and who was ranked among the greatest jockeys of all time and was one of the most famous athletes of the nineteenth century, were the most prominently displayed. That is, except for a large one of the new champion of the world, resplendent in street clothes, posing with his friend and patron, the proprietor of the establishment.

"This looks great," said a smiling Johnson, looking admiringly around the room. "Makes losing your money a little more pleasant eh Barron and I like the pictures, particularly that big one there," he added, pointing to his own photograph. "But where's the fellows?"

"Back here in the conference room," Wilkins replied, opening the door to yet another sizeable, high-ceilinged, richly-appointed room dominated by an enormous table at which the waiting sports were seated. Two young, slim, attractive and extremely tall, light-skinned black women in short, low-cut dresses had just started serving drinks and sandwiches when Wilkins and Souchon led the heavyweight champion into the room. Until then the room had been enveloped in an uneasy, somber silence that not even the appearance of the flirtatious and high-spirited young women had been able to break. Sitting quietly around a table in an office, even Barron's, made almost all of the sports uncomfortable; plus they had a lot on their minds. But Johnson' appearance dramatically changed the mood of the room. Quickly discarding their studied cool, to a man they leapt to their feet and rushed to the champion, shouting greetings, energetically competing with each other for his attention.

For a long minute the massive Wilkins watched the frenetic scene with the indulgent smile of a fond parent before interrupting with a gentle admonishment. "Let's get our business started boys," he said in a deep, pleasant voice, "we have a lot to do and Brother Jack and us have other business to take care of later tonight."

At three inches over six feet in his stocking feet and more than three hundred pounds, Barron Wilkins was an imposing figure but he was not a good-looking man, at least not in the traditional sense. In repose his lips were thick and wide and his nose large and broad. But when he smiled, which was more often than one would have expected on meeting him for the first time, the warmth and intelligence radiating from the large, wide-set, light-brown eyes unexpectedly transformed the heavy features into something approximating handsome.

Sitting at the head of the table with the champion to one side and Souchon on the other, Wilkins, his voice low and soft, his demeanor relaxed and matter-of-fact, began the meeting with what he promised would be a brief statement. "You' all know," he continued, "looking slowly around the table, his eyes pausing on each man, "why we're all gathered here and you' all know by now that the fight we've been waiting for, and some of us thought would never happen, is on, definitely on. Baby John and I were there to witness it for ourselves. And it was quite something to see. Those white boys gave the champ quite a reception but he knew how to handle himself and he gave better than he got, and made us proud, as usual. It will be next July, on the 4th or the 5th. I don't intend to say too much just right now, you 'all know that's not my style, I prefer to listen and a want everybody to 'ave a say. I know that you 'all have a lot of questions, so don't be afraid to talk up in front of the champ. I told him a little about what we've been talking about and some of what is on everybody's mind."

Except for the knowing chuckles that had greeted Wilkins' description of Johnson's response to his hostile reception, the sports had remained completely quiet and attentive during the low-keyed presentation. But, with his face hardening and his voice rising in volume, Wilkins ended with a pledge that drew the sports to their feet, stomping, clapping and shouting in approval.

"I just want to say to the champ in front of all of you and on behalf of all of you, that we fully understand the full power of what he's going to be facing in the weeks and months ahead. That we fully understand that every effort will be made—in and out of the ring—to humiliate him, to weaken him, to defeat him, to take away his will, his confidence and his title, in nefarious ways. Yes Sir, in dirty, low-down, sneaky, nefarious ways. But we want him to know that he will not be alone. No Sir, he will not be alone, because we will be with him, all the way, with everything we've got. And what we've got is a lot more than they think we've got... a lot more gentlemen...a lot more."

As the heavyweight champion of the world looked on in pleased amazement, the men, including Baby John, remained on their feet for what seemed like several minutes, shouting themselves hoarse, all pretense of cool discarded and forgotten.

One wild-eyed sport, even more animated than the rest, a shiny black, tall, gaunt, gravel-voiced man, inexplicably dressed in late October in a white suit, with a bold green shirt, a red tie and a jaunty panama hat, his voice carrying easily above the din, began a chant that echoed and reverberated in the room like the refrain of a song. "We with you champ, all the way, with everything we got. We with you champ, all the way, with everything we got. We with you champ, all the way, with everything we got." Soon it was picked up by the rest of the men and then some inspired soul added rhythmic clapping and stomping. Although not all of the sports proved capable of keeping a beat, their unbridled enthusiasm was so loud and infectious that the young women who had retired to another room, unable to restrain their curiosity, returned first to investigate and then to participate merrily in the fun.

Finally, a smiling Wilkins raised his hand to stop what he had started; he had meant to get the fellows riled up a bit but the intensity of the response had surprised even him. "Curly," he said, barely suppressing a chuckle at the sight of the aging sport in the white suit leaning against the wall in exhaustion after his brief but vigorous display, "I always knew you were a man of many talents but I had no idea song and dance was among them. Ladies and gentlemen," he added, turning to the rest of the group, "the champ thanks you and I thank you but remember we still have some business to discuss and the champ is the special guest at the Marshall Hotel tonight and most of us here, from what I hear, are planning to be there and out in Nassau County very, very early Saturday morning for the Vanderbilt. Isn't that right?"

"Most," Curly asked, as he walked slowly back to his seat at the table, his voice and entire persona radiating disgust and indignation. "Most," he repeated, as he sat down heavily and glared balefully at the other sports. "I don't believe dere's a single man around dis table dat 'as somethin better to do with 'is time tonight an tomorrow morning dan letting all dose white people see us supporting our champ."

"Everyone of us is going Curly, tonight and tomorrow morning" a short, heavily built man to his right, with a soothing manner, assured his glowering colleague.

"Nobody is not goin to be dere," the buddha-like Baby John agreed.

"Now that we're all in agreement gentlemen," Wilkins interrupted, "who's going to ask the first question."

"We only 'ave one question champ, only one," Curly responded, looking hard at Johnson and then slowly around the table at each of his colleague who one after the other nodded in assent.

The heavyweight champion who had been, mostly, uncharacteristically silent, replied quietly, "Go ahead Curly, ask it."

"It's about your manager, we don't trust him at all, not even one little bit," Curly replied, his voice blunt and pugnacious, as he stared at the champion.

"Because he's a white man" Johnson asked, his tone mild and soft.

His eyes fixed unwaveringly on the champion Curly nodded, drew a deep breath and began. "I ain't no racist, I don't hate no man jus for is color, although God knows wid what I've seen in dis here country I, jus like every black man in dis here America, 'ave every right to be. But I don't. But the truth is champ dis fight is goin to be about more than you against Jeffries, it will be us so-called Negroes against the so-called Caucasians, us so-called black people against the so-called white people, everyone of dem against everyone of us. That's 'ow it's goin to be."

"You all believe that," Johnson asked looking around the table.

"I, reluctantly and sadly, agree with them Jack," Wilkins added.

"You' all may be right," Johnson said, as he rose to his feet, "but I'm not sure yet. But I want to say," he added, standing to his full height and flashing his famous "golden" smile as he looked around the table, "that it makes me real proud to have the affection and support of real friends like all of you here. I want to tell you that I've often been obliged to listen, unfortunately, to a lot of professional politicians, but none, not even the best of them, ever made a speech as fine as the one you just heard. In fact," Johnson said, pausing to look fondly at his friend, "I have no doubt that if he had a lighter complexion the people of this great city would have long ago elected Barron Wilkins as their mayor, for what does he lack that the best of them have except the color of his skin."

"That is nothing but the godhonest truth my brothers," the heavily-built man with the soothing voice proclaimed fervently, leaping to his feet and then just as abruptly retaking his seat to the accompaniment of shouts of agreement and encouragement from around the table.

"Amen brother, amen."

"Tell it like it is Brother Bob."

"Witness Brother Bob, witness."

"Talk Brother Jack, talk."

"Don't hold anything back Brother Jack, let it out, let it all out."

The heavyweight champion greeted each declaration with a barely perceptible nod of his clean-shaven head and then with a small smile of satisfaction tugging at the corners of his mouth began again. "I don't believe every white person will be on one side and every black person on the other because," he said, pausing again, his eyes twinkling with mischief, "I know for a fact that come hell or high-water that there will be at least one Negro, who we all know very well, who'll be on any other side but ours. Sam Langford, I guarantee you, will be firmly in Jeffries' corner."

"That son of a whore is no Negro," one sport shouted fiercely, "He's nothing but a lowdown, self-hating nigger."

"Well, I don't know anything about his mother but I won't argue with you about the rest of it," Johnson replied with a chuckle. "But in all seriousness," he added, looking slowly around the table, pausing to meet each man's eyes before continuing, "I want to remind you all of something I said in March, right after I returned with the title, from the balcony on the second floor of this very building. Most, if not all of you were there. I said it then and I say it now: I am very conscious of the fact that I'm the first man of our race to wear this crown and while I wear it I'll do my best to defend it against all comers. I am willing to fight anybody and won't ask for money in advance as Burns did when he fought me, nor will I make or accept any deal to fix or predetermine the outcome of any fight, as Burns' manager tried to do when they offered me far more money than the size of my purse, if I was willing to throw the fight. Make no mistake about who is in charge at the Jack Johnson camp. Only one man is and his skin is black and his name is Jack Johnson. And one last thing," the champion said, raising his palms to hold back the applause, again pausing to look directly at each man, one-by-one, "and this is something I want not just you 'all but the entire world to know. I don't answer to my manager, he answers to me. He doesn't employ me, I employ him."

For the sports it was everything, and more' that they had wanted, had hoped to hear. And without waiting for the champion to take his seat they rose to their feet as one in a hooting, shouting, stomping, frenzy of delight and approval.

Fourteen

Dawn had not yet arrived but in Manhattan every road leading to the new Queensboro Bridge was filled for miles with what seemed to be continuous streams of light. Traveling bumper-to-bumper thousands of automobiles of every description, large and small, new and old, had converged on this entry point to Hempstead Plains, the site of the fifth driving of the country's premier automobile competition, the Vanderbilt Cup race.

The brainchild of William "Willie K." Vanderbilt Jr, a racer himself and a great grandson of Cornelius Vanderbilt, the vastly wealthy steamship and railroad pioneer, the race had been created, in Willie's words, "to inspire American automobile manufacturers and drivers to overtake the Europeans in motor racing."

The Vanderbilt Cup race eventually achieved a lot more than even that ambitious goal. First run in 1904, it excited the imaginations of the horse-and-wagon populace, popularized the automobile like no other event before, led to the building of the Long Island Motor Parkway, which was not just the first highway designed exclusively for automobiles, but was also the first to use overpasses and bridges to eliminate intersections, and ushered in the automobile age in America.

But despite the wealth and eminent surname of the founder, right from the start the inaugural race had faced enormous difficulties in the form of numerous court orders and threats of injunctions. In 1904 automobiles were still exotic playthings of the rich without any apparent practical usefulness to the vast majority of the American population. Not surprisingly therefore the very idea of an automobile race on a public road was angrily opposed in many quarters. Leading the public opposition was the creator of yellow journalism, Joseph Pulitzer's sensationalist *New York World*. "In order that the speed-madness monomaniacs may drive their man-maiming engines at an excessive and illegal pace, the residents and taxpayers of the island are bidden to keep off the road," it raged editorially. "It is an extraordinary condition of affairs when a coterie of idlers, rich men's sons and gilded youth can take possession of public highways."

Among the most passionate opponents of the race were local farmers. Since the route of the first race included the Jerico, Bethpage and Hempstead Turnpikes, roads the farmers used to take their produce to market, they tried to block it, arguing unsuccessfully in court that the Nassau Board of Supervisors had acted illegally in approving the route. The death of one of the drivers, who was thrown out of his car during a practice run after a near collision with a farm wagon, raised tensions further. And residents were outraged when signs were posted by the race organizers on the day of the race warning them to, "Chain your dogs and lock up your fowls."

Some farmers threatened to carry pistols to the race and on race day bent nails were scattered on parts of the course but the guns were left at home. Instead, in the best American tradition, they made themselves quite a bit of money by offering parking spots for the enormous sum of $25 per car to the wealthy spectators who lined the route, and circulated amongst the large standing crowds selling coffee and sandwiches. The majority of the curious without automobiles had been brought in by the Long Island Railroad, which ran full trains all night. "Almost everyone who could afford a holiday took it," a newspaper of the day reported. Adding that some onlookers had arrived on horses that "chafed impatiently on the bit, as if longing for a test of speed with these new things that man had made to take their place."

Seventeen entrants had lined up on the Jerico Turnpike at the break of dawn to face the starter on that frosty October morning on a course that had been sprinkled with 90,000 gallons of petroleum to keep the dust down. Willie K arrived from the Garden City Hotel in his trademark white Mercedes and at precisely at 6.00a.m., the first car, a red Mercedes, left the starting line to the roar of the crowd and what one reporter described as "a crash of exploding oil" and flames reaching out from the sides of the car.

Five hours, 26 minutes and 45 seconds later, the almost 300 mile, 10-lap race, was over and George Heath, driving a French 90-horsepower Panhard at an average speed of 52 miles an hour, claimed the silver Tiffany cup. The rugged course proved deadly to men and machines alike and the winner was determined more by attrition than skill. The mechanic for one of the French teams was thrown out of his car and killed and by the end of just the second lap six cars—more than a third of the field—were forced to retire because of a variety of mechanical problems.

The final laps were contested by just two drivers, Heath in the Panhard and Albert Clement in the Clement-Baynard. On the ninth and penultimate lap Heath managed to open a minute and a half lead and held it to the end.

Fifty thousand spectators watched the first race and over the next two years audience participation continued to grow. The deep roar of the exotic machines, the mind-boggling speed, and the ever-present possibility of witnessing an accident or even death itself, proved an intoxicating, irresistible allure for tens of thousands of ordinary Americans. In 1905, during the second race, the largest crowds gathered at the site most likely to produce a deadly accident, an S curve near the little town of Albertson. Commenting on the obvious bloodthirstiness of the crowd, the *New York Times* noted that they were rewarded for their efforts, as "two of the most sensational smash-ups of the day occurred at this point."

This morbid fascination with death and destruction would have fatal consequences in 1906. Vanderbilt had spent liberally on crowd control measures, hiring scores of men to keep order and installing wire fencing to restrain the multitudes, thousands of whom were inclined to run into the road to get a better look at the approaching cars. But a few determined spectators refusing to be denied the best possible view brought wire-cutters to the course and succeeded in breaching the fence. At 9:00 a.m., the liberated crowd spilled into the intersection of Willis Avenue and the Jerico Turnpike, just as Elliott Shepard was approaching rapidly in his 130-horsepower Hotchkiss. The powerful machine slammed into a group of people, killing Kurt Gruner of New Jersey and injuring two small boys. Considering the speed of the vehicle and the number of spectators who had gone onto the course, the newspapers proclaimed it a miracle that only one person was killed.

A shocked and distressed Willie K. responded by canceling the race for the following year and deciding with some of his wealthy friends to build a toll road that could be used as a racecourse. A corporation, capitalized with $2.5 million dollars of stock and boasting a board of directors with such notables as John Jacob Astor and Harry Payne Whitney, was formed to spearhead the venture. Since the building of the Long Island Motor Parkway, as the new road was called, was expected to dramatically increase property values along its route, property owners who were expected to benefit were asked to donate strips of their land for the right-of-way in a massive public relations campaign led by Arthur R. Paddington, the corporation's vice president.

Despite the enormous effort, the results were decidedly mixed, with some donating and others resisting. A letter-writer to a Long Island newspaper explained the reasoning of the resisters. "Mr. Paddington thinks landowners ought to give their land to millionaires for their pleasure. And I think the millionaires should pay for what they want."

The corporation declined to comply with this demand and consequently the final route of the Parkway snaked across the island, twisting and turning around areas where it was unable to get the land it wanted.

The construction, which began in mid-1908, introduced a new method of road paving, reinforced concrete. The procedure began with two layers of heavy crushed stone, separated by a sheet of mesh wire, being laid on the roadbed. That was followed with a thin, soupy mixture of cement and sand from Jones Beach that was poured over the stones. Finally, the surface was brushed for texture. The work went quickly and by October of that year the first nine miles of the Parkway were ready for use.

The nine miles of the Parkway allowed the race organizers to create a new, circular and more controllable route that also included some sections of the Jerico Turnpike. This change and greater attention to security allowed the 1908 race to proceed without incident. That year not only did George Robertson, driving a Locomobile, become the first American driver to win the Vanderbilt Cup driving an American car, but he also established a new average speed record of 64.38 miles per hour. And so by 1909, with the continuing rapid increase in the power and capabilities of the automobile and in the experience and skill of the drivers, the expectations of motor racing enthusiasts were extremely high and the *New York Times* estimated that 250,000 spectators would show up.

The practice sessions had not disappointed with one driver, Charles C. Metz in a National car, averaging ninety miles an hour for long stretches of the course. And another, Louis Strang in a Fiat, completing one-lap of the 12.64-mile course in the sensational time of 10mins and 10 seconds, for an average speed of 72.14 miles an hour, by far the fastest time ever recorded on that track.

It was the prospect of witnessing first hand such extraordinary speed and skill that had induced Jack Johnson, the heavyweight champion of the world and aspiring racing driver, to get out of bed before six o'clock in the morning after just a few hours of sleep.

Jack Johnson opened his eyes, yawned loudly, adjusted his goggles, took a long, deep gulp of the cold morning air flowing into the big car, glanced fondly at his traveling companions, Baby John Souchon and Barron Wilkins, looked out at the heavy traffic all around him and smiled contentedly. The three cups of coffee at breakfast and the brief nap had completely reinvigorated him. The event at the Marshall Club the night before had been far more fun than he had expected and he had stayed far longer than planned, into the wee hours of the morning. He had been stunned by the unique beauty of the music and the brilliance of the young piano player, the bellhop from the train station who he vaguely remembered meeting at Grand Central because of the youngman's exceptional politeness and good manners.

And then when he learnt that all the pieces the young pianist had selected had been composed by one man, a black man at that, he had decided at the urging of several of his friends to join in the fun. Somebody had supplied a big German bass viola and although he had never heard any of Joplin's work before, was not very familiar with ragtime and was more accustomed to playing solo or lead, he was able, to the delight of the audience, to accompany Patrick quite creditably by handling his bow as lightly as he could muster, content with adding an accent here and there.

He had hardly fallen asleep before the insistent ringing of the telephone by the side of his bed had signaled that it was time to rise. He had showered and shaved in just a few minutes, practiced strokes quickly removing the barely visible stubble from both his head and face. His body was almost hairless, naturally, and his beard and the hair on his head grew so slowly that often shaving was not necessary at all. He had then doused himself liberally with expensive French cologne and dressed carefully, selecting a pale-blue shirt to go with a pearl-grey suit made of Scottish tweed and a scarf and a long, black Burberry Ulster coat.

By the time he had made his way downstairs the entire group of sports, almost all of whom had prudently left the club hours before he did, were already there, ready and raring to go. They had decided to travel together in a 26-man, 10-car convoy that had, as the morning wore on, attracted widespread attention, favorable and unfavorable, from fellow auto enthusiasts, because of the ostentatiousness of the obviously expensive late model vehicles and the color and flamboyance of the occupants.

Now, as the convoy neared the dangerous Hicksville Corner, where during the race a short cut brought the cars into the speedway, the heavyweight champion spoke for the first time since the trip began. "Barron," he said, sitting straight up and looking through the window of the front passenger seat at the gathering crowd and then at his friend in the driver's seat, "judging from all those people out there I guess we're almost there."

"Yeah, Wilkins replied, "but we're going to park as near to the grandstand as possible. It's cold as hell outside; I don't know how those people standing out in the open can stand it."

"It's too late in the year," Baby John explained from the

backseat, "They used to have it at the beginning of the month."

"Well then I guess these will help today," Johnson answered, smiling broadly, as he pointed to the bottles of wine in the side pockets of his coat. "Where are the rest of them," he added, directing his question to Baby John. "I bought enough for everybody, more than a hundred bottles."

"I already gave some to the fellows champ," the big man responded, "Some of them didn't want to wait until we got here. But we got plenty left in the back."

The sun was shining brightly from a nearly cloudless sky when the men exited the car but a bitter west wind, blowing in at fifteen miles an hour, was sending all but the most hardy and dedicated auto enthusiasts scurrying for shelter.

"Jesus Christ," the heavyweight champion exclaimed, furiously stamping his booted feet, as he and his entourage of sports filed into the half-filled grandstand, entry into which they had paid the substantial sum of $50 per person, "I can hardly feel my goddamned feet."

"I propose gentlemen," Wilkins said, gravely, raising an unopened bottle of wine as soon as they had been ushered to their assigned box seats, "That we begin with a toast to the success of our coming venture and to a good day today."

The men had hardly swallowed their first sips and people were still pouring into the grandstand when the first thunderous roars announced the imminent start of the race. Most of the drivers had left the comfort of their beds long before daylight and the sun had just started peeping over the eastern horizon when many began their practice runs. Now, in the final minutes of preparation, the combined assault of twenty-five engines cranking and roaring sounded far more like the start of a battle than an automobile race.

Except for the biting wind, it was an ideal day for the race. The lowering temperature had chased away the mist that had hung over flat stretches of the course for most of the week, and the air was as clear as a bell even before the sun was an hour high. And, except for some grumbling about the turn from the Hicksville-Westbury Road back to the Parkway, which forced most of the cars to slow to ten or fifteen miles an hour and a patch of soft road from

Hicksville to Westbury, almost to a man the drivers had proclaimed their general satisfaction with the course.

Although all of the cars were lined up together only the most powerful fifteen were entered for the twenty-two-lap, 278.08-mile Vanderbilt, the others would contest the shorter Wheatley Hill and Massepequa Sweepstakes. First away in small clouds of smoke and fire were the Massapequa and Wheatley Hills contestants, who were sent off, one by one, at 15-second intervals. Then throbbing with impatient power and growling ominously the big Vanderbilt entrants moved, also one by one, to the starting line.

In the number one position, Louis Strang in the leading Fiat exploded away in a screaming, tire-burning display of raw power that brought the spectators in the now three-quarter-filled grandstand leaping to their feet in awe and excitement. Right behind and also blindly fast off the line were a Simplex, followed by another Fiat, then a Knox, an Atlas, and so on, for four more thunderous, smoke-belching minutes.

As the final racers tore madly down the speedway the heavyweight champion and most of the rest of the grandstand remained on their feet, transfixed. "Damn, damn, damn, hot diggety damn, that's some serious speed" a delighted Jackson shouted to no one in particular.

"You know what that calls for, don't you?" Wilkins asked, his deep tenor tones rising easily above the din.

"Another round" Johnson ventured, smiling, as they retook their seats.

"Damn right," his friend replied. Then with the eager assistance of Baby John and two other members of the festive party, several new bottles were popped open and their sparkling golden content poured carefully, almost reverentially, into the silver-plated, kidney-shaped hipflasks that each of the sports had brought along for this very purpose.

The pouring done Wilkins raised his arm as the replenished flasks were passed around the box. "Alright fellows, what's the toast this time," he asked.

Behind him, elegantly turned out in a full length, fur-trimmed leather motoring coat and goggles, Curly rose to his feet and made a counter proposal. "How about a wager instead," he suggested.

"Yes, but on what," another sport responded.

"Let's make it really interesting, how about the first car across the line at the end of on each lap," Johnson proposed to the smiles and nods of approval of his entourage. "Okay then," he added, his voice full of confidence: "I select Strang, the one who went first in the Fiat, he's the best driver and he has the fastest car, I don't believe anybody can beat him." Then, turning to Baby John, he briskly ordered him "to take the bets."

But on the track the champion's pick was about to disappoint his numerous supporters. On the very first lap a large stone that had either been thrown by somebody or had been dislodged from an embankment smashed into the radiator, doing so much damage that it would be a full two hours before he limped back, disabled and disgusted.

Instead, Louis Chevrolet, in a Buick, the last driver to leave the line, roared ahead to take the lead on the second lap and held it until the fourth, when he increased it even further with a lightning fast 9 minutes and 47 seconds lap, or about 76 miles an hour, a new course record. But the brutal pace was simply unsustainable. A cylinder went on the very next lap and his day too was officially over. A string of disastrous accidents followed, one after the other: The Simplex left with a broken shaft, another Fiat cracked its crank pin, the National car lost a wheel, a Marmon retired with radiator trouble, the Isotta broke its steering gear, and the Apperson turned over.

Outside the grandstand the largest crowds had gathered at the Westbury turn, the most dangerous of the course. There the skidding wheels of the speeding vehicles hurled volleys of stone and great clouds of earth and blue smoke at the enthralled spectators. Despite or because of the obvious danger, solid walls of people lined both sides of the curve for hundreds of yards and early in the race hundreds of them had surged onto to the road. Only the energetic work of an extra force of policemen, dispatched for the purpose after complaints by some of the drivers, had succeeded in getting them out of the way.

Long lines of automobiles, mainly expensive limousines,

stood side by side, packed in together as closely as they could get. And on their roofs in camp chairs sat the privileged young men and women they had brought. At the very apex of the curve, where the crowd was at its thickest and deepest, nothing separated the spectators from the hurtling missiles but a log fence and the uncanny skill of the drivers. Ray Harroun, driving a Marmon, somehow managed to maintain some control even after losing a rear wheel during a violent skid that forced the drivers immediately behind him into their own heart-stopping maneuvers. Perhaps most remarkably of all, William Knipper in a Chalmers-Detroit, driving furiously to make up ground after a slow start and encountering the same treacherous conditions, drew gasps and cheers by making the demanding turn on just one front wheel.

In the grandstand the heavyweight champion of the world was beginning to lose interest in the race and in the little betting game he had devised. Not only had he failed to correctly select a single winner but his attention had been diverted by something, or more accurately someone, far more intriguing, a beautiful, dark-haired young woman sitting nearby, who had not only noticed his less than subtle interest but with an occasional glance of the briefest duration in his direction, was seeming to signal that she might even welcome it.

She was decidedly not, Johnson had quickly surmised from a rapid but expert inventory of her tasteful, expensive clothes and air of genteel sophistication, the kind of white woman he had generally been successful with. But, then, he quickly reminded himself, he had not always been the heavyweight champion of the world.

But just going over and introducing himself might not be the best thing either, he decided. He knew enough about her world, he figured, to know that the right people got properly introduced. And so, after a small, wry smile in her direction and a whispered conference with his friend Barron Wilkins, both men got to their feet and went searching for someone who might do the honors.

Johnson was quickly recognized and almost immediately surrounded by well-wishers and the merely curious, one of whom was Lester Walton, or as the masthead on his weekly column in the

New York Age insisted, Lester A. Walton. The erudite, light-skinned Walton had only met Johnson, briefly, on a handful of occasions but Wilkins and himself had known each other for several years. More importantly, as he soon revealed, he had not only met the young lady, who they had discreetly pointed out, through mutual acquaintances but had gotten to know her quite well.

In addition to his column and a feature called "In the Sporting World," Walton was the paper's theatrical critic and it was in that role, he explained, that he had made her acquaintance. She had appeared on the stage herself and although a resident of Long Island was a regular visitor to the city during the theatre season. The bad news, he added, was that she, Mrs. Etta Terry Duryea, was her name, was married, to the scion of a prominent Long Island family; the good news was that they were no longer living together.

"Well, that's certainly good to know," Wilkins replied, "Jack has not been able to keep his eyes off her and I think she's looked back, kind of quick and sneaky like, a couple of times."

"She's pretty special gentlemen," Walton said, looking both men in the eye, "not just beautiful but a real lady, from a very good family, if you know what I mean."

"Look Lester," Johnson replied, holding the journalist's hard stare, his tone a bit defensive, "I know my reputation, what people say about me and women. But believe this, whatever you may have heard about me, I know a real lady when I see one and I saw that right away from just looking at Mrs. Duryea. That's one of the reasons I'd really like to meet her, in the right way. That's why I'm here talking to you about this Lester. Believe me; I don't normally go around asking to be introduced to women. That's not normally my style. I can usually take care of that myself and pretty good too. But I agree with you Lester…totally, that she's pretty special, maybe even very special. She's just the kind of woman I'm interested in at this stage of my life."

For an almost too long, almost uncomfortable moment neither the journalist nor the prize fighter would break their polite stare down. Finally, the journalist, having made his point, looked away and after a short pause responded quietly, "Okay Jack, good enough, I just wanted you to know that I think of her as a friend, let's go meet Mrs. Duryea."

"Lead the way Lester, we're right behind you," Wilkins replied, and then winked at the heavyweight champion, who not only did not respond to the wink but was, very uncharacteristically, smiling nervously, as the three men made their way through the thinning grandstand crowd.

On the track it was the fifteenth lap and only three cars were still in serious contention, Knipper in his Chalmers-Detroit, Edward Parker in a Fiat and Harry Grant in an Alco. But as the cars roared past the grandstand, hood to hood, mere inches separating them, the heavyweight champion barely noticed, far too preoccupied with the imminent introduction, far too busy thinking about just what to say.

As they neared their destination, Walton, who was walking slightly ahead, suddenly stopped and turned around to face his companions. "Gentlemen, she's not there" he gravely announced, I think she may have already left." The biting wind that had not eased throughout the day and the dwindling competition, had hastened the departure of thousands of spectators, from all along the course and even from the grandstand.

Johnson, following immediately behind, groaned softly, undisguised disappointment and dismay written all over his face. I can't believe it, he thought to himself, feeling sick to his stomach.

But just as he was about to thank the journalist and suggest to Wilkins that they also leave, Walton smiled and pointed to his left: "No," he said, "There she is, over there."

Etta, although she was too well brought up to let it show unduly, had been fully aware not only of Johnson's interest but also of the difficulty he was having figuring how to approach her. She would later tell friends that she had found his shyness both surprising and endearing. Like millions of other Americans she had read and heard quite a great deal about the new heavyweight champion, most of it unsavory, especially his relationships with women, white women in particular. And so she had been expecting someone quite different from the man she eventually met. At first, with his big entourage and noisy entrance, he had seemed to fit almost every negative stereotype of the Negro prizefighter she had ever heard.

There had been, however, one pleasant surprise right from the start. In person, he was not only more attractive than his photographs had indicated, but his lithe, broad-shouldered, athletic build, was the very opposite of the overly bulky muscularity she had pictured and so disliked. She had also been favorably impressed with his good taste and sense of style; from her point of view he was neither too stodgy nor too flamboyant, just right. His Ulster coat and the tartan-patterned Burberry scarf he had selected to go with it were just absolutely perfect and adorable. But, more than any other quality, what drew her to him so strongly was the raw power and strength of his masculinity. This was a man, she knew, who was not afraid of any man or anything. If she was going to be safe anywhere, she knew from deep inside, that it would be with him.

She had sensed when he left his seat with that enormous friend of his that he was trying to figure out a way of meeting her without just coming over and introducing himself. She had gotten up from where she had been sitting with some old family friends to make the meeting easier for both of them. She had already decided that she was going to make it clear that she welcomed his attention and wanted to see him again. And she didn't want them to start talking just yet and of course there was the question of his race. She was certain it was going to be a problem but, she had made up her mind that she was just going to follow her heart and ignore that kind of advice.

Now as she watched the approaching trio, Etta smiled warmly and took a few steps towards them. Lester was a really good friend and a good guy. Having him make the introductions would make everything a lot easier. "Hello Lester," she said brightly in a low but clear voice as they hugged briefly, "It's good to see you, I had no idea you were interested in auto racing."

"You're looking really great Etta, this weather may be too cold for the rest of us but it certainly agrees with you," Walton replied, his eyes sparkling, Johnson and Wilkins temporarily forgotten. Something's up, he told himself, I haven't seen her look like this before; the sadness is gone, she's glowing. Either she's met somebody new recently or Jack Johnson is truly the luckiest man in the world.

Then he heard something in her voice that had not been there before, a lightness, a suppressed excitement, and he knew. "Well Lester," he heard her saying, almost singing, "aren't you going to introduce your friends."

"Of course Etta," he replied smoothly, smiling easily, "please excuse my poor manners, but for a moment I was overcome by your beauty." Then turning to Johnson and Wilkins, who were standing behind him in a somewhat awkward silence, he said, "Gentlemen, this is my dear friend, the lovely and accomplished Mrs. Etta Duryea," and then turning back to Etta, added, pointing first to Johnson who was in front of Wilkins, "Etta, this is Mr. Jack Johnson, the new heavyweight boxing champion of the world, as you perhaps have heard, and our friend, Mr. Barron Wilkins, who is, although he will deny it, one of the most influential men of our race in the country."

Although she gracefully greeted both men her eyes never left Johnson's face. "Mr. Johnson, Mr. Wilkins," she said, extending a slim, gloved hand, "I hope you've been enjoying yourselves, the racing has been very exciting but it's been so very cold."

How large his hands are, the hands of a fighter, she thought, as her hand disappeared into his. But not his eyes, his eyes are gentle, sensitive, maybe too sensitive for what he does, she noted with surprise. He's not nearly the person he pretends to be, the toughness, the arrogance they accuse him of, she concluded, was just a shell, a wall to hide his true feelings behind.

For Jack Johnson, as he looked into Etta's large, dark eyes for the first time, time itself seemed to be standing still. Everything had slowed down, as it always did at the moments of his most intense experiences. It was one of his greatest strengths in the ring, for when the action was the most furious, when he was in the most danger, he was at his calmest, his best. Now, as he brought her hand to his lips for the briefest and gentlest of kisses, everything was clear and he knew that it was a moment he would never forget as long as he lived. She sees me, he exulted, as their eyes met in a flash of mutual recognition, me, not the fighter, not the heavyweight champion of the world, just me. Hundreds of words flooded his brain; there was so much he wanted to say, questions to ask, secrets to tell, but he heard his tongue, unbidden, reply in a voice that sounded only vaguely like his own.

"Let me assure you Mrs. Duryea," it said, "that this already has been the most enjoyable day of my life."

For the next thirty minutes the two were inseparable. The steady Grant in the Alco crossed the line first ahead of Parker in the Fiat, but neither Jack nor Etta looked nor cared. Exactly what they said to each other nobody knows, except that they exchanged telephone numbers and agreed to stay in touch and to meet again as soon as possible.

Fifteen

George Lewis Rickard took another look at himself in the big, gilt-edged mirror, poured a liberal splash of aftershave lotion from the blue-green bottle into his well tended palms and vigorously slapped his clean shaven, unwhiskered face, slightly raising the color in his tanned cheeks. Unsatisfied still, he carefully straightened his blue and red silk tie, placed his black silk tophat on his short-cropped, slightly graying hair, frowned and wrinkled his nose at the result. Then, after another long and critical examination, he fixed the offending headpiece at a more rakish angle by pulling it slightly lower over his eyes. Finally, with everything to his satisfaction, he grinned appreciatively at his own splendid image and stepped briskly out of his luxurious suite at the Waldorf Astoria.

He had dressed carefully; reluctantly rejecting his first choice, the mid-calf-length, unfitted brown and green checked wool overcoat, as too flamboyant for his purposes. The British, knee-length, double-breasted wool overcoat he was wearing, with its large astrakhan collar, cuffless sleeves and flap pockets, he had finally decided, perfectly complemented the three-piece checked suit and was just right for the impression he wanted to make: fashionable but serious. Few things irritated him more than the tendency in the Eastern papers to describe him, and thereby dismiss him, as some kind of picturesque cowboy.

While it was true that he had moved to Texas from Missouri as a teenager and had worked briefly as a horse wrangler and then as a frontier marshal, he had not lived in the Lone Star state for fifteen years. Since then he had traveled widely in and out of the country, tried his hand, without too much success, at mining, and then, finally, had made himself a lot of money in Alaska, running gambling establishments where more successful miners lost their gold to him.

But in 1903, tired of the cold and snow, he had moved his operation to the little mining town of Goldfield, Nevada, and opened the lavish Northern Saloon, a gambling palace which was soon raking in some ten thousand dollars a day. He had also become a successful boxing promoter. First, by staging amateur bouts as a way of attracting customers to his Alaskan saloons: And then, despite his lack of experience, by putting together a title bout between the two claimants for the disputed lightweight crown, the black Joe Gans and the white Oscar "Battling" Nelson.

As had been true of his amateur bouts in Alaska, Rickard's primary motive was the promotion of his Nevada gambling establishment. Making some money on the fight itself would be nice but putting his little town on the map would be far nicer and, of course, ultimately far more profitable. Although he, decidedly, was not, by the standards of the time, a racist himself, Rickard was fully aware that most white Americans were. So, to maximize interest in the fight, he decided to take full advantage of that dismal fact by promoting it as a battle for racial supremacy.

But, even that by itself, he decided, was not enough; he would settle for nothing less than commanding the attention of the sporting public like no other promoter had ever done before. Accordingly, the purse for the fight was set at the record sum of $30,000, a stupendous figure at the time for any weight class, unheard-of for a lightweight bout, and the entire amount, in gold coins, was stacked in his front window as dramatic proof of his means and sincerity. And to guarantee an endless stream of positive, invaluable, prefight stories, the wily promoter effectively courted the press by handing out twenty-dollar gold pieces to grateful and often thirsty sportswriters, whom, invariably, spent them right away in his saloon.

The strategy worked brilliantly. The eight thousand paying fans that turned up doubled the population of the little town overnight. The fight itself was long and savage, with Gans, the black fighter, getting the nod after forty brutal rounds. Across the country, here and there, in places like New York and Chicago, the Negro's triumph triggered arguments and fist fights between celebrating blacks and angry whites.

Rickard's attention to his dress was only one aspect of a program of relentless self-improvement begun several years earlier. Practice had modulated his diction, eliminating, at least when he chose, almost every trace of the range and the frontier. Extensive reading had considerably bolstered his meager formal education. His father had died when he was only ten and he had made himself a success by his own relentless efforts. Like many other successful men of the age Tex, as he was generally known, believed fervently in the Darwinian notion that society was the stage of a constant struggle to determine the weak and the strong, to pick winners and losers; and that government intervention, except for legitimate purposes such as the building of railroads, was almost always unwelcome meddling that interfered with the logical and efficient rendering of that salutary verdict.

His natural drive and ambition had made him rich and the attention and money that boxing promotion brought had proved addicting. Not surprisingly, the opportunity to stage the biggest fight in the history of the world proved irresistible. Richard had been galvanized into action by the terms of the articles signed by Johnson and Jeffries, opening the bidding to all comers. The most important qualification, it was clear, was the ability to guarantee large sums to the fighters and their representatives. In that game, he figured, he could play as well as anyone.

He had quickly devised a bold game plan, the first step of which had been to locate the champion and induce him to sign some kind of personal agreement. With the fight still nine months away and money still a problem, after leaving New York Johnson had returned to the stage, in Pittsburgh, in a revue called the Cracker-Jacks. Although Etta had aroused powerful emotions of a more tender kind than was customary for him, satisfying a less romantic, baser passion was no less necessary. For that he still had his old girlfriend, Belle Schreiber, who was with him at Frank Sutton's hotel the afternoon in late November when the intrepid promoter dropped by to introduce himself.

Johnson's welcome was warm and eager. The men had never met but Rickard's reputation had preceded him and it was a very favorable, fighter-friendly one. Everybody had made money from the Gans-Nelson bout and Gans had used some of his to open the Goldfield, an opulent café in Baltimore named in celebration of the site of his epic victory, and to which Johnson had been a frequent and conspicuous visitor.

The promoter had quickly sketched out his plan to make the champion and "Mrs. Johnson" very, very rich. The Goldfield fight, he had explained, had been a mere dress rehearsal for the upcoming showdown between he, Johnson, the "Negro's Deliverer" and Jeffries, the "Hope of the White Race." Rickard had pointed out that not only had the film of the champion's fight with Stanley Ketchel made hundreds of thousands of dollars, but it had also whetted the appetites of whites who desperately wanted to see him beaten. It was therefore inevitable, he had argued to the receptive champion, that the one between Jeffries and himself would make a great deal of money.

Although the bids were not due for more than another month, Rickard then spelled out the details of his proposal for the captivated champion and his "wife:" A purse of $101,000, by far the largest in boxing history; two-thirds of the film rights to be shared by the fighters; a $5,000 bonus for Johnson on signing ($2,500 in cash, to be paid immediately and the remaining half before he stepped into the ring); and the "finest sealskin coat he could find for "Mrs. Johnson." Without even bothering to consult with his erstwhile manager, George Little, Johnson, completely sold on the golden-tongued promoter, signed on the spot.

The estimable gentlemen of the New York press are due for quite a surprise tomorrow, Rickard thought, a small smile on his thin-lipped mouth, as he strode through the magnificent, marble lobby and turned into the long, cavernous, mirrored corridor that had been built to connect the original Waldorf to its recent Astoria addition. To Rickard's stunned surprise and delight, "Peacock Alley," as the corridor was popularly known, was filled with some of the most extraordinarily attractive and fashionably dressed women he had ever seen.

Dozens or scores of them he knew not which, being much too distracted to make such a fine distinction, each, it seemed to him, more beautiful than the previous, sauntered slowly past in a surreal and seemingly endless fashion parade. A few even carried parasols, although even outside the sun had already set. Many were in small groups; some had equally fashionable male escorts and a few of the most confident strutted on their own, unwilling perhaps to share any of the spotlight.

Most were too preoccupied with their own reflected images to acknowledge the admiration of the many men who stopped, or at least paused, to stare. But one particularly bold and lissome lass, with pouty red lips and shoulder length hair the color of burnished gold, rewarded Rickard's undisguised interest with a long look and a smile so inviting that only the importance of his mission and his iron discipline kept him moving determinedly forward.

He had little doubt, he thought, wrenching his head around and his mind back to business, with his agreement with Johnson in place, that he would win the bid and that the fight would be the biggest, grandest, highest-grossing, most-attended sporting spectacle the world had ever seen. And that everybody involved, including the fighters, his financial backers, and he himself, would make more money than anybody had ever before made from a sporting event. Afterall, look at what happened with the Jeffries tour. Even he had been surprised at the vast turnout across the country. It had been truly extraordinary, far better than anybody could have predicted.

White Americans were clearly avid to get the crown back. He had been reliably informed that the gross receipts were going to exceed the $200,000 mark, far more money than any fight had ever taken in. It had seemed an act of sheer folly when the William Morris Company had guaranteed the former champion at least $50,000 for a series of theatrical performances. But, from what he had heard, not only would Jeffries' share exceed the guaranteed amount but that, also, the company's share would be close to $150,000.

Even he had been surprised how well his meeting with Johnson had gone. The champion was quite a fellow, he had discovered. Nothing at all like his public reputation, or anything like the vast majority of the Negroes he had encountered in either this country or in South Africa. Most of them had tended, in his opinion, to be a little bit beaten down, a little bit subservient in manner. Although he had not, consciously anyway, formed any definitive opinion about them as a group, he had more or less accepted the prevailing view.

Apart from Johnson's obvious intelligence, what he had found the most surprising and what had impressed him most was the way the man handled himself. His ease with his new role, as if he had been born to it, was startling. The contrast with Jeffries was simply amazing. Even at his prime Jeffries had been uncomfortable with the attention and now, if anything, he had gotten worse. Jeffries' unease with attention was one of the reasons he had his doubts that the white fighter could win back the title. He had seen a few of his fights and there was no question that the man had been a great champion, but he was beginning to suspect that he was simply one of those people who did not handle pressure very well. There was, already, a brittleness about him that did not bode well for his ability to cope with all the craziness that lay ahead.

The only possible barrier to winning the bid, he had figured, was Jeffries' relationship with Jack Gleason. Rumor had it that the ex-champion had also signed a secret deal but for a signing bonus of $10,000, twice what he had offered Johnson. If that was true, he'd have to get the black champion another $5,000, and quickly. Nothing could be worse for their relationship than if Johnson discovered on his own that he had only been given a half of what the white fighter had received. The newspaper man he was about to meet had been described by people, whose judgment he trusted, as perhaps the best in the city. As somebody who'd know, if anybody on the outside knew, what was really happening in Jeffries' camp.

All the other loose ends that he was aware of had been taken care of. The other bidders were not really a concern, except perhaps for the rumors floating around that the Eastern promoters were going to pool their resources and form some kind of syndicate. The Easterners were at a distinct disadvantage because the various state laws made it easier to stage a title bout out West;

but that kind of arrangement might just give them a fighting chance to compete. He was hoping that that O'Brien fellow, the reporter, would also be able to shed some light on that subject. But, just to make sure, if all of that was not enough, he had a little surprise up his sleeve; call it the icing on the cake.

To Daniel O'Brien, meeting Rickard for the first time, the fight promoter seemed to defy almost every conventional image of his profession and region. As a species, the fight promoters he had previously met were, generally, repulsive, overweight, overdressed, untrustworthy, double-talking confidence men. Real Westerners, a category from which he had excluded most Californians, he had imagined, wore string ties with cowboy boots and hats. Rickard, on the other hand, was as tall and lean as any cowboy. But, as he noted, watching the sharp-featured Nevada resident being led over to his table by the pretty, young blonde hostess, that, except for his dark tan and a certain swagger in his step, the boxing promoter could easily have been mistaken for a wealthy English businessman.

"Welcome to New York Mister Rickard," Daniel began, rising slightly and gesturing unnecessarily at the chair across the table from his, which was already being pulled away from the table by the pretty, young hostess, whom, he noted, appreciatively, was even prettier, younger, blonder and bustier, seen up close.

"Thank you miss, you are very kind, and thank you sir, you are also very kind" Rickard said, removing his silken top hat with a sweep of his right hand. Then bowing slightly with a sort of old-fashioned courtesy that seemed a curious amalgamation of Western and European mannerisms, he smiled, alternately, at the suddenly flustered young woman, who blushed appropriately, and his bemused host.

"Well, Mister Rickard, what do you think of our weather, a good bit colder than what you are accustomed to I assume," Daniel replied in as expansive a tone as he muster, as he resumed his seat and gestured to the hovering waiter to come over to the table. The newspaper reporter was not a voluble man but his guest's elaborate manners seemed to require more than the standard greeting for such occasions, which for Daniel was rarely more than a brief, mumbled, "How are you." He normally preferred getting down to business as quickly as possible.

"Please call me Tex, all my friends do," Rickard responded, as he settled into his chair, looking directly at Daniel and smiling his dazzling straight-toothed smile. "You know of course," he added, leaning forward slightly to give the reporter his undivided attention, and sounding as if he sincerely believed him to be the very fountain of wisdom and information, "that I was once a gold miner in Alaska. But that was a long time ago and you're right, I've grown accustomed to the moderate climate of our western states."

"I may have picked up some vague rumors about your wide travels but they were more related to Texas than to Alaska," Daniel replied, his face registering his surprise at the Nevadan's clipped tone and cultivated manners. Then before Rickard could respond quickly added, "I hope I am not inquiring too much but the newspaperman in me can hardly resist... your tone, your speech seems very, well, un-Western, frankly... more British than American."

"Probably more South African," Rickard answered, smiling even more broadly," I spent several years there in the gold business, others have also made mention of it, my peculiar way of speaking, I mean."

"You are a man of many surprises, Mister Rickard," Daniel replied a bit churlishly, unable to prevent a slight accusatory tone from creeping into his voice. The man in front of him, it was becoming increasingly clear, was very different from the one he had expected to meet and he was already sensing that dealing with the fight promoter would not be the simple, straightforward business he had expected. He had been prepared for the normal self-serving bullshit that they all served up as a matter of course. That regular kind of crap he was always able to smell right away but Rickard's version, he was certain, would be harder to detect and could therefore be infinitely more dangerous.

" Daniel, it is Daniel, isn't it, please, call me Tex," Rickard interrupted, the big smile getting bigger, the sincere tone getting even more sincere, "Only people who don't like me, or who I don't like call me Mr. Rickard." He could sense Daniel's discomfort and he understood its source; that kind of response was not unusual for those with preconceived notions about people like him, and he had learned to use their confusion to his advantage.

"Very well... Tex," Daniel answered, his voice strained, sounding as if he thought he was being imposed upon. He was certain that Rickard's friendliness was contrived, artificial, designed to get his own way, to discourage tough questions, but he would not be deterred. "But," he said, his tone deliberately brusque, his manner, all-business, "Let me ask you about the matter that brought you here and will be decided tomorrow. My paper has been reliably informed that none of the responsible Western promoters will offer more than $75,000. Is that true, would you care to comment?

What the hell is wrong with this guy, Rickard thought to himself, as he listened in bemused bafflement to Daniel's formally structured question. What an asshole, invites me for drinks and then makes little speeches, what's the fucking point. At home not even a cub reporter would be so goddamned stupid. Everybody knows that you at least wait until your guest has had a drink or two. You don't just pounce, my god, don't these people know anything. But there was no use getting annoyed, he told himself, as he continuing smiling amiably, it was just their way. And, anyway, the business at hand was too important for petty piques. He too had questions he wanted answered and he had a few messages to send. He could play.

"You're aware aren't you," Rickard began, making his tone even crisper and more clipped, "that Jeffries' tour has already grossed more than $200,000, and the Johnson-Ketchel fight film has earned even more than that. There's never been anything like this fight in the history of sporting annals, nothing even close."

"Does that mean that the Western promoters will be bidding higher than $75,000," Daniel persisted. Then, after throwing a quick glance and waving a beckoning finger at the still hovering waiter, added, "What would you like, I'm having whiskey."

"The same," Rickard replied and for the first time leaned back in his chair and relaxed slightly, at least the man was going to observe some of the required rituals. "I can assure you," he said, looking directly at his questioner, "that all of the, as you put it, responsible Western promoters will be placing bids in excess of $100,000 tomorrow—at least that is what my colleagues have led me to expect—and some," he added, leaning slightly forward and whispering, an odd half smile on his thin-lipped mouth, "may even be significantly higher than that."

The surprise, perhaps even shock on the newspaperman's ruddy face completely restored Rickard's good humor. "Now it's your turn to divulge some information Daniel," he began, the dazzling smile returning, How high are the responsible New York promoters prepared to go, we've been reliably informed that they might be thinking of throwing in together to form some kind of syndicate, which is, I suppose, the only way they think they may be able to compete against us."

"Well, of course I do not pretend to know their precise intentions," Daniel replied, his voice and manner formal and unconvincing. Asking not answering questions was his forte and Rickard had been so apparently open and candid that he found it hard to believe that the man could be brazenly lying about a matter, which would either be confirmed or disproved the very next day. And yet what he had just said was so different from what he had expected to hear, that the newspaperman hardly knew what to think. "Why, they are no more willing to take newspaper reporters into their confidence than you and your fellow Westerners are," he added, a little bit defensively.

"Come now Daniel," Rickard said pleasantly as he took a tiny sip of the whiskey that had just been placed in front of him, "I was level with you, you might just need some more information from me one day, in fact before very long, maybe even tomorrow."

"Just let us say then that a bid of a $100,000 is a lot of money," Daniel grudgingly replied, knowing very well that we was either being bribed or threatened or both.

"Too much?" Rickard asked, arching one eyebrow, his tone gently mocking. Raising his glass he took another small sip and watched the play of emotions on Daniel's florid face.

The man drank as if he didn't really like whiskey, as if he was merely being polite, or probably like somebody who preferred to remain sober while his companions grew increasingly unable to restrain their answers to his clever questions, Daniel thought darkly before emptying his glass and acknowledging: "Yes Tex, too much, far too much."

"Another," Rickard asked with a big smile, pointing to the newspaperman's empty glass, "the rest of the night is on me. There is so much we need to talk about."

"Another," Daniel agreed. The newspaperman would say "another," and "another", many, many more times that night. In fact far more times than he had planned or would be able to remember the next day.

If Daniel had needed any further proof of the public's enormous interest in the Johnson-Jeffries contest, the huge crowd of onlookers, hordes of newspaper reporters, and battery of cameramen gathered in and around Negeli's Hotel in Hoboken on the chilly, overcast afternoon of November 30, 1909, was more than enough evidence for even as confirmed a skeptic as himself. Throngs had begun gathering at the tunnel stations and ferry landings before nine o'clock that morning.

At the nearby Myers Hotel, the initial site of the meeting, men, women and even children had elbowed savagely with rugged laborers in an attempt to catch a glimpse of the principals. The unruly crowd, many of them clearly inebriated at even that early time of the day, loudly and often profanely demanding that each bidding promoter be pointed out, had flocked into the corridors and café of the Myers.

Daniel had, literally, fallen out of bed several hours earlier, just before 10 o'clock, more than two hours later than was his custom, with a nasty, throbbing headache and a heavy, furry tongue that had rebelliously refused to do what it was told. A good, solid breakfast was his tried and tested antidote for a night of drinking but that morning the very thought of food had revolted him. But the passage of time, the chilly air and a little exercise--his home was a little more than thirty minutes away-- had helped to ease the throbbing pain that had gripped his temples and relentlessly burrowed its way into the sockets of his eyes. And so, by the time he arrived at the waterfront hotel, he had started believing that feeling like a human being again was not beyond the realm of possibility.

But much of what had happened the night before was at best a blur and after the fourth or fifth drink, a total blank. Fearful of what he might have revealed to Rickard, he had tried unsuccessfully all morning to reconstruct their meeting. He recalled, dimly, at some stage, repeatedly assuring himself that he had earned, for reasons he could no longer remember, the luxury of one night of overindulgence. Plus, he had reasoned with himself, the bidding, which had been originally scheduled to take place at the Albany Hotel in Manhattan, had been shifted across the Hudson and the additional time it would have taken to travel to the city could be used instead for recuperation.

Just before leaving for the meeting with Rickard, Murphy, the owner of the Albany and the stakeholder of the bids, had called to inform him of the change of venue. According to Murphy, William Travers Jerome, the city's District Attorney, had sent a police inspector to remind him that both boxing and the promotion of boxing matches were still illegal in New York, and warned that if the bids were opened anywhere in Manhattan that he and everybody involved would be promptly arrested.

The crowds had eventually spilled over into a banquet hall that had been prepared for the bidders and reporters. To escape the chaos the proceedings were moved across the street to Negeli's Hotel. There, after a brief but spirited battle with broad shouldered hotel employees, some two hundred persons had been wedged into the relatively limited quarters of the Hoboken Quartet Club. Mixed cheers and insults, with the insults exceeding the cheers, at least in volume, had greeted the arrival of the impeccably dressed black champion, who announced, to slightly more cheers, that every bidder would be given a chance and that the fighters themselves would make the final decision.

Johnson and a small party that included Barron Wilkins and his manager George Little, had traveled by specially arranged ferryboat from Manhattan that morning. Aboard the same vessel had been Murphy himself, Sam Berger representing Jeffries, bidders Rickard, Jack Gleason, and Eddie Graney of San Francisco, Tom McCarey of Los Angeles, and Phil King, the American representative of Hugh McIntosh, the Australian promoter who had staged the Johnson-Burns bout, and scores of newspapermen. But the man the crowds had really come to see, the people's champion, Jim Jeffries, was absent, to their intense and vocal disappointment, because of what was said to be a prior engagement in Pittsburgh.

It had taken Daniel several minutes and the usual brandishing of his press credentials to slowly work his way to the front of the dense, unyielding crowd. By then, Murphy, who was to open the sealed bids, had already taken his seat at the head of a large conference table in the center of the room. Seated at his right was Jack Johnson and George Little and on his left, Sam Berger and Tom McCarey. Too nervous to sit quietly, the other principals, including Gleason and Rickard, wandered restlessly among the newsmen and the onlookers. Conspicuous by their absence were Jim Coffroth and the unnamed New York promoters, who only the day before had been threatening to form a syndicate to outbid the Westerners.

The inside word from many of the more knowledgeable sporting men in the crowd had installed Jack Gleason as the prohibitive favorite. Reliable rumor had it that not only did he already have Jeffries under contract, but that he and the other leading Bay City promoter, Jim Coffroth, had already reached an agreement. McCarey had promoted several of Johnson's early fights and was expected to put in a large bid. But his longtime relationship with the champion was seen as more of a liability than an asset, because it was wellknown that the champion harbored grudges against many of the people he had done business with before he won the title.

The man had a long memory and slights were rarely forgiven. Graney and McIntosh were given little chance and few had even heard of Rickard, except that Johnson liked him but that hardly mattered since it was Jeffries not Johnson, conventional wisdom had it, who would have the most say in selecting the promoter.

Finally, with the crowd growing restive and a few not altogether sober voices calling for the proceedings to begin forthwith, Murphy, who had left his seat to confer with the promoters not at the table, sat down again, wrapped a broad palm around the fresh glass of water that had just been placed in front of him, took a tiny sip, and announced in a stentorian voice that the bids were ready and would now be opened. With that announcement a hush enveloped the room, and except for an audible intake of breath here and there, and the rustling of papers as Murphy struggled to open the first envelope, the silence was almost eerie.

The first bid opened was from the short, spherical Eddie Graney of the Tuxedo Club of San Francisco. As Murphy spelled out the details—80 percent of the gross receipts to go to the contestants, supported by a guarantee of $75,000 and the entire picture privileges—the more knowledgeable sporting men smirked, whispered and looked knowingly at each other. Graney's bid was a worthwhile one and under different circumstances might even have been a winning one, but given the stakes it was not nearly enough. He had confirmed what they already knew; he could not win.

At the announcement that the second bid would be from the pre-bidding favorite Jack Gleason, who it was explained would be bidding jointly with Jim Coffroth, silence again descended on the proceedings. Gasps of surprise greeted the revelations of the details, a guarantee of $125,000, but with all of the privileges including the picture proceeds going to the promoters. The fight they added would be held on July 4, 1910 at the Colana Club. Unlike the almost unanimous agreement that greeted Graney's bid, this one created sharp dissension among those who thought the fighters would be insane not to accept it and those who thought that Gleason had left the door open.

That view was quickly confirmed when the third bid, "Tex" Rickard's, was opened and, to cries of amazement, a flood of yellow currency notes flowed onto the table and Murphy announced that Gleason had joined with Rickard in the bid. Stupefied they listened, many with mouths literally hanging open, to the details: a guarantee of $101,000, two-thirds of the movie rights and a cash bonus of $10,000 for each fighter upon signing.

As it had the onlookers, the sight of the fifteen $1,000 bills carelessly thrown on the table in front of him immediately commanded the attention of the champion, who until then had been following the proceedings with almost sleepy indifference. *The New York Times* reported the following day that *"Johnson's eyes flashed brightly and a broad grin came over his dark face as Stakeholder Murphy counted the money."* The money and a certified check for $5,000 that accompanied it, the paper added, was the Goldfield miner's manifestation of good faith.

Rickard's bid added that they were also prepared to hold the fight on July 4, 1910, in Nevada, Utah or California. In Nevada, it explained, a fight to the finish would be permitted. Sam Berger, as recorded by *The New York Times*, then asked the first question of the proceedings: *"Berger asked Rickard when he would put up the purse, and Rickard offered to add $30,000 to the $20,000 already up in thirty days and the balance forty-eight hours before the fight."*

With the room still buzzing, the fourth bid, from Tom McCarey of the Pacific Club, was then opened. He offered the entire gate receipts and forty percent of the moving picture proceeds or a guarantee of $110,000 and fifty percent of the picture privileges. A good bid, everybody agreed but not nearly as attractive as Rickard's.

The final bid was from Hugh McIntosh. The Australian offered each fighter $37,000 if the fight was held in the United States. That one, everybody in the room agreed, had absolutely no chance and as one of the onlookers observed, demonstrated how much had changed in the year since Johnson had won the title.

After handing his bid to Murphy Rickard had continued standing; putting himself in position to watch the champion's face, to carefully gauge his reaction to his little bit of theatre. The promoter knew full well that his secret agreements with Johnson and Gleason and Gleason's with Berger were not legally enforceable. The little pieces of paper gave them the inside track but nothing else, theoretically anybody could still win. But he had done his best to leave nothing to chance. He had gone straight to see Gleason after leaving O'Brien. After the third drink or so the newsman had been remarkably forthcoming, confirming the rumors of the deal between Gleason and the former champion and adding some additional information. Gleason, O'Brien revealed, had also cut a deal with Coffroth and the two would be bidding jointly. Rickard had put his cards on the table, telling the San Franciscan about his own arrangement with Johnson and what he had learnt about Gleason's own deals, without revealing the identity of his source.

Although the men had agreed to become partners, Rickard was well aware that the deal would quickly fall apart unless the champion was still as committed to him after the bids were opened as he had been a month earlier in Pittsburgh. He had decided, even before his meeting with O'Brien, to include the $1,000 dollar bills and the cashiers check in his bid, a slightly altered replay of stacking the gold coins in the window of his saloon. But O'Brien's revelations had convinced him to add an additional $10,000 to the $5,000 he had originally planned. The champion's broad smile and quick wink in his direction as the thousand dollar bills floated onto the table told him all he needed to know. Now, he had a fight to plan.

Having assured Rickard that their deal was still in place, Johnson turned his attention to convincing the other promoters that they were still very much in the game.

PART THREE

SIXTEEN

Outside, as night fell on Georgetown an old man moved slowly and deliberately along a quiet P Street, pausing every so often to light the dim gaslamps that lined both sides of the nearly-deserted road. His only visible company was the driver of an almost empty, horse-drawn, fruit-and-vegetable wagon, wearily but contentedly making his way home. But inside, at 2902, the three-storey, New Orleans-influenced Federal style townhome of Richard and Alicia Barrington was filled with light and vibrant human energy.

Downstairs, four uniformed servants and a formally-dressed old man were fussily and sometimes rather noisily preparing the large house for the regular monthly meeting of the Wednesday Night Literary Society.

Always sensitive to their image in the white community, Washington's black elite had long been committed to aggressive programs of self-improvement. In 1872, students at Howard University had formed the Eureka Literary Society and during the next decade or so several of the District's leading citizens of color followed suit by starting literary societies and art and music clubs in their own homes. Among them were: The Carreno Music Club, which performed works by Beethoven, Chopin, Josephy, and Gottschalk; the Grimke Art Club, which studied subjects such as Italian art and assigned readings on which members were quizzed; and the Monday Night Literary Society, which discussed both history and race topics.

Literaries, as these literary societies were known, were usually both the most popular and the most lively, often attracting luminaries such as Frederick Douglass, representatives of the leading families and the most highly regarded Howard University professors.

Although it had been operating for slightly less than a year, Richard and Alicia's rare combination of wealth, status, personal attractiveness and intellectual achievement, had already made a visit to their Wednesday Night Literary Society one of the most sought after invitations among the black Washington elite.

Upstairs, the Barringtons were already dressed but not quite ready. Alicia wore a long white lingerie dress with a matching tunic style vest she had selected only after some hesitation and a great deal of encouragement from Richard; she had initially favored something a lot more tailored. He was in a light grey, two-buttoned spring suit and festive, multi-colored tie, she had purchased and selected. Surprisingly, the question of exactly which topic or topics would be discussed had not yet been settled. Richard, seemingly oblivious of that fact, was sitting at his desk in the small study adjoining their bedroom, intently pouring over a stack of automobile advertisements he had evidently clipped from several newspapers.

"Listen to this one about the Houpt-Rockwell," he called out to Alicia, who, after a series of critical evaluations, had removed her vest and substituted a narrow golden belt that emphasized the slenderness of her waist and was standing in front of the full length mirror in the bedroom, a slight smile indicating her approval of the change. "They claim that they spent a year and a half testing it before they put it out and that it ran 9,000 miles over the roughest roads without developing any defects."

"How do you know if all that's true?"

"Wait, I'm not done. Let me tell you some more and now I'm quoting exactly, it sounds really impressive... The result of this painstaking effort is a car embodying the most advanced ideas of motor construction, of exceptional strength. We believe it is the best car ever made. It has speed, plenty of power for the hills, is silent, easy riding and commodious."

"Sounds very, very expensive to me sweetheart, what does it cost?"

"Each model is offered with seven different styles of body, affording the widest variety of choice to the discriminating," Richard continued.

Apparently satisfied with the results of her fashion adjustments, Alicia nodded affirmatively at her image and walked barefoot into the study, hips swaying gently, eyes sparkling with amusement. "That expensive uh," she said, adding, "let me see what you're leaving out," as she snatched the newspaper clipping from her husband and began reading aloud, her eyes widening in alarm as she read. "The 4-cylinder 60 horse power $5,000 car is ready for delivery. We are now prepared to book orders for the 6-cylinder 90 horse power $6,000 car."

For one stunned moment, unable to believe what she had just read Alicia stood silent, staring at her husband, her mouth half open. "Oh my God Richard," she finally exclaimed, "that's absolutely obscene, do you realize that's a lot more than the price of most houses, more than most people make in several years. You're not seriously thinking about purchasing it are you? Can we even begin to afford something like that anyway?"

"Well I agree with you that $6,000 is far too much for even the best car in the world," Richard replied, his tone a bit defensive, "but when you consider the money we'll save on repairs $5,000 may not be such a bad deal afterall. And anyway we don't have to make a quick or rash decision. As the advertisement makes clear a telephone call or a letter to their offices will bring the car to our home and we'll have ample time to judge its merits for ourselves." Then looking up at his wife with his most winning smile, he added, "that's reasonable, isn't it sweetheart."

"Oh Richard," Alicia replied, smiling ruefully and reaching down to ruffle her husband's short-cropped, curly hair, "it's not just about the money darling. I know you've had money all your life. That's not it, that's not the problem. I just don't believe its right to spend that much on something, that's a mere machine, that's, let's face it, a little more than a toy."

"Did you really say," Richard asked, looking up at his wife, his voice brimming with indignation, "that the automobile, probably man's greatest invention to date, bar none, in my humble opinion anyway, is little more than a toy. I cannot believe you of all people, an educated, highly intelligent woman, just said that, at this time, at the end of the first decade of the twentieth century, I cannot believe it."

"I'm not saying cars are entirely useless Richard," Alicia replied, her voice soft, her tone conciliatory, "Just not $6,000 or $5,000 useful, that's all. But anyway," she added quickly before her husband could reply, "that's for another day. We've got to talk about tonight's discussion. We've got guests coming in a couple of hours, remember."

"You know what sweetheart," Richard said, all smiles again as he got up from his desk, kissed his wife affectionately on the cheek and walked across the room to remove a book from the ceiling-high shelves lining the entire back wall of the study, "I'm going to teach you to drive, getting behind the wheel of one of those little machines, as you call them, will prove to you pretty quickly that an automobile is, decidedly, not a toy."

Then, book in hand, Richard returned to his desk, retook his seat, placed the book on the desk, retrieved a sheet of paper from a drawer and turned to face his wife who had settled comfortably into a nearby leather sofa. "Anyway, about tonight, I came up with three topics and I jotted them down here," he began, referring to the paper in his hand. "I just completed the new Robert Waring book, *As We See It,*" he continued, gesturing vaguely in the direction of the top of his desk, "and while I'm not quite as enthusiastic about it as the *Bee* is, I agree with them that it presents a truer picture of the social, moral and economic problems facing Negroes in this country than one usually sees in print."

"Well you know the *Bee's* point of view, don't you," Alicia replied, a hint of disdain in her voice. "I read the editorial. I think they described it as the most remarkable and advanced book ever written and published by a Negro, which is clearly ridiculous."

"I know you think they're hopelessly bourgeois," Richard replied, smiling indulgently at his wife. "I also thought that it may be time for us to revisit the Heflin affair. The man has to be brought to trial; it's been more than a year, you just can't shoot a man in Washington DC, even a Negro, just because you're a Congressman and get away with it."

"In public, in a streetcar full of people, with a concealed weapon and he's walking around without a care in the world,"

Alicia added, her voice dripping with disgust. "The Attorney General ought to be horsewhipped."

"And tarred and feathered too," Richard replied teasingly. A light touch, he had discovered, was sometimes the best way of defusing his wife's more passionate outbursts. "My third and final topic idea," he continued, "concerns Mr. Mayer, the manager and I believe the owner of the Casino Theatre on F Street. As you know the gentleman does not admit colored persons to his theatre and he has just announced that he intends to put up a theatre for our exclusive patronage, in a rundown part of town no less."

"Even more insulting," Alicia responded, this time coolly and dispassionately, "is his disclamation of any anti-Negro feeling on his part. I prefer my bigots honest and straightforward."

"Well, what do you think," Richard asked. "Do you like any of them, do you have any ideas?"

"I like them all Richard," Alicia replied as she sat up straight on the sofa and looked at her husband with a mysterious little smile. "And at another time any, all of them, would be perfect. But tonight there's something even more topical and urgent that we must discuss."

"H'mm," Richard responded, looking at his wife speculatively, "I sense something out of the ordinary coming."

"You know that the Johnson-Ketchel fight film has been showing here in Washington and that even the women have been going to see it in large numbers don't you."

"You want to discuss the fight film?"

"Not exactly, I want us to discuss this question. "Who is the most important Negro in America, Dr. Booker T. Washington or Jack Johnson?"

"Wow, that's a good one, a really good one," Richard exclaimed as he looked admiringly at his wife, "and certainly topical. It should really set off some fireworks tonight. "But", he continued, "let me ask you something. Why the most important Negro, instead of the most important colored man. You know how many of our people feel about the Negro word."

"That's part of the point, isn't it," she replied, a hint of steel in her voice, "the answers to the most important Negro and the most important colored man may be quite different, don't you think. I mean there is a certain implication in the choice of nouns isn't there, as you just noted yourself."

"I assume from that response and your raising of the topic," Richard said, smiling at his wife, "that not only do you have pronounced views on the subject but that you would prefer to argue against Dr. Washington."

"You know Richard," she said quietly, a mischievous little smile tugging at her barely painted lips and reaching into her enormous hazel eyes, "you are so sweet and agreeable; you remind me every day why I love you so very much."

"And I love you very much too sweetheart," Richard replied as he walked across the room to replace the Waring book on the shelf, "but I must point out, at the risk of seeming ungallant, that I'll be at a severe disadvantage. I, afterall, have not previously given the matter any serious thought and, as you just pointed out, our guests are due in a couple of hours."

"I anticipated that problem dear husband," Alicia replied, her smiling widening as her eyes followed his journey, "and since I don't want you to have any excuse for the trouncing you're going to get tonight, I brought you some research I did for your side of the debate. And it even includes a quotation or two."

"Which means, I believe, dear wife," Richard replied, as he retook his seat at his desk, "that you'll be even better prepared than is normally the case, having carefully studied both sides of the argument."

"Dear me," Alicia responded teasingly, "do I detect a slight hesitation, a little lack of confidence from the brilliant Richard Barrington. I can hardly believe it. I'd have thought an hour or so more than adequate time for someone of your numerous accomplishments."

"Do you know Alicia," Richard said, looking at his wife with a wan little smile and a small shake of his head, "that women who look like you should not be so intelligent; it's an irresistible, even dangerous, combination."

"Oh Richard, I'm not trying to put you on the spot. I would never do anything to embarrass you," she replied as she stood up and started towards her husband, her voice and eyes filled with concern. "I really do believe," she continued as she plopped herself on his lap and locked her eyes on his, "that you're more than capable of pulling this off. You already know most of the stuff I found in my research. I've heard you make almost every point I've listed, at some stage, maybe not all at one time. I tell you what," she added, "I'll go first, that'll give you extra time to think about what you want to say. That should help, shouldn't it?"

With an impish smile making him look ever more boyish than usual, Richard responded to his wife's statement by kissing her on the lips and reaching into a drawer of his desk for pen and paper. "You've got it wrong kiddo," he said, grinning, as he eased her out of his lap and began jotting on his pad, "it's not my ability I doubt, it's your capacity to take a bad beating that's my concern."

Standing over her husband, relief flooding her face, Alicia ruffled his hair and started for the bedroom. "Let me get you the research material," she said and smiled happily as she paused at the doorway and watched him, already deep in concentration, rapidly fill the page.

As was their custom on the third Wednesday night of each month, at exactly eight o'clock, thirty minutes before the scheduled start of the proceedings, Richard and Alicia walked arm-in-arm down the graceful walnut spiral staircase to the first floor to begin overseeing the final preparations and to personally welcome any early arriving guests. Alicia, a vision of understated elegance, had selected three pieces of jewelry to complement her long white dress and golden belt—an exquisite four-strand pearl and diamond choker necklace, a pair of delicate pendant earrings with garlands of tiny diamond leaves and a pearl and diamond comb in her long, glossy black hair piled high on top of her head.

Waiting for them at the bottom of the stairs in the large, two-story entrance hall, its lustrous wooden floor glowing from the directed brilliance of a French, bronze d'ore, six-arm chandelier, was the ageless Mister Will, who had left his long employment with the senior Barringtons to take control of the household of the boy he had raised and loved like a son or more accurately given the differences in their ages, grandson. Alicia, who, unlike her husband, had not been raised with a retinue of servants, was initially appalled at the idea of a man closer in age to eighty than seventy working to near midnight. But she had been forced to withdraw her opposition by the old gentleman's deep unhappiness on learning that he was going to be prevented from doing something he regarded as both a right and a duty. Supervising the preparations for the monthly gathering and welcoming the guests, usually highly accomplished members of the city's colored elite, many of whom he had known since they were children, was both personally enjoyable and powerful validation of his continuing relevance and importance.

Despite his advanced years, the old man was almost as slim and ramrod straight as he had been sixty years earlier when he had first arrived in Washington from his native South Carolina. And the still tight skin on his slim, narrow, high-cheek-boned face was almost completely devoid of wrinkles. His only real visible concession to the irresistible demands of Mother Nature was the gleaming bald pate that had once been covered by a thicket of coarse, red-brown hair. "Good evening Master Richard, Miss Alicia, you is both looking particularly scrumptious tonight," he pronounced brightly in his customary greeting, as the Barringtons stepped into the entrance hall. Over the years, apparently to compensate for his almost total lack of formal education, Mister Will had, without mastering the basic rules of grammar, acquired a relatively extensive vocabulary that centered on a surprising number of fairly long, tongue-bending adjectives.

"Thank you Mister Will," they replied in unison.

"You're looking pretty outstanding yourself tonight," Alicia added, as the old man beamed benignly at his young employers. Although slightly frayed here and there, the well-fitting, freshly-pressed dark suit added to the air of conscious dignity that surrounded the old servant.

"Have any of the guests arrived yet Mister Will," Richard asked, pausing to straighten a large portrait of Frederick Douglass, one of several paintings that lined the walls of the hall.

"Yes Master Richard, four of dem, two couples, the Terrells and the Robinsons, the young ones," the old man replied in his usually brisk, efficient manner, "they is in the parlor."

"You go ahead Richard," Alicia said stepping away from her husband and heading for another set of stairs. "I'm going downstairs to check with Mona to see how the food is coming along." As was typical of homes of the period, the kitchen and pantry were located in the basement.

"Where's Johnny Mister Will," Richard asked, referring to the old man's grandnephew they had recently added to the household staff to both assist and understudy his granduncle.

"Helping out downstairs Master Richard," the old man replied, "Miss Mona she need some extra help tonight with all dem extra people coming."

"Extra people, what extra people are you talking about Mister Will," Richard asked.

"Dat's what Miss Alicia tell Miss Mona, Master Richard," the old man replied. "About six or eight more than usual is what I hear."

"I see," Richard replied thoughtfully as he began moving towards the parlor. "Thank you Mister Will," he said, glancing over his shoulder and smiling fondly at the old man who had resumed his lonely vigil in one of the two hall chairs. It had long been a rule in Barrington homes that when guests were expected the front door was to be answered almost immediately after the bell was rung. Anything less was seen as an act of gross discourtesy, an affront to the visitor and an indicator of poor breeding on the part of the host.

"The doors between the parlors are already open, aren't they," Richard added, in more statement than question. The old man, he knew, was even more of a stickler about enforcing a long list of arcane rules that governed how proper households were run, than even his parents had been.

"Of course Master Richard, dat is the proper thing when we is having guests," the old man replied without taking his eyes off the front door.

The little minx, Richard thought, a little smile tugging at his lips, as he walked into the enormous entertainment space that had been created by throwing open the double doors that normally divided it into two separate parlors. She must have been so confident of convincing me to accept her choice of topics that she advertised it before even discussing it with me.

"Great topic tonight Rich, Alicia told us about your idea a couple of days ago and I agreed to be the moderator; it's the right time man," a smiling and unusually animated Henry Robinson said as the two men briefly embraced. Tall and almost painfully lean, prematurely graying and normally quiet and reserved, Robinson, a law professor at Howard, whom he had known as long as he could remember, was still his closest friend. And his wife, Beth, whose family was part of the same Washington black elite and had known both men most of her life, and Alicia, had also, slowly, become close friends. Their mutual interests, both were professors in the history department at Howard, and the friendship of their husbands, had overcome an initial mutual antipathy, based, their husbands contended, on their amazing similarity of personality. Very unlike physically, Beth was smaller and darker, both were assertive, passionate, and outspoken. But, over the years—they had entered Howard the same year-- increasing familiarity and perhaps maturity had led to greater mutual appreciation and eventually to real friendship.

"Alicia told you it was my idea," Richard asked, surprise in his voice and all over his face.

"Yeah, wasn't it," Henry replied.

"No," Richard said, "it was hers."

"Okay," Henry said laughing, "it was from the both of you. I guess it doesn't really matter, you two function as one anyway."

Despite its size, the entertainment space was dominated by a single piece of furniture, a stunning, nine-foot, Steinway Victorian concert grand piano. Located directly across from the entrance of what was usually the front parlor, its almost-black ebonized finish shimmering in the soft light of two nearby Tiffany lamps, the Steinway commanded the immediate and rapt attention of almost every visitor. The rest of the space, low-keyed but tasteful, was a perfect counterpoint to the dramatic beginning. Persian carpets in muted colors and of various sizes and designs covered much but not all of the dark, wooden flooring, and buttoned-down, leather Chesterfield sofas and Queen Anne chairs were scattered with studied casualness throughout the big room.

By a quarter past eight, fifteen minutes before the scheduled start of the proceedings, all twenty-four guests had arrived and had been escorted to a seat and served a drink by either Mister Will or his grandson, Johnny, who had been summoned from the kitchen when an onslaught of arrivals had threatened to overpower the old man's physical resources. After personally greeting their guests and spending a few moments in pleasant chitchat with each, Richard and Alicia had taken their positions on either side of Henry, who was already sitting on a small, low platform strategically located in the middle of the room. In addition to the three chairs on the platform, there was a small table with three long glasses filled with some kind of iced drink.

The room had quickly fallen silent when Henry uncurled his long, loose-limbed body and rose to his feet. The murmur of conversation and the musical tinkling of ice in crystal glasses had given way to expectant silence. The general rules of debate were familiar to the guests, veterans to a man and woman of countless similar events in high school, college, and at this or other literary societies. But each literary society had its own peculiar set of conventions and regulations. And in the hermetic world of the black Washington elite where a premium was placed on good manners and "correct" behavior and where a social faux pas could be career-crippling, close attention was always paid to the rules.

"Good evening ladies and gentlemen, welcome to the Wednesday Night Literary Society," Henry began in his easy, laconic way, his baritone voice carrying easily across the room. "Our topic tonight, as you all already know, is a very timely and I believe exciting one that should spark some, and I use the word conservatively, interesting debate: Who is the most important Negro in America today, Dr. Booker T. Washington or Mr. Jack Johnson.? Some of you are here for the very first time and the rest of you may have already forgotten so I'll begin by explaining the rules of engagement, so to speak. There will be two opening statements, one on behalf of each man, by our hosts Richard and Alicia Barrington. No interruptions of any kind—no heckling, cheering or questioning—will be permitted during the statements. Applause, if warranted, will be allowed at the end of each statement.

The statements will be followed by a break of thirty minutes for refreshments and to give you a chance, since the floor will be open after the break, to compose your own statements or think about your questions. You've all, I'm sure, either know or heard of Miss Mona, since as the saying goes, her reputation precedes her. She is simply the finest cook I've ever known and for the past several hours she and her talented assistants have been fixing up some wonderful treats for us. And Mr. Will, who you 'all already know, and his grandnephew Johnny, will be around to help with the drinks and ice. After the break, as I already said, the floor will be open to everybody; so just raise your hand and I assure you I'll get to you. Everybody will get a chance to speak their piece. A time limit which has to be strictly adhered to, of three minutes, will be placed on each statement from the floor. The same rules as per the opening statements will apply, no interruptions of any kind during but applause after, if warranted. The floor statements and questions will be followed by closing statements from Alicia and Richard, only this time the order of appearance will be reversed, with Richard going first and, fittingly, Alicia having the final word."

Grinning at his own little joke, Henry glanced at Alicia over his shoulder before continuing. "Ladies and gentlemen," he concluded, "without further ado I give you the beautiful and brilliant Mrs. Alicia Barrington."

Instead of beginning her statement immediately, Alicia stood quietly, a little smile on her face as she looked around the room with her hands folded in front of her. Then just as the silence was becoming uncomfortable she began, quietly at first, with her surprisingly strong voice gradually growing louder and frequently dripping with scorn and anger.

"A recent editorial in the Bee began this way, and I quote:

"The national leadership of Dr. Booker T. Washington is acknowledged by the race. That's a fact. No other man of the race is in his class, except one. That's another fact; close quotes. That other man, Mr. Calvin Chase the editor and writer of the piece, informed us is Dr. James E. Shepard of Durham, North Carolina. What achievements, what qualities of mind, of character, you might ask, do these men share, which have inspired one of our leading newspapers to hold them in such lofty regard. About that there is no mystery at all; Mr. Chase explained it himself in that very same piece: the wonderful, transcendent quality Doctors Washington and Shepard share is their ability to attract the ardent support of the white community.

I'm not sure how those of you here tonight feel about such a measure for those who would be regarded as our leaders, but I for one reject it, contemptuously. Such craven behavior presumes the very opposite of the truth, that they—the rich and powerful white men who are the patrons of Drs. Washington and Shepard--know how best to fix the problems that beset our community. Nothing could be further from the truth; my friends they are not the solution, they are the problem. Our problems are not the result of any inherent flaw or fault in us but of their unmitigated greed and prejudice and the myths and lies they've invented to justify their vile and sinful conduct.

"Our topic tonight, as you already know, is: Who is the most important Negro in America today, Dr. Booker T. Washington or Mr. Jack Johnson? I intend to explain why I believe the answer to that question is, unquestionably, Jack Johnson.

Those who support Dr. Washington—and I grant that although his primary support comes from whites that there are many in our community who also fall into that category-- invariably do so because of what they claim are his accomplishments in the field of education. It is fair to say, I am sure you'll all agree, that Dr Washington's reputation and the value of his contribution to our race depends almost entirely on the quality of his contribution in this area. Dr. Washington has, afterall, advocated his view of education as an alternative to agitation for our civil and political rights.

Dr. Washington is, you'll all agree, the leading advocate, at least for our race, for what has been facetiously termed industrial education. And just what is industrial education? The term industrial education, I must confess, has a certain resonance, a certain heft, an undeniable ring of importance. Afterall, singly, both words are among the most important, the most meaningful in our vocabulary. Together, therefore, they should be describing something truly meaningful and wonderful. But of course, as you all are well aware, that is not true at all. In fact the very opposite is the case. Combining those two words have seriously diminished both and debased the very meaning of education.

Let us be clear ladies and gentlemen, preparing our children to be agricultural workers and domestic servants is not what I for one regard as educating them. Dr. Washington, as I said, is wildly popular within the white community. In fact it is they who first proclaimed him—after what has been kindly, in my view far too kindly, described as his Atlanta Compromise speech— the leader of the Negro people. And it their support, financial and otherwise, that has made his work at Tuskegee possible. It is not surprising therefore that it is their interests, not ours, that he serves. For that is what industrial education is, a design, a plot, a scheme, call it what you will, for preparing our people for what the white community sees as our proper station in life. Industrial education caters to the view, widely held in this country by a vast majority of whites, that the Negro people have a limited capacity for learning; that subjects such as Latin, literature, history and algebra are both beyond our grasp and useless for the base purposes they believe fate has reserved for our race.

But my problem with Dr. Washington goes well beyond his specific policies. It is my view that he has forfeited any claim he might have had to be considered a great leader of our people because of the negative impact his compromising meekness, his craven weakness, has had on the psyche of our entire people. Those who champion Dr. Washington's cause have even dared to compare him to our esteemed champion, our dear departed Frederick Douglass. That my friends is nothing less than heresy, or for those who prefer less religious terminology I refer them to the language of Kelly Miller's brilliant essay. Comparing the two men, he wrote, is like comparing a lion to a lamb. Douglass was like a lion, bold and fearless; whereas Washington is lamblike, meek and submissive."

Pausing briefly, Alicia bent gracefully and picked up a sheet of paper from the table in front of her chair, raised it to within a foot or so of her eyes and began reading. "I am quoting directly from Miller's essay," she explained, "to make sure that I get it absolutely right because I certainly cannot say it nearly as well as he did....Douglass escaped from personal bondage, which his soul abhorred; but for Lincoln's Proclamation, Washington would probably have risen to esteem and favor in the eyes of his Master as a good and faithful servant. Douglass insisted upon rights; Washington insists upon Duty. Douglass held up to public scorn the sins of the white man; Washington portrays the faults of his own race. Douglass spoke what he thought the world should hear; Washington speaks only what he feels it is disposed to listen to. Douglass's conduct was actuated by principle; Washington's by prudence."

Then, pausing again, Alicia replaced the sheet of paper on the table, picked up her glass, took two small sips with the glass barely touching her lips, returned it to the table and resumed her peroration.

"Let us now consider Jack Johnson. Like most of you I too am troubled by his seeming fixation on women of another race. And, frankly, the flamboyance of his lifestyle bothers me a great deal. But I also strongly believe that matters of the heart are personal and private and that Mr. Johnson's mistakes in his social life are—although Mr. Johnson who I've met and spoken to is neither an uneducated or uncultured man—to a great extent the result of the poverty and cultural deprivation of his early life. A fact which, of course, is the lamentable story of the vast majority of our people. I also note that in the white community no comparable disapproval was voiced when white men were taking our women, maybe not always, but often against their most fervently expressed wishes.

And I must confess that a part of me, the best part of me-- my heart—not my head, applauds Mr. Johnson's extraordinary courage in defying the approbation of Caucasian society. The masses of Negroes applaud him for his physical prowess but even more for his moral courage in defying the restrictive rules they have devised to keep us in what they impertently consider our place. Simply by standing up like a man: For refusing to bow or bend: For showing the entire world—and the entire world has been and is watching the Jack Johnson show—a vision of the Negro never before seen in the modern world, of a people strong, confident, unafraid, and unconquerable, I say that Jack Johnson is doing more to raise the spirits and hopes of our people, especially our young men who desperately need such an example, than Booker T. Washington ever has or ever will, and is therefore the most important Negro in the United States today."

Alicia's final syllable had hardly left her lips when the brief silence was shattered by a high, piercing whistle. Richard, who had been listening as impassively as a sphinx, only jotting an occasional note on the pad of paper resting precariously on his lap, had placed his index finger and thumb to his mouth the moment she was finished. And, as was always true of them, no one was more proud of the applause that flowed across the room in rolling, tidal wives and participated more loudly and enthusiastically, than Alicia's beaming husband.

"Well, ladies and gentlemen," a smiling Henry Robinson said after the applause had finally subsided, "I told you to expect something exciting and interesting and that Alicia is both beautiful and brilliant, but, I must confess, that even I did not expect anything quite like what we just heard. Now, it will be the responsibility, and I must say a heavy one, of my dear friend to reply in kind. But, I must tell you, if anyone here tonight is capable of doing so it is him. So, without further ado I give you the other half of this brilliant duo, Mr. Richard Barrington."

"Wow, that was something wasn't it," Richard said, smiling and shaking his head as he placed his pad on the table and stepped to the very edge of the platform. "It's probably not a good idea to concede that your opponent has just made probably the best speech you ever heard even if she's your wife. But I'm sure you'll agree," he added, as he looked around the room, his voice just loud enough to carry across the completely silent room, his tone conversational, "that she just made what was always going to be a tough job almost impossible. But it is my responsibility to try. And I believe that it is possible, difficult but possible, to convince those of you here tonight that Dr. Washington, not Mr. Jack Johnson, is the most important Negro in the United States at the present time.

I want to begin by conceding that Dr. Washington is not the perfect leader and that like my wife and, I assume, from the nature of your response to her, many of you here, that I have certain reservations about his leadership style. And I would be the first to admit that he does not compare favorably with the man I knew as Uncle Freddie, the incomparable Frederick Douglass, who was not just a great leader of his race but a great American. But whether or not Dr. Washington compares favorably with Ambassador Douglass, is not the topic; that is not what we are debating tonight. The question, the real question is, how does he compare to the pugilist Jack Johnson and other prominent men of our race. And that bar, you'll all agree I'm sure, is a far lower one to clear.

To his detractors, has Alicia has so eloquently explained, Washington has committed two unpardonable sins: his advocacy of what is now known as industrial education and his leadership style, his alleged accommodationism. Let me begin by gently pointing out a slightly important fact that my opponent conveniently omitted and might even surprise some of you: that during his own career Ambassador Douglass was just as supportive of industrial education for poor, rural Negroes as Washington is today. In fact, on that one subject, their views are virtually identical and I too have a quotation to prove it."

Casually turning his back on his audience, Richard picked up his pad from the table and returned to the edge of the platform. "The quotation I'm about to read to you," he said, smiling, "is from a letter Ambassador Douglass wrote to Harriet Beecher Stowe in 1853 while that good lady was attempting to establish an industrial school for Negroes…We must become mechanics; we must build as well as live in houses; we must make as well as use furniture. We need mechanics as well as ministers. We need workers in iron, clay and leather. We have orators, authors, and other professional men, but these reach only a certain class, and get respect for our race in certain select circles. To live here as we ought, we must fasten ourselves to our countrymen through their everyday cardinal wants. We must not only be able to black boots but to make them.

Ambassador Douglass therefore, it is clear, shared Dr. Washington's vision of devising practical, achievable steps to lift millions of our people out of the depths of poverty, ignorance and despair. And learning carpentry or needlework or some other practical skill might not seem like much to the privileged and educated members of our race, like those of us here tonight. It is easy for us to be contemptuous of Washington, to be disgusted at his fawning and bowing, to despise his caution and prudence as he wheedles and cajoles the tens of thousands, even hundreds of thousands of dollars he needs for his work lifting up the masses of our people from the degradation of poverty and ignorance.

It is not work that I could do, but not because I'm a better man than he but because I'm not nearly as good. I confess that I could not shed my pride the way he has for even a cause as noble as his. And let there be no mistake, his cause is noble and absolutely necessary. For the life of me I cannot understand why those of you who oppose him so fiercely cannot understand that you cannot, in the real world, wipe out all vestiges of hundreds of years of slavery and oppression in a single generation, regardless of how well-meaning you are. It takes time, patience, money, a great deal of money, and one other thing as important as the first three combined, an unblinking acknowledgment of reality, however unpleasant and unwelcome. And ladies and gentlemen, I am here to tell you tonight that there is one unpleasant reality that we must all face and acknowledge.

We, as a race, are not capable at this time, at this stage in our development, to save ourselves by ourselves. The unpleasant truth is that we are a small, poor and virtually defenseless minority in this country and to make the progress all of us so desperately desire for the poorest of our people we must make alliances with those who currently hold almost all the money and all of the power. And that is all Dr. Washington is doing, doing what he must, doing what he can, doing what he does better than any of us could, oftentimes no doubt gritting his teeth and forcing a smile on his face, to get the resources his people, our people, our poor, neglected, abused people, so desperately need. And I for one salute him for it."

Richard's voice had gradually risen in volume throughout the presentation and the easy smile and conversational tone had slowly disappeared. Pausing, he again turned away from his audience, replaced his pad on the table, winked conspiratorially at Alicia who returned a dazzling I-told-you-smile and a thumbs-up sign, picked up his glass, swallowed much of it in three or four quick gulps and walked back to the edge of the platform, smiling again.

"Alicia," he said, reverting to his conversational tone, "made an excellent point when she explained Mister Johnson's social shortcomings as the result of his upbringing and appealed for them to be judged in that context. The same is true, of course, for Dr. Washington, who was born in slavery and has lived his entire life in the South; no doubt those factors have influenced his leadership style to some extent. But, as I have tried to explain, it is my firm belief that the nature of his mission and the unfortunate and trying times in which we live are the dominant factors that have shaped his leadership style. In addition to all I've already said I implore you to consider one other factor as you compare Dr. Washington's style to our earlier leaders, particularly, of course, Ambassador Douglass. Ambassador Douglass lived and worked during a time of revolution and liberation, of war and controversy, and his job was to help destroy our enemies and liberate our people and he did it very, very well indeed. Dr. Washington, on the other hand, lives in a very different time, a time of construction and reconciliation, of making allies and building bridges, and I put it you that he too is doing his job very, very well: Different men, with different styles for different times.

As to the importance of Jack Johnson to our people, believe me I am not here to diminish it in any way. I was in Chicago when he returned to this country with the heavyweight title and I understand better than most his importance to the masses of our people. And I am not, I confess, personally immune to the seductive appeal of his defiance of white authority. In fact, and here is a bigger confession, if this debate was about which of the two men, Johnson or Washington, was more important to people like me and those of you here tonight, I would argue just as vigorously for Johnson as I now argue for Washington. I understand, believe me, Johnson's appeal to those of us who are sick and tired of seeing our people always on their knees and long to strike a blow or two against our oppressors. For those of us already gifted with the basics of a decent life, for those of us who can stand on our own two feet, for those of us who long for the respect our myriad contributions to this country deserve, the psychic satisfaction Johnson offers is as irresistible as opium must be to an addict.

But we, my friends, are a tiny, privileged elite and the great masses of our people cannot yet afford the luxury of pursuing psychic satisfaction, and certainly not at the expense of the things we take for granted--a safe and warm place to sleep, sufficient food to eat, clean clothes to cover our bodies, proper shoes for our feet, decent schools for our children and hope for a brighter future. It is because Dr. Washington understands this fact better than any other person and has made the empowerment of our people through the acquisition of basic education and vital skills his life's work that I say with absolute conviction that he, not Jack Johnson, is without question the most important Negro in America today."

Seventeen

The early afternoon sunlight peering determinedly through the towering roof had transmuted her long, flowing hair, from red to burnished gold and bronzed her pale alabaster skin. And when Daniel first saw her glowing like a Norse goddess, standing alone by the telephone booths, the meeting place of the city's lovers, surrounded by a sea of noisy "sunshine" children, he found himself thanking and cursing anew the gods of fate that had delivered so beautiful a creature to him. But had now cruelly decreed that he leave her on a trip he was determined to keep as brief as possible, but which he feared would almost certainly last for several months.

He had initially hoped to spend just a few weeks on the west coast on this trip and then to return a few weeks before the fight, maybe in mid-June or thereabouts, but with all the uncertainties and multiplying rumors that was no longer possible. Just getting there and back, six days in each direction, would take almost two weeks and he simply didn't have that kind of time now. It was going to be his first trip to the west coast and he had long wanted to visit San Francisco, a city that for years had assumed almost mythical proportions in his mind. But his priorities, he had begun to realize, had radically changed: And at a time when he was in the middle of the biggest story of his life.

Like any other sporting activity, the story of the Jack Johnson-Jim Jeffries fight had begun on the sports pages of the country's newspapers. But as the date of the showdown neared and the American people as a whole, black and white, male and female alike, became increasingly invested in the outcome of the bout that was now universally regarded as a defining contest between the races, the story had graduated to the front pages. And so, once again, as had been true throughout much of his professional life, fate had intervened on the side of his career.

This time was different however; for leaving Bridget behind, as Daniel was discovering now that the dreaded moment had almost arrived, was even more difficult than he had anticipated. His long years of carefree bachelorhood, when his career and the pursuit of pleasure were his almost exclusive focus, had not prepared him for the conflicting and unfamiliar emotions that were churning his stomach and making him strangely weak-limbed and lightheaded.

Despite the strong, widespread interest in the fight the promoters were having a great deal of trouble finding a suitable site, and even more unsettling, a serious rift seemed to have developed between the erstwhile partners, Tex Rickard and Jack Gleason. Rickard had been quoted as saying that he alone had put up any money for the contest, while Gleason had continued to assert that he was an equal partner and the men seemed to be barely on speaking terms. The situation had become so worrisome to many of the *Tribune's* readers that the editor had decided to send Daniel to the west coast to give the readers a first hand account of the state of the preparations for the fight.

There had also been wildly conflicting accounts of Jeffries' physical condition and readiness to fight. Not even a glowing report from the Chicago Athletic Association, based on a battery of tests by what was described as "unbiased experts", concluding that the former champion was in tremendous physical condition and retained his fighting power had been enough to quiet the rumors. Newspapers around the country continued to publish stories of a grossly overweight Jeffries despite photographic evidence to the contrary published by the *Chicago Daily Tribune*. The Chicago paper, which organized the tests on Jeffries, had carried photographs of the Californian's tremendously muscular and relatively lean upper body.

The disappointments had begun early in the year with San Francisco, the preferred site of all the principals. County Supervisor Johnny Herget, chairman of the police committee, the committee responsible for granting fight permits, who had been a fighter himself under the nom de plume "Young Mitchell," had at least temporarily taken the Bay City out of consideration. "If the

Johnson-Jeffries fight comes to San Francisco," he had told fellow supervisors at one of their meetings, "it must be directed by a San Franciscan man, and not by an outsider. I will not stand idly by and see Tex Rickard come in from the wilds of Nevada and secure a concession that should go to somebody who has been working for the good of the game here. From what I gather," he added, "Rickard and not Gleason, is the moving spirit of the combination. Now, let Gleason come forward and declare himself. If he can show us he is a bona fide promoter, well and good. But if Rickard is boss, then he will have to boss the match in some other place."

An angry Rickard, declaring that he was determined to keep the fight away from San Francisco because of Herget's actions, had then announced that the bout would be held in Utah, citing "positive assurances of businessmen, many of whom are close to the governor, that a forty-five round boxing contest can be held in Salt Lake City." Despite those assurances Governor Spry declared shortly after that he would not permit the fight to occur within the boundaries of his state under any circumstances. Reluctantly conceding defeat Rickard had then met with Gleason to iron out their differences and after a day of short conferences a gloomy Rickard and a cheery Gleason had called a press conference to issue the less than convincing assurance that the fight would be held either in San Mateo or in San Francisco.

Daniel had asked his new fiancée, they had been engaged for less than a month, to meet him at Grand Central for lunch. He was scheduled to leave on the Limited to Chicago at about four o'clock and that would have given them ample time for a leisurely meal at Mendel's, a couple of drinks at the Oyster bar and their favorite thing, a great deal of conversation. Of all Bridget's many virtues, the ones Daniel treasured most and were, initially, the ones he found most surprising, were the sharp native intelligence, almost insatiable curiosity and acerbic wit that made talking to her so easy and so such much fun. But Bridget's employer, she worked nearby as a secretary in a small, busy office on Madison Avenue, had refused to give her the half-day off she requested: And had only grudgingly agreed to let her off at two o'clock, after a call from Daniel explaining the circumstances. But, since she had worked through her lunch hour, it meant she had only been given an hour off, an hour he had made her promise to make up the very next day.

"She's going to have a glass of chardonnay, I'm having a whisky sour and we're both going to have the oyster stew," Daniel told the dark-haired waitress as they settled into their seats near the entrance from Grand Central, almost shouting to be heard over the cacophony of sounds and voices inside the busy restaurant and outside in the crowded terminal. "This isn't going to work, it's much too loud," he said, turning and leaning toward Bridget, "I'm going to get us moved further inside. I'll be right back," he added, as he got up from their table and made his way to the back of the restaurant.

"This is really a lot better, what did you do, how did you manage it so quickly," Bridget asked, looking admiringly at her smiling fiancé as they took their new seats in a relatively quiet area of the restaurant.

"Not much really," Daniel replied, his pleased smile and air of quiet satisfaction belying his modest words, "just one of the little benefits of my occupation you might say; just a tiny demonstration of the power of the press. Plus I know the manager quite well; I used to be a regular here at one time."

Although her sensual figure was still trim and youthful, Bridget, like her fiancé, had a strong appetite for and a keen appreciation of good food and drink. And for months she had been looking forward to trying the dish she had heard so much about from Daniel. Fortunately, their oyster stews thick with milk, butter and potatoes and spiced with garlic, onions, pepper and fresh chives, hers served with crushed crackers and his with thick, toasted bread, were every bit as good as promised, and between bites and sighs of appreciation they talked about San Francisco. About its birth out of the gold rush of 1849; about its amazing rise which made it the country's tenth largest city a mere twenty-one years later; about the utter destruction of its eastern half by earthquake and fire on April 18, 1906; and about its extraordinary, phoenix-like rise back to prominence in just a few short years.

Chewing slowly, large green-grey eyes wide with interest,

Bridget listened quietly and intently as Daniel described the Great Earthquake and the devastating fires that followed in its wake. "It began," he told her, "and this was the lucky thing, because as bad as it was it could have been much worse if it had happened earlier while it was still dark, at 5:12 in the morning when it was already getting light, with a foreshock that was itself strong enough to be felt throughout the San Francisco Bay area. Twenty to twenty-five seconds later the real earthquake began, and although it only lasted less than a minute the shocks were so strong they were felt all the way from Oregon to Los Angeles."

Pausing frequently to put a spoonful of stew or a piece of bread in his mouth and to chew and swallow his meal, Daniel continued his story. "More importantly, the quake ignited the fires that did the real damage. For three full days they raged out of control, ravaged the city, and destroyed almost 500 city blocks and 25,000 buildings. They say between 500 and 700 people were killed but nobody knows the real number. But it was probably a lot higher than that. Eyewitnesses described the most gruesome sights. Huge buildings shaking and waving and then crumbling like biscuits. Of the air being filled with falling stones and people being crushed like insects by giant pieces of mortar and concrete: Of the streets suddenly sinking by three or four feet in some places and rising in great humps in others: Of whole herds of cattle being swallowed up by great fissures in the streets; Of the rails of the street cars being bent and twisted like children's toys: Of horses and their drivers covered by bricks lying dead in the streets. But the worse, by far, were the fires. It was when they started that people believed that Armageddon had come, that the end of the world had arrived.

The fires began, one man said," he continued, smiling at the rapt attention with which she was following the story, "with explosions that sounded like 100 cannons going off at the same time. Then streams of fire would shoot out into the sky and then there would be other explosions and other streams of fire and on and on. All the water mains had been ruptured and destroyed and so the fire department was helpless to save the city. Their only weapon was dynamite. But time after time, after they had made what seemed at first like a successful stand to stop the fires from spreading, the flames would, almost diabolically, flank around on either side or come up from the rear and what only a few minutes earlier had seemed like certain victory would turn into defeat.

One woman, who had lost her own home and was sitting with her husband and son in a public park, described watching the long tongues of flame, shooting up into the murky, rolling clouds and enveloping the colossal mansions of Nob Hill, the palaces of the great families, the Floods, the Hopkins', the Stanford's, the Huntington and the Crockers', in a fire so mighty that even those formidable structures seemed like sediment at its base."

"That's such an extraordinary story," Bridget said, finally breaking her silence, her eyes glowing as she looked at her fiancé, "you have such wonderful powers of description and I don't know how you can remember all those details."

"I must confess," Daniel replied, with a pleased little smile, "that I refreshed my memory recently as part of my preparation for this trip."

"Nevertheless," Bridget replied and placed her hand over Daniel's. "And you say the city has been rebuilt already, after such terrible destruction: How?"

Just the touch of her hand, even in the crowded room, was enough to remind Daniel of the first time they kissed and to conjure up memories of the taste of her mouth, the heat of her skin and the surprising strength of her small, firm body. "The remarkable thing," he replied after a slight hesitation, wrenching his mind back to the present, "is that in most ways the city is better than it ever was. Corruption, especially governmental corruption, had been a real problem before the earthquake. After the earthquake they got rid of the crooked politicians, strengthened the building codes and financed a building boom with public bonds. The new buildings, from everything I've heard and read, are stronger and better looking than the ones they replaced; from all reports it's a beautiful vibrant city, by far the biggest and the best in the west."

"You make it sound so exciting," Bridget said with a small sigh, "I really wish I were going with you."

"And I wish you were coming too sweetie," he replied, his voice soft and low. Public displays of affection were still difficult for him. "The next few months are going to be a bit bleak to be honest."

Smiling and grey-green eyes sparkling mischievously, Bridget slipped her fingers between Daniel's, looked at him coyly and in her sweetest voice asked, "Do you think it's terribly selfish of me to say that I'm glad you're not going to be too happy while you're away."

"How could I," Daniel replied, smiling thinly at the little joke designed to hide his growing distress, as he signaled the waitress to bring the bill, "be not happy that you're happy that I'm not going to be happy."

As usual, in the human bedlam of Grand Central, the megaphone man on his pulpit-like platform, stentorian voice magisterially announcing the location and destination of each departing train, was the center of attention. Even as he called out "Track—number—-18," carefully spacing his words to allow the echo of each to return to its sender before issuing the next, a well-dressed, dark-haired young woman carrying a baby held like an ancient offering to an angry god, climbed timidly up one of the two sets of stairs leading to the platform. Below, on the ground, a young boy, no older than five or six, clung tightly to his mother's leg as he followed the woman's progress with wide-eyed fascination. Dozens, scores of women, seemingly representing every shape and size of their gender, many holding on to their hats, their high heels resonating almost musically on the mosaic floor, hurried along to mysterious destinations.

Men, large and small, young and not so young, with overcoats buttoned up to their chins, fumbled for tickets in voluminous pockets. And high-spirited "fresh-air" children shouted and teased and playfully pushed and shoved each other, to help ease the boredom of waiting to be whisked out of the noxious city to the alleged delights of the countryside.

Daniel had picked up his luggage from the amazingly efficient parcel-room of Mendel's, where he had left it earlier in the day, and had just purchased a large bunch of violets for Bridget from a vendor near the telephone booths where they had met earlier, when a vaguely familiar voice and a light tap on the shoulder brought him to a full stop.

"Good afternoon Mister O'Brien, I see you are the one traveling today. Would you like some help with your bags?" the polite voice said.

"Good afternoon to you too Patrick, I knew it was you, I recognized your voice right away," a smiling Daniel replied as he turned to shake the outstretched hand of the uniformed porter. "I can definitely use some help," he added, reaching for the suitcase Bridget was carrying, "this is a bit heavy for Miss O'Neill."

"Miss O'Neill? Her name is O'Neill," Patrick asked with a slightly startled look, as he slipped the suitcase's strap over his left shoulder.

"Why yes, she's my fiancée, Miss Bridget O'Neill," Daniel replied with a slight frown, "why do you ask, is something wrong?"

"No Sir, not at all," Patrick replied, his voice soft, his tone diffident, almost apologetic, "it's just that's my name also. I mean my name is Patrick O'Neill."

Bridget, who, until Patrick's statement, had been walking quietly beside Daniel and had seemed far more interested in the comings and goings around her than in the conversation of the two men, suddenly looked over at Patrick and asked: "Do you know anything about your family Patrick, where the name O'Neill came from."

"Came from Miss," Patrick responded quizzically, not quite comprehending.

"I was told," Bridget replied, "that many of your people have names that belonged to their slave masters; is that where your name comes from?"

"I don't think so Miss;" Patrick answered in the polite, almost servile tone he affected whenever he donned his porter's uniform, "my grandfather was certainly no slave-owner, spent his whole life at sea, just like my daddy and pretty much his whole family, or at least the men on his side."

Then shifting his attention to Daniel, Patrick reached for the larger of the two pieces of luggage the older man was carrying. "Let me take this for you Mister O'Brien," he said with a big smile, "I still have one hand totally free."

"Thanks Patrick, I really appreciate that," Daniel replied, as the trio, walking abreast, began making their way through the bustling crowds, with Daniel in the middle and the other two to his left and right. "Let me ask you something," he added, after casting a couple of speculative glances at the younger man, "do you know if your grandfather was born in Ireland."

"Yes Sir," Patrick replied, "when I was little my daddy used to tell me stories about over there that he learned from his daddy."

"Is that right," Daniel responded, his eyes fixed on Patrick, genuine interest in his voice. "What kinds of stories?

But before he could respond, Bridget, whose interest in the young black man had markedly increased with the revelation of his links to Ireland, interrupted with another question. "How does your family spell their name Patrick," she asked, almost shouting to be heard above the clamor."

"You mean O'Neill Miss."

"Yes Patrick."

"O- apostrophe- N-E-I-L-L Miss," Patrick replied, slightly slowing his pace and carefully pronouncing each letter as he turned to look at his questioner.

The final syllable had barely left his lips when Bridget followed with another question. "Do you happen to know where in Ireland your family comes from Patrick," she asked, the faint brogue in her voice becoming more pronounced.

"I think so Miss," Patrick answered, his tone still polite but with a hint of curiosity intruding, "if I remember right it's a man's name…a place called Tyrone, I think," he added after a brief hesitation.

Just then the rich, amplified voice of the megaphone man announcing the imminent departure of the Limited to Chicago ended any further conversation about Patrick's Irish ancestry. "Excuse me Sir, Miss," a smiling Patrick said, placing the bag in his right hand on the ground and holding it out to Daniel and Bridget, "I really enjoyed talking to you both and meeting you Miss Bridget but I've got to get these bags aboard right away. Mister O'Brien, please let me have your bag also," he added, pointing to the piece of luggage Daniel was carrying.

"Are you sure you can manage all of that by yourself Patrick," Daniel asked solicitously, as he watched the young man place the largest of the three bags over his right shoulder and pick up the two smaller ones with each hand.

"Do it all the time Sir," Patrick replied with a big, mischievous grin, as he moved away. "I'll go ahead Sir; I'm guessing you two would like to be alone for a while."

"That's so very strange," Bridget commented, her tone wry, almost melancholy, as they watched Patrick make light work of carrying the bags as he skillfully and effortlessly made his way through the crowd.

"Strange? You mean how he carries the bags," Daniel asked.

"No, not that," Bridget replied quietly, her eyes still following Daniel's rapidly disappearing form. It's just that I think I could be related to Patrick."

Eighteen

High up in the Santa Cruz Mountains of California the day had begun less than promisingly. At the break of dawn a clinging layer of crimson-tinged grey clouds had seemed determined to shut out the sun, while a lingering fog obscured the winding trails below. But fickle mother-nature soon changed her mind and by the time the heavily-swathed, grunting giants slowly emerged from their log cabins it seemed like one of those golden mornings that had slipped right out of paradise.

In the distance a solitary white hawk and a pair of great blue herons soared above the lake intently watching for any signs of life in the blue, chilly waters. As the men began their regular ten-mile run along the lightly-traveled trail, decorated with the pale purple of wild lilacs and the delicate rose of ripening blackberries, the air was moist and cool and fragrant, and the living cathedral of majestic redwoods whispered invitingly to all of god's creatures. Black-masked raccoons and wily gray foxes had been the first to rise and heed the call, but before long they had been joined by stately black-tailed mule deer, anxious gray squirrels, curious multi-colored chipmunks and even an occasional undistinguished-looking but bright-eyed brush rabbit. Here and there northern flickers appeared; their bright orange wings barely visible as they flashed through the trees and the laughing call of acorn woodpeckers resounded from the top of dead redwood trees.

It was here at the 300-acre Rowardennan Redwood Park resort, as far away from the maddening crowds as he could manage, that Jim Jeffries had come with a formidable entourage of trainers and sparring partners to begin final preparations for his historic contest with his detested foe, the black heavyweight champion of the world, Jack Johnson.

For Jeffries, increasingly short-tempered and irritable as the day of reckoning drew nearer, the isolated resort was the perfect choice. Rowardennan, the Scottish word for "enchanted forest," offered everything a fighter could possibly need or want. Its owner, Thomas Bell, had intentionally created a resort that cleverly combined the wilderness experience with substantial comfort and luxury, the kind of luxury and convenience that men of means expected and demanded. Tucked in between Highlands Park and the Ben Lomond Bridge, Rowardennan was surrounded on three sides by the San Lorenzo River and its architecture show-pieced the natural materials of the area. The redwood shingles and oak logs used in the buildings were left in their original colors and the foundations and fireplaces were constructed from rocks taken from the river.

Instead of a single building, the hotel consisted of sixteen log cabins with a combined total of 150 rooms, a main lodge that housed the lobby and a 200-seat dining room, a ballroom in a separate building, and a log-cabin Club House that contained a bowling alley and a library where books could be checked out by guests.

The grounds may not have been manicured but they contained well-maintained croquet and tennis courts, and a long, winding river trail, suggestively named Lover's Lane, which led to a pond where guests could go either boating or swimming. And at a time when electricity was still not widely available in many cities, the pond had been formed by the damming of the river to generate electricity for the resort. For guests who wanted a more authentic wilderness experience, horses and equipment for camping in the woods or touring the resort's extensive bridle trails were available.

It was the first week of April and Jeffries' retinue, which until then had been limited to his friend and manager Sam Berger, had expanded considerably. It now included the urbane Jim Corbett, himself a former heavyweight champion, who had been hired to help with Jeffries' training, and, perhaps even more importantly, to handle the newspapermen Jeffries so disliked and distrusted. Also there were: his brother Jack, himself a former heavyweight fighter who had lost on a fifth round knockout to Johnson in 1901; Joe Choynski, perhaps the greatest Jewish heavyweight boxer of all time and Johnson's onetime mentor; Martin "Farmer" Burns, a former wrestling champion; Bob Armstrong, a once-formidable black heavyweight, who had signed up with Jeffries after a quarrel with Johnson over back wages he claimed Johnson owed him; and two veterans of the stage, Walter Kelly, who had become famous for his vaudeville character "The Virginia Judge" and whose yet unborn niece, Grace Kelly, would become a Hollywood legend and a member of the European royalty, and Eddie Leonard, a longtime blackface minstrel.

The showmen had been given the difficult assignment of amusing and relaxing the relentlessly dour Jeffries, which they sometimes temporarily managed with their after-dinner performances built around the usual fare of crude anti-Negro jokes about watermelon eating and chicken stealing.

For days sleep for the former champion had been fitful at best. So instead of just lying in bed staring at the ceiling, during the last few nights he had begun getting up and going out on the fancy log porch of his shingle cabin. There he could be alone with the sounds of the forest and the river of stars that filled the ink-black sky. It was the only time he was really alone and, already, it was time he was beginning to cherish. He needed the time away from everybody, even his dear wife Freida, his constant companion for the last six years.

Sometimes, sitting alone and listening in fascination to the howling of the coyote, he wondered about his craving for privacy. He knew it wasn't just the burden of fame; in truth he'd always been like that, perhaps not quite so much so but enough to set him apart even then from his siblings and friends, ever since he could remember. Perhaps it was just his nature and the size of the family, he mused, with four brothers and three sisters there was always somebody around.

But the fighting and all the unwelcome attention it had brought, he knew, also had something to do with it, a lot to do with it. He had never wanted to be a fighter. He had never wanted to be famous. He had never even wanted to be rich. But now he was all three, the envy of most of the men on earth, and he was absolutely miserable. He'd made more money in the last year than he had in his whole life before that, all without throwing a single punch in anger. He'd made a lot from the first tour, more than sixty thousand dollars. But that was nothing compared to the second tour. At the end the promoters wrote him a check for $112,500, (more than two million dollars in 2010 currency) more money than he could have even imagined just a few months earlier. But, as he knew only too well, all that money came with a price, a very heavy price; the hopes and expectations of almost every white man in the country.

Sometimes it was all too much to bear. Everybody wanted so much from him, expected so much of him. They didn't just expect him to win; they expected him to destroy the fucking nigger, to demonstrate the superiority of the white man, their superiority, he thought bitterly, in the clearest and most violent manner possible. Sometimes, in his blackest moods, in his bleakest moments, he wondered who he hated most, his most ardent supporters, those who so desperately wanted him to win for the goddamned white race or that fucking nigger, Johnson.

Much of the time, the truth he told, he just wanted to disappear, to give back the money, to be left alone, to be allowed to go about his business unnoticed and unmolested, just like everybody else. And anyway it wasn't as if it was really him they were cheering for; he knew better, had always known better. It was for themselves they cheered, their sense of themselves, their image of the Caucasian race. He was nothing than an instrument, a tool to boost their self-esteem, and he was sick of it.

The burst of confidence of October and November had almost completely dissipated and he really didn't know why. It wasn't as if his body was failing him, far from it. He was every bit as strong as he ever was and his wind, while not yet quite where it was at his peak, was good and getting better. The ridiculous rumors that he weighed over 300 pounds or that he was just an empty shell didn't really bother him, the world would see for itself on the fourth of July. What made him sick to his stomach were the attempts to make him into some kind of superhuman being, a superman.

Like the article in that Chicago paper, after the tests they had talked him into undergoing, which had described him as a gorilla man of the Stone Age brought back to the flesh: And ridiculously compared him to the mythical Hercules. How could Hercules lose against a mere man, a nigger at that. The pressure never stopped, it only grew more and more intense every fucking, goddamned day with the arrival of the letters, hundreds, maybe thousands of them, that never stopped coming. Telling him that it was his responsibility as a white man to shut the mouth of that grinning, cocky nigger once and for all. Finally, he had ordered that all letters from people he didn't know personally were to be dumped in the trash, unopened.

He had even heard that bartenders around the country were passing on the most ridiculous, unbelievable stories about him: That he had cured himself of pneumonia by drinking a case of whisky in two days: That he had fought on a broken leg and still beaten a top heavyweight contender: That a doctor who had examined him had declared that he was not human. Hearing stories like that it was no wonder they expected him to kill the nigger. Sometimes it was all just too much. It wasn't as if he was afraid of Johnson. He believed he could win, most of the time anyway. But deep in his heart he also knew he could lose. And that was what he was scared of; letting everybody down, his family, his friends, his race, himself, in front of the whole world.

I wonder, he thought to himself as the plaintive howling of the coyotes echoed through the night, if they are as unhappy as me.

Nineteen

Upstairs, in the big front bedroom of the large and imposing three-storey Victorian house at 3345 South Wabash Avenue on Chicago's South Side, Etta Duryea was reclining on a massive four-poster bed, propped up by a half-dozen oversized, feather-filled pillows. After taking one long, last drag on her third and final cannabis cigarette she crushed the red-tinged butt in the crystal ashtray on the bedside table, smiled enigmatically, and slowly removed the small wet towel covering her eyes. The drug was beginning to work its reliable magic. The familiar euphoria, the overwhelming sense of wellbeing, was beginning to take over.

The pain that had gripped her eyes in its ruthless embrace had gone away, and so had the flashing silver lights, the aversion to the faintest sound and the relentless waves of nausea. Gone too was the unease, the anxiety, the vague sense of dread, the ephemeral, indefinable fear that had stalked her for much of her adult life. And which, after a brief hiatus, had returned in just the past month to precipitate her increasingly frequent headaches.

When her relationship with Johnson had just begun, his wealth, enormous confidence, personal physical power and, most of all, his generosity and obvious devotion, had helped to make her feel safe and protected, especially when they were alone together. But she had soon discovered that life with the black heavyweight champion of the world was unpredictable at best and held its own unique dangers. The crash on the way home from Milwaukee had been absolutely terrifying. They had been traveling at a high speed, too fast for the road conditions. The car had hit a muddy spot, suddenly swerved, plunged into a bank of snow and overturned. They had been thrown out violently and both had been badly bruised but fortunately, almost miraculously, not badly injured.

And then there had the incident in front of the pub in Minneapolis, which still made her shudder with fear and revulsion just to think about it.

She knew that she was a bundle of contradictions, constantly in search of peace and tranquility, but also, easily bored and always attracted to men who were not exactly pillars of tradition and conformity.

The cannabis had been a last resort for the lifetime non-smoker. She had first tried every other known natural remedy, including drinking powdered ginger mixed with water, sipping tea made from feverfew leaves and chewing on juniper berries, without even a semblance of success. Desperate, she'd even had her neck roped and manipulated, to, the eminent physician had gravely explained, "suspend the action of the great occipital nerves and harmonize the flow of arterial blood to and through the veins." She'd had her colon flushed, "vibratory friction" applied to her spine and given complete bed rest "to reduce the demand on the weight carrying function of her spine." None of it had worked. Only the cannabis had made a difference.

Getting out of the bed, Etta walked over to the windows facing the side of the house, pulled the heavy drapes aside, and energetically flung them open. Sunlight, the strains of the popular song, "In the shade of the old apple tree," a medley of voices, male and female, laughter, and other sounds of merriment, came pouring in. Downstairs, the all-day party, the barn dance, to celebrate Jack's thirty-second birthday was in full swing. All morning she'd helped to complete the transformation of the training quarters he'd built behind the house he had bought for his mother into, if she said so herself, a very realistic-looking barn.

She had enjoyed working with Jack and his mother and brother and sisters, feeling like one of the family. The headache had come on suddenly, without any warning, right there in the middle of the barn, just as they were finishing up and getting ready to go upstairs to get ready for the first guests. Jack knew about the headaches but had never personally witnessed the onset of one her attacks before. Even in her distress she had seen the shock, the concern, even the fear, in his face and she had gloated in painful triumph because she knew that no other woman, certainly not those two common whores that would not leave him alone, could have inspired that kind of response from him. It, that unguarded moment when his soul was revealed, was, for her, confirmation that there was something very rare and very special between them.

After their first meeting at the Vanderbilt Cup race on Long Island the telephone calls had quickly escalated into personal meetings and less than two months later, just before Christmas, Etta had moved in with him at his home away from home, Barron Wilkins' Little Savoy hotel in Manhattan. Friends and acquaintances who had previously been introduced to other Mrs. Johnsons, a list that included long-time girlfriends Hattie McClay and Belle Schreiber, were summarily informed that this was his "real" wife and warned not to mention other women in her presence.

It was quickly obvious to Johnson's wide circle of friends, acquaintances and business associates, that the relationship with the glamorous, elegant and well-spoken Etta Duryea was unlike any other the champion had had before. Johnson had always been fairly generous with his lady friends but he lavished gifts of expensive dresses, furs, and diamonds on Etta, who wore them with a flair that turned heads wherever they went. For the new heavyweight champion of the world, she was everything and more that a public man could have hoped for or wanted. With her on his arm, he finally had a female companion who was worthy of his new elevated status, a trophy he could proudly display to the entire world.

Etta Terry was born in 1881 at her family's comfortable summer home in the fashionable Long Island community of Hempstead. Her father's position as the superintendent of a large, Brooklyn-based company that manufactured milled door frames, window sashes and decorative mouldings, allowed the family to live in the kind of upper-middleclass comfort that the champion and the women he had previously been intimate with could only have dreamed of. Independent and headstrong, she had impulsively began a romance with a handsome young man who turned up on the doorstep of the Terry family home asking if he could water his limping horse. Intrigued, she not only readily agreed to the stranger's request but brought him a glass of water for himself. Enchanted by her beauty, the young man asked if he could call again and so began a courtship which ended in a wedding ceremony in the parlor of her family's large and well-appointed Brooklyn home, in June of 1903.

Etta's husband, Clarence E. Duryea, was the dashing and charming but unaccomplished son of a wealthy real estate man. Young Duryea unabashedly enjoyed all the good things of life. He was a yachtsman and a member of the exclusive Meadow Brook Hunt club, whose membership included people with the surnames of Vanderbilt, Belmont and Roosevelt. But, despite his personal charm and his family's wealth and connections, the young man was unable to duplicate the success of his father. Instead of applying himself to business or a profession, Clarence tried, against the advice of his parents, to parlay a modest talent for singing—he had been good enough to be a tenor soloist at the Garden City Episcopal Church—into a career in show business.

Etta, who, played the piano and sang, like her husband with only modest talent, was obviously as stagestruck as he was: And similarly disregarding the wishes and advice of her parents, plunged into a career on the stage. Predictably neither was successful and after a period of about four years, and mutual disillusionment, they seemed to have simply drifted apart.

Despite his admiration, great affection, and perhaps even genuine love for his new female companion, Etta's arrival did not immediately end Johnson's dalliance with Hattie and Belle. Both women were deeply entrenched in his life and ending those relationships would take time, effort and not least of all, money. While Etta was the only "Mrs. Johnson" in New York, back at home in Chicago things were different. He had bought his mother the big, three-storey house at 3344 South Wabash and for the first time in seven years he was going to be at home with his family for the holidays. Etta had stayed in New York to celebrate Christmas with her family and a photograph in the Milwaukee *Evening Wisconsin* showed the champion at home, embracing his mother and "wife,"—Hattie McClay— while manager George Little and a niece looked on.

But Hattie would not have him to herself for long. Alerted by the photograph of Johnson's presence in Chicago, Belle Schreiber, accompanied by her younger sister, arrived unexpectedly from Milwaukee a few days later with startling news. She was pregnant, she said, and the baby was Johnson's. Belle would later claim that the childless Johnson was pleased and asked her to have his child and not to do anything to get rid of it. But the chaos and confusion that surrounded Johnson was just beginning. Later that very day, Barney Gerard, the theatrical impresario, who had arranged for the champion to star in a touring show called the *Atlantic Athletic Carnival*, followed by seven weeks with a burlesque revue, *Follies of the Day*, arrived from New York to make sure that Johnson would be able to start his tour on New Year's Eve as scheduled.

But after an unusually brief and terse greeting, the normally affable champion, looking uncharacteristically harried, pulled him aside to explain that he had a serious problem and to ask for his help. Etta was due, he said, at any moment and, as had been the case in New York, he did not want her to know about his relationship with the other women. Gerard was to pretend that Hattie and Belle were with him. The impresario agreed to play along but the women would have none of it. Like much of the country they had read and heard a great deal about Johnson's new "wife," and they deeply resented the special treatment the newcomer, the interloper, received from the champion. When Etta arrived from New York only moments later, to her horror and the champion's embarrassment and distress, they not only attacked her verbally but threatened to beat her up.

For Hattie and Belle this was nothing new; they had long fought each other for Johnson's attention, but as Johnson understood only too well, Etta was in an entirely different league. She would never have tolerated that kind of treatment and he, to his credit, never expected her, never wanted her to. She was far too special for that. Knowing that he had to act quickly and decisively if he wanted to salvage his relationship with Etta, Johnson, after a long, private conversation with the woman who was claiming to be pregnant with his child, calmed her down and sent her away with what Gerard later described as a "large amount of cash."

Hattie, who had grown accustomed to playing a secondary role to Belle and was not claiming to be pregnant, was far easier to handle and left, it seems, without causing any undue trouble. With both women finally out of the way, a relieved Johnson moved Etta and her belongings into his mother's home.

In marked contrast to Jeffries, who spent the first three months of 1910 traveling the country awash in the uncritical adoration of the media and the American people and amassing enormous sums of money, as he begun his own tour Johnson was repeatedly confronted with the unyielding hostility of white America. In Cleveland, he was forced to dress in the cellar because blacks were not allowed in the theatre's dressing rooms; in Boston, he smashed the windows of a cab when a taxi driver refused to pick him up; in Detroit, it took Gerard three days to find a hotel willing to accommodate both Etta, who by then had joined him on the road for the *Follies of the Day* tour, and himself in the same room; and, most disturbing and hurtful to him, his income, despite his best efforts, was only a fraction of what Jeffries was so effortlessly collecting.

Despite the slights, injustices, and inconveniences of the road and his occasional dalliance with other women, the relationship with Etta continued to grow and develop. On the road they always registered as husband and wife and the happy couple spent every night together. With the assistance of friends and associates like Sig Hart, the other women, which still included Belle, who were stashed away at other hotels and rooming houses, were kept well away from Etta and the apparently insatiable champion was careful to only visit them during daylight hours.

But it was on the final day of Johnson's engagement in Minneapolis and St. Paul that Etta had her first, terrifying experience with the burning anger that her relationship with the black champion would arouse in much of the white population. On their way home to Chicago, the taxi that was taking them to the railroad station broke down in front of a saloon. When the word got out that Johnson and a white woman were inside, a sizeable crowd the *Police Gazette* described as "deckhands, wharf wallopers, timber jacks, mill hogs and bar flies," quickly surrounded the vehicle, jeering, hurling obscenities, screaming racial insults, threatening to lynch the nigger and his white whore. Only the unexpected intervention of the police, who escorted the shaken couple to the train station, had saved them from serious harm or worse.

For Johnson, inured to white hatred and discrimination by long and bitter experience, the incident was unsettling, but not particularly surprising or unexpected. It was the price he paid for living his life his way, without restrictions, limitations or apologies. But, for Etta, it must have been devastating. Nothing in her privileged existence as a white woman of education and means had prepared her for anything like the scorn and fury white men, men of her own race, men who would have been polite and deferential in almost any other circumstance, directed at her that day. It was, however, but the beginning of the abuse and ridicule that would be heaped on her for the rest of her life. That she persisted in the relationship with Johnson after this harrowing incident speaks volumes about the nature of the relationship and the surprising grittiness of her character.

Later in the day, in fact within an hour of getting out of bed, Etta was downstairs playing, to the enormous pride and satisfaction of her new beau, the welcoming hostess with all the charm and grace of a lady of her upbringing. Dressed simply but elegantly in a Gibson Girl-influenced high-necked embroidered blouse, a long, draped bustle skirt, boots, cotton kid gloves and a pair of large diamond earrings, Etta personally greeted each arriving guest. As the day wore into evening and then night, as people, black and white, came and went, she circulated tirelessly, smiling constantly, seemingly enjoying her role as the champion's official hostess.

Except for one small incident the party was an enormous success. At some stage during the festivities the champion and Sig Hart were inspired to test the speed of two of Johnson's newest racing cars, on the public roads. The merry pair drove to nearby Michigan Avenue. And the car Johnson was driving sporting a hand-lettered sign on its hood, which read, DON'T PINCH ME TODAY. I AM NOT SPEEDING. BELIEVE ME.

But the sign only seemed to have attracted the immediate attention of the police, in the person of a foot patrolman named Flynn who, Johnson claimed, had long been out to get him. Before they were able to do much racing both men were arrested. When Johnson adamantly refused to allow the police officer to ride in his car to the police station, Flynn summoned a patrol wagon. As a crowd gathered while they waited, a jovial Johnson smilingly turned to the officer and said. "Stand back, Mr. White Officer, and let the colored people have a look at me."

Twenty

What had surprised and somewhat disappointed Daniel most about San Francisco, as he strode eagerly through its bustling streets those first few days after his arrival, had been its absolute and utter newness; how little remained either of the old city or any evidence of the terrible destruction that had befallen it just four years earlier. He had, of course, expected the city to be dotted here and there by shiny new buildings, but he had also expected it to be strewn with the dust and rubble of destruction and construction. He had hoped to describe both the demolition and the rebuilding, as the scavengers and the carpenters and the bricklayers and the plumbers went about their work; to paint word pictures for his readers of the city's painful but glorious rebirth. For none of the research he'd done, nothing he had heard or read or imagined, had prepared him for the enormous ambitiousness and breathtaking scope of the transformation that had already taken place.

It was as if, he'd thought, as he walked around the city, along Market Street, and through Downtown and Chinatown and the Financial District, the sites of so much of the destruction, but now clean and glittering with handsome, new steel-framed buildings, that the gods of fate and destiny had shaken the earth and sent the fire to the golden city not in hate and anger but out of unrequited but undying love.

The destruction of the old city had only been a prelude to the rising of the new and vastly improved San Francisco, the newspaperman had decided, while gaping in awe at the architectural marvels of the Financial District. Montgomery Street by itself, he discovered, had some of the finest buildings in the world, with four of them, the Anton Borel, the Alvinza Hayward, the Bank of Italy, and the Italian American Bank, on one spectacular block.

Incredibly, twenty thousand new buildings had been erected in just three years and in October of 1909 the justifiably proud city fathers had celebrated their achievement by throwing a grand, five-day party, the Partola Festival, to show-off their new city and loudly announce to the world that the golden city was back in business.

The brand-new metropolis of broad streets, neoclassical public buildings and arterial thoroughfares, old residents assured him, many with proud smiles but some with sad little shakes of their heads, was nothing like the old one. Within the neighborhoods the earthquake had destroyed, just over 300 of 28,000 buildings had been left standing. Thousands of the city's two-storey Victorian houses, her "painted ladies," constructed almost entirely of wood from the local redwood forests, had perished in the fire. And the gilded structures, with their gingerbread latticework, gabled roofs and bay windows, had been replaced, to the horror of some but the approval of many, by buildings far less ornate and romantic but much more utilitarian and practical.

The fanciful style of those destroyed Victorian homes, examples of which remain even today in neighborhoods, such as Haight-Ashbury, that the fire did not reach, reflected the grand style, untested optimism, even naiveté, of nineteenth century San Francisco. By 1906 the rough frontier town of fifty years earlier had been transformed into what some with considerable justification called the Paris of the West. Like Paris, San Francisco was grand enough and famous enough to attract the eager attention of the most illustrious performers from other parts of the world, people such as the Italian tenor Enrico Caruso and the doyenne Sarah Bernhardt. And like Paris it had its own, homegrown contingent of famous writers and artists. It even had its equivalent of the Parisian cafes where young intellectuals, writers and artists gathered to meet, greet, jovially trade insults, exchange ideas and eat and drink merrily well into the night.

The most famous of these was Coppa's. Located in the basement of what was said to be the city's first fireproof structure, the four-storey, Montgomery Block, the restaurant was, by far, the city's most important bohemian rendezvous. Considered an engineering marvel at the time of its construction in 1853 by General Henry W. Halleck and for a time the largest building west of the Mississippi, the Montgomery Block also provided office space for the *San Francisco Argonaut*, where people like Mark Twain and Ambrose Bierce, author of the Devil's Dictionary, sometimes worked. Also among Coppa's regular patrons were literary stars such as: George Sterling, whose poetry was said to compare favorably with Milton, Keats and Spencer, and who was hailed by Bierce as the future "poet of the skies, prophet of the suns;" the writer Isabel Fraser, who was christened "Queen of Bohemia" on a ladder at the restaurant; Nora May French, the flamboyant journalist and poet, who was said to have prophesied the city's destruction over lunch; and the dashing journalist and novelist Jack London, who had summoned Jim Jeffries out of retirement to rescue the Caucasian race from the despised Jack Johnson.

It was not uncommon for these luminaries and others less wellknown, to gather around a great table strategically located in the middle of the restaurant and over dishes of Pappa Coppa's famous Chicken Portola fire volleys of always blistering, often witty repartee at each other, while patrons, many of whom had come specifically to see the celebrities, watched and listened in undisguised delight and admiration.

But entertainment in pre-earthquake San Francisco was hardly limited to the banter of writers and poets. The city's ethnically diverse population included people of Italian, Russian, German, Mexican and Chinese backgrounds, and almost every group could attend some kind of artistic production performed in their own native language. Particularly popular, with San Franciscans of all ethnic backgrounds, was Chinese opera at the venerable 1,500-seat Royal China Theatre. And on the night before the earthquake, two of the biggest shows in town were Enrico Caruso's performance of Bizet's *Carmen* at the Grand Opera House on Mission Street, and the operatta *Babes in Toyland* at the Colombia Theatre downtown.

The city also had less artistic offerings centered in the notorious neighborhood known as the Barbary Coast, just down the road from Coppa's and for decades one of the most exciting but dangerous places on the face of the earth. There, at nights, among the seamy waterfront dives, opium dens, gambling houses, brothels, dancehalls and concert saloons, men, with regular jobs and everyday lives but with a taste for the bawdy and the forbidden and perhaps a certain kind of female companionship, furtively rubbed shoulders with a motley, unsavory crew of sailors, gamblers, habitual drunks, lewd fallen women, chorus girls, pickpockets, house burglars, cutthroats and murderers.

That world, artistic, exciting, bohemian San Francisco, was utterly destroyed by the great earthquake and the fires that roared uncontrolled for several days through the city in its wake. All eight of the city's eight downtown theatres, the Grand Opera House, the Royal China Theatre, even Coppa's in its supposedly fireproof building, and much of the Barbary Coast, perished during those awful days. In fact, almost all of the city's great public buildings were lost, most in the conflagration: City Hall, the city's most ambitious public building; the new Post Office; the 20-storey "Call" Building, the Parrott Building, which housed the largest department store in the West, the buildings housing the city's leading newspapers, the Chronicle and the Examiner, Stanford University at Palo Alto and St. Ignatius Church and all the buildings, laboratories, libraries and art treasures of the University of San Francisco, then known as St. Ignatius College.

In the spring of 1910, the city that Daniel visited was very different from the one it had replaced. The new San Francisco was, unquestionably, far more modern, cleaner and less politically corrupt. But it was also, undoubtedly, less brash, romantic and blindly optimistic. Commerce and its concerns, like in every other major city, were always important in San Francisco; but now the interests of business would become supreme.

Perhaps nothing symbolized the city's new culture more accurately than the rebuilding of Chinatown. An enterprising Chinese businessman, Look Tin Eli, convinced his fellow merchants to redesign their neighborhood with an eye on attracting tourist dollars. The idea was to recreate a little piece of China right there in San Francisco. But very little attempt was made at authenticity. In most instances American architects designed regular American-style buildings and simply placed colorful pagodas with curled eaves and dragon motifs on top of them; creating what was, in effect, an Oriental Disneyland.

Like Chinatown, the banks and the theatres and all the public buildings would be built again, bigger and better than ever. But something important about the old spirit, the bohemian creativity, would be lost, for a very long time. In 1910, most of the buildings were back but the spirit was not.

It was just past midday when Daniel strode into the vast, crowded, dining room for the second time that day. Soft, amber sunlight filtered through the towering, iridescent glass ceiling and the soft buzz of foreign tongues and unfamiliar accents rose above the musical tinkling of crystal glasses and goblets. Already almost every table and chair was taken, many by some of the most elegantly dressed men and women Daniel O'Brien had ever seen.

That morning it had taken him several long seconds to recognize the vaguely familiar, bleary-eyed and jowly middle-aged man staring at him from his bathroom mirror in startled disbelief. It was as if he had gotten fat and old overnight, he thought, as he examined the mottled skin of his bloated face and the fine red-blue veins in his swollen nose with growing disgust. He knew that the eating and the drinking, especially the drinking, had been getting out of control. And after the first week or so he had done very little walking; he had been taking the ever-present streetcars or cabs everywhere. If he continued the way he was going, he told himself, Bridget wouldn't even be able to recognize him when he got back home let alone want to marry him. So with images of his beautiful fiancée burnt into his brain as incentive, Daniel had vowed to begin the job of losing the unwanted pounds that very day. Not being physically attractive to her was a prospect he could not face.

He had been surprised at the extent of his homesickness. He had fully expected to miss seeing Bridget, watching the sun in her hair, touching her, tasting the sweetness of her lips, talking to her, just listening to her voice, just sharing the same space and breathing the same air, just being with her. But he had not expected, especially in the first few weeks, the visceral sense of loss, as if a limb, some piece of his body, was missing, that numbed every sense and diminished every experience. Her long, chatty letters, arriving after the first fortnight at a rate of one every other day had helped, somewhat. Knowing that she was well and that she missed him every bit as he missed her was deeply satisfying. But her vivid descriptions of the small details of her day also reminded him of just how much she meant to him.

Although he had been a registered guest there for more than five weeks, for the newspaperman just sitting in the Palace Hotel's magnificent Garden Court was still as impressive as it had been on that very first day. He had known quite a bit about the hotel and its storied history before his arrival: That it had been the largest, costliest, and most luxurious hotel in the world when it first opened in 1875 and that William Ralston, who exhausted his banking empire building it, had been found floating in San Francisco Bay just weeks before it opened; that Presidents Ulysses S. Grant, Benjamin Harrison and Rutherford Hayes had stayed there; that it had the first hydraulic elevators in the West, electric call buttons in every room, a pneumatic tube system throughout the hotel and air-conditioning, fireplaces and bay windows in each room.

The new Palace Hotel which opened on the same site in 1909, approximately three years after the destruction of the first, was, in some ways, as Daniel had learned, a very different structure. Constructed of steel, concrete and brick, it had a far plainer exterior than Ralston's original caravansary and rose to nine floors, two more than its predecessor. But the interior was every bit as opulent and with its beaux arts style that combined Greek and Roman architecture, dome stained glass ceiling, and massive Austrian crystal chandeliers, the new Garden Court was judged by many who knew both to be even more magnificent than the original.

But as Daniel discovered soon after his arrival, the Garden Court was only one of several extraordinarily beautiful public rooms in the new Palace Hotel. The Rose Room, which featured the same iridescent glass ceiling and old-ivory toned woodwork as the Garden Court, the magnificent white and gold Ball Room, the Grill, with its heavily carved panels and beamed ceiling, the delightful gray and ivory French Parlor, and Daniel's absolute favorite, the Pied Pier Room, named in honor of Maxfield Parrish's magical depiction of the children's fable of the Pied Piper of Hamelin, were all absolutely stunning. Since the famed American's massive seven-by-sixteen-foot oil on canvas painting hung above the club-like bar that dominated the room, the homesick Daniel soon became exceedingly familiar with its inspired charms.

Daniel had debated with himself whether to even bother having lunch. The truth was he was not really hungry; in fact he was not hungry at all. He had supplemented the Palace's truly extraordinary Continental buffet breakfast with a perfect crab omelette that was served with chardonnay cream sauce and the tenderest of tiny, breakfast potatoes. He had gorged himself on an enormous plate of mouthwatering fresh fruits—pears, grapes, apples and slices of cantaloupes, watermelons and mangoes--all the while assuring himself that fruits were not only not fattening but healthy. But then he had been unable to resist the fresh, house-smoked Pacific salmon, which he had with the kind of crisp but tender bagel he'd thought you could only find in New York. And he had finished it all off with two steaming hot cups of coffee, dark with three spoons of sugar, just the way he liked it. He had returned to his room stuffed and absolutely disgusted with himself.

"Sir," the voice said, "Are you ready to order."

Looking up at the pleasant, smiling face of the young waiter, Daniel hesitated briefly before replying. "I'll have the calamari salad and the roasted breast of chicken."

That was a good decision, Daniel assured himself, as he looked around the room, a little bit guiltily. Not too heavy, not too light. He had thought about going with something lighter, and he would have if he knew with any certainty what time he'd be back. But with Jack Johnson you never knew what would happen.

Summers are cold and foggy and springs are warm and dry in San

Francisco. Daniel, who had first become aware of the city's peculiar weather by learning of Mark Twain's famous quip that the coldest winter he had ever spent was a summer in San Francisco, was wearing one of the several light-colored linen suits he had purchased specifically for the trip as he left his hotel and began walking eastwards on Market Street towards San Francisco Bay. Since the Seal Rock House, where Johnson and his party had encamped, was on Ocean Avenue on the city's western edge, far too far for walking, he had decided to walk to the Ferry Building at the eastern end of Market Street, a distance of some two miles from the hotel. From there he would the take the Number One California Street Car, past the Golden Gate Park and the Sutro Baths, all the way to the Lands End Station at the very end of the line.

It was just past the middle of May and for San Francisco a perfect spring day, cloudless, clear, and mild. Market Street, the city's great transit artery, which runs diagonally across the city for more than three miles from the waterfront to the hills of Twin Peaks, was, as usual, a beehive of activity. Electric and horsedrawn streetcars, motorized vehicles, and humans of almost every age, size, shape and shade, moved tirelessly up and down the 120-foot wide boulevard. Advertisements were plastered on every building and flying banners denoting some public holiday swooped and streaked between the buildings.

At the corner of 3rd Street, at the intersection known by locals as Newspaper Row, a policeman and two-well-dressed businessmen carefully followed the progress of a dark-haired young woman daringly dressed in a gauzy, sort of semi-transparent long white frock and broad-brimmed white hat, as she crossed from one side of the street to the other. The men's eyes continued to follow the young woman, who was nonchalantly smoking a small, dark cigaret, until she disappeared into the white-walled Examiner Building. Across the street was the rival Call newspaper in its domed 12-storey building, and a block further west was the building housing the third of the city's three leading newspapers, the Chronicle. All three buildings were either badly damaged or destroyed by the earthquake and fire but were quickly rebuilt or remodeled.

For Daniel, much needed exercise was only one of the benefits of a long walk that day. He also needed to compose his thoughts, urgently. Despite his best efforts he was still as uncertain about the fate of the fight as the day he arrived. He had visited the champion at his home in Chicago, spent a week up in the mountains at Rowardennan with Jeffries, or, more accurately, since he so rarely actually met with or even saw the ex-champion, at Jeffries' camp, interviewed both promoters several times, met with the Governor in Sacramento and spoken with scores of local officials in both Oakland and San Francisco. And although he had filed more than a dozen stories since his arrival, he had been unable to give his readers or his editor the kind of definitive assurance that all was well with the fight, as he had hoped. While the promoters, Rickard and Gleason had, seemingly, patched up their differences nothing else seemed to be going well.

Just the day before Thomas Williams, president of the New California Jockey Club, had announced that the fight would not in fact take place at the Oakland race track or, for that matter, at any other place in Alameda County. In one of the most mealy-mouthed statements Daniel had ever heard, Williams announced that he had been willing to stand by his personal agreement to lease the track on July 4th, but that the promoters had accepted his advice against holding it there. The problem, he claimed, wasn't with him or with the clergymen who had been agitating against it for several weeks, ever since the death of young Tommy McCarthy in San Francisco on April 29th, from injuries received during a bout with the British featherweight Owen Moran. It was instead, Williams insisted, the solid opposition of the businessmen of Oakland, many of whom, he admitted, had initially favored bringing the fight to their city, and the unwavering hostility of the Attorney General, who was threatening arrests, that had doomed the fight, at least in Alameda County. So, amazingly, unbelievably, with less than six weeks to go, the fight had still not found a venue.

True, after a hurried conference with Gleason and other unnamed parties, Rickards had confidently, if tersely, announced that "the fight would be held in California." And there were unconfirmed rumors that a deal had already been made to stage it in San Francisco, although, unlike their counterparts in Oakland, the merchants of both Richmond and Emeryville were anxious to bring the fight to their cities. Despite the soothing words Daniel had not been reassured. An earlier interview with the Governor of the State, James Gillett, had left him shaken and deeply pessimistic, a pessimism he had tried unsuccessfully to squelch, about the fight's prospects in the state. Daniel had interviewed the Republican, who had taken office in 1907 as the candidate of the Southern Pacific's Political Bureau, to assess the extent of his support for the fight and had been shocked by Gillett's response that it was, in his opinion, "simply a scheme to make a lot of money out of the credulity of the public."

When pressed to explain why he had come to that conclusion, if he had some kind of inside knowledge of a deal, Gillett, who had been an affluent lawyer with a successful practice before assuming the political leadership of the state, had blithely replied that "Anybody with the least sense knows the whites of this country won't allow Johnson or any other Negro to win the world's championship from Jeffries. Johnson knows that. He's no fool. He knows that to win that fight he would have to whip every white man at ringside. So he has agreed to lay down for the money."

Since the governor had admitted that he had no special knowledge of any "fix" and was just expressing his personal opinion, Daniel had decided after long consideration not to use the governor's startling statement in any of his articles. But the Wisconsin native had obviously said the same thing to at least one other reporter because it eventually made its way into print. Although the governor, under intense pressure from Rickard, later claimed he had been misquoted, the damage had already been done. His original statement was widely regarded as the real truth and it, seemingly, validated the whispering and rumors of a deal and intensified the national campaign being led by white clergymen against the bout.

But it is still far too early to conclude that the fight will not take place, Daniel told himself, as he made his way through the wholesale district and glanced at the attractive Chinese woman standing uncertainly outside one of the district's spice companies, clutching two teenaged children pressed tightly against her. The three, dressed in traditional Chinese costumes, eyes carefully cast down at the pavement and standing as closely together as possible, seemed intent on occupying the smallest possible space and not offending any passerby. A few yards away but a world apart a giggling group of young white girls, a few holding umbrellas as protection against the overhead sun, waited impatiently for a streetcar.

Surely, Daniel told himself, as he neared the Davis and Pine intersections, a rabidly pro-business Republican like Gillett would not lightly deprive the state of the kind of revenue the fight was expected to generate. Tens of thousands of people from all over the country and the world would be pouring into the city, most of them by railroad, and were expected to spend millions of dollars with the city's hotels, bars, brothels, restaurants, groceries, night clubs etc. Just ahead a Negro in a dark blue uniform driving a 1909, six-cylinder, fifty-horsepower Touring car turned to smile at the laughing young white boy in the backseat, who was pointing at the sidewalk. The source of the amusement, Daniel noted, as he glanced across the street, were two unusually ungainly human beings: an extremely tall, thin businessman walking slowly and gingerly in shoes that were clearly too tight, and his companion, an enormously overweight woman, in an even larger hat smothered with artificial flowers, who was obviously struggling to keep up with even that very modest pace.

As he passed East Street and an advertisement for Nathan Hale Havana Cigars on a wall to his right, Daniel increased his pace and lengthened his stride. But the problem is not just with the venue or the odd behavior of the governor, the fighters' attitudes may be just as big a problem, he reminded himself as the Ferry Building came into view. Johnson's refusal to begin serious training despite the pleadings of the promoters was feeding the rumors that the fight was fixed. But more worrisome than Johnson's casual arrogance had been Jeffries' strange regression to the sullen, withdrawn fighter he had seen in Boston more than a year earlier. When Daniel had last seen him in the fall, at Jack

Cooper's gymnasium in Manhattan, the former champion had been calmly confident and almost cheerful. Then, he had been almost talkative, regaling the newsmen with a mocking description of Johnson's pugilistic shortcomings and a quietly confident explanation of why he was going to regain the title he had never lost in the ring. Now, inexplicably, at Rowardennan with the date of the fight rapidly approaching, he was more tightlipped and irritable than ever, steadfastly refusing to meet with the press, sending out former champion Jim Corbett to speak on his behalf instead, even building a fence around his cottage.

He had, at least, been able to assure his readers that the rumors that the reclusive former champion was either grossly overweight, or a spent, empty shell, were simply not true. From what he had observed Jeffries was, physically, in excellent condition, especially considering that the fight was then still almost two months away. The Californian's wind seemed good and his power was as impressive as ever. Some ringside observers claimed that the former champion's judgment of distance was not what it used to be and worried aloud that their champion would be unable to catch-up with the elusive Johnson. But, in Daniel's experience, Jeffries' ring rustiness was typical of fighters at an early stage of preparation. In fact, in his opinion, it would have been far more worrisome if he was too sharp too soon. What concerned him, although not a word had ever made its way into any of his dispatches, was not Jeffries' physical condition but what seemed, at least to him, to be the fighter's fragile mental state.

He would have liked to have been as reassuring about the rumors of a fix as he had been about Jeffries' physical readiness. Not that he believed it himself, not for a moment. Johnson was far too egotistical. The people who believed the black champion would take a dive in a fight of this magnitude just didn't know the man and the fierce pride that drove him. But his behavior, he had to admit, was provocative. The whispers that a deal had been done started almost immediately after the fight contracts had been signed. The willingness of the fighters, both Jeffries and Johnson, to accept a share of the fight film's proceeds as part of their compensation was cited as proof that the fix was in. Even a fool knew, the reasoning went, that the film of the fight would be almost worthless if Johnson won. Nobody, except a bunch of poor, broke niggers, would want to see it. On the other hand, if Jeffries triumphed, millions of white people would line up at theatres all over the country and around the world to see it, many more than once. Johnson, the story went, had decided to go for the money instead of the glory.

The rumors eventually became so rampant and widespread that Gleason had made a special trip to Johnson's Chicago home in late March to remind the champion of the clause in his contract that required both fighters to begin training no less than ninety days before the stated date of the fight, and to urge him to pack his belongings and leave for the coast at once. According to newspaper reports, the promoter had told an indignant Johnson that while he had no fear that he would not be in proper shape to defend his title that it was only fair to him and to Rickard, considering the large purse they had put up and the lengths to which they were going to promote the fight, that he show the public that he was serious about defending his title.

The enormous clock on the slim, grey tower read 1:20 when Daniel arrived at the loop in front of the Ferry Building. A major terminal for the busy Market Street Line, and for ferries carrying passengers across the bay to Oakland, Almeda and Berkley, it had survived the earthquake and fire virtually intact. The cacophony of sounds and variety of sights that greeted him was like nothing he had ever experienced before. Even for a New Yorker the high-pitched screeching of the streetcars, the constant clanging of their bells, the copious dust stirred in their wake as they rumbled slowly around the loop to begin their return trips to the city, the discordant shouting of the numerous newsboys aggressively hawking their wares, the meandering commuters, the intermingled horsedrawn and motorized vehicles, and the chiming of the bells of the ferryboats, was more than a little disorienting.

After taking a deep breath, narrowly dodging a People's Express Van, pushing through the chaos of commuters, streetcars and vehicles, and getting to the relative safety of the sidewalk in front of the building, Daniel checked the watch he had pulled out of his pocket and smiled happily. There was no mistake, he had gotten there quite a bit faster than he had expected. The newspaperman was pleased with himself, for good reason. He had been walking briskly for almost forty minutes and despite the overindulgence of the past weeks and the extra pounds he was carrying, mostly around his middle, he had barely broken a sweat. The long walk, thanks to the cooling breeze blowing off the bay, had been unexpectedly pleasant. And now he had enough time and plenty of energy left to look around the famous building and walk up to the observation deck in its tower. The view of the bay from that height, he knew, had to be spectacular.

Up close, the Neo-Romanesque building, with its formal Colusa sandstone façade, was extremely impressive. The main structure was only three stories high, but the clock tower, modeled on the Giralda Tower of the Cathedral of Seville in Spain, reached 245 feet into the sky. Inside, the soaring two-storey public area, the 660-foot long Grand Nave, with its repeating interior arches, overhead skylight and mosaic floor, was even more impressive. After a quick, admiring trip around the magnificent space and the delightful and busy retail outlets, restaurants, cafes and specialty shops it housed, Daniel began the difficult climb up the narrow, winding staircase to the observation deck on the twelfth floor.

Sweating profusely, his chest heaving and his knees aching from the unaccustomed exertion, Daniel staggered out onto the observation deck, stopped briefly, drew a deep breath and took his first good look at the green-blue waters of the great, landlocked harbor known as San Francisco Bay. His first startled impression of a vast limitless horizon, where out in the shimmering distance, in defiance of the very laws of nature, the waters and the clouds seem to meet in mutual agreement and perfect harmony, was one of those indelible images he would cherish forever.

Like every other corner of San Francisco on that fine spring day, the rippling waters of the bay and the pale blue skies above it were bursting with life and frenetic activity. On the water, white flat-bottomed ferryboats with black smokestacks moved with solid purpose to and from the wharf: And what seemed like, at least, hundreds of fishing vessels, most powered by sails but some by the new marine engines, swarmed about like eager flocks of butterflies. Above the water, hundreds of thousands of waterbirds tirelessly searched for food. But while the murres, cormorants, loons and grebes dived and swooped to hunt their own, the spoiled seagulls doggedly followed the ferries around. They had been taught to depend on man; snatching up food thrown from the cook's galleys; darting after breadcrumbs tossed from the decks, sometimes skillfully catching them in mid-air; and, even, to the delight of the passengers, plucking tasty morsels from outstretched hands.

    Coming back down the narrow stairs was a lot easier on his lungs and knees than going up and by the time he took his seat in the open side trolley Daniel had almost fully recovered his wind and strength. The light tropical suit had been perfect for Market Street and the cooling breeze coming off the bay, but it was, he soon discovered, totally inadequate protection from the chilly winds blowing, sometimes with almost gale-like force, off the grey, choppy Pacific Ocean. Fortunately for Daniel, the streetcar was packed with far more warmly dressed passengers until almost the end of the line, most of them getting off at the Golden Gate Park and the Sutro Baths stations. So he was able to remain reasonably warm until he arrived at his destination, the one-storey hexagonal building at the Lands End station, and, with more than a dozen fellow passengers, began his hike down the rugged walking trail to Seal Rock House.

Twenty-One

Etta Duryea closed her eyes and shivered in delight as the magnificent voice of Marcella Sembrich flooded, then overpowered the enormous bedroom of the suite in the Seal Rock House that she shared with her lover, the heavyweight champion of the world, Jack Johnson. The Polish soprano, who she had once been fortunate enough to hear in person at the Met, was one of her absolute favorite vocalists. And Sembrich's bravura rendition of Arditi's "Parla," she considered one of the very best of the great artist's recordings, many of which had not, unfortunately, captured the true quality of that unforgettable voice. Listening to the woman, who had conquered Europe before becoming a permanent resident of the United States, soar so effortlessly into the high Ds was Etta's idea of a supreme spiritual experience.

Jack had loaded the expensive, late model Victor-Victrola phonograph they brought with them from Chicago with selections from Sembrich, Enrico Caruso, Mary Garden, the Scottish-American soprano and others of that ilk immediately after returning from his morning run. Jack's musical tastes, so similar to hers, had been quite a surprise, a very pleasant surprise for Etta. And it hadn't been, at least not so much, that he was a pugilist or a Negro either. But mostly because he was a man, a real man, not one of those sad creatures, for whom she had the utmost sympathy, who belonged, she believed, because of no fault of their own, to neither gender. Not even her former husband, somebody who'd had the finest of upbringings and education and a singer and a man of the theatre himself, had such a fine ear, such highly developed appreciation for operatic talent as her new lover.

And it was not all a pretense, a way of gilding his image, as she had quickly discovered. Not only did his record collection include the finest operatic music and the greatest vocal talent from around the world, but, as his Sembrich collection proved, he was able to select the very best of an artist's recordings. Although Madame Sembrich had made quite a number of recordings much of it had failed to capture the brilliance and range of her amazing voice. Her "Parla" was probably the finest of her commercial recordings.

This was Etta's first visit to a training camp and it was, fortunately, nothing like she'd feared. Other fighters might hide away like hermits and subject themselves and everybody around them to the most disagreeable of conditions, but not her Jack. The Seal Rock House was a wonderful place, right on the beach, and since they had taken the entire place so they could keep everybody together, the trainers, the sparring partners, the cooks, the maids, everybody, it was almost like having their own private residence. They even had a suite of rooms, like their own regular little flat, on the second floor. In addition to their bedroom and bathroom, there was a massage room for Jack, a lounging room, a dining room and even their own kitchen.

The privacy had been her idea and not everybody liked it, but that's the way it was going to be from now on. She was simply not going to tolerate all those people coming in and out of her private quarters as they pleased. She had made it known that when the doors were closed, especially after hours, that it meant that they didn't want any visitors, that they wanted to be alone together. She had been told, she remembered, a small, sly smile tugging at her lips and a faint blush spreading across her face, that fighters were not supposed to have sex during training for a big fight; because, supposedly, the loss of semen drained their strength away. But Jack had only laughed and said that he would prove to her that it was all just superstitious nonsense. He intended, he told her, to make love to her at least once every single day until the fight and then go out and give Jeffries the whipping of his life. And so far he had been as good, and many days better, than his word.

But it had not been only the sex, or even primarily the sex, as wonderful as that had been, that made those evenings alone in their little flat so unforgettable. Even more special had been the extraordinary level of intimacy they had managed to achieve. They told each other everything there was to know about the other, revealing themselves as neither of them had ever done before, to any other man or woman. The feeling of dread and the headaches had disappeared, the cannabis cigarettes were forgotten and she told herself that she had never been so much in love in her entire life.

The only real sour notes, she thought, as Mary Garden's hauntingly beautiful, ethereal voice replaced Sembrich's more powerful one, were the problem with that horrible little man, so aptly named Little, and all that shit that was always being written about Jack. She had been urging Jack for some time to get rid of the man and now it seemed that he would. Firing him would probably cause some problems, particularly with the newspapers, because he had some kind of contract that Jack had signed that gave him 25 percent of all of Jack's earnings for another year, but it had to be done. From what she had seen Jack was really his own manager. He did all the real negotiations himself; George was just an assistant, an errand boy. She had long wondered what Jack saw in him, why he had ever made him his manager. She knew that they used to go out drinking and whoring together; that had been their bond. But she had a put a stop to all that nonsense, Jack's life was now totally different and she knew that Little resented her for that, but she didn't care, he had to go.

As for the newspapers, they always seemed to find something to criticize Jack about. Now it was that he wasn't training because he intended to throw the fight, when the truth was that he had slipped and hurt himself outside Tex Rickard's office the day after they arrived. And all that nonsense that he was fat and out of shape, when the truth was, as she knew better than anybody else, was that he had a wonderful body and he was, as always, in wonderful condition. But they really didn't care what they wrote in the newspapers about them, at least Jack didn't, although it still made her crazy. The accident turned out not to be all bad. Since he hadn't been able to train seriously for a while they'd had a chance to spend a lot of time together. She loved just walking on Ocean Beach holding hands, listening to the crashing of the waves and breathing in the cool, tangy air. They had gone for long drives in and around the city—Jack loved San Francisco and had so many friends there—and through the beautiful Golden Gate Park, which she learned was filled with lakes and fishing ponds, was even larger than Central Park, and had something like a million trees in it.

But her absolute favorite thing was dining at the very famous Cliff House. The meals were even better than she had heard, and she adored how the building had been designed to blend in perfectly with the ocean and the cliffs around it. And, best of all, from their table they were able to see miles and miles of the coast and watch actual seals sunning themselves on seal rock and ships off all sizes sail in and out of the Golden Gate strait, while they talked and talked and sipped a bottle of wine. It had been two of the happiest weeks of her life. Out here in California, especially here in San Francisco, was like being in another country, another world, where skin color didn't matter all that much, where she could forget for even a little while that he was black and she was white. Back home in Chicago and New York and everywhere in that part of the world, it was always there, always intruding in their lives. If only, she thought, she could freeze time.

Mary Garden was singing "And there's none in the world can wi my sweet love compare, Oh what tell me what if your heelin' lad be slain," when the damp, lean and naked heavyweight champion of the world, the muscles in his arms, shoulders, abdomen and legs rippling with every movement, emerged from the bathroom with a large, fluffy, white towel slung around his neck.

"Have you eaten yet Princess," he semi-shouted, smiling solicitously at the small, slim figure stretched out on the sofa with her eyes tightly shut. Etta, he had discovered, aroused unfamiliar and sometimes uncomfortable emotions in him. She was not the most knowledgeable or skilful of lovers but her lack of experience only endeared her more to him. She often seemed so frail, so fragile, that he was always afraid of hurting her in any way because her wellbeing, her happiness had become the most important thing in the world to him.

Lost in her reminiscing and transported by Garden's powerful and emotional delivery of John Mcdermott's "Blue Bells of Scotland," Etta turned towards the bathroom door, more sensing her lover's presence than hearing his question.

"Oh Jack," she said, eyes shining as she stretched her arms to him. "It's so sad and I'm so happy. I think I'm going to cry."

"I know, I know, my lovely little Princess," he said, smiling still as he reached down and effortlessly swept her into his powerful arms and carried her to their bed. "Come and let me make it better."

The trek along the winding, sandy trail from the Lands End Station to the Seal Rock House on Ocean Beach was longer and more difficult to navigate in his thin-soled leather shoes than Daniel had anticipated. But the proceedings, in the big pavilion, were just beginning when he arrived out of breath and with his feet aching from the pebbles along the way and made his way to the press enclosure. The converted dance hall was jammed with some 2,000 paying fans, several hundreds of them, to Daniel's surprise--since he had seen so few since his arrival-- local Negroes, most or all of whom were, judging from their cries of encouragement and admiration, rabid fans of the black champion.

Up on the stage the heavyweight champion of the world was just beginning his routine when Daniel settled into place and pulled a battered notebook and a pen from the right pocket of his jacket. Johnson, who, as Daniel would later learn, had completed his 12-mile run along Ocean Boulevard that morning in the excellent time of 1hour and 40 minutes, began slowly by working on the pulley and tossing around the medicine ball for about ten minutes. Then, gradually stepping up the pace, he moved to the speed bag and treated the spectators to an exhibition of manual speed and dexterity, hand-eye coordination and sheer stamina, which frequently had many of them shouting in delight and astonishment. For fifteen uninterrupted minutes, showing absolutely no signs of fatigue or distress, Johnson rhythmically pummeled the leather bag with both hands, sometimes using one hand repeatedly, sometimes alternating with his left and his right, before ending with a sizzling left hook that sent the bag flying off its hook and far over the heads of the crowd.

When it was announced that the champion would be following his "warm-up" with eight rounds of boxing with three training partners and that there would be "no cutting of the time" of the rounds, there were audible expressions of surprise from many of the numerous newspapermen and professional gamblers in the audience. The reporter sitting next to Daniel, a grizzled fellow from Minnesota with an enormous belly and, to Daniel's disgust, a bad case of body odor, let it be known to everybody within reach of his alcohol-and-cigarette-scarred vocal chords, that "This was going to be quite an unexpected show, especially if the big Smoke went at it pell-mell," since it was customary "at the start of training to only go for three or four short rounds."

Johnson's opponent for the first three rounds was George Cotton, a scrappy Negro fighter from Chicago, who had obviously been instructed to press the champion and try to get inside his defense. The game Cotton gave a good account of himself the whole way but the champion, sweating freely by then, handled the 185lb fighter like a sack of wheat, moving him around easily in the clinches and drew blood from his sparring partner's mouth in the second with a wicked uppercut.

Next up for another three rounds was a white fighter, Marty Cutler, also from Chicago, who was introduced as one of the champion's regular sparring partners. Cutler's instructions were to jab, move and throw as many punches as he could physically muster. In the first round the champion was content to work on his defense but in the second round a short right uppercut to the jaw dropped the white fighter to the canvas. It took some time to revive the unconscious fighter and a worried looking Johnson was among those who administered aid. After getting unsteadily to his feet Cutler asked the champion to take it easy, which he did. Nevertheless, by the end of the third, the white fighter was visibly spent and clearly relieved to get out of the ring.

The champion's partner for the final two rounds was Denver Jack Geyer, a big, strong, white heavyweight from Los Angeles. Instead of concentrating on his defense as he had done in the previous six rounds, Johnson attacked from the opening bell, landing punishing lefts and rights to the white fighter's body. Only Geyer's excellent conditioning, ringsiders agreed, kept him on his feet.

Afterwards, sitting in his crowded dressing room, surrounded by friends, well-wishers and about a dozen members of the press, the champion, who was breathing easily and normally despite the exertions of the previous hour, was clearly pleased with his performance.

"It went better than I expected," he began, looking slowly around the room, a big smile creasing his face.

"Are you going to be spending more time in the gymnasium from now on?" was the first question, delivered in an aggressive, almost accusatory tone, from the representative of the *Oakland Tribune*, a rather pompous, well dressed, heavyset man with carefully-groomed, graying hair.

The champion's big smile quickly vanished. "I'm going to train to suit myself and not the public," he replied, anger tightening his mouth and narrowing his eyes. "As I first said when I came to California," he continued, looking directly at his questioner, "no one in the whole wide world is going to dictate the amount of work that is done except Jack Johnson. I have always attended to my own training and I am too old to let the public disturb me. I haven't been in the gymnasium before today simply because I did not need the work."

"How much do you weigh now Jack," a tall, bespectacled man in a jauntily-angled straw hat asked in a high-pitched Midwestern accent.

"Well," Johnson replied, smiling again, as he affectionately rested a big right arm on his little trainer's narrow right shoulder, "I was weighed in this morning by Sig Hart here, at 214, and I since I figured on fighting Jeffries at about 206 I guess I don't have too much to go. Isn't that right Sig," he added, as he stood up from the massage table he'd been sitting on and began moving towards the door, signaling that the interview was over.

But before the trainer could reply or the champion could get out of the room, the reporter from the *Oakland Tribune* shouted one last question. "Jack, there's a lot of talk on the streets that there's trouble between your manager George Little and yourself, is there any truth to any of it."

"Gentlemen I assure you," Johnson began, pausing to look around the room, his tone even, his manner relaxed and frank, "that there's not a word of truth to any of it, it's all pure baseless rumor. You saw him yourself taking the tickets today didn't you? Now, I ask you in all good common sense, would I have him collecting my money if there was anything wrong between us?

Then, as he slowly made his way out of the room accompanied by his entourage, the grinning heavyweight champion of the world glanced at Daniel, who had been standing at the very back of the room, stopped, and with recognition lighting up his eyes, turned his head toward the startled newspaperman, and whispered "bet everything you have on me" and winked conspiratorially as he disappeared through the door.

When he finally began typing his dispatch later that evening, Daniel had been sitting at his desk for almost an hour. He had left the Seal Rock House in a state bordering on euphoria, confident that Johnson's whispered admonition was the Negro's way of assuring him that the fight was not fixed. That after all had been among the subjects they had discussed in Chicago. But he was a cautious man and his career, the reputation he had worked so hard to build, would be seriously hurt if he made the wrong call, if he was made to look the fool. But Johnson, he finally decided, had simply confirmed his own intuition. So, with a deep breath, he began:

> *I am now confident that the great pugilistic showdown between the undefeated Jim Jeffries and the current champion Jack Johnson, to be staged appropriately on our national holiday, will be worthy of the great interest it has excited in a broader section of the American people than any previous sporting event in the history of our country.*
>
> *This afternoon, fanned by the cooling winds of the Pacific Ocean, I and 2,000 other fans of the pugilistic arts watched Johnson demonstrate in his first serious session*

in the gymnasium why many veteran followers of the game believe he'll be a formidable opponent for the former champion. For those who were inclined to be taken in by the rumors of a "fix" let me be the first to dispel them. Not only is the Negro champion, as is his great Caucasian opponent, in excellent physical condition but I am now of the firm opinion that he is as determined, in his own way, to prevail in this battle of physical supremacy between the white and colored races.

For eight rounds with three opponents....

Twenty-Two

The secretary had the look, dark hair and bold dark eyes with fair skin and long legs, that normally would have commanded his full attention. But this was, decidedly, not normal times. It was late afternoon and instead of overseeing the construction of the colossal arena on Eight and Market Street or the myriad other details that required his urgent attention, he was sitting in the surprisingly small and modestly furnished anteroom of the Attorney General of the State of California. He had been summoned by both telephone and telegram to meet with the State's second most powerful elected official at his earliest possible convenience. And from the tone of both messages, Tex Rickard, the promoter and referee of the most anticipated sporting event in American history, knew that something was terribly, terribly wrong.

He had been waiting for only a few minutes when after a brief conversation on one of several telephones on her desk, the secretary smilingly indicated that the Attorney General was ready to see him.

"Could you please come this way Mister Rickard," she said, rising from her desk and leading the way to a door just yards away from where she sat. "Attorney General Webb asked me to apologize for any inconvenience we may have caused you by scheduling this meeting at such short notice," she added in a slightly accented voice, as she turned the big brass knob and pushed the heavy door open.

A big, paper-strewn, mahogany desk and two walls of leather-covered books dominated the room, which looked far more like the office of a law professor from a small college than that of the giant state's chief legal officer. A much-used leather couch, a small conference table with eight chairs, a couple of lamps with fraying shades, a modest chandelier and heavy drapes over the big windows behind the desk, completed the no-frills furnishing.

But if the room was nondescript, the man who occupied it was everything but. Forty-six-year-old Ulysses S. Webb, a man of strong and outspoken convictions but courtly manners, had already been Attorney General for eight years and would serve in that position for another twenty-eight before relinquishing it, after nine terms, to Earl Warren, the future Chief Justice of the Supreme Court of the United States. The descendant of an old Virginia family, whose father had been a Confederate captain in the Civil War, Webb would devote much of his considerable physical and mental energy to keeping his adopted state white and healthy by vigorously enforcing various anti-Asian and involuntary sterilization laws.

But Webb was more than just an enthusiastic enforcer of racist and eugenic laws. He was also the proud and unapologetic author of California's Alien Land Law Act, the first of its kind and the model for the rest of the country. He once explained its purpose this way: "The fundamental basis of all legislation upon this subject, State and Federal, has been, and is, race desirability. The simple and single question is, is the race desirable. The law seeks to limit their presence by curtailing their privileges which they may enjoy here; for they will not come in large numbers and long abide with us if they may not acquire land."

"I regret having to ask you to attend this meeting at such short notice," the shirt-sleeved Attorney General, who had left his desk to meet his visitor halfway into the cavernous room, said in a grave, quiet tone, as he extended his right hand to the fight promoter.

"It sounded urgent, I came as quickly as I could," Rickard replied, a slight but audible tremor in his voice.

"It is, unfortunately, certainly that Mister Rickard," the Attorney General said. "Let us sit over here," he continued, pointing to the conference table. Then glancing at the hovering secretary, asked in the same grave tone, "Is the mimeographing finished Miss Ruhl?"

"I'll get them organized right away," she responded quietly, no longer smiling.

"I know that you must be wondering what this is all about, so I'll get to the point immediately," Webb said in a voice now brisk and businesslike, as soon as they had taken their seats facing each other across the table. Then looking directly at the promoter, he added: "The Governor has instructed me to stop the fight between Jeffries and Johnson and I intend to carry out his instructions."

The words struck with the force of a sledgehammer, exploding in his brain, disassembling the carefully constructed arguments he had arrived with. He had tried to anticipate the worse but in his fevered imaginings it had all been about money. He had come fully prepared to be told that there was something wrong with one or more of the numerous applications his company had made to the state and city, that documents had not been properly filed, that regulations had been breached, that construction permits had been improperly acquired, and that additional fees and penalties would have to be paid. And since whatever it was had attracted the attention of the Attorney General himself, his greatest fear had been that the amount would have been substantial, perhaps substantial enough to make the whole venture unprofitable. So, he had come prepared to bargain, negotiate, compromise. There was going to be enough money for everybody, everybody just had to be reasonable.

The shock drained the blood out of his face and froze his tongue against the roof of his mouth. And when he finally spoke it was, at first, in a voice he did not recognize as his own.

"But why," Rickard finally gasped in a strangled voice, "why now?"

In his head cogent thoughts and full sentences were forming again. There has to be some mistake, this has to be some kind of negotiating ploy, he told himself. They couldn't seriously want to stop it now, not with less than three weeks to go. Neither the politics nor the economics makes any sense. It doesn't add up. Just about every businessman in the city is going to lose a lot of money. Gillett himself said again and again that he wouldn't interfere. Now this shit, just when everything was going so well. The fucking protesters had finally given up. The constructions of the arena and ticket sales were ahead of schedule. People were going to be coming from every corner of the civilized world to spend money, a lot of money, right here in this city. Just this morning some of the richest men in Canada had bought a thousand tickets. The hotels, the restaurants, the clubs, the bars, the shops, would all be full. Everybody would be making money. It just didn't make any fucking sense.

"Because of the numerous complaints made to the governor's office, and under the laws of this state prizefighting is a felony," the Attorney General replied coolly, noting with grim satisfaction that his blunt, aggressive opening statement had had the desired effect of discombobulating the normally confident and verbose promoter. It was a tactic he had learned, during twenty years of service as District Attorney and Attorney General, to use with devastating effect.

"But the law was changed some years ago," Rickard replied, in a voice that was beginning to return to its normal jaunty confidence. "Just the other day Mr. Fickert, the District Attorney, assured me of that fact. That is why you have more fights arranged in this city than anywhere else in the whole country."

For the first time since his visitor entered his office the Attorney General allowed himself to smile, a triumphant flicker that bared tobacco-stained teeth for a fleeting moment. The discussion was quickly moving to the area he always felt the most comfortable, the letter of the law. "You are right about the amendments of the original law," he began, leaning back in the chair, his voice and manner almost professorial, "but none of the amendments ever allowed prizefighting. In 1903, the date of the last amendment, the Legislature agreed to permit sparring exhibitions for a limited number of rounds, but it, emphatically, did not remove the restrictions against prizefighting which remains, as I indicated earlier, a felony."

"So are you saying that if the fight, the bout," Rickard asked quietly, hesitantly, a touch of optimism creeping back into his voice and manner, "was advertised as an exhibition instead of a prizefight that it would be okay to go ahead." Maybe this is what it was all about, he thought, giving the governor political cover. A sparring exhibition didn't quite have quite the same catch but he could do that. And it wouldn't change anything about what would happen in the ring, so it wouldn't matter what they called it. Not really, especially at this late date.

"I'm sorry Mr. Rickard, it is not as simple as that," Webb replied, his tone curt, almost brutal. "The governor in his letter to me, and Miss Ruhl will have a copy for you shortly, has asked me, commanded me, not just to investigate the legal facts of the case and to present them to the court for its decision, but also to have all interested enjoined pending the hearing."

"You say investigate," Rickard asked, his voice still soft and tentative, "does that mean that you haven't yet decided what the facts are and therefore what you'll finally recommend?"

The poor bastard just doesn't get it, Webb thought, as he studied the promoter dispassionately. He's having a hard time believing that somebody like Gillett would choose morality over money and deliberately antagonize the businessmen of this city, some of his most important supporters. And, of course he's right in doubting that Gillett would ever make that choice. What the poor son-of-bitch doesn't know is that Gillett hadn't chosen morality but more money. It had been made clear to the governor that the Panama Exposition would not be awarded to a prizefighting city. And that event was going to bring in a lot more money than any prizefight. But Gillett's motives didn't matter, he told himself, stopping the fight was the right decision, morally, and Rickard must be made to understand the futility of resisting.

"Mr. Rickard," he began, in a noticeably frostier tone, "I want you to understand that it is extremely unlikely that the fight will take place on July 4th, if ever."

"But I thought you said you were going to investigate the facts," the promoter replied with a touch of indignation, "but it seems you've already made up your mind."

"Allow me to be very clear Mr. Rickard," Webb responded, sitting straight up in his chair, his tone even frostier, all pretence at professorial detachment discarded. "My charge from the governor pertains not just to the Jeffries-Johnson fight but to prizefighting in this state as a whole. Governor Gillett and I believe, strongly, that the people of California have the right to demand that prizefighting shall cease in their state. Ever since the first amendment of 1899 permitting sparring exhibitions, prizefighting under the guise of that amendment has greatly increased and has been tolerated to an extent that our state is now the Mecca of prizefighters, a development that both the governor and I believe is much to our discredit. Our Supreme Court has never defined a prize fight and we believe it should be given the opportunity to do so. I intend to issue a formal finding on the legal facts of this matter within two days. But I do not wish to mislead you or provide any false hope about the intentions of this office. In all candor, I expect to find positively in favor of the governor's request. And I must warn you that I also intend to seek an injunction barring the staging of any prize fight anywhere in this state until our highest court has had a chance to rule on this matter."

It's all over, there's no point in prolonging this, the fucking bastards really intend to kill prizefighting in this state, Rickard told himself, as he listened impassively to the Attorney General's peroration. But they're not going to fucking kill this fight, he vowed silently.

"Mr. Webb," he said, getting to his feet, his quiet, even tone disguising his rising anger. "I think that as a gentleman you know that after all the money I've spent and the lateness of your decision that this is a most untasty morsel I'm being asked to swallow. But swallow it I will and without choking I assure you. This will be the greatest fight, the greatest sporting event ever staged anywhere in the world and even at this late hour it will go on, elsewhere. Good day Sir, I have urgent business to attend."

PART FOUR

Twenty-Three

Nevada had always been good to Tex Rickard. It was where he became a rich man: And not just a rich man but an important rich man. And it was where he staged his first big, important fight. It was also home and now in his moment of crisis, with failure on an unimaginable scale a distinct possibility, it was where he turned for help and redemption.

The role of redeemer was not a new one for the Silver State; it was, in fact, part of its very essence. Its stunningly premature birth, just eight days before the presidential election of 1864, had been driven by urgent political need. Because its mining-based economy tied it to the industrialized Union rather than the agricultural Confederacy, it had been seen in Washington by the embattled Lincoln administration as politically reliable. And its votes and taxes had been desperately needed to help defeat slavery and prosecute the war. So, despite a population of a mere 40,000 souls, far less than the minimum required by Congress to place a single member in the House of Representatives, Nevada became the Thirty-Sixth State in the union on October 31, 1864 and voted, as expected, solidly Republican.

But by 1910 the state, where the Comstock Lode, the richest known deposit of silver ore in the United States had been discovered, was itself in desperate need of redemption. For two giddy decades, between 1859 and 1878, it had yielded $400 million—several billions in today's currency—in silver and gold, generated enormous fortunes and spurred the development not just of Nevada itself but also its neighbor to the north, San Francisco. However, wasteful and intensive exploitation quickly exhausted the mines. And after the lode was finally abandoned in 1898, the economy of the state collapsed so completely that Congress seriously considered stripping it of its statehood, the first and only time such an act was ever contemplated. Fortunately, rich discoveries of silver in Tonopah and gold in Goldfield and Rhyolite between 1900 and 1904 revived the economy and helped to salvage its status. But by the time Rickard came calling in 1910, the population of the entire state was still less than 82,000 souls and its biggest cities little more than large villages.

Despite this considerable limitation, Nevada was in many ways an attractive site for a major prizefighting event. Most importantly, unlike its larger and far more populous northern neighbor and most of the states of the union, prizefighting had been legal in the Silver State for thirteen years. Since Governor Reinhold Sadler signed an enabling act in January of 1897 to facilitate the staging of the heavyweight title fight between champion James J. Corbett and challenger Bob Fitzsimmons in Carson City. Also strongly in the state's favor was the advantageous location of its largest and most dynamic city. Reno was not only a mere one hundred and eighty-seven miles from the original site in San Francisco, but it was also on the main overland line of the railroads. And Southern Pacific's depot at the little town of Sparks, which had ample facilities to accommodate a large number trains, was only four miles away.

Named after General Jessie Reno, a Union Officer who had died at the Battle of South Mountain in 1862, Reno was a communication center for the agricultural and mining industries and the true center of the state. Situated at almost five thousand feet in a high desert valley on the eastern slope of the Sierra Nevada Mountains, it was glorious in summer and its low humidity made even the coldest winter days bearable. Not surprisingly then, by 1910, its population of almost eleven thousand included a majority of the state's movers and shakers. All of whom, almost to the man and woman, unreservedly welcomed the opportunity to stage the biggest prizefight in history. An event, they were confident, which would not only pour riches into Reno's coffers, but also, they hoped, focus the eyes of the world on their state's almost limitless space and myriad but largely unknown opportunities.

The hour was late, nearing 10 o'clock at night, and Tex Rickards was in a reflective but expansive mood. "You'll see the difference when we get to Reno," he assured the dozen or so wide-eyed newspaper correspondents, who were gathered around him like eager schoolboys in the plushly decorated dining-room of the powerful train hurtling through the cool, thin desert air. Then, after a leisurely sip of the golden beverage nestled in the crystal glass in his right hand, he continued in a light and confident tone: "No more knocking, none, only boosting with everybody glad to see Nevada get the match. I was a fool ever to think of taking a big fight to the coast. Never Again."

He had spent the earlier part of the trip locked away in his private suite in a series of meetings. First with Tom Flanagan, the man Jack Johnson had selected to replace the fired George Little, and J.M. McLaughlin, the contractor he had hired to build the Nevada arena. And then with two of his former business partners, Ole Elliott and E. S. (Kid) Highley, who had been selected by the Goldfield delegation to present the little town's long-shot bid to their fellow Goldfielder. But now with the trip nearing its end he had summoned the correspondents for a little chat.

It had been five long days since his traumatic meeting with Attorney General Webb and with the scheduled date of the fight only two weeks away he was finally on his way back home. It had taken longer than he had expected, when he angrily walked out of Webb's office, to end the proceedings in San Francisco. The Democratic, pro-labor major of the city, P.H. McCarthy, a bitter political opponent of the Republican, pro-business Governor, had been out of town when the decision to stop the fight had been made. Immediately on his return the furious mayor, declaring that San Francisco was "his town," had vowed to reverse the governor's decision. And with the city's normally Republican-leaning business community rallying to his side it appeared, for several days, that he would have been successful. Only Gillett's preemptory threat to use the National Guard to impose his ban had ended the rebellion.

"But regardless of how well things go here, you're going to

lose money aren't you Tex," Daniel asked from his seat at the big dining table, where the newspapermen had all gathered to meet with the promoter.

"You're darn right I'm going to lose a lot of money Danny," Tex replied, his casual use of the diminutive signaling just how far the relationship had developed since their first contentious meeting in a Manhattan bar some eight months earlier. "I figure my actual loss, money straight out of my pocket that's been spent already and cannot be recouped, to be about $75,000. But when it comes to my prospective loss, what I figure I'd have cleared if I didn't have to move the fight, that is a hell of a lot higher, I figure close to a quarter of a million dollars."

"What about Dickerson," asked a little sharp-featured man with a distinctive southern accent, who, inexplicably, had elected not to remove his black overcoat and fedora throughout the trip.

"What about him," the promoter replied after a languid sip of the golden liquid in the crystal glass.

"Well," the little sharp-featured man began, squirming uncomfortably under the steady gaze of the promoter, "there was rumors, just rumors mind you as far as I know, but people in the know was sayin' when we was leaving San Francisco that that feller from Columbus, George Rockwell I think 'is name is, you know the one that's been runnin' the Stop the Fight post card movement, that he 'as been puttin' a lot of pressure on Governor Dickerson and that he's feelin' the heat already and may stop the fight here too."

The flicker of irritation that clouded Rickard's pale blue eyes was almost imperceptible, vanishing as quickly as it had appeared. But the smile that followed was full and brilliant, revealing a full set of white, well-tended teeth. "You obviously don't know much about the people of our state," the promoter began, a little chuckle taking the place of the smile, "there's absolutely no chance, zero, that the fight will be canceled."

"But how can you be so sure," the little fellow pressed, a nervous tic in his left eye betraying his unease, "I mean you haven't talked to the governor yet have you?"

Before Rickard was able to reply, the loud, high-pitched shriek of the Limited's whistle announced their arrival on the outskirts of the city. "Fellows," the promoter said, smiling and almost shouting as he got to his feet, "you've got to excuse me, I'd have liked to continue this a little longer but we're almost there and I have a few things to do before we leave."

The familiar sound of the train's whistle had also galvanized the more than 10,000 persons who had gathered along several blocks of Center Street and filled the enormous outdoor plaza in front of the Golden Hotel, the city's pre-eminent hotel and meeting place. Before long, as the luxury train made its way slowly and noisily through the center of town, Rickard was spotted and even before it came to a stop cries of "Reno wants the fight", and "Hooray for Tex," shouted passionately from thousands of throats, filled the air.

Then, abandoning all pretenses at restraint thousands of men and women surged towards the train as it ground to a halt and massed around the promoter's Pullman car, making it impossible for him to leave for several minutes. Finally, smiling and waving, Rickard, surrounded protectively by several associates, shoved his way through the delighted crowd that surged along the sidewalk as he passed, hundreds reaching out to grasp his hand and call out his name as he walked to the hotel just a half block away.

The strongest, the boldest and the most advantageously placed followed him into the Golden's huge marble lobby, filling it until it could not hold a single other person. People stood on the reception desk, the settees and on the window seats, refusing to budge until Rickard answered their impassioned cry of "Reno wants the fight." Outside thousands blocked Center Street, making it impassable to all vehicular traffic and all trains. They too refused to budge for the very same reason, chanting "Reno wants the fight" over and over.

As he had so confidently predicted to the newsmen less than an hour earlier, Tex Rickard had expected a positive reception but nothing even approaching what he was witnessing. For several minutes, pinned and trapped against the reception desk by a sea of humanity, he simply stood silent, too overcome with emotion to speak. Finally, with tears dimming his eyes, he raised his hand and everything suddenly went silent.

"This is no bidding proposition," he began, his voice loud and clear as he lifted his glistening eyes and looked around the room. "I'm not asking Goldfield or Reno to bid against each other. I'm going to meet the committees from both places tonight and I'll hold the fight in the city that will draw the largest gate. I'm through with California and every other state. Nevada is good enough for me."

The final words had hardly left his mouth before the room, and then the streets outside, erupted in a wild frenzy of cheering, whooping and hollering. "Hooray for Tex" was now the only cry and it was repeated over and over and over again, louder and louder, fiercer and fiercer, like the war chant of the Indian tribes-- the proud Paiute people--who had first roamed the lakes, rivers, marshes, mountains and plains of the land that would be known by the Spanish word for snowy. And through it all, they kept coming forward, grizzled old miners, suave gamblers, well-dressed businessmen, even a few bold women, with hands outstretched and heads slightly bowed, to pay homage to the man who was about to make their state and perhaps their beloved city famous around the world.

Twenty-Four

So much had happened and so quickly that he had hardly slept for two full days. He had been so completely spent, in both mind and body, that when he was finally able to throw himself onto his bed it had been like falling into a deep, dark hole, more like lapsing into unconsciousness than falling asleep. For seven straight hours he had remained there, exactly where he had fallen, nearly motionless, lost in that dreamless, timeless nirvana that is normally the province of infants, fools and saints.

After what seemed to him like just the blink of an eye, he had arisen, wide awake, nudged perhaps by the fingers of light that had crept through the drapes on the windows and had been playfully caressing his face, fully refreshed and ready to go. Jim Jeffries was due in town that very morning, he soon remembered, and he had to be there, on time, because, from every indication, the people of Reno were going to give the Great White Hope the kind of rapturous welcome normally reserved for crowned heads of state, popular presidents of the United States, and, of course, hometown promoters of world heavyweight title fights.

In his long and distinguished journalistic career, Daniel had never witnessed anything even approaching the excitement that had seized the good people of Reno. And in the pieces he had filed he had exhausted his not inconsiderable storehouse of superlatives trying unsuccessfully, he had ruefully concluded, to convey to his readers the fervor, the mad intensity with which Tex Rickard had been greeted on his return to Nevada and the single-mindedness and sheer exuberance with which Renoites had pursued their goal of hosting the fight. He knew that despite his best, bravest efforts, the people of the New York area would never be able to fully grasp just how much the staging of a mere pugilistic contest, even one as rich and of such enormous social and perhaps even political implications, meant to the isolated people of Reno.

Although it was summer his room on the top floor of the four-storey Riverside Hotel, was, he discovered, as he pulled off the light blanket and walked over to the windows, delightfully cool. That must be why I slept so well, that, and the exhaustion, he thought, as he pulled the drapes open, inhaled deeply and then stood transfixed in awe at the glistening, trembling, silvery wonder flowing restlessly beneath his window. The Truckee River, fed by the eternal snows of the Sierra Nevadas, was a whirling crystal stream that furnished Reno with a water supply of the finest quality and, along with the surrounding broad, green meadows, made the little, three-square mile city one of nature's finest gems.

He had selected the Riverside, one of only three decent hotels in the city, for no other reason than he preferred its name to the other two, the Golden and the Overland. Riverside Drive in Manhattan, with its graceful brownstones, wide, tree-shaded sidewalks and spectacular views of the mighty Hudson, had long been one of his favorite addresses. And he and Bridget were hoping to find a suitable place there after their marriage. Unremarkable in appearance, the squat red brick building had only one truly distinguishing characteristic, its location on the south bank of the Truckee, on the exact site where Reno began in 1859. Nevertheless, its rooms were spacious and comfortable and the electric elevator, supposedly the first installed in the state, smooth and efficient.

The tiled floor of the bathroom was almost too cold for his bare feet, and the water that poured out of the polished nickel faucet was initially almost ice cold. But after a little adjustment of the hot and cold knobs he produced the perfect temperature; neither too cold nor too warm, just invigorating. Standing there in the tiny shower, with the water pounding a soothing rhythm on his naked skin, the extraordinary events of the past two days seemed distant, surreal. He even wondered briefly if it all been some kind of mad dream or if he had simply been hallucinating the whole time.

It had had begun with their hurried departure from San

Francisco early Monday morning and the day-long trip, with the gatherings of people at every stop along the way, small at first, but getting ever larger, calling for Rickard, intimations of the amazing outpouring of emotion at Reno that night. Then it had continued throughout the night and into the morning with the comings and goings of the dueling delegations from Reno and Goldfield, amidst the whisperings, the wild rumors of which city was up or down. It was all over, Goldfield had won. No, Reno had made the stronger bid. Nobody had won; Rickard was still unsure which city he favored. Reno would get it, if they could meet the terms. What terms, nobody knew exactly, just more rumors, the delegations weren't talking. Goldfield must be ahead, didn't you seeing the smiles on the faces of the delegates. That doesn't mean anything, yes it does, no it doesn't.

Then, in the morning, for the first time, signs of real movement towards Reno; bands, people in the streets, and confirmation from the delegation that the fight was theirs with one daunting condition: That they raise all the funds, every penny of it, for the construction of the arena and the licensing fee, by noon that very day. So there had been marching, and cheering, and bands heralding on every street, as the whole city joined in. And, finally, when the word finally came down from on high, from Rickard's suite on an upper floor at the Golden, that the high honor of staging the fight was officially theirs, there had been the ear-splitting cheers, the dancing in the streets, and the raucous celebrations in saloons and hotel bars throughout the city that went on and on and on.

The day began, like so many others in Reno, as a perfect summer morning, cool and dry under an almost cloudless pale blue sky: The best kind of day, if there ever was such a thing, for standing in the sun. After a hurried breakfast, Daniel stepped onto Virginia Street and began the relatively short walk, of about eight blocks, to the Southern Pacific Station in the heart of the city's business district on East Commercial Row. But he had only traveled a few yards when he noticed a half dozen or so fashionably-dressed women, raised floor-length dresses revealing an ankle or two, laughing and giggling as they gingerly picked their way along the slippery surface of the grassy bank overlooking the Truckee. Curious, and ever the newspaperman, he immediately turned to his left and began moving toward the women, who had quickly attracted a small crowd of mostly male onlookers.

The women, acutely aware of the attention they were attracting, soon found a suitable location for whatever they were planning and began, rather ostentatiously, to remove their gloves and then their rings, a few with a little difficulty, from the second fingers of their left hands. Then, after considerably more laughing and giggling, the women, almost as one, a few with surprising athleticism, flung the rings into the deep waters of the Truckee. As the women walked back to the street to scattered applause, wearing various forms of facial expressions, from triumph to relief, Daniel asked an older man in the crowd, whose broad, florid face was a mask of disapproval, if he knew what the women were doing.

"Throwing away their weddings rings an makin' a foolish spectacle of themselves is what," the older gentleman replied, then stalked off abruptly, muttering fiercely about the sad pass the world and the city of Reno, had come to when women were allowed to behave so shamelessly in public.

"It's becoming something of a ritual here, tossing their wedding bands into the river I mean, it's been happening quite a lot recently," an attractive, dark blonde young woman, one of a handful of the women in the crowd, explained.

"But why," Daniel asked and pulled his notebook, battered as usual, out of a jacket pocket.

"You're one of those newspapermen from out of town for the fight," she asked, a note of interest in her voice.

She's more than plenty attractive but nothing like my Bridget, Daniel found himself thinking, as mental images of his fiancée flooded his brain and set off waves of longing and the only too-familiar queasiness in the pit of his stomach, that he had come to recognize as the most common physical symptom of his loneliness and homesickness.

"Yes, from New York," he heard himself answering in a voice

that sounded oddly strained. "But do you know why," he quickly added, determined to prevent the encounter from becoming too personal.

"They're part of our divorce colony," the blonde explained, "and its not just women either. They're quite a few men too," she added, "but the women are the most numerous and they're the ones that throw away their rings, at least from what I've seen."

"Thank you, thank you very much," Daniel replied, quickly turning away as he replaced his notebook in his pocket and fled precipitously from the clear evidence of the young woman's interest in him he had discovered in her eyes, without asking the obvious question of why was there a divorce colony in Reno.

Reno had never before seen anything like it so early in the morning. They had begun gathering, in just trickles at first, but then in floods as the morning wore on: Lining up patiently in front of the stores, banks, restaurants, saloons, hotels, rooming houses, barbershops and stockyards, almost as soon as the first rays of sunlight had peeked above the crimson-streaked eastern sky. Well before the anointed hour, the three blocks of East Commercial Row had been lined with more than five thousand excited and expectant men, women and children. The colorful crowd, representing the full spectrum of Reno society, had gathered in front of the Southern Pacific Station to welcome, pay homage to, or simply get a glimpse of the fearsome giant they all had been assured would soon be restoring the honor of white American manhood.

In the meantime, while they waited for the main attraction to arrive, the focus of attention was on hometown hero, Tex Rickard, who only a day earlier had granted the city the right the host the most important sporting event of the young century. With some difficulty the promoter, dressed jauntily in a belted sports coat with creased, cuffed trousers and a grey derby hat, had slowly made his way through the adoring crowd and out to the track, where he was interviewed and re-interviewed by several of the scores of journalists who had already arrived in town.

"No, there is absolutely no chance the governor will interfere," was his unvarying response, repeated quietly but firmly again and again, to the common question of whether Governor Dickerson was likely to yield to the mounting pressure from groups across the country to stop the fight. "Not only had Governor Dickerson himself, when asked that very question at a stop in Boise, denied that there was any truth in the San Francisco reports that he intends to interfere," he patiently explained, "but the governor has even volunteered the information that there is no state law in Nevada preventing prizefighting."

And occasionally, to some of the newsmen he knew quite well, Rickard added: "It is also the case that Finch, the governor's private secretary, has publicly said that not only will the governor not interfere. But even better, that he could not, because the law does not empower him to do so. Finch told me himself that he has been assured of this, privately, by the justices of our Supreme Court and other eminent jurists throughout the state with whom he has consulted. Believe me gentlemen, the only way to stop the fight in this state, if the governor was determined to do so, would be to call a Special Session of the Legislature and have them rescind the existing law. But doing so and before July 4, given the overwhelming sentiment in favor of this fight, as you saw Monday night and are seeing against this morning, would be all but impossible."

Also attracting attention from the newspapermen were some of the country's best-known and most prominent gamblers and a substantial contingent of female members of the city's growing divorce colony, easily identifiable by their pale skins, elaborate hairdos, fashionable frocks and colorful pongee parasols. But when the long scream of the steam train's whistle announced the approach of the Overland, these sideshows were quickly forgotten. Cameras were quickly unlimbered and the photographers led a general charge toward the Pullman cars as the big black engine finally groaned to a stop.

Inside, the man they had come to worship was not at all pleased at the overwhelming reception. Looking out of the grimy, dirt-streaked window at the thousands of eager upturned faces, distaste evident all over his own, he snorted in disgust, scowled menacingly and turned to his wife sitting next to him in the dining car.

"Goddammit," he growled, "so many of them so early in the goddamned morning. What more do they want of me anyway. They already got what they goddamned wanted, haven't they. I'm fighting the godddamned nigger just like they wanted, aren't I. Now why can't they just go away and leave me the goddamned hell alone."

Only minutes earlier the former champion had seemed unusually relaxed and carefree, wolfing down a big breakfast while animatedly, for him, trading fishing stories across the table with Jim Corbett. The lighthearted banter with Corbett, himself a former heavyweight champion of the world, was a rare and brief sunny interlude in a particularly gloomy period for Jeffries and his camp. He had been deeply and relentlessly despondent for more than a week, barely able to summon the energy to train, ever since he had been notified that the fight would not be held in San Francisco. He had repeatedly threatened to pull out of the contest, because, as he mutteringly repeated again and again, he had signed to fight in California and nowhere else. The very thought of leaving the sheltering isolation of Rowardennan had made him almost physically ill. And he complained over and over that all the progress he'd made in his almost three-month stay would be undone by the altitude and greater heat of Nevada.

It had taken every bit of Tex Rickard's legendary charm and persuasive powers to convince him to make the move to Reno. Jeffries' antipathy for the Silver State was not surprising since, with the sole exception of his fishing exploits, his memories of Nevada were not exactly pleasant. In one highly publicized incident he had managed to run up $25,000 of unpaid gambling debts while attending the Nelson-Gans lightweight title fight in Goldfield four years earlier. One measure of Rickard's powers of persuasion was his success in talking Jeffries' debtors into settling for fifty cents on the dollar, despite the riches the Californian had already raked in during his exhibition tour and the additional fortune he was about to make in his contest with the black heavyweight champion.

But nothing seemed to lighten the big man's dark mood, to lift the gloom that clung to him like a shroud. Not the settling of his debts, not the waves of adulation that had followed him along the entire three hundred miles of the journey, from Rowardennan to Reno. In truth it had only made things worse; the mantle of savior of the white race was a too-heavy burden that was clearly wearing him down.

The innocent inhabitants of the nearby little town of Ben Lamond had unknowingly precipitated his misery by taking the day off from work to participate in the sendoff ceremonies the town fathers had organized for their departing champion. The entire town had been at the little station when he arrived that morning and he been given three rousing cheers as he boarded the train with his training party. The cheers had followed throughout his home state, far into the night, and all the way into Nevada. The cries of "Three cheers for Jeffries," and the hopelessly optimistic "O, Jeff, come out and show yourself," became a familiar refrain at every stop. That Jeffries never bothered to show himself or acknowledge their cheers seemed not to faze the crowds or dampen their extraordinary enthusiasm.

But now he was in Reno, at his journey's end, and he no longer had the option of hiding away onboard. He had no choice but to disembark but he was determined to avoid the agony of coming face to face with his admirers if he possibly could, and he had a plan.

"Go on and get off first," he barked at his wife and the rest of his party. "All you people get off first," he repeated, as he stealthily made his way to the rear of the train.

Outside, the anxious crowd cheered loudly for the first celebrity who stepped off the train, Bob Armstrong, one of Jeffries' primary sparring partners, nattily dressed in a dark suit enlivened by a purple shirt and a tan colored derby; their hero, they figured could not be too far behind. Some in the crowd mistaking the black Armstrong for the heavyweight champion yelled "Johnson." Amused, Armstrong grinned widely and replied "Not guilty, gentlemen, not guilty."

Next was Jim Corbett, resplendent in a gray traveling suit, pausing briefly to modestly acknowledge the cheers with which he was greeted.

Sam Berger soon followed and halfway down the steps he also paused, but for a considerable period, apparently to give the waiting photographers a chance to get a shot under the most favorable circumstances. But their only interest that morning was the big game still on the train and Berger dropped into the crowd unrecorded on film or plate.

Not far behind was Mrs. Jeffries, who was greeted by loud applause, some no doubt in anticipation of the imminent appearance of her husband, and Mrs. Rickard, an extremely attractive young woman in a gray traveling suit and a Russian turban.

Following closely behind his sister-in-law was Jack Jeffries, who, because of his likeness to his brother, was greeted, initially, with a hopeful explosion of cheers that soon turned tentative and then stopped altogether as the crowd got a closer look at the former champion's smaller sibling.

Then came a long, painful wait amidst an eerie silence, as the enormous crowd seemed to hold its collective breath: But nothing happened, absolutely nothing.

Finally, one of the correspondents, a big beefy guy, standing in front of Daniel broke the silence. "Wise old fox," he opined. "He'll appear just at the last minute and get a terrific hand. Wonder who stage-managed this part of the show."

But the suspense continued; the mystery deepened: No Jeffries. Ten thousand eyes, all watching for a big man with a deep tan and a cauliflower ear, were, however, riveted on the wrong end of the train. So nobody saw Jeffries slip quietly out the other end. But before he could tip toe away unnoticed, he was spotted by a keen-eyed photographer who recognized the former champion despite the big floppy hat he had pulled low over his face. Within seconds there was a mad rush from all directions and he was quickly surrounded and rapturously welcomed by the adoring horde, for whom he obviously could do no wrong.

After a few minutes of stoically enduring the seemingly

endless backslapping and rib-prodding Jeffries had had enough. Barely controlling his anger, he turned to Rickards, who had fought his way through the crowd to stand at his side, and growled through gritted teeth, "Let's get out of this." With the promoter leading the way, the two men finally broke free of the throng and walked rapidly to the hotel where another big crowd was waiting, expectantly. But whatever they were expecting, a brief speech, a round of handshaking, a smile or two, whatever, Jeffries was not delivering. Without even glancing in their direction, the people's champion hopped into the elevator and disappeared.

Twenty-Five

The small, fair-haired boy, seemingly not a day older than twelve, the fraying, olive-green Western Union uniform draped loosely around his slender body like an oversized sack, was staring at the heavyweight champion of the world in undisguised, wide-eyed awe, and gasping as he fought to catch his breath. "You Mister Jack Johnson," he asked, breathlessly, in his high-pitched pre-puberty voice. Only seconds earlier he had been racing through the train, shouting "Western Union for Mister Jack Johnson", speeding from car to car, as if his life depended on locating his quarry.

"That for me son," the heavyweight champion asked, smiling broadly in evident amusement, as he took the proffered telegram from the boy's tiny hand. "And I have something for you," he added, handing over the silver coin he had fished out of the pocket of his jacket.

"Gee, wow, thanks Mister Johnson, a whole dollar," the little boy said, looking with something between amazement and disbelief at the shining object cradled carefully in the palm of his hand, before stuffing it into a trouser pocket, turning and bolting off the train, his exit every bit as rapid as his entrance had been.

Chuckling and muttering "that one is going to go far," to himself, the heavyweight champions stepped back into the private compartment in which Etta and himself were traveling, sat next to the window and tore the envelope open. "Jesus Christ," he groaned after quickly scanning the five or six teletyped lines, "not a fucking roadhouse."

"It's from Tom isn't it," Etta asked, her tone sharp, the smile disappearing, as she placed the two long glasses, brimming with some kind of iced drink that she had apparently brought from the dining room, on the small table in front of her lover. "What does it say, tell me," she demanded, fiercely, while bending down to retrieve the small piece of rose-colored paper Jack had crumpled and thrown on the carpeted floor.

But the first black man to be crowned heavyweight champion of the world, staring fixedly through the window as the train began pulling slowly out of the station, was, at least for the moment, beyond seeing or hearing. For several minutes, an interminably long time for him, he neither moved nor spoke. And Etta, after a quick perusal of the offending missive, sensing his distress, sat quietly at his side.

Finally, slowly shaking his head, again and again, he turned away from the window and to Etta's shock and dismay his eyes were welling with tears. "Sometimes," he said, as she reached out to embrace him, "this whole thing is just too hard."

"I know sweetheart, I know," she murmured, pulling him closer, gently cradling the enormous round head on her breast. "But don't let them know, don't let them know, that's what they want sweetheart, that's what they want."

"It's not because of me," he began, sitting up, his tone soft but bitter, "god knows I've seen a lot worse, and I know how to deal with it. But you deserve better, a lot better, at least as good as she is getting. You're from a much better family, accustomed to much better things, much more of a lady, than she is, or will ever be, and I'm the champion, not him. But they're staying at Moana Springs, the best place in the state, and we get Rick's roadhouse."

Smiling, she leaned over and pressed her lips against his cheek. "You're so sweet," she said, "I loved Seal Rock and I hated to leave but, as you already know sweetheart, I'm a lot tougher than I look. We're going to get through it just fine; it's only for a few weeks, thank god. So we'll just play pretend. You're going to smile, I'm going to smile and not a word of complaint will pass either of our lips. And when you beat him, and I know you'll beat him whatever the advantage these pathetic country bumpkins believe they're giving him, we'll have, as the saying goes, the last laugh."

"I'll tell you something I've never said to anybody else," the champion replied, the hurt and bitterness in his voice giving way to a cold steeliness. "All the things they do to me, the humiliations, the slights, the harassments, I smile like the fool they often think I am. And I lock them up, all the feelings, deep inside. Sometimes I want to explode, just let go, smash my fist a million times into somebody's face, and damn the consequences. But I've trained myself for a long time and I keep everything inside, for the right time, inside the ring. In there it's legal to let go, and I get paid to beat the shit out of them. That's where I get my revenge. You know the other night I was trying to think about all the times they've arrested me or turned me away from a hotel or a restaurant or somewhere since I got the title and I couldn't even remember all of them. I don't think a month has passed that I haven't been arrested or, at least, threatened with arrest. But I like thinking about those things, I can't afford to forget any of it, not one single incident. That's how I keep going, that's my motivation, my edge."

Etta had placed her hand on his leg just above the knee, squeezing and stroking as he spoke. Now, as he finally ended, she murmured, her soft voice gentle and soothing, "It will be alright sweetheart, it will be alright. Remember now you're not alone anymore sweetheart. We'll fight them together. I promise sweetheart, I promise. I love you very, very much, more than you know. I'll always be here for you sweetheart, I'll always be right beside you."

"You promise," he asked, sounding like a little boy.

"I promise," she answered, snuggling against him, moving as close as she could, until their bodies were pressed against each other, placed her head on his shoulder, closed her eyes and sighed in deep contentment.

Daniel pulled the kerchief out of his pocket, folded it twice, and patted repeatedly at the beads of sweat on his forehead. Grimacing, he unfolded it, loosened his tie, opened the two top buttons of his shirt and wiped the back and front of his neck, again and again. Then, with his nose wrinkling in distaste, he plucked ineffectively at the front of the damp shirt clinging stubbornly to his belly, before replacing the small piece of now thoroughly sodden cotton material in his pocket. There was nothing, he realized, to be done about the tiny rivulets making their way with ever-increasing force and urgency down his back, chest, arms and legs.

It was almost one o'clock and the heat from the overhead sun, unfiltered by a single cloud, was stifling. The train, delayed by a wreck in tunnel number thirteen, was already three hours late. The heat rising in shimmering waves from the pavement, the thin air, the peculiar white light that accompanies the sun on June afternoons in Nevada, and several long glasses of whiskey, were threatening to overwhelm his senses, casting a hallucinatory glow on everything around him. Damn you Daniel O'Brien you goddamned drunk, you weak, pathetic bastard, he cursed himself silently, as he struggled to keep the nausea at bay and the bile out of his throat. Determined to lose weight and get himself into decent shape before returning home to Bridget, Daniel had vowed not just to exercise more but also to eat and drink less and he had been doing an excellent job in the five days since leaving San Francisco.

Just when he had concluded that he had to get out of the sun and find somewhere cool to sit, somebody in the crowd of several hundred people shouted that the train was coming. And as the Overland rumbled into view and screeched slowly down East Commerce, Daniel allowed himself to be carried along as a tide of boisterous humanity surged ever closer to the train station.

This time, unlike Jeffries' arrival two days earlier, the crowd comprised of correspondents, photographers, professional gamblers, celebrity stalkers, the merely curious, and most surprisingly, an unusually high number of enthusiastic female fans, did not have to wait long for the appearance of the principal. A smiling Johnson, in a white linen suit and a white panama hat, led his party of eleven off the train and quickly forced his way through the densely packed crowd, using his strength to shield Etta who was immediately behind him.

Waiting for the champion was promoter Tex Rickard, but minus his wife, and two automobiles. After assisting Etta into a bright red, late model vehicle, Johnson, smiling broadly, stepped onto the running board, turned to face the cheering crowd, doffed his hat and bowed with what one newspaper described as "Chesterfieldean grace." Somebody called for a speech but the champion compromised by again removing his hat and posing patiently for a battery of cameras that were directed at him from various elevated positions.

Finally, after several minutes, with beads of moisture forming on his shaven head and Etta visibly wilting from the stinging warmth of the sun, Johnson had had enough. Jamming his hat over his ears he dropped into a seat and the chauffeur, with his horn tooting hoarsely, fought his way, inch by inch, through a blockade of automobiles and a jam of humanity that filled the street from curb to curb. As the champion's automobile wended its way to the Hotel Golden, several young men in their frenzy to get as close to the champion as possible leaped onto the running boards and wheel guards, momentarily interfering with the driver's ability to steer and operate the gears.

Another fairly large crowd, including scores of the city's tiny black population, had gathered outside the hotel. After pausing briefly to smile and wave, the champion, accompanied by Etta and several members of his party, followed Rickard into the lobby and like Jeffries before him quickly disappeared into the elevator.

Twenty-Six

The day was cool, cloudy, and humid. The towering Capitol, the nation's magisterial seat of power and influence, hovered clearly in the background, a mere three blocks in the distance. But here, almost within the reach of its long shadow, raggedy children, bony arms and legs and distended bellies visible, were playing listlessly, and mangy dogs, scrawny and dirty, yelped at their heels weakly.

The decrepit condition of the buildings, if such an appellation could still be accurately applied to the filthy, tottering, broken-down structures that lined both sides of the dark, narrow lane, testified eloquently to the complete triumph of an especially brutal and pitiless species of poverty. Many were held together precariously by scraps of timber, pieces of tin and patches of cloth scavenged from here and there. Adults, threadbare and empty-eyed, wiser and less hopeful than their children, moved about slowly, if at all, a few with an exhausted furtive air, but most seemingly without care or purpose.

Except for one perilously thin, doe-eyed young woman, no, a mere girl, perhaps no older than seventeen, with matted hair and three young children, almost naked, runny-nosed and dirty. None seemingly older than three and the youngest, an undernourished infant pulling weakly and absentmindedly at his mother's prematurely withered tits. But, as she smiled lovingly at the baby balanced in her right arm and reached down with her left to tenderly stroke the little ones snuggling by her side, the light in her light-brown eyes shone startlingly bright.

Louse Alley had the highest rate of abject poverty, disease, despair, hopelessness, drunkenness, immorality, and crime, in all of Washington. But it was only the filthiest of the filthy; the most degraded of the degraded; the very worst of the worst. Originally designed by the great architect of the city, Pierre Charles L'Enfant, as the home of artisans, horses, and gainfully employed servants, the alleys of Washington had, in large part, become by the closing decades of the nineteenth century crumbling, soulless slums inhabited almost entirely by those who had absolutely nowhere else to go, no other option.

All over the great city the spring flowers, the yellow daffodils, the pink magnolias, the purple azaleas, and the myriad others, were blooming in all of their fragrant glory. But here in the dark, narrow, crowded alley, the mingled, gagging stink of human, animal, commercial and industrial waste was pervasive, inescapable, and overpowering.

Alicia Barrington, elegant and businesslike, in a tailor-made dark blue suit and a white shirtwaist blouse, her face a mask of determination, stepped gingerly around and between piles of rotting garbage and recently deposited dog feces. Twenty feet ahead were a pair of reeking box privies covered by hundreds of flies, fat and lazy from the human excrement they had been devouring. And as she drew near this abomination, despite her preparation and resolve and the eyes that she knew were following her every move, she flinched visibly and took a half-step backward, as if struck by a physical blow, the color draining from her face rapidly.

In one involuntary reflex she both exhaled sharply and tried desperately to hold her breath. Then, in another autonomous response she, briefly, lifted the large, perfumed lace handkerchief to her nostrils, all in a futile attempt to ward off the poisonous, noxious fumes. Oh dear god in heaven, she whispered to herself as she fought to regain her composure, why have you so forsaken these poor neglected creatures, why have you condemned these innocent children to this living hell. What sins could they have committed, what could they have done to deserve to be consigned to this hell on earth.

How do these poor people, endure such conditions all day, every day; how does a just and all powerful god, she thought bitterly, permit such manifest evil and why does he always seem to visit it so disproportionately on my poor, long-suffering people.

"Richard," she said, turning to her husband strolling with apparent unconcern at her side, her large hazel eyes flashing with pain and anger, the color rushing back into her cheeks, "I cannot believe that in this country, in this city, that people, children, babies, are made to live in conditions as deplorable, unhealthy and inhumane as these. It is simply unacceptable, unconscionable and ungodly. I know what you said but whatever the reason, we cannot condone this, whatever the cost, we just cannot."

"Alicia, you don't understand, not all of these are ours, in fact…" he began.

Without waiting for her husband to finish, Alicia spun sharply on her heels, turning around to confront the extremely large, dark-skinned black man walking several paces behind them, "Mr. West," she exploded, her voice shaking with anger, "this is disgusting, disgraceful, filthy beyond belief, an absolute outrage. You must have known about this. How long has it been like this? This has got to be fixed immediately."

"Yuh talkin' bout the privies Miss Alicia," the big man asked quietly in the mildest of tones.

"Those in particular Mr. West," she replied, her voice and manner oozing outrage, "but also this whole vile, stinking mess," she added, making a sweeping gesture with her right hand.

"Well Miss," he responded in the same mild, unruffled tone, "with all due respec' but cleanin up de privies is not goin to be such a simple matter."

"Whatever do you mean Mr. West," she asked, her voice quivering from barely restrained anger.

"Weh can duh some general cleanin up Miss Alicia but dere is not much weh can duh bout the privies because dey is no runnin' water or no power anywhere roun ere. An in any case 'as Mr. Richard was bout to tell yuh, dis is not part of our properties anyways. Mos o ours is on de Maryland Avenue side, dis is de Maine Avenue side. Some o ours is pretty bad too but nuttin like this, dats whats I mean," he replied, a tiny hint of triumph in his voice.

"Oh I see," she answered quietly, before rejoining her husband who had been watching the exchange in silent amusement. Like most of the people in his employ, at his home and in his office, Richard had known Overton West for much of his life. Now in his mid-forties, West had worked for the Barringtons for more than thirty years. He had been an unusually tall and gangly 12-year-old living with his mother and five younger siblings in a small, two-room shack owned by the Barringtons when he entered their employ. His father had died suddenly a few months earlier and with his mother unable to manage on her own, he had decided that he had to become the man of the house and convinced the senior Mrs. Barrington—Richard's mother—to take him on as a messenger. Naturally shrewd, hardworking, trustworthy and ambitious and blessed with uncanny mechanical ability, West had risen to managing supervisor of all of the Barrington properties, responsible for both maintenance and rent collection, despite having only a few years of formal education.

Alicia's outburst had come despite Richard's warning about the desperate conditions in the alleys. He had explained that after the Civil War tens of thousands of penniless and illiterate former slaves had poured into the city searching for a better life, hoping for a new beginning. But they were, almost all of them, to be bitterly disappointed. Rampant discrimination and the city's limited housing stock had made it impossible to adequately accommodate such an enormous influx of poor Negroes, many of whom were former field hands without the skills required to thrive in a sophisticated urban environment. As a result many, if not most of them, had ended up in the alleys, where conditions had gradually deteriorated over the years and which had become the home of both the poorest and the most depraved: mothers overwhelmed by the burden of raising children without fathers or support, aging prostitutes plying their trade on the meanest streets, petty pickpockets, hopeless drunks and vile cutthroats.

She had insisted however that such depraved qualifications made it even more incumbent on her to see for herself and make her own judgments, if she was to, as he had requested, make a meaningful contribution to the changes they had discussed in what he had first described, jokingly, as his investment philosophy. Although the matter had been raised, at least initially partly in jest, soon after returning home from Chicago Richard had sat down with Alicia to explain, in considerable detail, just what he was hoping to accomplish as the relatively new chairman of his family's real estate corporation.

He had explained, as they sat together on the well-worn leather sofa in the small study off their bedroom as she listened in rapt, wide-eyed silence, that his family over a period of many decades and several generations had accumulated a considerable real estate portfolio. But that while the properties had steadily increased in value over the years and were now worth quite a great deal, that they produced, relative to their value, only a very modest cash flow and that he was determined to change that despite very determined opposition from his siblings.

But the problem, he told her, speaking slowly and deliberately, was not limited to low return on investment. There was also the question of the extremely poor condition of many of the properties, something he found both embarrassing and morally offensive. But fixing it was not a simple matter. On one hand while it was true that maintenance had been neglected, it was also true that the rents had been kept as low as possible, just a little more than was needed to pay the mortgages. His choices as he saw them were stark and extremely limited. He could leave things as they were, which he found repugnant and unacceptable. He could improve the properties but that would also mean raising the rents and, inevitably, displacing hundreds of their tenants; and he also found that repugnant and unacceptable. Or, he could, sell off the properties and reinvest elsewhere, most likely in the stock and bond markets. And that, he told her, was the option he favored.

The money markets, he pointed out, were the only areas of the economy where the color of his money and the content of his knowledge mattered more than the color of his skin. But he had also become firmly convinced, he added, his voice still grave and serious, that the country was about to enter a new phase, a new industrial age where science and machines would play a far more important role in the everyday lives of most Americans, regardless of class or skin color. The great inventions of the old century, electricity, the telephone, the automobile, would be developed further and be used by many more people. This new scientific era, he said, repressed excitement beginning to lighten his voice and speed the pace of his delivery, would have to be financed and huge profits would be made. Inevitably, education and knowledge would spread, ignorance, superstition and prejudice would gradually diminish, and the world would become a far better place.

"I admire your vision and passion Richard," she had said, "and I trust what you say about increasing your company's earnings in the stock market. But sweetheart," she had added, looking up at him in that wide-eyed soft reproach he had begun to know so well, "how is selling off the properties and just walking away going to help those poor, helpless people."

The ride had been short, just over six miles, less than a half of their usual distance, primarily in deference to their companions, Henry and Beth Robinson, who had been cycling for only a few months. But the day was also unseasonably warm and Richard and Alicia Barrington were unusually distracted and were anxious to discuss the perplexing moral dilemma they had been wrestling with for several months with their best friends.

Burrelle's, the neighborhood drugstore and soda shop, housed in a solid but undistinguished two-storey red brick building, had in recent years become one of the foursome's favorite destinations, especially in the summer. The introduction of a counter-service soda fountain had dramatically transformed what had been a particularly staid and uninspiring interior. Although the drugstore still did a steady business, the first floor was visually dominated by the soda fountain, which had taken over more than fifty percent of the floor space. An enormous mirror stood behind a 20-foot green-and-white Italian marble counter with gooseneck spouts. Coca-Cola glasses and pewter holders were stacked behind the counter while spinning stools lined the front. Round marble-topped tables with wireframe sweetheart chairs provided additional seating on the floor.

It was still late morning, just after 11 o'clock, when the foursome entered Burrelle's and the soda fountain was little more than half-filled. The room was cool and dark. A big fan whirled noisily from the high tin ceiling and the dark-stained wooden floor shone from a recent bout of polishing. After briefly greeting a few friends the foursome headed immediately for an empty table at the back of the room and summoned a hovering waitress within seconds of taking their seats.

Beth, still slightly flushed from the morning's exertions, began the ordering without even glancing at the menu. "I don't know about the rest of you" she said, glancing at her companions, "but I'm so thirsty I'm skipping my usual chocolate malteds and milkshakes, I'm getting an ice-cream soda to start."

"That sounds very inviting to me too," Alicia responded. "Exactly what's in it?" she added, looking up at the young waitress.

"Well Miss," the waitress replied, her voice brisk and confident, "you ave to start with a little soda water, den you squirt in some chocolate syrup and a little vanilla ice cream. You mix them together with a big spoon, den you fill up the glass with carbonated water, plus two scoops of vanilla ice cream, and some whipped cream, and den top it off with a cherry."

"I'll definitely have one of those," Richard said.

"Me too," Henry added.

"We'll have four," Alicia said, smiling at the young waitress, "and then you can tell us about your sandwiches."

Richard took a long, hard pull at the two drinking straws, swallowed the thick, sweet, cold liquid slowly and smiled appreciatively before returning the nearly-empty glass to the marble-topped table. "The truth," he began, his voice soft and low, his eyes fixed on the table, "is that I've never been less certain of anything in my whole life. I know it's absolutely ridiculous for somebody like me who has long fancied himself a supreme rationalist, but I no longer seem capable of rational thought. I even, in a moment of weakness, you'll be surprised to learn," he added, briefly flashing a crooked little smile, "consulted the scriptures. Which were, as I had expected, of very little help since they, as we all here know, freely contradict each other. Nevertheless, and here's the thing, a little voice in my head keeps repeating over and over, drowning out every attempt at logic, just as you did to one of the least of these who are members of my family, you did to me. So for reasons beyond my comprehension that particular scriptural admonition has inserted itself, deeply, very deeply, into my psyche."

"What about you Alicia, where are you on all of this" Henry asked, glancing across the table at his uncharacteristically somber friend.

"To be honest Henry," she replied, as she picked up the two-tier club sandwich and replaced it on the plate without taking a bite, "more than a little confused and guilty; I started it all, badgering Richard and now I don't have an answer. What I've discovered, painfully, very painfully, is that whether we sell or not won't make much of a difference, the problems are far too big for our actions to have any real impact. What we do or don't do is pretty much irrelevant in any kind of grand moral statement. At best, or perhaps more accurately, at worst, we could make their miserable lives a little more miserable. We could make a gesture by hanging on to the properties and spending a little more money on repairs and such. It would make us feel better about ourselves; but I also understand that Richard is running a business, not a charity. And I don't really believe in gestures."

"I think you guys are being far too hard on yourselves, even Jesus said that the poor will always be with us," Beth commented between bites, sips and small sighs of appreciation.

"This may seem particularly cold and hard-hearted," Henry said, digging into his glass with a large spoon, "but at this stage of our development, our race's development, visible symbols of success, clear evidence of our race's abilities, are more important, far more important, than the individual welfare of any particular Negro in this or any other country."

"I'm not sure I understand," Richard said, looking up at his friend.

"What I mean," Henry said, pausing briefly to shove a spoonful of ice-cream in his mouth, "is that the eventual success of our entire race will be better served if businessmen like you are successful at building large successful businesses, than if you sacrifice that to try to help a few hundred poor people. It's like that Negro preacher, I think in Ohio, said the other day in the papers about his opposition to the efforts of all those white ministers to get the governor of Nevada to stop the Johnson-Jeffries fight, the way they had in California. Some of them were trying to justify their racist actions by claiming they were concerned about the violence that would follow the result of the fight, whoever won. It was better, he said, and I most heartily agree, for a few Negroes, even for more than a few Negroes, to sacrifice their lives than for the world to be denied the opportunity to witness the extraordinary bravery, skill and power of that great Negro pugilist. White writers and others have been claiming for some time as you know that Jeffries' membership in the so-called Caucasian race, his supposed linkage to the founders of modern civilization, is the greatest asset he takes into the contest with Johnson. Viewed through those lenses, the lives of even hundreds of Negroes are less important than the triumph of a single Negro pugilist. Unfortunately, that is the truth, bitter as it may be, about the condition of our race. Those precious few of us with the opportunity to strike a blow on behalf of our entire people must not, cannot, shrink from doing so, however challenging to our natural, understandable sympathies. So my advice to you my dear friend is that your real responsibility is to succeed as spectacularly as you can, to let your light shine as brilliantly as it can, and hopefully become a beacon of hope illuminating the darkness our poor people are lost in."

Twenty-Seven

The ivy-covered cottage had been cleverly designed to offer its patrons both the amenities of a fine hotel and the seclusion of a solitary residence. Set amongst majestic trees, native cottonwoods, ponderosas, and western junipers, and imported maples and elms, it stood aloof from the main building and well away from the nearest road, a narrow dirt lane. In the front yard the big, new sign on the picket fence read 'Private, Keep Out' in large, clear letters. In the spacious backyard swings, rolling chairs, benches, a late model automobile and an enormous dancefloor nestled under the protective shade of massive, spreading branches.

The occupant of this little slice of paradise, Jim Jeffries, the former, undefeated heavyweight champion of the world, trailed closely by a friendly, black and white terrier puppy, stepped outside into the aromaic, sylvan setting, looked around, drew a long, deep breath and allowed himself the luxury of a brief, thin smile. He was pleased, very pleased. Life, he had to admit, was pretty good. Tex Rickard had just called him to let him know that he had sold his one-third share of the fight film for $66,666.00, which was, most satisfyingly, $16,000 more than that ignorant nigger, who had negotiated his own deal several weeks earlier, had received for his one-third.

On top of that his roadwork had gone well, really well, that morning and he'd just finished a great breakfast of smoked trout. None of his fears of the city's heat or altitude had been realized. In fact from his first run, the day after his arrival, his lungs had somehow just opened up and he had been able to perform as well as if he had been a native of Reno his entire life. His new training quarters at the Moana Springs resort on the Truckee River Basin was, the truth be told, everything he had expected and more. And, at least for now, the crowds had not yet started to arrive and he could venture out safely into his own backyard.

Stooping in one fluid motion, the big pugilist swooped up the squirming puppy with his powerful hands, lifted him to his face and touched his nose to his, all the while murmuring in the same tone of voice mother's normally reserve for their babies, "You're getting to be a big boy aren't you, aren't you," as the excited animal licked his hands and face furiously in delight.

Returning the puppy to the ground, Jeffries picked up a small stick, the remnant perhaps of a broken branch, and gently tossed it into the slightly overgrown grass about fifteen or twenty feet away. "Go get it boy," he yelled and then smiled indulgently as he watched the little creature charge away on his too-large paws in his enthusiastic, uncoordinated puppy way.

Jeffries and his party had been in residence at the Moana Springs resort for a week and to his surprise he had not missed Rowardennan nearly as much as he had feared. In fact, the truth was he preferred being in Moana Springs. The fishing was undoubtedly the biggest difference, particularly pulling those long fat trout out of the Truckee. The really big brown ones especially, they were not just fatter and tastier, he had discovered, but they were also, undoubtedly, a hell of a lot more fun to catch. Nothing was better, he had decided, than just sitting on the bank of a river when everything was still and quiet, just him and his tackle, waiting patiently to feel that special tug on the line. Then battling, matching wits with the big ones, and there were plenty of big ones in the Truckee, more than anywhere else he knew of, and finally, winning, reeling them in, and tossing them triumphantly into his waiting basket.

There was no finer enjoyment available to man on God's good earth, he thought, as he watched the puppy make his way back in tail-wagging triumph with the stick clamped firmly between his tiny teeth, than hunting or fishing for one's own food: Except, of course, for devouring it, which was definitely the best part of all; especially when one had a wife who was as fine a cook as his Freida. She knew more ways to fix trout, he was convinced, than any other cook in the entire world. That thing she had done this morning, cold smoking she called it, with the red onions piled on top, had been as delicious as anything he'd tasted in a very, very, long time. He must have put away a couple pounds just by himself.

Just sitting around in the backyard, at least when the crowds weren't around, wasn't too bad either. The cooling breeze off the river and the shade from all those trees made the backyard a pretty pleasant place indeed. But, apart from the fishing, what he particularly appreciated was the hot waters of that pool in the bathhouse. It reminded him of the spa he and Freida had visited in Germany. Nobody knew exactly what was in it, but everybody knew it had some pretty miraculous way of healing the body, of restoring its powers. He was convinced of it. In fact he could feel it working as he took his long soak every single day.

They had come in their hundreds from every direction and by every available means. They had come from the city, the suburbs and the countryside. They had come by train, by automobile and on foot. The crush of automobiles around Moana Spring was so great that it reminded him, one newsman was overheard telling another, of an opening day at the race track or an eastern football game. Extra cars had been run on the trolley line between Reno and Moana and for hours long lines of pedestrians had been spotted making their way there.

Long before the hour set for Jeffries' appearance, the crowd had occupied every inch of every available space and more. The only seats, wooden benches placed on either side of the training platform--a 40-foot by 100-foot converted dance floor that sat directly behind the former champion's cottage--went in minutes. Many of them to well-dressed women, some of them local, others from the divorce colony, all of them seemingly just as eager as the men for the show to begin.

The newsmen, for whom the benches had been originally set aside, were reduced to kneeling or sitting on the dance floor itself. Packed tightly around the 24-foot square mat that had been daubed red, sprinkled with resin, and designated the 'ring', they were nevertheless far more happily situated than most of the other spectators. The vast majority of whom were forced to stand, frequently ten deep, on the grass surrounding the dance floor, and peer over the heads of those on the benches in order to see what was going on. Others, mostly young boys and agile young men, had climbed into the trees surrounding the ring and even astride a ridge pole on the small cottage behind the dance floor, for a less unrestricted view.

An earlier rumor that Jeffries would not be working out that day had whittled down the numbers of the crowd somewhat. But more than a thousand of the hopeful and the faithful were still there when the trio of Bob Armstrong, Jack Jeffries and Farmer Burns, emerged from the cottage at exactly four o'clock. Then, to the instant cheers of the crowd, following almost immediately behind them, came the man himself, dressed in long flannel underwear and looking, as usual, straight ahead, studiously ignoring every attempt to compel his attention.

The cheers continued to swell as he made his way past the gawking, squatting newsmen, to the big, leather punching bag that had been erected on a massive frame in one corner of the floor. But before he could begin his assault on the bag, Farmer Burns, carefully dressed in a three-piece suit, quickly raised his right hand and placing two fingers to his lips, signaled that quiet should be preserved.

"I want to say that Jeffries will take off his shirt," he began, looking hard in the direction where most of the women were seated, "and that any ladies who object will have ample time to leave." But not only did not a single woman even stir but they all looked absolutely unconcerned, as if they had not even heard the announcement.

But, to the vocal disappointment of some of the women, Jeffries did not take off his shirt right away. Instead, fully dressed, he began hitting the heavy bag lightly with both hands as he moved around in semi-circles, back and forth, shuffling his feet, gradually building up a rhythm, slowly working up a sweat. Soon beads of sweat were forming on his brow, then flowing down his face, wetting and matting his slightly thinning hair. At the end of three minutes, the retired champion stopped, drew a deep breath and leaned forward, his enormous arms outstretched.

Farmer Burns and Joe Choynski, who had joined the others on the converted dance floor, each grabbed a side of the soaked and clinging flannel shirt and quickly pulled it over his head. Then Jeffries, who had bent over at the waist to facilitate the removal of the offending garment, straightened up and took a great deep breath. And many in the crowd got their first look at the uncovered upper body of the man on whom they had placed so much of their race's hope of reasserting what they regarded as its unquestionable physical and moral superiority. For a few, brief seconds there was silence as more than two thousand eyes feasted hungrily on the magnificent specimen revealed before them. Jeffries, an infinestimal smile on his face, turned around slowly, showing off the hard, flat belly, the great hairy chest glistening with perspiration, arms as large as small tree trunks, and the thick rope-like muscles of his back and shoulders, slipping and sliding beneath the healthy tan. With every movement, the muscles protruded to a degree that seemed abnormal to the uninitiated. The thick pads of sinews and muscle covering his chest and abdomen seemed bullet proof. The only visible blemish was the celebrated boil on his back which seemed red and angry. Then, with a single voice, the crowd roared in an elemental scream of triumph, the ageless war cry of the victorious, marauding warrior. What mortal man, it said, could possibly stand before such a superman.

But again, as he had done earlier, Burns quieted the crowd by raising his hand to his lips and without even a trace of irony in his voice said, "When you get a chance to see the best man in the world for nothing don't cheer when he don't want you to. And by the way," he added, "it may be mentioned that no admission was charged, even to the common people."

Having made nonsense of the silly rumors that he was fat and out of shape, Jeffries made his way back to the punching bag, while the trainers and attendants scattered resin on the floor and stomped it into powder. This time there was no warm-up. He assailed it from the start, banging away with crashing lefts and rights as if the leather bag was his mortal enemy. For thirteen unbroken minutes, the sound of the heavy bag slamming against the wooden platform was as loud and as regular as the footfalls of a marching regiment. To demonstrate his tremendous fitness, Jeffries doubled his pace in the last thirty seconds, ending the session with several particularly brutal blows that threatened to tear the bag from its mooring.

The skipping rope was next. After some adjustments a slightly too-long rope that a trainer had handed him, Jeffries began, to the immense amusement of the women in the audience, with the kind of straightforward skipping that most of them had probably performed as schoolgirls. The routines quickly became far more complex and difficult however, as he ran forward and backward and dodged sideways, from left to right, over and over again, all with astonishing skill, for a full ten minutes.

Sweat streaming from every pore, the former champion was swiftly attacked by his trainers with big, rough towels and wiped dry. Then after slipping on a clean flannel shirt he moved smoothly into the third phase of his workout, shadowboxing. Because the giant cottonwood trees beside the ring was casting shadows over the dance floor, the big fellow was obliged to pick out places where the sun was able to break through, to find his own shadow. Soon, to the astonishment of the locals, he was darting, and dodging and shifting, back and forth, with remarkable grace and ease for a man of his size. As he moved, rising up and down on his toes, the muscles in his calves, heavy and steely in their hardness, followed in unison, bunching up and stretching out. Finally, towards the end of this phase of his workout, Jeffries gathered himself at one end of the floor and raced madly toward the other. Halfway through, while at full speed, he leaped in the air and turned nimbly in the opposite direction. He repeated this stunt four other times, landing precisely where he intended each time.

Without even pausing to catch his breath, Jeffries moved from shadowboxing to real boxing, the final phase of the session. Joe Choynski, in long white tights and stripped to the waist was the first to face the master. The men went two fast rounds with Joe mostly jabbing and moving, doing his best to avoid the charges of the bigger man. By clutching and covering up Choynski was able to land a few light blows to Jeffries face without being hit solidly himself, until near the end of the second round when a short right from Jeffries exploded into his midsection and had him gasping and holding on. Two more fast rounds, these with his brother, Jack, followed. This time, Jeffries seemed content to work on his defense, dodging and feinting, as he easily evaded the best his hardworking but less talented sibling had to offer. Another two, with Sam Berger had been scheduled. But the end of the session was called before the first was over, when a short, sharp right, which could not have traveled more than nine inches or so, to Berger's body doubled him over, leaving him unable to catch his breath or stand upright, eloquent testimony to the undiminished power of the man who had never been defeated in the ring.

Twenty-Eight

As soon as he spotted the sprawling gathering on Center Street, Daniel O'Brien got out of the car he had hired for the day, spoke briefly to the driver and stepped onto the busy sidewalk. Showing up at Tex Rickard's hotel with a car and driver was probably not the best way, he figured, of keeping his assignment a secret.

Daniel had arranged to spend the day with the promoter, who had arranged to visit the site of the arena and the camps of both fighters, in the company of Governor Dickerson himself. The elusive chief executive had finally returned to town a few days earlier. The hope was that not only would Dickerson's mere presence at these venues finally put to rest the persistent rumors that the fight might still be canceled, but that the Governor would, for the first time in public, actively deny that he had any such intention. While there would be other newsmen at all three venues, Rickard had been promised his friend special access to both the Governor and himself.

It was still only mid-morning, but already the crowd was spilling over from the broad sidewalk into the street itself, slowing traffic and turning heads. All around him, as he made his way to the Golden, was bustling and chattering and comings and goings. There were men with briefcases and cameras and notebooks. Some gathered in groups, others stood alone. Some were involved in animated discussions, some scribbled notes, others smoked, and some seemed lost in thought while others merely looked on.

Adding to the surprisingly cosmopolitan, big-city cast of the gathering were screeching little newsboys all the way from San Francisco, darting through the crowd, aggressively hawking their wares. It was as if, he thought, he had stepped into the middle of a great railroad or national political convention. Not that he was entirely surprised. The lobby of his own hotel, the Riverside, had been unusually crowded that morning, but nothing like what he was now witnessing. But the Golden, he reminded himself, was Tex Rickard's headquarters, the primary source of almost all reliable information about the fight, and as the name of the street constantly reminded, it was also located in the very center of downtown.

They had been arriving in steady droves by train and automobile for days, filling the better hotels in town, and some lesser ones too, to overflowing. These were not yet the bright-eyed fans come to cheer for their champions; those innocents had not yet arrived. These were the scribes and the pundits, the opinion-shapers and the odds-makers, cool-eyed professionals who knew an opportunity when they saw it. They were from very different places and they spoke with very different accents. They were tall, short and medium, heavy, slim and average. They were Roman Catholics and Protestants, Deists and Atheists. They were Republicans and Democrats and of no political persuasion. They were, in short, very different men, except that almost without exception, they were white men of a certain age and certain shared beliefs: That the almighty in his ultimate wisdom had made the white man physically, morally and intellectually superior to the Negro: That a black heavyweight champion violated the very laws of nature and represented a dire threat to the established order and civilization itself: And that, therefore, the coming contest between Jim Jeffries and Jack Johnson was not merely a personal struggle between two skilled pugilists, but a matter of transcendent political and social importance to the nation itself.

And so by the week before the fight more than three hundred of the country's most prominent journalists, the best of the best and the brightest of the brightest, had set up shop in this dusty little town. Following hard of their heels had been countless hundreds of the smartest and most successful of what were then quaintly known as "sports," gambling men who had no other profession. Just about every major daily newspaper in the United States had sent their own reporters, so too had papers from Britain, Australia and France. But, testifying to the enormity of the event, the skills of the traditional newspaper fraternity had been deemed inadequate. Some of the larger newspapers and magazines had recruited prominent literary figures to lend their fame and powers of description to the coverage. None did so more memorably than the best-selling novelist, Rex Beach.

Beach wrote immensely popular adventure stories that would be made into successful Hollywood movies featuring major stars such as Gary Cooper and John Wayne. He told the readers of the Atlanta Constitution, that the little city of 11,000 people had been transformed into "the precise magnetic center of the civilized world." And he vividly captured the extraordinary worldwide interest in the fight with this elegant paragraph. "In a single day, one hundred and fifty thousand words went out from here over the wires. The fall of Port Arthur (China, during the Russo-Japanese War) did not take one quarter that number of words to tell and every day it is the same. In other words, two novels are written every twenty-four hours, dealing entirely with the question of individual superiority."

Similarly, with singular skill, he described the differences in the fighters' personalities and the contrasts in the environments of their training quarters this way: "At Jeffries' quarters you behold a vine-embowered cottage surrounded by a fence with a large readable sign 'Private, Keep Out,' and inside the cottage there is silence, peace. He has the white man's sense of privacy." At Rick's Roadhouse "You find yourself in a honky-tonk. A pair of muscular pianists and a fiddler poison the air with ragtime. There are two roulette tables going constantly, drunken men abound. The rooms, the porches, the yards, are packed with all classes and conditions of people. They elbow their way upstairs to the quarters of "Lil Artha." They pinch his muscles and prod him in the ribs to discover his condition. I have a mental photograph of the distorted remains of the stranger who would presume to thrust a curious finger into Jeffries' rib."

"Johnson," Beach wrote, has the "soul of a joy-rider." But the glowering, taciturn Jeffries evoked a very different image. "I saw that which I never expected to see, a man who has come back. Jeffries has renewed youth. Ponce de Leon should have gone west in his search for that fabled fountain, the waters of which he believed could roll back the years from human shoulders. I believe Jeffries to be the most dangerous and most rugged fighter the world has ever seen."

When his car turned on Fourth Street and he got their first close-up view of the immense, hexagonal amphitheater, Daniel could hardly believe the evidence of his own eyes. Less than a week earlier nothing had been there except an empty, fairly small field strewn with rubble. Now, packed in tightly between the Sparks Trolley Line and the Asylum Road, the arena towered over the blighted neighborhood like some wooden colossus.

The contractors, Messers Freidhoff and McLaughlin, were already greeting Rickard, Governor Dickerson and his security officer, Captain Cox of the State Police, when the mesmerized newspaperman was finally able to tear his gaze away, get out of his car and hurriedly catch up with the others.

The construction site itself was a frenzy of noise and motion. Dirt and dust was everywhere, making it difficult for the uninitiated to see or breathe. What seemed like hundreds of men were engaged in a whirlwind of activities, hammering, cutting, fitting, measuring, shaping and joining. In all of his fairly long life Daniel had never seen anything quite it before. Unlike the sites he had been on in the New York area, and he had been to more than quite a few, nobody was taking any time off. Everybody seemed to be working at full speed at the same time. And, best of all, there were no other newsmen there. He had the field to himself.

Governor Dickerson, who seemed remarkably unaffected by all the noise, dirt and swirling debris, was expressing his admiration for the speed with which the arena had been erected. "I must tell you in all frankness gentlemen," he was saying, shouting above the din, "that what you've done, erecting this enormous stadium in such a short time is quite remarkable and well beyond what most of us thought possible. I'd like to hear how you managed to pull off this little miracle."

At first, the chief executive's lavish praise seemed to freeze both men into tongue-tied silence. But after exchanging a series of glances and gestures with his partner, Freidhoff, obviously the designated speaker, spoke up, slowly and haltingly at first. "To be honest Governor," he began, his voice so soft as to be almost inaudible, "the most credit we deserve is for puttin together as skilled and dedicated a group of men as we've ever had the pleasure of workin with. They've been goin at it hard, jus as you see them now, with no let up, for ten hours a day and no days off."

"How many men Mr. Freidhoff," the smiling Governor asked.

"Sir, one hundred and seventy-five of the best men in the state," the contractor replied proudly.

"Governor let me add something to that, and I'd like my friend here from the press to make a special note of what I'm about to say," a pleased-looking Rickard interjected as he nodded in Daniel's direction. "Mr. Freidhoff and Mr. McLaughlin are being far too modest. In just a few short days these two gentlemen have somehow managed to fashion 400,000 square feet of lumber and five tons of nails into this magnificent arena you see before us today. Which will be able to safely, and I underline safely, accommodate up to 25,000 men and women."

Knowing that his friend's comments were meant as much for the Governor as it was for him, Daniel suppressed a smile as he pulled out his notebook. "Actually you anticipated my question," he said, "I was about to ask if there were any formal safety inspections planned, by the city or any other such body."

Looking as self-satisfied as the cat that has just swallowed the canary, the promoter paused briefly, glancing over at the Governor to ensure he had the chief executives full attention. "I'm glad you asked that question my friend," he replied, raising his voice just enough to be clearly heard, "because I want to place on record my high regard for the outstanding job being done by the Washoe County grand jury. They came yesterday for the first time and they'll be back two more times. I must tell you those men know their stuff, they really do. They knew what they were doing and they did it right. They read the blueprints and then they discussed in a lot of detail, frankly more than we were expecting, the methodologies we'd used for the construction and the bracing. And their inspection of the quality of the lumber and the workmanship was as thorough as any I've seen."

"And the results," Daniel asked, unnecessarily, for Rickard's demeanor had already telegraphed the answer.

"Well," the promoter replied with something between a smirk and a smile creasing his long, lean face, "Despite the limited time we've had the work was judged as sound in every respect and would have been completely satisfactory under normal circumstances. But you know the eyes of the world are going to be on this little city. And so they decided, very sensibly in my opinion, and I immediately agreed although it was, all the parties agreed, not strictly necessary, that because the arena was designed with a great deal of sloping so as to give every customer a clear view of the ring, that the joinings between the flooring and the upright posts should be reinforced."

"From this layman's perspective it looks just about finished, what's left," Daniel asked.

By then many of the workmen had seemingly become aware of the identity of the visitors and some had even paused from their labors to point and gape.

"It seems we're becoming somewhat of a distraction gentlemen," Rickard observed dryly before turning to Daniel and pointing to the top of the arena. "Look up there," he said, "at the uppermost tier of benches; ticket sales are going so well we're going to be adding a gallery right behind them. It will be six feet wide; it will run around the entire arena and accommodate another 3,000 people, but it will be standing room only."

Daniel had awoken that morning with a sense of wellbeing he had not experienced in months. After more than a week in Reno he had, finally, gone to bed the night before confident for the first time that not only would the fight take place on schedule, that every available ticket would be sold, and that both fighters had gotten themselves as ready as they could. There would be no quarter given by either man, of that he had become certain. It would be, he hoped, as brutal a test of strength and skill, of will and endurance, of cunning and intelligence, as the world had ever witnessed.

And most satisfyingly of all, as he had slowly read and reread her two most recent letters before switching off the lights, the belated realization came that his long, enforced separation from Bridget would soon be coming to an end. Now as he watched the beaming Governor throw a friendly right arm around the shoulders of the triumphant promoter, he knew that his newsman instincts and the piece he had filed that very morning predicting that the coming contest was going to be the greatest sporting spectacle the world had ever seen, would soon be validated.

Twenty-Nine

The reigning heavyweight champion of the world stepped briskly into the room, took his seat behind the big roulette table, looked around at the assembled crowd, picked up the gavel and pounded loudly for order. "Ladies and gentlemen," he said gravely, "we are gathered together here for a matter of the utmost seriousness and importance, electing a new judge—close the door Burns—a man of the highest and best legal mentality, absolutely of honor: A man of impeccable credentials, unassailable honesty, unimpeachable integrity, complete reliability, whose word is his unbreakable bond."

Johnson's soaring oratory, delivered in a pompous tone and accompanied by grand, theatrical gestures, was too much for the crowd, many of whom were soon convulsed with laughter or wonderment or both at this unexpected entertainment. And when a wild melee broke out between members of the champion's entourage who were obviously supporters of competing candidates for the judgeship in question, and the champion waded into their midst after they had repeatedly ignored his admonitions from the bench to come to order, the cheers, laughter and applause grew louder and louder.

The audience, a broad cross-section of Reno's population, had come on foot, carriage, and automobile to see the black champion. The word had gradually gotten out that Johnson's workouts, unlike the Californian's, always began on schedule and many in the big crowd at Rick's that day had finally deserted the favored but elusive and unfriendly Jeffries for the punctual, friendly Johnson.

For almost a week stories had been circulating around the city that if you arrived at Johnson's training quarters early, before his afternoon workouts began, there was a good chance you'd be able to catch him doing something like playing baseball, playing his big bass fiddle or shooting craps. And that unlike his remote, unapproachable challenger, he didn't seem to mind, in fact seemed to enjoy, interacting casually with the fans, answering questions, even swapping jokes. So, well before noon, a long caravan of pedestrians could be seen all along Laughton's Road making their way to the roadhouse. The automobile and carriage crowd followed later, passing most of the walkers on the way.

Johnson's day had begun early, when the grass and leaves were still damp from the morning dew and the sun still low in the eastern sky. Accompanied by several of his trainers and braced by the cool, fragrant air, he had reeled off the approximately ten miles to Laughton Springs and back in just ninety minutes. Perspiring freely but breathing easily, the champion had finished with a strong sprint from 200 yards out that swept him past the rest of the party.

Despite this early morning exertion and a planned 10-round workout with five different sparring partners that afternoon, Johnson, after a quick rubdown, had spent the rest of the morning and early afternoon engaged in a blur of activities that would have by themselves exhausted many a lesser man. But for the champion, extensive, even exhaustive human contact was a kind of physic tonic, paradoxically recharging his batteries and buoying his spirits.

Etta sat at the dark oak dresser and stared critically at her image, reflected from multiple directions in the large, beveled, tri-view mirror on her dresser. Frowning, she pulled the brush through her long, glossy, black hair several more times. Jack always liked it down but today she had to be perfectly fashionable. And that meant piling it up on top of her head in a high pompadour, just like in the magazines; that was an important part of the Gibson look she liked to effect. The Governor and many other important people would be coming. Even more snapshots than usual would be taken and printed god knows where. And a lot of people would be looking at her, most of them in envy or disapproval, as they always did, just because she was with Jack.

But she really didn't care she told herself, as she got up and walked over to the matching dark oak, tallboy chest, she had gotten past all that. After searching through several drawers, and picking up, examining, and then rejecting several garments, she finally settled on a pale blue, tailored shirtwaist blouse with a high collar and leg-of-mutton sleeves, and added it to the collection of blouses and dark, floor-length skirts already covering the king-size bed.

She had to admit though, she thought, as she retook her seat at the dresser and examined her face in the mirror, that the sun had been good for her complexion. She had never really liked the ultra pale look that so many favored. She tanned well and her newly bronzed skin went well with her dark hair and blue eyes. All in all Ricks had not been as bad as she feared, at least for her. Their suite was the best part of the whole resort; it was large, airy, and high-ceilinged and fairly well furnished.

But the training conditions for Jack had been perfectly awful. The ring, set out in the open behind the old barn, was completely unshaded. After just a few minutes even the spectators would be sweating profusely and the glare from the new canvas on the floor of the ring was blinding. But somehow in a way she just didn't understand, he didn't seem to mind that much. In fact, he was, inexplicably to her, having a really good time.

The memory of Jack's tears on the train brought on a little smile as she opened a drawer of the dresser and pulled out a large bottle labeled 'Recamier Cream, for the complexion,' and what appeared to be a fairly recent newspaper clipping. Nothing seemed to bother him except when he thought some insult was being offered to her. Nothing made him angrier faster than even the hint of a slight aimed at her; those directed at him elicited little if any response. He had, she mused, as she picked up the clipping, the most remarkable disposition of any man she had ever known, and one of the local papers, the *Nevada State Journal*, had finally admitted as much a few days ago. Although the paper had insisted on referring to him by that repulsive tile, the Big Smoke, that they all obviously thought was so funny, she had decided to keep it, because it was the first acknowledgement of his true character she'd ever seen in the papers.

"Never was there a fighter with such a wonderful disposition," she murmured to herself, her eyes lighting up as she scanned the section she had carefully underlined. *"There never is a growl or murmur of any sort and when he isn't grinning over the shoulders of his trainers in the ring he's busy with the big music, in which he insists that everyone take part. Everyone usually does and enjoys it. The whole camp seems imbued with the great Smoke's wonderful spirit. There is constant music and it is seldom that the hearty laughter of the members of the camp doesn't ring out."*

It was high time for Jack to get his due, even if in a little way, because there were so many hateful, untrue things written about him just about every day, she said to herself, a little smile of satisfaction on her face, as she replaced the clipping in the drawer, wiped her hands on a small towel, opened the bottle and reached in with her index and middle fingers. Imagine, she thought, a flash of anger darkening the blue eyes as she began dabbing some of the cream on her nose, forehead and cheeks, describing a man as well read and intelligent as Jack as behaving like a happy and carefree plantation darky at watermelon time.

Etta was almost fully dressed and her maid had already left when Jack finally entered the bedroom, wearing blue tights and a short dressing gown. Her hair was done and she had selected the pale blue blouse and paired it with a floor-length black skirt, but she had been waiting for Jack to help her decide just which pieces of jewelry to wear. It was a delicate balance and she had to get it just right. She wanted to show-off some of the finer pieces Jack had lavished on her. They were, after all, probably the most tangible expression of his love and regard. But she didn't want to overdo it, especially since it was still broad daylight, like some poor misguided parvenu.

"Oh Jack darling," she said, turning away from the full-length mirror, relief flooding her face and voice, "where have you been, I've been besides myself waiting for you. I need your help desperately. I..."

Interrupting his girlfriend's complaint with a short, sharp

whistle of appreciation that drew a dazzling smile in response, the heavyweight champion of the world followed up with a brief apology as he walked towards her, hugged her briefly and planted a quick kiss on her right cheek. "Sorry sweetheart," he began, his eyes beaming, as he took a half step back to get a better look at her. "I swear," He said, interrupting himself, "you're the most fantastic looking woman I've ever set eyes on. But I was waylaid by a Baptist minister, a Reverend Wilson, if I got his name right."

"A Baptist Minister, what in the world did he want with you," she asked sharply, her tone hinting at something less than total respect for the gentleman's religious affiliation.

"To tell you the truth sweetheart," he replied distractedly, taking a seat on the bed as his eyes continued to pour over his lover's slim but curvy figure, "even now I'm not sure but since one of the local newspapers brought him over I guess he must be somebody pretty important."

"Jack, he must have said something," she replied in the same sharp tone, then quickly added in a voice suddenly soft and seductive, "Do you really, really mean what you just said darling. There's been some really pretty girls coming over here in the last few days and I've seen you looking."

"Which is why I can say with authority that you're the very best I've ever seen," Johnson replied, chuckling softly. "One of the things the Reverend asked me," he added after a brief pause, "was what religion I belonged to."

That piece of information seemed to make Etta, who had begun trying on rings from a large jewelry box sitting on the tallboy chest, genuinely angry for the first time. "He did, how incredibly inappropriate and impertinent," she said hotly, "I hope you told him that in this country one's religious affiliations like one's political views are a personal, private matter, and certainly not the concern of total strangers. I tell you," she added, " I'll be glad to get out of here next week, these frontier people are far too self-righteous and gauche for my taste."

"I did even better than that," Johnson replied, chuckling at the memory, "I told him I was a Roman Catholic. You should have seen the look on his face, like he swallowed his tongue and found out that it was too hot for his mouth. It would have been better if I'd been a heathen, at least he would have been able to save my immortal soul. But here I was an apostle of the Roman devil and he couldn't say a word, not with all those newsmen listening."

"But you're a Methodist, I'm the Roman Catholic" she said, smiling.

"Well, Methodists haven't been too good to me," he replied dryly as he got to his feet, "plus I remembered all those stories you told me that some Protestant Churches don't even believe Roman Catholics are really Christians, and I just wanted to shut him up."

Smiling broadly and shaking her head in amusement, Etta raised her hands with her fingers slightly spread to display the rings, encrusted with diamonds and expensive colored stones, which adorned several fingers of both hands, to their best advantage. "You're quite the devil Jack Johnson," she said, "but a clever one. But tell me," she added, dangling her fingers in front of his eyes, "do you think this would be just too gauche."

"Yes," he replied, "just a half will do."

"That's what I thought too," she said happily.

The air was still and hot. The sun, three hours past its apex but still extraordinarily potent, was unfiltered by a single tree or cloud. The scent from the nearby barn was pungent and powerful. The assemblage was already perspiring; some were even beginning to pant. But, despite it all, there was gaiety and expectation in the large crowd. It had overflowed from the barroom into the dancehall and piazzas, before gathering on the lush, green lawn that circled the uncovered ring. Large numbers of bright summer frocks and colored parasols announced the presence of an unusual number of women, including a bevy of divorcees. Just outside the fence a long line of automobiles and wagon teams from distant ranches also patiently waited.

A few minutes after three o'clock, Tex Rickard's late model auto carrying the promoter, Governor Dickerson, and Captain Cox of the State Police, drove into sight just as the heavyweight champion of the world, accompanied by Etta and his entourage, emerged from the rear end of the roadhouse. Despite the unexpected convergence of these happy events, it was the black champion, dressed as was his custom in brilliant blue fighting togs with an American flag knotted around his waist, who attracted the vast majority of the attention. Necks craned in his direction and generous applause from his overwhelmingly white audience accompanied him as he walked, smiling broadly with both hands carefully taped, to the platform that had been set up near the ring. But of course the identity of the distinguished passengers in the car had not yet been revealed.

Johnson began with a slow, almost gentle warm-up, shadowboxing and going through a routine of light calisthenics for a few minutes, all the while holding a light dumbbell in either hand. Sufficiently limber for something somewhat more strenuous, the heavyweight champion summoned two of his trainers for a game of throwing the ten- and- a- half pound medicine ball. Each, both big, strong men, took a corner of the ring and began slamming the big sphere into the champ's lean and muscular torso with as much force as they could muster, competing to outdo the other. Grunting softly after each enormous impact, designed to simulate the hardest blow from even as powerful a fighter as Jeffries, Johnson willingly endured the beating for several minutes.

By then Governor Dickerson, Tex Rickard and Captain Cox, accompanied by Etta and several other notables, had taken their seats on the grass just ten feet away from the center of the action, on the north side of the ring, to relatively little excitement. That is until they were surrounded by dozens of newspapermen and photographers, including one Daniel O'Brien, eager to listen to the chief executive's views of the manly art and record the event on film. Despite the considerable distraction to which he was being subjected, Johnson spotted the party almost as soon as they took their seat and on a couple of occasions playfully sent the medicine ball in their direction instead of immediately returning it to his tormentors.

Finally, the champion deemed himself ready for the main event, twelve rounds against four opponents, Al Kaufman, George Cotton, Walter Monahan and David Mills. First up was Kaufman, a big, strong white Californian and a top heavyweight contender in his own right. Kaufman was more than an adequate opponent to begin the proceedings, having held Johnson to a ten-round decision in a non-title bout only nine months earlier. As the two men moved into the center of the ring a brisk, cooling breeze mercifully began blowing off the river. The first consequential blow was struck by the champion, a right hand cross that drew blood from his opponent's nose.

Out on the grass, Etta was telling the Governor and the others that she "had never seen Jack bleed yet, in a fight or out," when a Kaufman left hook drew a thin red line from the champion's mouth. Annoyed at the unaccustomed sight of his own blood, Johnson picked up the pace considerably, pressuring his opponent relentlessly, repeatedly landing so many stiff blows to his head and body that Kaufman was puffing and blowing and unable to speak when time was called at the end of the first round.

Three more hard fought rounds followed, with Johnson concentrating primarily on honing his considerable defensive skills, but going on the offensive sufficiently often to badly bloody his opponent. More often than not the champion, when Kaufman swung at him, was content to block the blows with his great, muscular arms, or to laughingly move out of the way, sometimes by what seemed with just the slightest shift of his head or feet. Occasionally, he would take the lead, peppering Kaufman with short left jabs and straight rights, inflicting enough damage that the white fighter's nose, mouth, chin and cheeks were smeared with gore by the end of the fourth, when he stumbled out of the ring, visibly relieved that his ordeal was finally over.

George Cotton was next. Cotton was described by one of the local papers this way. "George is a young Negro as black as the seven of spades and about as lumpy. His muscles are thick and knotty and he is as willing as they make them." Cotton quickly proved his mettle by immediately taking the fight to the champion, shaking him with several hard blows, one of which reopened the cut on his lip and restarted the flow of blood. Stung and annoyed by the young man's impudence, Johnson stepped up the pace considerably, driving him around the ring at will, punishing him with left-right combinations. In the fourth round, seemingly determined to end the bout on a decisive note, the champion chased the tough, game youngster into a corner and unleashed a particularly lethal left-right combination. Blood gushing from both nostrils, Cotton clutched at Johnson with determined strength, desperately trying to save himself. But after easily extricating himself with one of his surprising displays of strength and smeared with the young Negro's blood, the champion unleashed a devastating double left hook. The first exploded on the side of the jaw, and the second, coming so quickly after the first that some in the audience claimed to have seen a single blow, landed right on the point of the chin.

Cotton, who until then had been, improbably and inexplicably, smiling widely, suddenly closed his eyes and wobbled at the knees as both hands fell to his sides. Several of the trainers alertly leaped into the ring and reached him just as he collapsed. They then dragged him to the edge and hung him over the ropes, where they placed ice water on his neck and smelling salts to his nostrils. In the meantime, Johnson had casually walked back to his corner, serenely confident that it had been all over as soon as the punches landed. Fortunately, young Cotton was as good as new after a minute or so and the champion signaled for the next victim, Walter Monahan.

After quickly blooding the tall, slender Irishman, who although a former amateur heavyweight champion, seemed far too frail to withstand a prolonged pounding and with four rounds of his scheduled twelve-rounder still to go, Johnson backed off the attack and concentrated on polishing his defense and showing-off his clever feinting for the rest of the workout.

As always, within minutes of his arrival, his dressing room was filled with a bedlam of noise, conversation, and people coming and going--trainers, newspapermen, photographers, sports, assorted friends, and even a few of the bolder women from the audience. Serenely indifferent to it all, the heavyweight champion of the world, naked except for his blue tights, sat quietly on the rubbing table while his hands were unwrapped by a trainer, his breathing easy and unhurried. A fine sheet of moisture on his heavily-muscled upper body and tiny beads of perspiration on his dark, flat face, with its almost oriental cast, were the only visible indications of his just concluded exertions. His hands finally free of the gauze and adhesive tape that had protected them, Johnson was about to get off the table and step on the nearby scale, a twice-daily training ritual, when Tex Rickard, accompanied by the governor and his party, entered the room.

After a brief introduction by the promoter, Johnson smiled broadly as he firmly grasped the chief executive' right hand. "I'm glad to meet you Governor Dickerson," he said, and the governor returned the compliment while sizing up the champion's impressive muscular development from close range. A visibly impressed Captain Cox congratulated Johnson on his ring work. And with another member of the party, Frank Golden, the owner of the famous Golden Hotel, chorusing his agreement, and the governor nodding in approval, Cox added that the exhibition was better than any of the many actual fights he'd seen. Having paid their respects to Johnson, the governor and his party started for the door but the genial champion would have none of it.

"Don't rush off gentlemen," he said, almost shouting as he stepped off the scale which had registered his current weight at 209 lbs, "I must give the governor a good chance to look me over." With all eyes intensely focused on him, the chief executive smiled gamely and with both hands took hold of the world champion's enormous right bicep, squeezed briefly, then nodded his head sagely in apparent satisfaction at whatever he had discovered and turned to go.

But the garrulous Johnson was obviously loath to see this new friend leave. "Goodbye governor," he called out cheerfully, as the chief executive waved goodbye, "I have a good many words to say to you but I guess I'll have to write them to you."

The next morning the *San Francisco Examiner*, a hotbed of unabashed support for Jeffries, carried the following statement from the governor. *"My visit to the training camp of Johnson yesterday was the first time I had ever seen a boxer in the course of preparation for combat. I was greatly interested in the exhibition. With my party I watched Johnson go through his paces and I must say that the work of the Negro was a revelation. I never knew that a man of Johnson's size could be so wonderfully clever at defending himself. My impression of the fighter is that he is the embodiment of strength, agility, aggressiveness and perhaps most of all good-natured. He went at his work willingly and his sparring partners were as playthings in his hands. Not being a judge of the physical condition of athletes I can't give an expert opinion as to Johnson's fitness for his meeting with Jeffries, but so far as my opinion goes it may be said that Johnson is an excellent specimen of physical manhood. He amused me greatly. His wit is keen and I rather enjoyed a little of it yesterday."*

Thirty

In just one extraordinary day, on the final Saturday before the great event, the population of Reno doubled. In Rex Beach's slightly ominous phrase: "An army of unknowns is rapidly gathering." They were gentlemen of leisure, and adventurers, there were some who rarely left home, more than a few hoboes, and many others of a more dubious character. Very different men, of very different circumstances, largely united only by one common, powerful passion: To personally witness the great Jim Jeffries mercilessly whip the uppity nigger pretender Johnson into submission and appropriate humility, and return the heavyweight championship where it naturally belonged, in the control of the white man.

They came from everywhere and by every available means. They came by big, touring automobiles and by far more modest private cars, by luxurious Pullmans, by less comfortable day coaches and smokers, and even off the top of flat-topped box cars. They came from every part of the country and from many foreign lands. And they just kept coming. Between midnight on Saturday and nine o'clock that Sunday morning, fifteen special trains from San Francisco, Sacramento, Los Angeles, Vancouver, Seattle, Portland, Spokane and other points beyond, deposited another vast army of sweating humanity, most of them wearing buttons inscribed "Oh, you Jeff," onto the already overcrowded streets of the little city, precipitating a traffic jam that lasted for several hours.

Hundreds of Reno residents, including the mayor, had already supplemented the city's meager store of hotel rooms by offering rooms in their own homes. But for most of these latecomers there was often no place to sleep, except in their own automobiles, or on a billiard table, in a hammock, or on a park bench; or for the affluent, lucky few, on a cot in the marbled lobby, or on the flat graveled roof, of one of the better hotels.

For black fight fans the problem of accommodation was particularly acute. There were few Negro families in Reno and racism was widespread and unapologetic. To fill the breach an enterprising real estate entrepreneur rented three abandoned storefronts and filled them with three hundred cots. Such meager fare, for the daring few of African descent who ventured into the little mountain city, was deemed luxury enough.

But to Daniel O'Brien, on his reporting rounds, it seemed that Reno was far too excited on those two final nights to do much sleeping anyway. Surging throngs, giddy with anticipation, restlessly roamed back and forth on the city's brilliantly lit main thoroughfare into the wee hours of the morning. The normal distinctions of class and financial rank, but not of race, were temporarily suspended. Hoboes and miners and cattle herders, rubbed shoulders with businessmen, major politicians, expensively-dressed women, and prominent visitors from across the country and around the world.

But it was not only on the streets that there was little distinction between night and day in Reno. On Commercial Row, where the traditional gambling houses stretched out for several blocks across from the Southern Pacific tracks, the electric lights at night shone almost as brightly as the noonday sun. And the sharp slap of falling chips and the shouts of gamblers continued all day and throughout the night. But the action was hardly limited to Commercial Row. In full swing too were the roulette wheels and other games of chance that every saloon and hotel in town had graciously installed, to give out-of-town fight fans even further opportunities to enjoy themselves and lose their money.

Among the crowds filling the saloons and gambling houses, lining up four-deep as early as noon around the roulette and faro tables, were cold-eyed, hard-faced men who were known throughout the world of the pink sheet. And others too, sharper-eyed, more furtive and watchful, who were all too well-known to the police departments of all the great cities. But the miniscule local police force, a mere fifteen men and twenty-five hastily deputized assistants, despite heroic effort, simply lacked the experience and the manpower to keep even the best-known grafters and thieves out of the city.

The not much larger state police did what they could to help, even stopping and searching trains at the state border. And ten members of the elite State Police Rangers were dispatched to the city under the command of Captain Cox himself. But Cox himself readily admitted to the considerable limitations of the police operation, telling Daniel that he deeply regretted the fact that detectives had not been sent from San Francisco and other coast cities and from Chicago.

"We know," he told him, "the class of crooks who operate exclusively in this territory, and we can keep them under strict surveillance. But it is the pickpockets and hold-up men from the cities we are especially concerned about, and we would be a much better position to cope with their activities if detectives from large cities were here to cooperate with our efforts."

With little to restrain them, the light-fingered gentry descended on the helpless city like a swarm of locus, expertly working the big crowds, lifting wallets and watches from countless unsuspecting fight fans. So many, one wag noted, that "if a hand was not dipped into your pocket sooner or later it was almost a sign of disrespect."

Daniel stood motionlessly at the window staring morosely into the surging, crystal waters of the Truckee. Then, after several minutes, he lifted the mug in his right hand to his lips, took a long sip, swallowed audibly, and grimaced as the potent liquid coursed a fiery path down his gullet and into his rebelling stomach. For more than an hour he had moved back and forth between the window and the dented and peeling Remington typewriter on his desk. A single bare sheet of white paper sat unmolested in the typewriter, and the lone trashcan under his desk was just as empty and forlorn.

He had already decided to perpetuate a fraud on his readers, but not a real fraud, he had been telling himself, since he simply intended to tell them what they wanted to hear. That he their trusted correspondent believed, like they all did, that Jim Jeffries by dint of the superiority of mind, body, and temperament—natural endowments of his Caucasian ancestry—would almost effortlessly vanquish his Negro opponent, who, however strong and clever—in a primitive, elemental way—simply lacked the mental power, the iron determination, unbreakable will, and the genetic link to the founders of western civilization. That his childish bravado would begin to crumble the moment he stepped in the ring and finally came face to face with the most formidable and fearsome fighting machine the world had ever known.

He wanted, desperately, to embrace the racial theory his friend Arthur Ruhl had so confidently outlined only hours earlier in a nearby bar. That Johnson, while unquestionably fast and clever, simply lacked the dogged courage and intellectual initiative which is the white man's inheritance. Jeffries on the other hand, Ruhl had explained between sips, to the consenting nods of several of their colleagues, would be able to summon thirty centuries of tradition, all of the supreme efforts, the inventions and the conquests of the Caucasian race. It was Bunker Hill and Thermopylae, and Hastings and Agincourt against the primitive jungle; Jeffries could not lose.

In fact he had arrived at exactly the opposite conclusion. Against every instinct of his Irish soul and every fiber in his Irish body, he had become convinced that the Negro was going to win and fairly easily. Jeffries, he had concluded, simply lacked the skills, had probably never possessed the skills, to defeat a fighter of Johnson's caliber. At his best, at the height of his physical powers, Jeffries had indeed been a formidable fighting machine. Big, rugged, immensely powerful, tough, dogged and virtually tireless; but he had never been a particular clever boxer or a fearsome puncher. Now, he was just as big, rugged, tough and powerful as ever. And, if anything, judging from his physique which was even more impressively developed than before his retirement and the feats of strength and agility he regularly performed at his training camp, he was probably stronger and more powerful than ever.

But it was also clear that he no longer had the extraordinary stamina of his youth, and it was doubtful that he would be able to withstand the relentless pressure, round after round, that the superbly conditioned Negro would certainly apply. The truth was that Jeffries had simply refused to put in the long hours of actual glove work in the ring, or the daily early morning road running, that his trainers had demanded. Too often opting instead for the fishing pole in the mornings, and for wowing the adoring fans in the afternoons with impressive displays of power and agility. He had, at the end, it seemed, become a victim of his own myth.

His only chance of victory, Daniel decided, would be to somehow overwhelm the Negro champion very early in the contest and score a quick knockout. Likely only, he allowed, in the unlikely, very unlikely scenario: that Johnson, unnerved by the hostility of the crowd and the enormity of the occasion would freeze. And Jeffries, emboldened and rejuvenated by its support, would be able to turn back the clock, at least for a few rounds. But, given the Negro's considerable experience with hostile crowds, unflappable personality, and great defensive boxing skills, the likelihood of a Jeffries victory seemed too remote to seriously consider.

Yet that, he knew, was exactly what was required of him; nothing less. To find clever words to persuasively, even passionately, argue in favor of a proposition he did not believe, did not accept. Perhaps, he thought, as he took a great gulp of the potent liquid and winced again as its passage scorched his throat and stomach, the words would finally come when he was no longer fully conscious.

THIRTY-ONE

The gods of the winds, and the sky and the clouds smiled benignly on Reno on the morning of Monday, July 4th, 1910. It was the height of summer but at daybreak the skies were mostly clear and a cooling westerly wind heralded moderate temperatures throughout the day. And soon the foothills were mottled with the gold of sunlight and the blue-black of wispy cloud-shadows. But not many of the little mountain city's citizens or the tens of thousands of their guests were awake at that early hour to take note of such favorable auguries. For after days of all-night celebrations the exhausted city had finally fallen asleep. The calm before the storm, which was scheduled to begin promptly at 1:30 that very afternoon.

The thick blue smoke rising over the Reno rail yards signaled that not everyone in town was asleep. There, in the dining cars of scores of special trains parked along a siding three miles of downtown, breakfast was being served by uniformed Negro porters. Among the porters was the familiar face of Patrick O'Neill, who had finagled the assignment with a combination of charm and moxie; repeatedly explaining to his supervisors that he had become personally acquainted with the champion at the Marshall Club and by volunteering, for several weeks, to work some of the least popular shifts.

He too had barely slept in several days, at most no more than a few hours a day, and only in brief snatches. But as he moved around the noisy, crowded dining car, resplendent in his spotless white jacket, efficiently dispensing eggs, bacon and coffee to bleary-eyed fight fans, a wide smile seemingly permanently plastered on his face, he had never felt more wide awake and full of energy in his whole life. The night before had been beyond his wildest expectations, and in just a few hours he'd be doing what he had promised himself, so many months ago, on that fall night at the Victoria Theatre at Broadway and 42nd Street. Profoundly moved, after watching the film of Johnson's remarkable bout with Stanley Ketchel, in a way he had never been before in his young life, he had vowed that the next time his hero stepped in the ring he would, if at all possible, be there in person to support him.

And now here he was, in Reno, mere hours before the scheduled start of the 'Fight of the Century,' with a $10 ticket he had purchased the night before, only hours after arriving in town, sewn firmly into the pocket of his trousers. His train, one of two dozen or so of the latest arrivals, had gotten into town just after four o'clock on Sunday afternoon after a grueling three-day trip across the country. He, like other members of the crew, had been told repeatedly about Reno's legendary inhospitality to members of their race and warned to be extremely careful if they ever ventured downtown. Nevertheless, he and several of the younger cooks and porters, determined "to see the sights and stake a bet on their champion," as they put it, had, almost immediately after their arrival, set out by foot for downtown.

But for these native New Yorkers, denizens of glittering Broadway and Times Square, Reno's dusty little downtown was quite a disappointment. Even more so was the quick discovery, by the now ravenous young men, that it was almost impossible for anybody, of any race, to find decent food, at any price, anywhere in the city. Saloons and gambling establishments were packed to the rafters. But all over the city dozens of restaurants had simply run out of food and closed their doors. And long, slow-moving lines snaked around the ones that were still open. Reno it seems was rapidly running out of everything to eat.

Disgusted and determined to get out of the little mountain town as quickly as possible, Patrick and his friends were on Center Street, on their way to an establishment called the Tom Corbett Poolroom, where they had been assured they would be able to both place their bets and purchase tickets of any price, when a sudden commotion several blocks ahead attracted their attention.

They had all but decided to ignore whatever it was that was getting the "country hicks" all worked up, when several teenage boys, narrow white faces flushed with excitement, ran past them shouting in high-pitched voices, "It's Jack Johnson, It's Jack Johnson. Jack Johnson is down at the press center."

Unwilling to accept such extraordinary news from such an apparently unreliable source but intrigued despite himself, Patrick, closely followed by the others, broke first into a slow trot, then a full sprint, as other voices joined in the proclamation that the champion was at the press center and crowds continued to pour into the area.

The incredible news, a panting Patrick soon discovered, was only too true. There, right in front of his startled eyes, sitting in an open automobile on the busiest street in a city overwhelmingly supportive of his opponent, on the evening before the most important fight of his life, was the heavyweight champion of the world, smiling and chatting amiably with members of the press and the public. He had heard, he told them, that twenty thousand people had come to Reno for the fight and he wanted to see the crowds for himself. He also wanted, he added, smiling even wider, to personally place a twenty thousand dollar bet on himself with funds that been wired to him by his friend Barron Wilkins, and to send two telegrams to his family in Chicago.

The first, he announced to generous applause from the crowd, would be to his mother, to assure her that he was in great condition and fine spirits and that he felt right at home having ridden into town and gotten a fine reception from the people. The second, he said, this time to almost total silence, would be to his brother Charles, urging him to bet his last copper on him.

Very aware that he and his friends were, from what he could see, the only black faces in sight, and strategically located at the very back of a crowd some ten rows deep, Patrick was initially content to simply listen. But, finally, too excited to constrain himself any longer and determined to attract Johnson's attention, he raised one long, bony arm as high as it could reach, added several inches to his already considerable height by standing on the tips of his toes, and shouted as loudly as he could manage, "Mr. Johnson, do you have a message for your friends and supporters from 53rd Street."

The impact of the distinctive New York accent delivered in a strong, clear tenor voice, of the dark-hued Irish face towering over much of the crowd, and the long, thin, dark arm that seemed to reach into the sky, was astonishing and a great deal more than Patrick could ever have expected. The noisy throng immediately fell silent and every head and all eyes turned, expectantly, in his direction.

Time slowed, milliseconds became eternity. For the longest time the loudest sound on that street that night, Patrick would later recall, was the beating of his heart. Finally, the champion, who had gotten to his feet and had been staring intently at the source of the disturbance, spoke. "Are you the young man from the Marshall Club with the magic fingers," he asked. "The young man who kept me up all night playing some of the finest music man ever composed on this good earth."

"Pleading guilty as charged Sir," Patrick answered, his voice strained, almost breaking, hardly believing that the heavyweight champion of the world knew who he was, personally remembered him. "It was a great privilege Sir," he added after a brief pause, gradually regaining some control of his voice, and speaking loudly enough to be heard above the buzz of the crowd, that had provided enough space for Patrick and his friends to make their way to within a few feet of the champion's automobile. "I'll never forget it as long as I live, and I just want you to know that they're a lot of us here, back at the train yard, supporting you as best we can. From what I hear there's been a whole lot of praying and a whole lot of wagering goin' on. Me and my friends here were just about to put down our stake on you and get a few tickets for tomorrow."

"Well fellows," the champion said, smiling broadly as he resumed his seat, "I'd better be going. As you know I have a little bit of business to take care of tomorrow afternoon. Wager what you can and tell all my friends at the train yard that I sent them a personal guarantee that they're going to have a lot more dollars in their pockets tomorrow than they had today. The odds are still heavily in favor of Mr. Jeffries, 10 to 6, as of this moment. Every six dollars placed on me will return ten dollars, almost doubling the stake. Not bad business you'll agree."

As the champion's car wended its way slowly through the crowd, "Magic Fingers" and his friends were surrounded by scores of suddenly friendly well-wishers. Politely declining numerous invitations "to come have a drink" with the explanation that they had to get back to work, they quickly completed their business in town and set out, again on foot, for the rail yard.

Later that night, the story, embellished with each telling, of how their champion, unarmed and alone, had faced down an entire town of hostile white folks, spread like a summer brushfire, among the delighted cooks and porters. It was a sure sign, they all agreed, that one white man would not be able to do what thousands of them could not.

Thirty-Two

The giant threw off the light blanket, scratched his great hairy chest vigorously with both hands, yawned with a roar as loud as a lion's, swung his legs off the bed, glanced at the clock on his bedside table, frowned, walked barefooted and shirtless to the half-opened double window, threw it open, pulled aside the curtains, glanced outside and drew a deep, appreciative breath as the mingled aroma of elms, juniper, and maplewood, filled the room.

It was just past eight o'clock, a late morning for him, but he had not slept particularly well, waking several times to repeatedly adjust the window, closing then opening it, before finally settling for leaving it half-open. He had slept alone, as he had for the past several weeks. Frieda's soft, curvy presence in their bed was just too much temptation. Hoarding his manly juices, he had long believed, not only preserved his strength, but increased his ferocity and determination, and was as important a part of the training ritual as running and sparring.

The day before had been upsetting. He'd had that turncoat Stanley Ketchel thrown out of his camp. Coming around laughing and smiling as if nothing had changed between them, as if he wasn't on that nigger's payroll; that was just too much. But what had made him sick to his stomach was the news that his mentor, the man who had molded his fighting skills and nursed and guided his career, Billy Delaney, had not only announced to the press that "Johnson will win. There can be no doubt about this point," but would be in the nigger's corner during the fight. True, they'd had their differences, but there was a time when white men would have been expected to stand together against a nigger, no matter what.

Well he was going to show them, he vowed, as he began a series of piston-like pushups, the enormous muscles in his back and arms bulging and rippling with every movement, that fucking

Delaney and all the doubters. He was going to lick that nigger so bad he would never want to see a boxing glove again. He was so sick and tired of all the talk about his condition. The fact was he had never felt better in his life. But no matter what his condition was or wasn't, he was going to give that nigger the beating of his life. It didn't matter to him whether the fight lasted four rounds or forty. It was going to be his last fight and it might just be Johnson's too. He'd had to do a lot of training and give up a lot of pleasure and he was going to make that son-of-a-bitch pay for it.

But now he was as hungry as a bear waking from a long hibernation. And there was another aroma, a deliciously familiar one, of fried pork chops, floating into the room. Jumping to his feet and quickly dragging on a worn flannel shirt and a pair of old corduroys, Frieda didn't like him coming to the table in just his underwear, Jeffries walked barefooted down the short hallway leading to the kitchen shouting "Frieda is it ready yet."

He had somehow thrown off the bedcovers and discarded his pillow during the night, and was lying flat on his back, naked, except for a tiny pair of shorts. One arm, the left, was bent and tucked under his head, the other stretched out at his side. As she watched, the tiniest of smiles on his lips, his breathing quiet and almost imperceptible, his skin, paper-thin from the weight-loss of his grueling training regimen, revealing almost every tendon, muscle fiber and vein in his lithe muscular frame, he seemed more a statue carved from black granite, than a man of human flesh. Until she placed her hand on his shoulder and wondered anew at the warmth of his body and the silky smoothness of his skin.

They had not gotten to bed until well after midnight and had not fallen asleep for at least another hour. Their lovemaking had been the way she liked it best, slow, gentle and almost agonizingly prolonged. And they had laughed at the vision of poor old Jeffries, probably cold, alone and miserable, with his long-suffering wife locked away in an adjoining room.

Her touch was enough to wake him. It was late in the morning and the sun had pushed its way through the curtains into every corner of the room. "Good god, what time is it," he asked, as he lifted his head, abruptly sat up, stretched his arms above his head and looked around the sun-drenched room. "I overslept and it's all your fault," he added, as he rolled out of the bed, stood up, and smiled at the slight figure still snuggling under the bedcovers."

"You mean tiny little me wore out the toughest, strongest man in the whole world,' she asked, the innocent tone belying the devilish gleam in the large dark eyes.

"Enough that I slept like a baby," he acknowledged. Chuckling, he opened a wall closet, one of several in the suite, packed with bathrobes of various lengths and colors, pulled several off their hangers and laid them out on the large sofa in the sitting room.

"Are you doing what I think you're doing before you've even had a chance to wash, eat or go to the bathroom," she asked, smiling incredulously, as she got out of bed to take a closer look.

"Just deciding which one to wear today," he explained matter-of-factly, as he began holding them up to the light, examining them, one by one. "What do you think of this one" he asked, picking up a full-length black and white silk garment.

The strap of Etta's baby blue nightgown had slipped off her left shoulder, revealing one small, pert, perfectly-shaped breast. Her hair, black, glossy and unbound, tumbled down her back and around her pale, thin, lightly-freckled shoulders. She glanced at the bathrobe and looked up at him, and their eyes met and locked.

"You're so very beautiful," he said, his voice thick, as he allowed the robe to fall onto the carpeted floor. "And these are very beautiful too," he continued, tugging gently at the right shoulder of the nightgown until it too spilled its delicate secret. The enormous hands, the knuckles scarred, battered and misshapen, and the fingers, long, tapering and almost delicate, reached down and stroked and then cupped the quivering objects of his desire.

"Jack don't, please don't, we should not be doing this, not now" she said, even as, with a little cry, she threw herself against him, and with surprising strength pulled his head down and hungrily locked her half-opened lips against his. He had scooped her into his arms and was on his way back to the bed with their lips still desperately locked together when two thunderous knocks on the door stopped them short.

The voice of his friend and trainer, Sig Hart, loud and dripping with suspicion and exasperation, quickly followed. "Jack, Etta," he shouted, "for god sakes you two lovebirds aren't still in bed are you? My god, don't either of you have any fucking sense? Don't you know what time it is? Jesus Christ, we have a fight in a few hours."

Giggling madly like teenage lovers, they tumbled onto the bed still locked together, reluctantly separated and, in unison, shouted. "Why you dirty old man we're playing tiddlywinks."

Thirty-Three

The gates were scheduled to open at noon. And by midmorning the exodus from the city to the great wooden amphitheater, one-and-a-half miles away, had begun. For several hours, a vast sea of humanity of every race and major ethnicity, twenty thousand strong, made its tumultuous way along the single broad street that was the only direct route to the arena. Everything with wheels was loaded to capacity. Some of the more adventurous even sat on the roofs of the two street cars that comprised the entire rolling stock of the tramline serving the arena. Taxis, reveling in the situation, repeatedly raised their fees throughout the day, from $3 dollars for a single passenger in the morning, to $5 at noon, and as high as $10 an hour later.

But most, by choice or necessity, made the journey by foot, Daniel, amongst them. The noise along the route was deafening, as a kind of manic, celebratory, good humor became the order of the day. Automobile drivers blew their horns madly, indiscriminately. Betting men cried the odds through megaphones. Experienced hawkers aggressively pushed iced watermelon and photographs of the combatants. And small boys with pitchers and tumblers darted through the crowds offering water for a nickel.

After all the doubts and apprehension, all the loneliness and the occasional exhilaration, Daniel's only emotion when he awoke that morning, head throbbing and stomach churning in resentment, was an empty sense of relief. The alcohol had worked its magic, as it always did. Seemingly unbidden, the appropriate words had poured out of his typewriter, as they always had. But now, the time for prognosticating and dissembling was finally over. The truth, whatever it was, would finally set him free.

Well before midday, thousands of boisterous fans, including

hundreds of women, most wearing pictures of Jeffries on their coats, had already gathered outside the great wooden amphitheatre. Giant American flags floated gently over all four gates, which swung open, exactly on time, at noon. Carpenters were still busy hammering and applying finishing touches as the wild rush for the turnstiles began. Because of the numerous threats to shoot the black champion, would-be spectators, although they were not searched, had to get past the expert scrutiny of armed deputies posted by promoter Tex Rickard to ensure that no firearms got into the arena. Nonetheless, in less than fifteen minutes the cheapest seats on the top tier of the arena were half-filled.

The private section erected especially for women was also quickly filled. The boxes were located well away from ringside, toward the back of the arena, to protect the ladies' supposedly delicate sensibilities from too close an encounter with the expected gore and mayhem. Despite their banishment to the outer regions of the amphitheatre, the gaudy hats and colorful frocks of these female fight fans, many of them reputedly from the sizable divorce colony, added a vivid and welcome splash of color to the proceedings. Before long, the ladies were seen demonstrating their ability to protect themselves, by creating their own awning from strips of white muslin, to at least ameliorate the impact of the meridian sun.

But female spectators, as Daniel noted were hardly restricted to this special section. Hundreds of bolder types were scattered about in every section of the arena, from the cheapest seats to ringside. Far more women, he was assured by several older male fans, some in obvious disapproval, especially for the ones outside the private boxes, than they had ever seen at a boxing contest before.

By 12:30, a full hour before the scheduled start of the contest, the amphitheatre was three-quarters filled, without a single disturbance. As the afternoon wore on there was only the faintest hint of a breeze, and as the sun heated the wooden structure the raw-pine seats oozed pitch and the smell of fresh pine became overwhelming. To cope with the increasing heat, restive spectators peeled off their coats, wrapped handkerchiefs around their necks, donned smoked glasses, green shades, and wide-brimmed straw hats, and bought thousands of palm-leaf fans and copious amounts of lemonade, the strongest beverage allowed in the arena.

Messenger boys stalked the aisles selling newspapers and shouting the latest odds in the betting, which after midday had suddenly increased to 2 to 1 in favor of Jeffries. Greatly alarming those with money on the champion, who feared, understandably, that something underhand was afoot.

John. L. Sullivan was the first big-name celebrity to enter the arena and he was lustily cheered, as much out of boredom as in tribute, as he took his seat directly in front of the moving-picture machines, and opposite the official timekeeper. The squat, powerfully-built, almost rotund former champion had been hired by the New York Times as a Special Correspondent. Well known for his strong antipathy to Negroes in general and Johnson in particular, and his initial strong support of Jeffries, the former "Boston Strongboy's" columns had cautiously reflected, as the fight grew nearer, his growing doubts about his friend's ability to regain the title for the white race.

Bowing to the protests of spectators whose view of the ring was obstructed by the moving picture booths, Tex Rickard ordered one dismantled. At ten minutes past one, while several thousands were still waiting in line at the ticket booths, correspondents were informed that every seat in the arena was sold.

At 1:30 p.m., the scheduled start of the fight, Rickard dispatched the Reno Brass Band into the ring, apparently with instructions to arouse the passions of the crowd. Their very first selection, a powerful rendition of the emotional Civil War favorite, "Just Before the Battle, Mother," moved grizzled, hard-eyed men to tears. Then "America" and "Dixie" repeatedly brought the audience to its feet in a frenzy of foot-stomping, hand-clapping, flag-waving, patriotic fervor.

With the emotions of the crowd at a fever pitch, Rickard now sought to cool them down just a bit. Twenty-five minutes after the fight should have started, at 1:55, the aging, former wrestler, William Muldoon, climbed slowly into the ring to praise Nevada and ask for a fair deal for Johnson. Muldoon, an unabashed Jeffries partisan, who had publicly questioned the black champion's courage, began by describing Nevada as "the only free State in the Union" for permitting the staging of the fight. The man, who had once trained John L. Sullivan, then asked the crowd to remain peaceful so that "no one should be able to say after it was all over that the Negro had not been given a fair deal."

No sooner had Muldoon ended his little speech, than the attention of the ringside patrons was riveted by Etta's glittering entrance. Murmurs of "Mrs. Johnson," and innumerable involuntary expressions of male approval of her singular beauty, spread through the crowd as, with her friend and constant companion, Mrs. Sig Hart at her side, they made their almost stately progression to their sixth-row seats. Fully aware of and delighted by the stir their arrival had created, both women turned and waved gaily to the crowd before taking their seats.

"By gad, is she really a white woman or one of those New Orleans high yellers," one paunchy, silver-haired ringside patron, who had been paying particularly close attention to Etta's arrival and progress, asked of nobody in particular.

"White woman or not, she sure cuts a damn fine figure" another admirer noted.

"Say O'Brien, you should know if she's really a white woman or not," the tall, painfully thin, correspondent from the Los Angeles Examiner, sitting immediately behind Daniel, asked. "I hear she's from your part of the world."

"I'm not sure, but I believe she is," Daniel replied, quietly, uneasily.

"Goddamn outrage, that's what it is," the paunchy, silver-haired patron—the original questioner—growled. "Damned indecencies like that ought not be allowed."

Daniel had not been fully truthful. He did, in fact, know quite a bit more about Ella's background than his response indicated. He had known almost from the first moment he had spotted her at Johnson's camp at Ocean Beach that she was the living embodiment of the deepest fear of almost every white American male; an apparently "decent" white woman, seemingly of sound mind, who had on her own accord, openly, inexplicably, in defiance of what was probably one of her society's most potent taboos, taken up with a Negro. He had, for the first few days, watched her carefully, almost surreptitiously, as she watched, usually with a surprisingly quiet intensity, and invariably in the company of the blonde woman he would learn was Sig Hart's wife, the muscular exploits of her black lover in the gym and ring. It had not taken long or much, a few overheard words between the women and a gesture or two of hers, for him to recognize her, at least her type, as one with which he was only too deeply, painfully, personally, familiar. A wellborn, educated, headstrong, rebellious, "modern" woman, whose privileged upbringing, had only made them bitter and dissatisfied with "their menial, subservient role in society." The type, to put it mildly, was not his favorite. He had in his earlier, less formed, years met many and, disastrously, dated a few.

As if Etta's arrival was a signal to ramp up the pace of the proceedings the main announcer, Billy Jordan, took over the ring and began an interminably long introduction of celebrities, major and minor. A big, fleshy man with an even bigger voice, Jordan led each man—they were all male—to the center of the ring for an elaborate tribute. The novelty of so many famous men in one place at the same time soon wore thin however and scattered booing and shouts of "don't introduce everybody in Reno" signaled the growing impatience of the spectators. Unfazed, Jordan, a decades-long veteran of big West Coast fights, simply raised his extraordinary voice and continued along his merry way, introducing even the person supervising the battery of motion picture cameras that had been set up on a platform thirty feet from the ring as "Rock, the moving picture man."

With Jordan droning on and on, neither fighter in sight and the scheduled start of the bout already delayed by almost an hour, a rumor sped through the crowd that a doctor had found Johnson in his dressing room near "nervous prostration," too frightened to even leave his dressing room.

Up in the rafters Patrick and a small contingent of his friends and colleagues, huddled protectively together in a few adjoining rows, had, initially, received the news in stunned silence. But quickly regaining their equilibrium, they had begun softly chanting "bullshit, bullshit" in quiet defiance of the shouts of "coward, coward" that were spreading rapidly through the overwhelmingly white crowd.

But that brief excitement was over almost as soon as it started. Johnson's entry into the arena at 2:28 was greeted by an explosion of cheering, more from pent-up excitement than from any particularly widespread support for the Negro champion. Two minutes later when he climbed into the ring wearing the same floor-length black and white silk bathrobe with violet lining he had picked out that morning, their true sentiments were unmistakable. The reigning heavyweight champion of the world was greeted with taunts of "Cold feet, Johnson," and "Now you'll get it you black coward." Here and there a few friendly voices urged fairness.

In a brazen contravention of established etiquette, the challenger was the last to arrive, from the opposite side of the arena; a full four minutes after the champion had already taken up his position in the ring. As soon as he was spotted the crowd rose as one to its collective feet and greeted their champion with a roar of such ancient tribal power that Daniel shivered slightly as he described it as "the first great blood cry of the aroused white masses."

To all outward appearances completely unperturbed by the intensity of the welcome accorded to the challenger, the amiable champion, also stood, smiled and clapped as Jim Corbett led the Jeffries party though the crowd. Immediately behind the former champion was Jeffries himself, dressed, inexplicably, for golf, in an old grey suit and a checked golf cap, chewing furiously on a big wad of gum. One of his seconds, the Negro heavyweight Bob Armstrong, carried a giant paper circus hoop mounted on a stick that Mrs. Jeffries had supposedly helped to design to protect her husband from the ravages of the early afternoon sun. As was his custom, the great man paid absolutely no attention to his adoring supporters, looking neither left nor right, uttering not a single word to anyone.

The ring was quickly crowded with the trainers and seconds of both fighters. The normally dour Jeffries seemed in unusually fine humor, laughing as he passed through the ropes, and stamping heavily on the platform to satisfy himself that it was strong enough. With an almost theatrical flourish he jerked off the suit, glared viciously at his black opponent on the other side of the ring, stood as erectly as he could manage, puffed out his chest and twice raised his great arms above his head in the traditional gesture of triumph.

Electrified, the crowd responded with what Daniel described as a "terrifying, wolfish cry" and another round of taunts and insults. "He daresen't look at him! O-o! Don't let him see him! Don't let him see him."

Sam Berger then approached Johnson, who, with back turned and surrounded by his trainer and seconds, had not witnessed Jeffries' histrionics, and asked him to toss for corners. "Take any corner you want," the champion replied nonchalantly, barely glancing at his questioner, "it's all the same to me."

Surprised and relieved, Berger quickly claimed the southwest corner for Jeffries, leaving the northeast, the direction from which the sun was directing its still potent rays, for Johnson.

His stentorian voice easily reaching every corner of the packed stadium and over the vocal objections of the Negro fighter, Jordan introduced the reigning champion of the world as "the colored heavyweight champion of the world," and Jeffries, to the enormous delight of the shamelessly partisan crowd, as "the champion of champions, the great unbeaten white champion of the world, James J. Jeffries."

Promoter Tex Rickard, battling the heat in shirtsleeves and a straw hat, then announced, in his dual role as referee, that at Jeffries' insistence they would be eschewing the normal preliminaries of handshaking and picture posing. Finally, at 2:46, an hour and sixteen minutes past the scheduled time, Jordan bellowed "Let 'er go" and the combatants raised their hands and moved into the middle of the ring.

Jeffries, who had been perching on the ropes, bypassing the stool in an apparent eagerness to get at his black opponent, wore purple tights and his enormous hairy chest and back rippled with enormous cord-like muscles.

Johnson was clad in blue tights with an American flag wrapped around his trim waist. As he moved into the middle of the ring and the white light of the afternoon sun lit the chiseled muscles of his naked upper body involuntary murmurs of admiration spread through the hostile crowd.

The great showdown between the black and white races, the supposed Battle of the Century, was on.

Thirty-Four

It was neither the largest nor the grandest but the pale-blue, fifth-floor bedroom with its towering ceiling, entire wall of windows, enormous marble fireplace, adjoining bathroom and sitting room and relative privacy, was their favorite room in the big, old house. They had spent two, glorious, unforgettable weeks there shortly after their marriage, much of it in the king-size, mahogany four-poster canopy bed, and shortly after his return to Washington Richard had made it clear to his siblings that as the only married member of the trio he was laying immediate claim to its exclusive use.

The Murray Hill townhouse, near 37th and Park, had been in the Barrington family for almost forty years. Purchased as a home away from home by Richard's grandfather, Dr. Anton Barrington, during the optimism of the Reconstruction period, the nation's brief racial honeymoon, the house had been almost abandoned by the family in recent years, leaving its upkeep to the ancient couple Dr. Barrington had hired as caretakers almost two decades earlier. But Richard, as was his wont, intended to change all that. The neighborhood, once on the outer edges of the city but only blocks away from the newly refurbished Grand Central Station, had become increasingly fashionable and centralized as the city expanded northward. Just the kind of location in fact a wealthy and ambitious young businessman with a keen interest in New York's burgeoning financial markets might consider ideal for a new home.

The Barrington's had spent the entire week in New York, interviewing brokerage houses and assessing the feasibility of transferring the headquarters of the Barrington Development Company from Washington to Manhattan. The trip had gone remarkably well, with brokerage houses, large and small, including the venerable J.P. Morgan and Company, competing avidly for what, from every indication, promised to be a very large and very profitable account. But the highlight of the trip for Richard and Alicia was the discovery that it would be unnecessary to sell off the properties to finance their foray into the money markets. Their trading accounts, they were repeatedly assured, could be collateralized by properly notarized mortgage documents.

And as the week wore on and they were literally besieged with invitations for lunch, dinner and even the theater, it had slowly dawned on the Barringtons, proud pillars of the Negro community in Washington, that their racial identities had been mysteriously transmuted in this new city. Here, they came to realize, in this metropolis of ceaseless immigration, of boundless ambition and relentless striving, of invention and reinvention, that the past was not prologue, just the past, that history was only for books and museums, that yesterday meant nothing and tomorrow everything, unless, of course, you were cursed with the gross misfortune of bearing the unambiguous markings of the Negro race. In this citadel of commerce, however, they, wealthy, educated and cosmopolitan, more than adequately Europeanized in facial features and sufficiently light of skin, could, fortunately, be whatever and whoever they chose to be.

"Have you ever noticed," Alicia asked, glancing over her shoulder at her husband who was still in bed, lying with both hands tucked behind his head, staring fixedly on the ceiling, a contented little smile on his face, "that it always seems to be better when we are away from home."

"Particularly in this house," Richard agreed, the little smile getting wider. "There's something special about it, last night was almost magical."

"Almost?" Alicia asked softly, pausing briefly from the ritual brushing of her long and already glossy black hair, to turn away from the mirrored dresser and look directly at her husband. As she turned the tops of her pale brown breasts spilled over the low-cut neckline of her dark blue nightgown and her large hazel eyes seemed aglow.

God, Richard thought, shifting his eyes from the ceiling to his wife, she is so damned beautiful, even in the morning. "Sadly my darling," he said, sitting up to look directly at his wife, a pained look flooding the handsome brown face, "I seem to be far better, freer anyway, at expressing ideas than my deepest emotions. I can only explain my qualifying of what happened between us last night as an unfortunate habit of speech. In truth not even magical adequately."

"Oh Richard," she interrupted, smiling, eyes glowing, I was just teasing, you're so sweet and silly," the nightgown falling open to reveal a pair of long and surprisingly firm legs as she rose from the dresser and approached the bed. "You don't have to explain, I know how you feel, just show me, again. You do that very, very well."

The great metropolis in its long public history had never seen anything like it before. The thirty thousand generally well-dressed men and women surrounding the New York Times building, was, in the expert opinion of Inspector Richard Walsh, the largest daytime crowd ever assembled in the state. It was also, according to the Inspector, commander of a fifty-man police force dispatched to Times Square to maintain public order, the best-behaved one he had ever seen. "It is all the more remarkable," he explained to the small group of newspapermen covering the event, "when we consider how worked up practically every one of these people are over the battle."

The fans, many among the city's business, social and political elites, had begun gathering soon after 4 o'clock. The earliest arrivals had quickly filled every square inch of the block of Broadway fronting the Times building, widely considered as the most advantageous position from which to view the newspaper's startling innovation, the Automatic Bulletin, which described in large, clear, easily readable type, in almost real time, exactly what was happening in the arena in distant Reno, before, during and after the fight. The Bulletin, the first and only one of its kind in the world, had been installed at the beginning of the week in one of the large Broadway windows of the Times Building. All week, the extraordinary spectacle of the strange machine printing bulletins in letters an inch and a half high in the full view of onlookers, without the intervention of a even a single human hand, had attracted the excited attention of thousands of passersby.

The second wave of arrivers had gathered on the Forty-third Street side of the newspaper building, flooding Times Square and two blocks beyond. There, the news from the Automatic Bulletin was displayed on an enormous revolving blackboard that was operated from the north side of the Times Building. The laggards were forced to settle for the least attractive site, along Seventh Avenue, where there was a smaller bulletin board and displays in the windows, but even here the crowd extended in an unbroken mass between Forty-second and Forty-third streets.

Richard and Alicia, who had spent much of the late morning and early afternoon in an alternatively anguished and triumphantly anticipatory debate regarding the possibilities and betrayals of accepting new racial identities were among the laggards. As too were perhaps a half-dozen well-dressed but unambiguous Negro faces, slightly uneasy, unsure of their welcome, the only visible ones in the enormous crowd, but proud of their material accomplishments and determined to stand their ground.

Preoccupied with their own uncertain fate and with a fierce buzz announcing the imminent start of the contest, the Barrington's, like the rest of the crowd, paid scant attention to these Negroes, as the first cry of the crowd signaled that the first blow had been struck.

Thirty-Five

Back in Reno, despite the howling of the near-demented crowd, the first real blow of the battle, a light, glancing hook, from Jeffrey to Johnson's neck, came only after long seconds of wary sparring and feinting between the extremely cautious combatants. Energized, Johnson quickly responded with his left and both men exchanged largely ineffectual short lefts and rights from very close range. To the surprise and chagrin of many of his supporters, instead of rushing at Johnson and exposing the Negro's genetically endowed "yellow streak", Jeffries seemed content during much of the round to use his greater weight—227 to 208—to shove and push his opponent around the ring. Although he did most of the backing up, Johnson gave a convincing demonstration of his own strength, effectively pinioning the white man's arms to prevent him from punching. Round one of the historic bout ended tamely and inconclusively with the men locked defensively in a tight clinch.

Not all of the white fighter's supporters disapproved of this unexpected tactic. One prominent ringside observer, Johnson's estranged former manager, George Little, not only gave the round to Jeffries but made a four hundred dollar bet with entertainer Al Jolson that the former champion would win the fight as well.

Round two, like its predecessor, began slowly. Jeffries crouched and feinted and Johnson circled warily before suddenly swooping in and landing twice to the challenger's chin, the second blow delivered significantly faster and harder than the first. The champion also feinted and ripped in a favorite punch, a short uppercut, to notable effect, to the body of his powerful challenger. But first blood, a trickle from Johnson's bottom lip, to the savage delight of the crowd, went to their "white champion," who reopened an old training cut with a short brutal right.

By the third Johnson had visibly relaxed. Initially throwing few punches but feinting repeatedly he managed to keep Jeffries off-balance while talking almost nonstop to the challenger or his supporters outside the ring. Finally, changing tactics in the middle of the round, Johnson landed again and again with lightning quickness to Jeffries' neck and upper body before the older man could react. Visibly stung, Jeffries tucked his head behind his enormous shoulders and doggedly kept moving forward, aiming powerful lefts and rights at his elusive opponent but with stunningly little success.

As the round ended, Daniel, who had been dictating to his telegrapher at a furious rate, paused briefly and shook his head sadly. Its over, he's done, he's hardly thrown a meaningful punch, the veteran journalist told himself, as he watched the challenger return slowly, stoically, to his corner. It's only a matter of time. Mentally, he's just going through the motions. The burden of expectations, the hopes of an entire race, is just too much for the poor man. Johnson is lucky, he can be himself, there's no real pressure on him. Almost nobody really expects him to win, even among his own people. Even now they're Negroes all over the country in churches praying for him. They'll be delighted if he wins of course but most of them, especially their best educated and most prominent people don't see him as some kind of savior.

The fourth, like the others before it, began slowly with neither fighter trying to force the pace. Nevertheless, Corbett, whose primary responsibility was to annoy and rattle the champion, and had been stalking all four corners of the ring, swapping insults with the unfazed Negro, inexplicably asked Jeffries to take it easy. Annoyed, referee Richard ordered the challenger and his second "to quit this motion work; get busy boys." Aroused by the admonition Jeffries rushed Johnson, swinging powerfully from his crouch, as if aiming to end the contest with one great blow but once again the black man was not there, his shadow fell across the spot where Jeffries' blow had been aimed. Increasingly confident Johnson threw and missed a hard right uppercut and began testing his new blow, a left uppercut, all the while keeping up a fire of jokes and repartee with Jeffries, more often with Corbett and even with sporting writers.

As the bout progressed, a sportingman, who had let it be known that he'd placed a $10,000 bet on Jeffries, in a typical exchange with the amiable champion, yelled "He'll kill you Jack."

"That's what they all say," a smiling Johnson replied lightly, then underlined his growing dominance by landing a short, snappy left hook to Jeffries' reddening face. But the powerful and determined challenger was far from beaten or discouraged, and as they came out of a clinch seemed to hurt the champion for the first with a punishing right to the body that echoed throughout the stadium and drew a wince from Johnson and hopeful cheers from the now largely quiet crowd.

Trying desperately to rally his fading fighter, Corbett responded to stiff left that cut Jeffries' cheek to the bone in the sixth by taunting the champion. "That left was a joke," he shouted. "You big stiff, I always knew you were a faker."

In Johnson's corner, Delaney was literally hopping with glee. "Go in and finish him," he whispered to Johnson at the end of the round.

At the start of the seventh Johnson was off his stool and into the middle of the ring in a flash. "It's all over for you Jim," he announced, smiling broadly, to the gum-chewing challenger before landing a vicious right hook on the big man's rapidly swelling right eye. Clinching desperately, Jeffries pawed at his eye as he leaned on the glistening shoulder of the black champion. Retreating, Jeffries feinted in an attempt to draw Johnson in but the champion declined the bait. The challenger tried a left to the body but missed and took a sizzling left-right combination to the head and his mouth was streaked with blood as he returned to his corner at the end of the round.

Noting the hesitancy in the challenger's walk, a number of sporting men observed somberly that "it looks bad for Jeffries."

"Remember how much he took from Fitzsimmons and then landed," said the more hopeful ones.

A somber Corbett huddled with a weeping Jack Jeffries, the challenger's younger brother. "Jack," he told him, "your brother's whipped. What are we going to do?"

Johnson began the eighth with yet another jarring left to Jeffries' face. "Did you see that one, Jimmy," he asked Corbett as he leaned over the challenger's shoulder and grinned. Warming to his task, the champion increased the pace of his attack, the blows coming faster and harder, repeatedly hurting the tiring challenger. Summoning every bit of his great strength, Jeffries continued to resist what increasingly seemed as his inevitable defeat, rushing in with more conviction than he had earlier in the fight and occasionally landing to the champion's body.

Desperately trying to maintain his equanimity and speaking with difficulty through bloodied lips, Jeffries did his best to reply to the champion's taunts and punches. "Ain't I got a hard old head," he said defiantly, after absorbing a withering series of hooks and uppercuts.

"You certainly have Jim," a smiling Johnson replied and snapped the challenger's back with another volley of punches.

An excited Etta leaped to her feet and shouted "keep it up Jack."

By the eleventh the relentless beating had taken a terrible toll on the visibly weakening challenger who seemed at times barely able to lift his arms. Johnson began by blocking Jeffries' attempt at a left hook to the body and responding with a series of blindingly fast hooks and uppercuts to the challenger' swollen face. Another volley of left hooks and uppercuts from the champion, coming out of a clinch, drew a copious flow of blood from the challenger's nose and mouth and a scattering of cheers from a few at ringside and the more expensive seats, reluctant admiration of the Negro's great skill.

A frantic, red-faced, Corbett dashed furiously back and forth, screaming and waving his arms. "I thought you said you were going to make me wild," Johnson laughingly noted.

Up in the rafters the mood was grimly different. Patrick sat quietly, barely able to breathe or contain his growing excitement. All around him, the once loud and raucously confident Jeffries partisans were sullen and silent. The impossible, the unthinkable, was unfolding in front of their incredulous eyes. The reviled nigger was not just outmaneuvering and outboxing their previously unbeaten champion, but was administering the beating of his life with what seemed like effortless ease. Cheering, clapping, even smiling, appearing to celebrate in any way, would, in the event of a Johnson victory, Patrick and his friends had agreed, threaten their safety, their very lives. Now, as the battle drew to a close, Patrick became increasingly aware of the hostile stares being directed in his direction.

Johnson, still breathing easily, continued his furious onslaught throughout the twelfth, thirteenth and fourteenth rounds, effortlessly blocking Jeffries' attempts at offense while pouring in left hooks and uppercuts to the challenger's face and body. In the fourteenth, as the game but hopelessly outclassed challenger shambled forward on shaky legs still trying to land one lethal blow, he was met with three jarring lefts to the head, so fast they seemed a single punch. "How do you feel, Jim," the champion asked, as they clinched. "Do they hurt?"

"No they don't," Jeffries replied. But many clearly did, one even drawing a grunt of "Oh! from the rugged challenger. And by the end of the round his nose was broken, both eyes were swollen almost shut and his shoulders, chest and thighs were covered with his own blood. Balanced uncertainly on his stool between rounds and gasping for air, his arms hanging limply at his side, only an immense well of pride and courage seemed to be keeping the former champion upright. Corbett, finally accepting the inevitable, suddenly seemed grey, drawn and old.

Like a man marching to his own funeral, Jeffries began the fifteenth by wading, stiff-legged and resolute, into Johnson's corner and throwing the first punch, a weak, tentative right, the champion easily avoided. Coming out of a brief clinch, Johnson forcefully shoved away the fading challenger and unleashed a volley of punches that drove the big Californian stumbling into his own corner. Sensing the kill, Johnson quickly followed and with panther-like quickness, unleashed the most deadly blows of the contest, a left-right combination that exploded on Jefffries' jaw like gunshots. As the man who had been celebrated for his indestructibility crumbled to the canvas, one arm tangled in the lower strands of the ropes, a great silence fell over the crowd. And, as Daniel described, "a great, guttural gust of pity came, as if from one, from thousands of manly chests. It was," he noted to his telegrapher, "a queer, uncanny, almost indescribable, sound— a long, deep, aw-w-w-w—from profoundly affected men."

Slowly, with a supreme effort, shaking his massive head, just before the timekeeper counted ten, Jeffries staggered to his feet, tree-trunk legs trembling uncontrollably. Spitting blood, he tried, desperately, unsuccessfully, to clinch. Another vicious left sent him sprawling through the lower ropes on the east side of the ring, onto the platform, where he lay dazed and confused as the count began.

"Don't let the nigger knock him out," the chant began, every syllable dripping with anguish, "Stop it; don't let the nigger knock him out."

But a few supporters, including younger brother Jack, unwilling still to concede defeat, in contravention of every rule and etiquette of boxing, leaped onto the apron of the ring, pulled their champion to his feet and pushed him toward the center of the ring, where a relaxed and confident Johnson waited.

As the champion moved in, Corbett waved frantically his arms and cried out. "Oh, don't Jack, don't hit him."

A pitiless flurry of punches sent the Great White Hope reeling along the ropes, collapsing on the opposite side of the ring. Johnson followed, ready to strike again, should the challenger somehow manage to rise. Richard pushed him back and began the count, but Jeffries' seconds had seen enough. Sam Berger climbed into the ring. Bob Armstrong threw in a white towel. Richard clasped Johnson's shoulder, the traditional gesture of victory. The Fight of the Century was over. In the great battle of civilizations, Hastings and Agincourt against the primitive jungle, the primitive jungle had prevailed.

Jeffries struggled to his feet and wobbled back to his corner. "I'm no good as a fighter any longer," he said quietly, shaking his head. "I couldn't come back boys. Ask Johnson if he'll give me his gloves."

Johnson was ecstatic. "It was easy. I could have fought for two hours longer." he boasted to his cornermen, declining to sit on his stool. "I was having lots of fun. Not one blow hurt me. He can't hit. He won't forget two punches I landed on him. He was only half the trouble Burns was."

"Somebody wire to my mother," he added.

The ring was filled almost immediately with scores of spectators; all, to a man, bitterly disappointed Jeffries supporters. Fearing for the champion's safety, Johnson's seconds quickly formed a protective cordon around him; but he would have none it, he wanted to shake Jeffries' hand. Unfazed, he pushed his way across the ring to Jeffries' corner, where the defeated challenger was still slumped forlornly on his stool, but the Great White Hope's glum-faced seconds flatly refused to allow him to even get close.

Outside the ring a few fans offered up a few desultory cheers for the black champion. Another small group, enthusiastic souvenir hunters, began energetically cutting up the ropes. But the vast majority of the once raucous, confident, crowd filed out of the vast, wooden arena in what Daniel described as "funeral gloom, grim, hostile and silent."

At ringside, too stricken to move, a well-dressed white woman and beside her, an enormous white man, both sobbed inconsolably.

Downtown, the streets were densely packed. The great contest was over and the race to get out of Reno before the night was over was on. Leading the charge was the champion himself, surrounded by Etta and their entire entourage. As they made their way to the train depot, a skinny, freckle-faced paperboy raced alongside the champion's automobile until the grinning champion reached out and shook his hand. And thousands in the crowd, who, only hours earlier, had been his bitter foes, now acknowledged him good-naturedly with cheers. But cheering the longest and loudest were a surprising number of Negroes, many of whom had come to Reno for the fight but had been too afraid to actually enter the arena.

The cheering continued unabated as the champion and his party hurried on foot through the crowded station. The powerfully-built Kid Cotton, a big Victrola under one arm and the leash of

Johnson's bulldog in the other, struggled to keep pace. Just before getting on her train, a light-skinned woman ceremoniously removed her hat to reveal her frizzy, Negroid hair, explaining loudly that she was a nigger and "proud of it." For now, at least in Reno, it seemed it was no longer dangerous to openly proclaim support for the black champion.

Watching all of this, Daniel smiled in bemusement. It seems Americans love a winner, even a previously detested black one, at least for a while, the veteran newspaperman mused as he made his way to the Overland Limited to Chicago, the same train that would be taking Jack Johnson on his triumphant journey home. His own long journey was, finally, almost over. Without even closing his eyes he could see her face, hear her voice, feel her skin, smell her breath. Bridget, he thought, smiling to himself, increasing the pace of his long stride, I'm coming home, I'm coming home.

The highly-polished black-oak floor of the dining-room, only partially covered by a slightly worn green and crimson Turkish rug with a woven border, glittered like a giant diamond. Light from the harsh mid-summer sun had slipped through the ruby-and-amber stained glass of the bay window and past the faded, silk-lined green velour curtains. Black-oak, with dividing bands of lighter oak, was also the theme of the ceiling and wainscots the walls, which were covered by a slightly soiled, cream-colored embossed fabric touched with gold and ruddy brown. The box seats in the windows on both sides of the room were lined with brown leather and stacked with green and crimson pillows.

Standing amidst this fading magnificence, Richard stared hard at the face in the gilded mirror above the elaborately carved sideboard, the brown skin, the short blunt nose, the wide, thin-lipped mouth. All my life, he thought, running his hand through his loosely curled dark hair, a hint of puzzlement in the wide-spaced, light brown eyes, this was the face of a Negro. I knew who I was, everybody knew who I was, a proud member of the Barrington family; there was never any doubt, any confusion. But here, in this strange city, there is no historic memory, nothing is fixed, you are what you seem to be. And now, pathetically, having briefly tasted the sweet fruits of universal acceptance available only to members of the Caucasian race I'm no longer sure of who I am or, even, who I want to be. But I do know that being a willing party to the humiliation of the Negro people is a greater price than I'm willing to pay.

The memory rankled. The tall, gangly, hollow-cheeked, furniture salesman had oozed obsequiousness. After their explanation that they were thinking of redecorating and refurnishing their townhome, he had trailed eagerly after them, his prominent Adam's apple bobbing nervously in his long, narrow neck, breathlessly extolling the virtues of his establishment. He had been in the full flight of his presentation, his deep tenor voice rising and falling several octaves, when an older black couple showed up and dared to ask a few questions. The transformation had been sudden and startling.

"You people," he had snarled, literally baring yellowing teeth, "better be careful of getting too swellheaded and big-chested jus' because of what went on in Reno. Jus' because you have the same complexion as Johnson. You're jus' the same this week as you were last week. You're not on a higher plane of society. Nobody thinks any better of you now than they did before. You didn't do anything. You don't deserve any new consideration, and you won't be getting any in this fine establishment."

The older couple had retreated in alarm and confusion, and they had, to the puzzled consternation of the salesman, quietly, without a single word of explanation, walked out.

Seated at the large oak dining table with its highly polished ornamental top, Alicia glowed from the softened bands of light streaming into the room. But her expression was grim and her large, hazel eyes moist with tears. "As many as twenty-six killed, more than two hundred and fifty seriously injured, more than five thousand arrested, almost all of them Negroes, she intoned, gesturing at the open newspaper lying on the table. While we were basking in the privileges of our lighter skin, safely pretending to be white people, real white people, all over the country, from the Atlantic to the Pacific, in the South and the North, in the East and the West, in Washington, right here in New York City, were shooting, stabbing, burning, lynching, real black people."

Richard walked across the room to the western window and looked down at the crowded, teeming thoroughfare. To conquer such a city, he thought to himself, would be a rich prize indeed. But what does it profit a man to gain the whole world and risk losing his immortal soul.

Epilogue

Chicago, September 1912

The spell of silent, body-shaking sobs had finally stopped. Sometimes, when the crying fits, as her mother had labeled them, took hold of her she felt that they would only stop if she could expel the grief filling her insides by screaming as long and loudly as she could manage. But that, she knew, would mean that they would never leave her alone, for even a second. Instead, Etta Johnson wiped her tears, sat up in the big four-postered bed, her legs dangling over the floor, glanced again at the Rudd mechanical clock on the marble mantelpiece, pressed the open palm of her right hand against her face and with the three middle fingers slowly and gently massaged the fragile space between her eyes.

Against her bidding, the words were filling her head again: Around and around they went, pressing hard against her eyes, refusing to stop. *The moving finger writes and having writ moves on; Nor all thy piety nor wit shall lure it back to cancel half a line, Nor all thy tears wash out a word of it.* From the first time she had heard them, she had been struck by the timeless wisdom of the prophet. The words had seemed to be directed just at her. *Ah, my beloved, fill the cup that clears, today of past regrets and future fears; Tomorrow? Why tomorrow I may be myself with yesterday's Sev'n thousand years.*

Her bare feet sinking into the thick carpeting, Etta made her way across the room and sat heavily on the padded stool of her dressing table. In the mirror, she could see that her eyes were dark and heavy and spent. For much of her life men had admired her, had complimented her on her beauty, but she herself had never, she thought, leaning forward and staring with wide-eyed disapproval at the sunken-cheeked woman confronting her, liked anything about her face. Her eyes were not large enough, her face far too thin, her nose too long. The meaning of the prophet's words she had understood instinctively, without even really thinking about it. The moving finger was the hand of God, relentlessly recording in some eternal book of life each of our fates, and nothing we did on earth could change that heavenly judgment.

Straightening up, her hands moving to the long, thick dark hair, which Jack loved so much, she smiled thinly at the memory of her mother's furious objection to her obsession, she had called it, with the poem. Faithful Roman Catholics, good Christians, did not, her mother had insisted, even read let alone give credence to the words of a heathen. The Lord had allowed his only son, Jesus Christ, she had reminded her, to perish on the cross to absolve the sins of the world, to show the way to the paradise of heaven. Salvation was hers for the asking. But the words had continued to haunt her mind with an even greater power. *Nor all thy piety nor wit shall lure it back to cancel half a line, nor all thy tears wash out a word of it. Nor all piety nor all they tears, cancel half a line, nor wash out a word of it.* She wasn't sure if she believed it, but she accepted it, the mystery of her own life was testimony to it. Predestination. Free will, what free will. *The moving finger writes; and having writ moves on.*

Outside, in downtown Chicago, the night air was hot and heavy and muffled sounds of merriment and bustle, of people laughing, of vehicles moving, floated lazily through the open windows of the big, high-ceilinged, second-floor bedroom, but Etta was only listening to the voice inside her head. Immediately below, at 41 West 31st Street, at the *Café de Champion*, frequently described by the ladies and gentlemen of the popular press as the most famous nightclub-saloon in America, people were dancing to the rich sounds of the orchestra Etta's husband had so proudly assembled. But sitting alone at her elegant and expensive rosewood Renaissance Revival dressing table, in her fashionable blue, short-sleeved nightdress, staring fixedly at the blank sheet of paper in front of her, Etta Johnson was too preoccupied to take note of such earthly matters. Then, narrow lips set with determination, she slowly began writing, frequently stopping and mouthing the words, getting what she wanted to say just right before continuing.

My Dear Mother,

I am writing this and I am going to have Jack put in his safe, so if anything should happen to me there will be no hard feelings left behind me. I would send this letter to you, only I know how much you worry and I do not want you to know how sick I really am. Jack has done all in his power to care for me but it is of no use. Since Papa's death I have worried myself into my grave. I haven't been worrying over Papa's loss, only over some horrifying dread-I don't know what, I want to be buried here in Chicago. Never try to take my body to Hempstead only to be a mark for curiosity seekers-let me rest for once. With love and always the sweetest to you.

I am your loving daughter

Drained by the effort, Etta allowed the pen to fall from her long, pale fingers and on to the plushly carpeted floor. This time, she knew deep inside, as she slowly rose and closed the folds of her nightdress, that Jack would not be on time. Glancing again at the clock and folding the letter in two while searching distractedly around the room for an envelope, she wondered if he had ever understood why she had made him promise never to leave her alone. She had told him about the inexplicable dread that she could not explain even to herself. She had wanted him to understand what was happening to her and he had hired maids to watch her.

Living had become too difficult and nobody understood, not even Jack. She had grown so tired of being an outcast. She was, afterall, a white woman. But nobody respected her, not even Jack's people, and all because she had married a black man. Her people, were even worse, she thought bitterly, as she pulled open the top drawer of her night table, they hated her, called her a traitor to her race, a dirty, nigger-loving slut and even worse: words that sickened her just to think of them. She had heard them, heard them all over the years: vile, filthy words, spewing like poison from the mouths of even the most well-dressed, respectable-looking, supposedly god-fearing, men and women. Not even Papa had understood or approved, but, because he loved her so much, she thought fondly, a small smile tugging at the corners of her mouth, he had been cordial, even kind, to Jack. Her mother, though, had not been quite as forgiving. She was convinced, she had told her, that she was not herself, that that terrible fall when she was a child had damaged her brain and made her crazy.

Then, as if she had suddenly remembered something of the utmost importance, Etta abruptly turned, walked back to her dressing table, reached for the late model Bell telephone, impatiently removed the barbell shaped receiver from the switch hook, placed it at her left ear and in a little burst of frenzy leaned forward slightly and rapidly dialed an obviously familiar number with her right index finger. Pulling the phone closer, after a brief wait, in a soft, almost listless voice she whispered into the transmitter, "Jennie, can you please come over, now. I am afraid I might kill myself" Then after another brief pause, "Yes, its Etta." Then without bothering to wait for a reply she replaced the receiver on the switch hook and resumed her meandering search for an envelope.

Threatening to kill herself was nothing new for Etta. In fact, in the two years since the Jeffries fight, she had already gone further by actually making two attempts, sort of. Once, in London, after an argument with Jack, she had tried to jump through the window of their hotel room. And again, during one of Jack's tours out West, after another argument, she had tried to throw herself under a train. But Jack had always been there to restrain her and to beg and plead for forgiveness. And that, for her, had always been the best part of it; it was only then when she saw his tears and smelled his fear that she really felt that he cared. The letter, even the telephone call to his sister, might have been just another warning to Jack to mend his wandering ways. She had always been jealous of the attention he received from other women, of the attention he paid other women. Once, during one of his visits to Europe she had become enraged when the famous French actress, Gaby Deslys, became enamoured with him. The French siren's unabashed admiration of the heavyweight champion had been widely reported in the Parisian press. "His great staring eyes," she supposedly said, "simply devours one... he evokes a desperation in a woman for utter fulfillment."

Her search, which had progressed to the bottom left-hand drawer of the elaborately carved dresser had turned up no envelopes but an item that she had not been able to find during another search several days earlier, her father's self-winding Breguet watch. Knowing how much she had admired it, he had given it to her just before his death. Pressing a button at the top of the watch sounded the exact time, to the hour and minute. She had been enchanted when as a child he had showed her how to use it; and he had not forgotten his promise that one day it would be hers. With tears welling at the memory and murmuring "dearest Papa," Etta gently lifted the watch, cradling it in her palm and even more gently, almost reverently, pressed the big button and brought it to her ear, as a soft smile suddenly lit up her eyes. But that quickly disappeared, as evidently startled by what she heard, Etta turned sharply and glanced again at the clock on the mantelpiece, as if for confirmation, and if as seeing the open windows for the first time walked over, leaned outside and stared upward into the darkening night.

To the west, grey-streaked crimson bands still marked the recent passage of the retiring sun. But, already, through the thicket of the mighty buildings guarding downtown like giant sentinels, flickering stars were beginning to announce their imminent arrival. It had all, Etta thought, long been written in the stars. *The moving finger writes and having writ moves on; Nor all they piety nor wit shall lure it back to cancel half a line, Nor all thy tears wash out a word of it.*

Things had changed between them, she knew, since she changed her mind about having children. Jack had wanted children, desperately. She had been surprised at first by the intensity. Everybody had been surprised, even his family. They had argued about it for months; he insisting, entreating, she resisting, then weakening. Opening the *Cafe de Champion* had been part of what he had described as his master plan for settling down and raising a family. Finally, in Paris, she had given in. In that great city of romance love had overcome reason and they had even started thinking about names. In Berlin, they had gone shopping for baby clothes and she had bought a whole trunk full of the most delightful creations. They had even ordered a cradle and a rattle. And she had even teasingly begun calling him "Papa."

Nothing had seemed impossible over there but almost as soon as they returned to America she knew that for her, knowing what they would go through, the insults, the disdain of both races, it became impossible. To his claims that they'd go through no more than he had and that they'd have a head start because of what he would be able to provide, she'd replied, again and again, almost mockingly "You can't even protect me from what I have to go through. How do you think you could protect the children we'd have." He had taken the rejection badly; becoming even more reckless, speeding through the Chicago streets in his powerful automobiles; getting arrested repeatedly and paying huge fines in court.

She had done what she could to try to make up for the children. She had let him know that she wouldn't mind too much if he had to, sometimes, see other women, discreetly. She knew what he was like about women; she had been warned about him even before they got together. That he couldn't be satisfied with just one woman, black or white. In a way it was what drew her to him, his manliness. And when she had become so afraid of becoming pregnant that she no longer wanted him beside her at nights, she had even allowed him to set up what he laughingly called his harem room here, right across the hall from their own apartment. But nothing had worked and now she was too tired to keep on fighting the entire world. *The moving finger writes and having writ moves on; nor all they piety nor wit shall lure it back to cancel half a line, nor all they tears wash out a word of it.*

"Miss Etta, Miss Etta, Miss Etta."

At first, the voices had been so faint she had not been sure if they had come from far away or had been conjured up by her mind. But now she could feel hands on her arms pulling her, gently but firmly, back from the window, and turning around she looked into the anxious faces of the two live-in maids, Mabel and Helen, Jack had hired to take care of her every need, night and day.

"Miss Etta," Mabel asked, worry and reproach tightening her voice, "what you doing at the window, is everything alright."

"Don't worry yourself Mabel," voice soft but edged with sarcasm, "it's not high enough to jump from here."

"You mustn't say things like that Miss Etta, Mistah Jack is mighty worried about you."

"Are you sure about that Helen, I'm not sure that Mister Jack still bothers his head about me. I'm just so tired and lonely. Have you ever been lonely Helen?"

"But Miss Etta," Mabel interjected scoldingly, rolling her eyes at her partner in exasperation, "with all the friends you have, and all the travel you do with Mistah Jack."

"You may not know this Mabel," Etta replied, in a voice suddenly fierce and accusatory, "but everybody hates me. Your people hate me too Mabel, I've seen the way some of them look at me, especially the women. I'm a white woman, Mabel, but nobody respects me, and just because I married a black man."

"That's not true Miss Etta, you shouldn't say things like that, Negro people don't hate you Miss Etta. Me and Mabel.. we don't hate you… we care about you… we doing our best to take care of you." And with a reproachful look at the suddenly chastened Mabel who sheepishly and silently nodded her assent, "Isn't that right Mabel, Negro people don't hate Miss Etta. We care about Miss Etta, don't we?"

"I know you don't hate me Helen," and then hurriedly as the mortified Mabel was about to interrupt, "nor Mabel either, although she is not as patient with me as you are. But I know both of you have taken good care of me. I tell that to Mister Jack almost every day. But you know, sometimes I need something more. I want to pray, will you both help a poor woman pray for her sins."

Outside, on the streets below and in the saloon downstairs, the night was coming into its own; people were pouring into the streets and the sounds of revelry seemed to be everywhere. But, at the side of the bed, the three women were kneeling in a tiny semi-circle of anguish. With an arm draped lightly around the waists of her maids, eyes tightly shut and head bowed in submission, Etta, in the soft hesitant voice of the confessional began to pray. "I believe in

God, the father almighty, creator of heaven and earth." Searching still for the once familiar words, but her voice growing slightly stronger, she continued. "I believe in Jesus Christ, his only Son, our Lord. He was conceived by the power of the Holy Spirit and born of the Virgin Mary." Then in a flood of memory, her eyes opening and her head lifting, slowly, she continued in a voice growing steadily louder and more mournful. "He suffered under Pontius Pilate, was crucified, died, and was buried. He descended to the dead. On the third day he rose again. He ascended into heaven, and is seated at the right hand of the Father. He will come again to judge the living and the dead."

Seemingly oblivious of the stares of the other women, her hands now clasped in front of her, her body rocking gently from one knee to the other, her eyes wide open, her head tilted upward, Etta, in a near shout ended her profession of fate. "I believe in the Holy Spirit, the holy Catholic Church, the communion of saints, the forgiveness of sins, the resurrection of the body and the life everlasting."

Suddenly, it was over, and for a long moment nobody spoke. Finally, as if waking from a trance or a dream, Etta, with a little smile of reassurance, turned to each of her companions, nodded and whispered, "Thank you." Then, struggling to her feet, she quickly sat on the bed, pressed her hands to her face and in a loud voice cried out: "God pity a poor woman who is lonely."

Disconcerted, Mabel and Helen furtively exchanged long stares as they, too, struggled to their feet. But as Helen knotted her brow in worry and Mabel resumed the rolling of her eyes, Etta soothingly announced, as she stretched out on the bed, that she was feeling a lot better and almost apologetically asked them to fix her "a little something to eat."

"Would you like one of us to stay with you Miss Etta."

"That's not necessary Helen, I'm just going to lie here and rest for a while. You go along and help Mabel."

"Are you sure Miss Etta, it don't take two of us to fix you a little supper."

"I'm sure, Helen, I'm just going to close my eyes for a few minutes, I'm a little bit tired, take your time and close the door behind you.

After waiting for their voices and footsteps to fade away, Etta rose swiftly from the bed, purposefully strode across the room, quietly closed the door her maids had deliberately left ajar and carefully locked it. Then, with one last glance at the mantelpiece, removed the revolver from the dresser drawer, raised it slowly to her right temple, closed her eyes and, before the words could return and reclaim her mind, unhesitatingly, pulled the trigger.

The crowd outside the imposing wrought-iron fence of the large three-storey Victorian house at 3345 South Wabash Avenue, on Chicago's South Side, had begun gathering from as early as eight o'clock that morning, although it had been announced that the services would not begin until eleven. From the time Etta's body had been taken to the house after the completion of the coroner's inquest thousands of people, friends, acquaintances and the merely morbidly curious, had besieged the home he had purchased for his mother and the streets around it, in a desperate attempt to view the corpse.

All day Friday, until the wee hours of the morning, endless waves of people had sought admittance; but all, except friends had been turned away, and those relative few had been permitted to view the remains in private and commiserate quietly with the grieving husband and the rest of the family. Inflamed rather than deterred by their failure on Friday, the crowd began gathering early on Saturday morning. When the police detail from the nearby Stanton Avenue station, dispatched early in an effort to control the expected hordes, arrived, the crowd had already reached a thousand; and by 11:00 a.m. it had swollen to more than 10,000 men, women and children, black and white alike.

Inside the residence, in the spacious front parlor, the Reverend John W. Robinson, stood beside the coffin, which was framed by a solid wall of floral designs in the background. In a revival of a very old funerary custom, the pictures and other ornaments in the room were draped in white. At the head of the casket the heavyweight champion of the world stood ramrod straight, listening intently, his mother-in-law, her face contorted with grief, tightly gripping his arm. On the completion of the prayer, which comprised the simple service at the house, husband and mother united in grief, bowed over the corpse. Then, his eyes glistening with tears, Jack kissed his wife, the casket was closed, and the undertaker efficiently gathered the mourners together for the trip to the church.

In life, Etta Johnson had been harshly punished for the social sin of crossing the color line. Now in death, Johnson bitterly noted, as the funeral cortege made its way slowly through the enormous crowds lining both sides of the streets, the very people who had shunned or ignored her were now making a spectacle of her death and funeral. Drawn, no doubt, by a mixture of curiosity and sympathy, vast throngs jammed every street on or near the route, rendering many of them virtually impassable; and forcing the mounted police into service outside the Loop district for the first time in city history. The crowds were particularly dense along 50th Street, from State Street to Michigan Avenue, where pedestrians of every race and gender competed with each other and well-dressed sightseers in autos with Michigan license plates, for the most advantageous positions. Eventually, the crowds became so large and unruly, the jostling so intense, that the police station at 50th and State Street was obliged to summon their reserve force.

Etta's funeral, the arrangements for which had been handled by Jack Curley, the white fight promoter, was a spectacle worth fighting to see. Her husband, dogged by rumors that marital discord had contributed heavily to his wife's unhappiness, had clearly decided to send her off in high style. At a time when automobiles were still rare luxuries, well beyond the reach of average Americans, the procession to Saint Mark's African Episcopal included twenty-three expensive, late model vehicles. Three automobiles filled with flowers led the way, followed by a magnificent auto hearse carrying the body and finally, eighteen cars filled with mourners and one with newspaper reporters. It was, according to every daily newspaper in the city, every one of which had a reporter at the funeral and whose reporters filled one large touring car, easily the largest auto funeral ever seen in the city.

Despite published reports that the service was to be held at

Saint Monica's Roman Catholic Church at 36th and Dearborn Streets, Saint Mark's was surrounded by large crowds that had somehow found out that it would be held there instead. The misleading reports had not been intentional. Father Morris, the priest in charge of Saint Monica's had administered extreme unction to Etta on her deathbed, and some newspapers had understandably assumed that the funeral would be held at the local Catholic Church. A sizeable crowd had also gathered at Saint Monica's but many later found their way to Saint Mark's.

After agonizingly slow progress, the funeral cortege finally arrived at Saint Mark's, where the Johnson family, his mother and sisters, regularly worshipped. After the noise and confusion of the streets, the small church was, for the mourners, an oasis of tranquility and meticulous organization. The automobiles pulled smoothly into the spaces that had been reserved for them. The hundreds of floral offerings, which were in every conceivable size and shape and had been sent by individuals and organizations both near and far, were not displayed in the church itself. Instead, the three automobiles that they filled to overflowing were parked at a conspicuous place on the corner nearest the church.

Onlookers gasped, apparently in sympathy, surprise and some amazement, as the grieving husband, smooth black skin shining from a film of sweat on the brutally hot day, half-carried his white mother-in-law, leaning heavily on her son-in-law for support, from the automobile. And, some of the white mourners and reporters would note, often with surprised approval, the heavyweight champion's solicitous attention, throughout the funeral services, to Mrs. Terry and her daughter, Miss Elaine Terry. Once the funeral party had all gathered in the church, the Reverend Robinson led the mourning line to the altar, and after what had seemed like interminable delays, the service actually began. The church was filled but only to its seating capacity, there was no standing in the aisles. Scores of prominent people from the boxing establishment, a great many of them white, were among the mourners, but every church and choir member was seated comfortably.

The service began with a reading of the Nineteenth Psalm and was followed by a short but eloquent sermon, titled "Hope Thou in

God" by Pastor Robinson. "Is there anyone in this church who can be so cruel as to deny the star of hope to the weary one," he asked in his tender but powerful voice. Then, after waiting for the chorus of "no, no one" to recede, he asked again, his voice throbbing with emotion, "Is there any who cannot let the great mantle of charity cover the call of a disquieted heart." Again, a chorus but louder now and more heartfelt, of "no, no one" rolled across the church and embraced the altar. Here and there a quiet sob and a dabbed tear assured the pastor that his job had been well done. But when the choir filled that consecrated space with the bittersweet strains of "Nearer, My God, to Thee," the pent-up passions of the week broke wide open and men and women, black and white alike, wept unashamedly and uncontrollably. And there, in the front pew, the chief mourner, his powerful shoulders trembling, sobbed like a child. Overcome by both heat and emotion, a few women fainted inside the church. Others, including Johnson's sister, Mrs. Jennie Roach, the last person Etta had called that final night of her brief life, feeling themselves growing faint rushed outside to gasp fresh, reviving air.

Finally, after two solos, the family and friends in the church stood in line to view the body, which had been very capably prepared, all agreed, by the undertaker, Daniel Jackson, for one last time. The formal french-grey state casket, handles and nameplate gleaming in solid silver, was almost completely covered by a blanket of flowers, the final gift of her husband who tenderly kissed her goodbye. The racially mixed group of pallbearers then placed the body in the hearse for the short trip.

At Graceland cemetery, in an all-white neighborhood, the funeral cortege was greeted by yet another throng; primarily comprised, this time, of local residents. The heavyweight champion had selected a lot in the exclusive section of the cemetery, adjoining the family plots of some of Chicago's wealthiest families, as his wife's final resting-place. The body was placed in a vault with a handsome monument, which reportedly cost three and a half thousand dollars, a sum three times the cost of an expensive automobile. A caretaker, who had been employed by the cemetery for thirty-four years, told reporters covering the funeral that he had never seen a larger or better conducted funeral, nor so many beautiful floral designs.

As the funeral party left the cemetery, the champion, as if in agreement, was heard to say as he slowly walked away: "That's all I can do."

He had, again and again, over and over, replayed the events of that fateful day, examining and re-examining, every word she had said, everything he had said and done, wondering, speculating, about what he could, should, have done differently to save the woman, he told himself, again and again, that he had genuinely loved. She had seemed happy enough, for her, all day before the headache began. Certainly, nothing in her demeanor or actions, had aroused his suspicion. They had entertained their friends, the sportswriter Ed Smith and his wife, for several hours that day. In fact she had planned to leave with the Smiths for a vacation in Las Vegas, New Mexico, that very night and had only begged off at the last moment, and he had taken the Smiths to the train station by himself.

The street in front of their home was already filled with people and police wagons when he returned. Friends in the crowd had ominously advised him to hurry upstairs, that something had happened to Etta. Almost numb with fear and apprehension, his chest pounding, his knees buckling, he had somehow found the strength to bound up the stairs, dreading all along what he would find. When he entered the bedroom, she was still lying on the floor, her beautiful long hair covering her face, a small black revolver by her side. At first, from what he could see, there was no blood, except for a single red spot on one bare, exposed arm. For one hopeful moment he had believed that the bullet had not been fatal. But, as he gathered her in his arms, her hair had fallen back from her face, abruptly revealing the ugly wound in her head and the eyes that no longer saw him, abruptly crushing his hopes.

The final sight of his wife's pallid face, the knowledge that he could, should, have been more attentive, had brought back the brain fever that had led him to contemplate suicide in the months after the Jeffries fight. It was Etta who had taken care of him when he was at his lowest; she had rarely left his side for a whole year.

He had not been as faithful; true he had done everything the doctors had ordered. He had been generous with everything, except what she needed most, his time.

Daniel O'Brien slipped the wireframe reading glasses off his face, briefly massaged the outside corners of his eyes with the tips of his index and middle fingers, walked over to the big bay windows overlooking Riverside Drive, pulled one of the curtains aside and quietly stared into the starless night. Outside, a young couple strolled hand-in-hand, shoulders and hips in gentle constant contact, shining eyes devoted only to devouring the wonder of the other's face, oblivious to the mad swirl of traffic, pedestrian and vehicular, around them. So much had changed in just two years, he thought. For a brief while after that extraordinary day in Reno it had even seemed possible that America would have embraced Johnson, or at least reconciled itself to the idea of a Negro champion. But the continuing provocations with white women had been too much. His second marriage, to a mere girl, just weeks after Etta's death had been the last straw; the actions of the government were perfectly understandable.

Behind him, an apple-cheeked toddler, a redhead like her beaming mother, tottered across the thick carpet as quickly as her stubby little legs could take her. Turning away from the window, Daniel smiled fondly at his wife and daughter, resumed his seat at the mahogany desk, pulled his battered, old Underwood typewriter closer and began typing, slowly and hesitantly at first, then with increasing speed and conviction.

> *As regular readers of this paper may be aware I've often written quite sympathetically, perhaps, in retrospect, far too much so, about the Negro pugilist Jack Johnson. But by cowardly and illegally fleeing the country of his birth, the country which had provided him with a level of wealth and fame that few men of any color even remotely approach, to escape a modest and just sentence, after a fair and open trial, for a crime of moral*

turpitude, he has forfeited forever any small, lingering claim to the goodwill or sympathy of the citizens of this great nation of ours. We must, especially those of us who have championed fair treatment for the Negroes in this country, sternly and often remind ourselves that the national trafficking in women that has come to be known as the White Slave Trade, is as mercenary and fiendish as was the African slave trade in its blackest days.

We can now expect Mr. Johnson to be warmly welcomed in foreign capitals, none of them, incidentally, with our long and intimate knowledge of the Negro and his true character, that are so fond of lecturing us about our so-called racial problems. And for him to claim, loudly and repeatedly, that he was ill-treated and abused in this country for no reason other than his race.

That of course, as we are all well aware, is not true and what will make the claim particularly ingenious and pernicious is that Mr. Johnson, an intelligent man by the standards of his race, knows very well it is not true. The truth, as evidenced by the universally high regard in which the revered Negro leader, Dr. Booker Washington, is held by every sector of our society, is that the Negro pugilist was condemned for his outrageous behavior and not his race.

Unlike Dr. Washington, who has wisely tried to raise up his people by practical and gradual means and counsels patience and modesty in their behavior while they acquire the means to play a fuller role in our society, Mr. Johnson was constantly immodest, provocative, irresponsible, and immoral. He never understood or perhaps cared that the chastity of women is at the very foundation of Anglo-Saxon society. Our laws are based upon it, and it is not only the finest but the most binding of our social relations. Nothing could be more menacing to a civilization than the sale of this bedrock value as a commodity.

There may well come a time, a distant time, well

beyond the lifetimes of any of us now alive no doubt, when society will no longer frown on the social intermingling of the races. But that time, I'm happy to say, has not yet come and for very good reason. Certainly not because of any active spite or negligence on our part, but because the Negro has not yet advanced to a stage of development, intellectual, emotional or moral, to make that possible, despite the best efforts of Caucasian society.

And sadly Mr. Johnson's behavior and the unfortunate example he provided for many untutored and impressionable young men of his race has undoubtedly helped to delay, perhaps for many, many more years, the time when Negroes will be able to assume a more responsible place in our society. And that in the end, for those many, many of our race who wish the Negro well, is, I believe, a great pity.

Finally, the danger of Johnson's example should not be underestimated. It is not only unrestrained Negroes who threaten the very existence of our country. We no longer draw our immigrants from the Northern people. Today this enormous influx hales from Russia, Austria, Hungary, Italy, and the Southern countries from the eastern end of the Mediterranean. As much as it pains me to write this, we must admit, especially those of us of a more liberal cast of mind, the hard truth that these are men of alien races, mixed in blood, of many tongues, and often the last remnants of effete and decaying civilizations.

The inescapable truth is that we no longer receive accessions from the best people beyond our borders, but from the mediocre and worse. Jack Johnson was merely a symbol of the lurking dangers. For America's sake, we, all of us who love with all our souls this greatest of all countries, must be vigilant.

ABOUT THE AUTHOR

Patrick Cooper was a writer his entire adult life. A native of Jamaica, Pat began his professional career as a journalist on the sports desk of the Gleaner, the oldest and largest daily newspaper in the British Caribbean. His long and varied career also included stints in advertising, marketing and politics. In 1968, at the age of 25, Mr. Cooper was hired by the People's National Party (PNP) - as its first fulltime Public Relations Director and Editor of its start-up newspaper, *The New Nation*.

Pat emigrated to the United States in 1978 with his wife Juin and children Gregory, Rachel and Charles and became a naturalized American citizen. In the United States Pat worked, primarily, as an advertising copywriter in New York, and owed his own agency in Houston.

His first book *Black Superman: A Cultural and Biological History of the People who Became the World's Greatest Athletes* explains the biological and biomechanical basis for the disproportional success of blacks of West African descent in sports that require speed and power and has gained international acclaim and inspired research on the subject.

In the final days before his death in 2009 Pat finished his most personal book, *From the Sceptre to the Rod*. The memoir spans Pat's idyllic childhood in colonial Jamaica, to his days in the leadership of the PNP and his ringside view of history and the events that shaped modern Jamaica.

www.ingramcontent.com/pod-product-compliance
Lightning Source LLC
Chambersburg PA
CBHW030212170426
43201CB00006B/66